The Cambridge Companion to Recorded Music

From the cylinder to the download, the practice of music has been radically transformed by the development of recording and playback technologies. *The Cambridge Companion to Recorded Music* provides a detailed overview of this transformation, encompassing both classical and popular music. Topics covered include the history of recording technology and the businesses built on it; the impact of recording on performance styles; studio practices, viewed from the perspectives of performer, producer and engineer; and approaches to the study of recordings. The main chapters are complemented by 'personal takes' – contributions by different practitioners, ranging from classical or pop producers and performers to record collectors. Combining basic information with a variety of perspectives on records and recordings, this book will appeal not only to students in a range of areas from music to the media, but also to general readers interested in a fundamental yet insufficiently understood dimension of musical culture.

Nicholas Cook is 1684 Professor of Music at the University of Cambridge.

Eric Clarke is Heather Professor of Music at the University of Oxford.

Daniel Leech-Wilkinson is Professor of Music at King's College, London.

John Rink is Professor of Musical Performance Studies at the University of Cambridge.

The Cambridge Companion to

RECORDED MUSIC

....

EDITED BY
Nicholas Cook,
Eric Clarke,
Daniel Leech-Wilkinson,
and
John Rink

CAMBRIDGE
UNIVERSITY PRESS

CAMBRIDGE UNIVERSITY PRESS
Cambridge, New York, Melbourne, Madrid, Cape Town, Singapore, São Paulo, Delhi

Cambridge University Press
The Edinburgh Building, Cambridge CB2 8RU, UK

Published in the United States of America by Cambridge University Press, New York

www.cambridge.org
Information on this title: www.cambridge.org/9780521684613

First published 2009

Printed in the United Kingdom at the University Press, Cambridge

A catalogue record for this publication is available from the British Library

ISBN 978-0-521-86582-1 hardback
ISBN 978-0-521-68461-3 paperback

Contents

[v]

Illustrations

Notes on contributors

Roger Beardsley is a recording engineer specialising in the restoration of older formats of recording including 78 rpm discs and analogue tapes at his own studio in Lincolnshire. Current positions reflect this specialism: he is a member of the boards of Music Preserved (a broadcast performances' archive), Historic Masters (re-pressings of 78s direct from original masters) and the Historic Singers Trust. In addition he is technical consultant to the Sound Archive at Kings College London and York University Sound Archives. He is a lifelong music lover with a wide range of tastes, but with a bias towards vocal and opera.

Arild Bergh is currently working on a PhD on the topic of music and conflict transformation at the University of Exeter, with fieldwork in Norway and Sudan. He is an editor of the journal *Music and Arts in Action* (www.musicandartsinaction. net). He has previously worked as a music journalist and researched and written on topics ranging from immigrant music in Europe to cassette music culture and underground music in communist countries. Recent published work includes 'I'd like to teach the world to sing: Music and conflict transformation' (*Musicae Scientiae*, special issue, 2007) and 'Everlasting love: The sustainability of top-down versus bottom-up approaches to music and conflict transformation' (*Sustainability: A New Frontier for the Arts and Cultures*, 2008).

Andrew Blake is Associate Dean of the School of Social Sciences, Media and Cultural Studies at the University of East London. For a while in the 1980s he was a professional saxophonist. His writings on music include *The Music Business* (1992); *The Land Without Music* (1997); *Living through Pop* (1999, as editor); and *Popular Music: The Age of Multimedia* (2007), alongside numerous chapters and articles including a contribution to *The Cambridge History of Twentieth-Century Music* (2004). He has also written widely on other cultural matters; his book *The Irresistible Rise of Harry Potter* (2002) has been translated into five languages.

Georgina Born is Professor of Sociology, Anthropology and Music at Cambridge University, and Honorary Professor of Anthropology at University College London. She has been a Fellow of Emmanuel College Cambridge (1998–2006), Senior Research Fellow, King's College, Cambridge (1997–8), and a Fellow of the University of California, Humanities Research Institute (2002–3), and is an International Fellow of the Australian Sociological Association and of Yale University's Center for Cultural Sociology. Her books are *Rationalizing Culture: IRCAM, Boulez, and the Institutionalization of the Musical Avant-Garde* (1995), *Western Music and Its Others: Difference, Representation and Appropriation in Music* (2000) and *Uncertain Vision: Birt, Dyke, and the Reinvention of the BBC* (2005).

Born in 1946, **George Brock-Nannestad** graduated in electronics and signal processing in 1971 and is a European patent attorney, focusing on musical acoustics.

From 1981 to 1986 he carried out the project 'The establishment of objective criteria for correct reproduction of historical sound recordings', funded by the Danish Research Council for the Humanities. From 1991 to 1998 he was responsible for research and tuition in preservation and restoration of carriers for sound, moving images, and data at the Royal Danish Academy for Fine Art. Since 1997 George has been providing consultation and research on patents, restoration concepts and the history of AV technology. He is a member of several academic and professional organisations, including the Acoustical Society of America, the Audio Engineering Society, the International Council of Museums, and the Danish Musicological Society.

Eric Clarke is Heather Professor of Music at the University of Oxford, having previously held posts at the University of Sheffield and City University, London. He is the author of *Ways of Listening: An Ecological Approach to the Perception of Musical Meaning*, is co-editor with Nicholas Cook of *Empirical Musicology*, and has published papers and book chapters on various topics in the psychology of music. He was a member of CHARM; is a co-investigator on the successor Centre for Musical Performance as Creative Practice; and is an associate editor for a number of journals including *Music Perception*, *Musicae Scientiae*, *Empirical Musicology Review* and *Radical Musicology*.

Nicholas Cook is 1684 Professor of Music at the University of Cambridge. He was previously Professorial Research Fellow in Music at Royal Holloway, University of London, where he directed the AHRC Research Centre for the History and Analysis of Recorded Music (CHARM). He is the author of articles and books on a wide variety of musicological and theoretical subjects, and his *Music: A Very Short Introduction* has been translated into eleven languages. His latest book is *The Schenker Project: Culture, Race, and Music Theory in Fin-de-siècle Vienna*. A former editor of *Journal of the Royal Musical Association*, he was elected Fellow of the British Academy in 2001.

Tia DeNora teaches music sociology, research methods and social theory in the Department of Sociology and Philosophy at Exeter University. She is the author of *Beethoven and the Construction of Genius* (1995), *Music in Everyday Life* (Cambridge University Press, 2000) and *After Adorno: Rethinking Music Sociology* (Cambridge University Press, 2003). She is part of the editorial team of *Music and Arts in Action* (MAiA). Her ongoing research is in the area of music, health, well-being and disability studies and she is currently collaborating with the Nordoff Robbins Centre for Music Therapy in London on a project that examines music and identity work in a mental health setting.

Martin Elste (born in 1952) studied musicology and mass communication in Cologne, London and Berlin, where he concluded his studies with Carl Dahlhaus in 1981 with his doctoral thesis on 'Bach's Art of Fugue on Records'. Since 1982 he has been working at the Staatliches Institut für Musikforschung, Berlin, as curator in the Museum of Musical Instruments. Elste was Chair of the Discography Committee as well as Vice President of the International Association of Sound and Audiovisual Archives, and is an Advisory Board member of the Comité International des Musées et Collections d'Instruments de Musique. He acted on the Advisory Boards of the *Encyclopedia of Recorded Sound in the*

United States (1993) and the revised edition of *Die Musik in Geschichte und Gegenwart*. Since 2000, Elste has been President of the German Record Critics' Award. Besides working as a music and record critic, he has written more than 200 articles as well as ten monographs. For his book *Meilensteine der Bach-Interpretation 1750–2000* he was given the Association for Recorded Sound Collections (ARSC) Award for Excellence in Historical Recorded Sound Research.

Lewis Foreman's many books and articles include the standard biography of Bax. He has produced over 250 CD booklets and programme notes for organisations as varied as the London Symphony Orchestra and the Nash Ensemble. Associated with the Kensington Symphony Orchestra and Opera Viva/Pro Opera in the 1970s, he helped programme over 300 revivals for the London 'fringe'. Now a full-time writer, he is also A&R consultant for Dutton Epoch, advises various record companies on new repertoire and booklet notes, and writes musical obituaries for the *Independent*. Long a record collector, he has sourced many historical CDs.

Jonathan Freeman-Attwood is Principal of the Royal Academy of Music. He is producer of over 100 commercial recordings, many of which have won Gramophone Awards and other international prizes. As trumpet soloist, he performs in a series for Linn Records including his re-working of Fauré's late violin sonata in *La trompette retrouvée* and a radical view of the seventeenth century in *Trumpet Masque*. He broadcasts regularly for BBC Radio 3 and writes as an established authority on Bach interpretation. In 2001 he was appointed a University of London Professor.

Simon Frith has been Tovey Professor of Music at the University of Edinburgh since 2006, having previously been Professor of Film and Media at the University of Stirling. He was for many years a rock critic, writing for a variety of publications in Britain and the USA, and now chairs the judges of the Mercury Music Prize. He is presently directing an AHRC-funded research project on the post-war history of live music promotion in Britain. His most recent publication is *Taking Popular Music Seriously* (2007).

Donald Greig is a professional singer with twenty-five years of concert and recording experience, most notably – though by no means exclusively – in the field of early music. A former lecturer in film studies and semiology, he has published several articles in both film and musicological journals.

Michael Haas, now a freelance producer of important classical artists, has worked as an executive and recording producer for both Universal Music Group and Sony Classical. He was producer for Sir Georg Solti for over ten years, winning several Grammies, before leaving for Sony to work with Claudio Abbado and the Berlin Philharmonic. His most regarded work has been in the rediscovery of music lost during the Nazi years in Europe. The recording series *Entartete Musik* is seen as a groundbreaking recovery of works thought lost, forgotten or destroyed. The series has won most major awards and created an opportunity for launching artists as diverse as Ute Lemper and Matthias Goerne. The *London Evening Standard*, in their 'Millennium List of London's Movers and Shakers', named Mr Haas as one of classical music's most influential entrepreneurs.

Roger Heaton, clarinettist and conductor, performs with many groups including the Fidelio Trio and the Kreutzer and Smith String Quartets, and has been a member of the Gavin Bryars Ensemble since the early 1980s. He was a member of the London Sinfonietta and Ensemble Modern, has played with the Arditti Quartet, was Music Director and conductor of Rambert Dance Company during the 1990s, and was Clarinet Professor at the Darmstadt Ferienkurse für Neue Musik, 1982–94. He records regularly for CD and radio and is currently Professor of Music at Bath Spa University.

Peter Hill is a pianist and writer on music. He studied at Oxford University, and at the Royal College of Music with Cyril Smith and Nadia Boulanger, and was awarded first prize at Darmstadt for his performances of Cage and Stockhausen. His complete recording of Messiaen's solo piano works was made with the composer's help and encouragement, and has been described as 'one of the most important recording projects of recent years' (*New York Times*). Other recordings include CDs of Beethoven (the Diabelli Variations), Stravinsky, and the Second Viennese School (Schoenberg, Berg and Webern). He has made over a hundred programmes for the BBC, and among his broadcast talks was the 2,000th edition of 'Building a Library' (Radio 3). His books include *The Messiaen Companion*, and *Stravinsky: The Rite of Spring* (Cambridge University Press). Research on Messiaen led to a biography of the composer (*Messiaen*) – co-authored with Nigel Simeone – which was published in 2005 and has been reissued in translation in both Germany and France. A further joint-authored book, *Olivier Messiaen: Oiseaux exotiques*, was published in 2007. Peter Hill teaches at the University of Sheffield.

During the seventies **Mike Howlett** played bass and wrote with esoteric space-funk group Gong. After leaving Gong Mike put together his own group, Strontium-90, with musicians Sting, Andy Summers and Stuart Copeland, who went on to enormous success as the Police. Mike began producing records in the 1980s and had a string of Top Ten hits, receiving a Grammy award for his work on *A Flock of Seagulls*. He is currently Chairman of the Music Producers Guild and lectures in Audio Technology at the University of Glamorgan and at Thames Valley University.

Ted Kendall grew up surrounded by music and electronics. After gaining a degree in electronic engineering, he joined the BBC Transcription Service, where he received a thorough training as a recording engineer. A chance meeting with John R. T. Davies combined latent interests in jazz and archive sound, and since 1990 he has remastered material for hundreds of CDs including complete editions of Fats Waller and George Formby, BBC radio comedy (*The Goon Show, Hancock's Half Hour, Round The Horne, The Navy Lark*), and classical material for Conifer and Teldec. His Front End transfer preamplifier is relied upon by transfer engineers the world over.

Colin Lawson is Director of the Royal College of Music, London. He has an international profile as a period clarinettist and has played principal in most of Britain's leading period orchestras, notably the Hanover Band, the English Concert and the London Classical Players, with whom he has recorded extensively and toured worldwide. Described recently as 'a brilliant, absolutely world-class player' (*Westdeutsche Allgemeine Zeitung*), he has appeared as soloist in many international venues, including London's major concert halls and New York's Lincoln Center and Carnegie Hall. Colin has published widely on historical performance practice, especially for Cambridge University Press.

Daniel Leech-Wilkinson is a professor of music at King's College London. As a medievalist he is the author of *The Modern Invention of Medieval Music* (Cambridge University Press, 2002). His more recent research, dealing with musical communication, is focused on the changing relationship between expressive performance and meaning.

While studying architecture in 1965, **Nick Mason** became one of the founding members of Pink Floyd, and is the only member to have played on every album. Throughout Pink Floyd's four-decade history they have achieved a blend of both creative and commercial success: *Dark Side of the Moon* still holds the record for the longest continuous period any album has remained in the American charts, and the band's last two tours played to over 9.8 million people. Nick has produced albums by Robert Wyatt, Steve Hillage and the Damned, as well as a West End musical, *Return to the Forbidden Planet*. In 2004 Nick wrote *Inside Out: A Personal History of Pink Floyd*, which has been published in ten languages and sold over 300,000 copies worldwide.

Louise Meintjes is Associate Professor of Music and Cultural Anthropology at Duke University and the author of *Sound of Africa! Making Music Zulu in a South African Studio* (2003).

David Patmore's research interests focus upon commercial and cultural interactions within the history of the recording industry. His work has been funded individually by the Economic and Social Research Council and by the Arts and Humanities Research Council. He is a research fellow at the Centre for the History and Analysis of Recorded Music (CHARM), based at the University of Sheffield. He has been reviewing and writing about recordings for over twenty-five years and has contributed to numerous consumer magazines and academic journals. He is the author of *The A–Z of Conductors*, published in 2007 by Naxos Records.

Tully Potter, born in Edinburgh in 1942, spent his formative years in South Africa. The human voice was his first musical interest. A serious record collector since he was twelve, he has made a special study of performing practice, especially of vocal, string and chamber music. Over more than forty years he has contributed to international musical journals, notably *The Strad*; from 1997 to 2008 he edited *Classic Record Collector*. He has lectured on historic recordings in Britain, Italy, Austria, France, Belgium and Switzerland. His biography of Adolf Busch is to be published soon by Toccata Press.

John Rink is Professor of Musical Performance Studies at the University of Cambridge. He studied at Princeton University, King's College London, and the University of Cambridge; he also holds the Concert Recital Diploma and *Premier Prix* in piano from the Guildhall School of Music and Drama. He specialises in the fields of performance studies, theory and analysis, and nineteenth-century studies, and has produced numerous books for Cambridge University Press, including *The Practice of Performance* (1995), *Chopin: The Piano Concertos* (1997), *Musical Performance* (2002), and *Annotated Catalogue of Chopin's First Editions* (with Christophe Grabowski, 2010).

Steve Savage is an active producer and recording engineer. He has been the primary engineer on seven CDs that received Grammy nominations. These include CDs for Robert Cray, John Hammond, the Gospel Hummingbirds and Otis Rush. Recent projects include CDs for Elvin Bishop and Sista Monica. Steve is a former Chapter President and National Trustee of the San Francisco Chapter of the Recording Academy (the Grammy organisation). Steve is the author of *The Rhythm Book*, published by Electronic Musician Books, and a lecturer in the Humanities department at San Francisco State University.

Nigel Simeone is Professor of Historical Musicology at the University of Sheffield. He has published extensively on the life and music of Olivier Messiaen (notably as co-author with Peter Hill of *Messiaen* and *Olivier Messiaen: Oiseaux exotiques*) and on other twentieth-century French composers; he is also co-author of the standard catalogue of Janáček's works. At present he is writing a monograph on Bernstein's *West Side Story* and working on other projects related to the sources and recording of Broadway musicals.

Susan Tomes is a concert pianist internationally renowned for her achievements in chamber music. For fifteen years she was the pianist of the innovative group Domus. Since 1995 she has been the pianist of the Florestan Trio, winner of a 2000 Royal Philharmonic Society Award and one of the most recorded piano trios in the world. Susan has made nearly fifty CDs, winning awards in various countries. She is also the author of two acclaimed books on music, *Beyond the Notes* and *A Musician's Alphabet*. She writes occasionally for the *Guardian* and the *Independent*.

Simon Trezise was born in Brighton, England. He studied at Keble College, Oxford, where he wrote his dissertation on Schoenberg's *Gurrelieder* under the supervision of Derrick Puffett. Since 1984 he has lectured at Trinity College Dublin. He has published books on Debussy, the Cambridge Music Handbook on Debussy's *La mer* and the *Debussy Companion*. Interests include Elgar, Wagner, romantic opera, music and text, film music and, more recently, the study of performance through recordings, which is reflected in a number of articles, papers, a book project on the conductor Eugene Ormandy, and the creation of an audio archive at Trinity College Dublin.

Following an early career working with computers, **Martyn Ware** went on to form the Human League (1978), production company/label British Electric Foundation, and Heaven 17 (both 1980). He has written, performed and produced two Human League, two BEF and nine Heaven 17 albums. As a producer he has worked with artists such as Tina Turner, Terence Trent D'Arby, Chaka Khan, Erasure, Marc Almond and Mavis Staples. In 2001 he founded The Illustrious Company with Vince Clarke to exploit the creative and commercial possibilities of their unique three-dimensional sound technology in collaboration with fine artists, the performing arts and corporate clients around the world.

Chris Watson is a sound recordist with a particular and passionate interest in recording the wildlife sounds of animals, habitats and atmospheres from around the world. As a freelance recordist for film, TV and radio, Chris Watson specialises in natural history and documentary location sound together with track assembly and sound design in post-production.

Richard Witts is a music lecturer at the University of Edinburgh. His first book, a contextual biography of the anarchist chanteuse Nico (1993), was followed by a history of the Arts Council (1999), and his most recent book has been a cultural study of the Velvet Underground (2006). As a musician in Manchester he was a member of both the Hallé Orchestra and the post-punk band the Passage. His next book considers music in Britain, 1940–2000.

Albin Zak holds degrees in composition and performance from New England Conservatory, and a PhD in musicology from the City University of New York. He has taught at the City College of New York and the University of Michigan, and is currently chair of the Music Department at the State University of New York at Albany. His publications include two books, *The Velvet Underground Companion* and *The Poetics of Rock: Cutting Tracks, Making Records*. He is currently at work on a book for the University of Michigan Press entitled *'I Don't Sound Like Nobody': Remaking Music in 1950s America*.

Acknowledgements

This book is one of the outputs of the AHRC Research Centre for the History and Analysis of Recorded Music (CHARM), and the editors wish to acknowledge the financial support of the AHRC (Arts and Humanities Research Council) in making this book, as well as the larger programme of research of which it forms part, possible; further details of the Centre, and its successor centre CMPCP (the AHRC Research Centre for Musical Performance as Creative Practice), may be found at www.charm.kcl.ac.uk. We would like to thank Penny Souster and Vicki Cooper, successive Music Books editors at Cambridge University Press, for their help and patience during what turned out to be a rather prolonged period of gestation. Finally we owe a particular debt of gratitude to Carol Chan, the Centre Coordinator, who made the whole process of bringing the book together into its final form much smoother and easier than we could ever have expected it to be.

Introduction

The Cambridge Companion to Recorded Music is a very broad title. On one interpretation it might take in just about all popular music, the development of which was largely conditioned by recording; on another you might expect an annotated guide to the recorded repertory. We are offering neither of these. Our aim is rather to promote an understanding of the ways in which recording has both reflected and shaped music throughout the twentieth century and into the twenty-first: that is, how it has reflected and shaped not just the music itself, but the ways in which it is produced and the ways in which it is heard. That involves a lot of background information about recording and recordings, which we also try to cover. And 'music' in this context is a very inclusive term, encompassing the countless different genres of classical and popular music, all of which have been shaped by the development of recording technologies, originally in North America and Europe, and their subsequent spread across the globe. The way in which music has been shaped by recording is not uniform, however, and comparison of the impact of recording on different classical and popular traditions brings home the variety of conceptions that exists of what recorded music is and might be.

The appearance of this *Companion* is a symptom of – and, we hope, will further contribute to – the increasing interest of musicologists in music as performance. To someone outside musicology it might be odd to think of it as anything else, but the traditional focus on scores as the repositories of compositional creativity has led musicologists to think of performance as something that happens after the event, so to speak, rather than being a creative practice in its own right. It also signals the discipline's increasing concern with reception, with the way in which music is given meaning in the act of listening to it, and in the other acts that are informed by listening, ranging from dancing to it to writing about it: recording has fundamentally changed the reception of music, in terms of its nature, its conditions, the places where it happens. Other recent symptoms of this disciplinary development range from the establishment of an academic journal on the work of producers (*Journal on the Art of Record Production*) to publicly funded initiatives to disseminate the heritage of recorded music (such as the British Library's 'Archival Sound

Recordings' project) and the establishment in the UK of a dedicated research centre, the AHRC Research Centre for the History and Analysis of Recorded Music (CHARM), from which the four co-editors of this book are drawn.[1] At the same time the focus on recordings is establishing new interdisciplinary links, for work on recorded music is carried out not just – not even mainly – by musicologists, but also by cultural and media theorists, sociologists and historians of technology. All these fields are represented in this volume.

Like most collaborative books, *The Companion to Recorded Music* consists of a variety of complementary perspectives on a common subject, with individual contributions being relatively self-contained. (The contributors also write from a variety of geographical perspectives – North America, Britain, Ireland, continental Europe – and this explains some variations in terminology which we have not attempted to standardise.[2]) The main chapters are counterpointed by a series of shorter essays which offer personal (sometimes contradictory) takes on different aspects of recorded music. Most of them reflect a practitioner's viewpoint, the practices in question including performance, record production, sound engineering and record collecting. Several have a strong autobiographical dimension, illustrating how a lifelong enthusiasm for recordings typically takes root at an early age; others are first-hand testimonies of particular moments, whether in the development of recording practices or the discovery of historic recordings long thought lost. All this means that the book can be browsed rather than read straight through, but we have laid out the chapters and personal takes in such a way as to provide, when read in sequence, a possible trajectory through the varied and often complex world of recorded music.

Since the main chapters are designed between them to cover those areas most essential for an understanding of recording and recordings, they provide a convenient structure around which to pick out some of the principal themes that weave in and out of the book. We begin where recording began: with the live performance of which the recording is, literally, a record. It is well known (and quite possibly true) that the first reproduced sound – dating from 1877 – was of Thomas Edison reciting 'Mary had a little lamb', but in chapter 1 Donald Greig writes about performing for the microphone from the perspective of a present-day singer specialising in early music, yet with experience in pop session work as well. Central to this chapter is the contrast between classical and pop performers in terms of their attitude towards both the process of recording and the technologies involved in it: classical performers tend to see recordings as in essence reproducing concert performances, whereas for pop performers the recording is, so to speak, the primary text. Linked to this is a distinction between two essentially different, though often overlapping, orientations, one towards the event that is recorded, and the other towards the musical work embodied in the recording. As will become plain, these different conceptions of what recorded music is are fundamental to an understanding of the whole field.

Rather as orchestral performance is mediated by the silent yet crucial figure of the conductor, so both classical and popular recordings are mediated by the producer, who is the focus of chapter 2. There is something shadowy about the figure of the producer: Andrew Blake entitles the final section of his chapter 'So, what do producers actually *do*?', and there are many answers to the question. At one extreme the producer's job is to keep the artists happy; at the other it merges into sound engineering. But the producer's central role – like the conductor's – is perhaps as an expert listener able to focus on the larger context as well as the details of the recording as it develops. Yet expert listening is also an essential part of how, in chapter 3, Albin Zak characterises the work of the sound engineer, citing Chick Plotkin: 'That's what you do ... Listen hard.' However, Zak stresses the specifically analytical nature of engineers' listening, oriented towards those aspects of sound that are amenable to technological control: the fact that digital technology puts more and more aspects of sound under the engineer's control is one reason why the distinction between producer and engineer is becoming increasingly hard to draw.

But the most important feature shared by Blake's and Zak's chapters is their emphasis on the creative dimension of recording: as Blake puts it, producers, not just performers, 'make music', while Zak emphasises how all technical decisions made by engineers are at the same time 'aesthetic choices'. Both Blake and Zak refer to sonic 'signatures', so underlining the extent to which producers and engineers, like film directors, might be viewed as authors. There is, however, a paradox here. These creative professions have been brought into being by successive developments in technology, yet the digital revolution is now undoing them. By bringing studio-quality recording and editing into garages and teenagers' bedrooms at ever decreasing prices, and by offering integrated interfaces for sound design and manipulation, computers are turning sound engineering into part of general musicianship. If, like producers, sound engineers make music, then increasingly anyone who makes music is likely to be their own sound engineer.

In the early days of recording, the technology was intrusive and could not cope with ensemble performance – at least not without significantly disrupting it. Electrical recording, from about 1925, alleviated the situation, and for two decades the relationship between live performance and recording was arguably at its closest. But, as emerges very clearly from the three opening chapters, the general adoption of tape recording from the late 1940s initiated a process by which the relationship between live performance and recording became increasingly tenuous. At first this was because tape editing allowed a form of time shifting: mistakes could be overdubbed, or a recording could be assembled from any number of separate takes, resulting in what was heard as a performance – but a performance that had never in fact happened. The introduction around 1970 of multitrack recording (with sixteen or more channels) took things a stage further: musical textures could be built up from layers recorded at different times, with reverberation and other effects being used to generate an acoustic which, again, didn't necessarily exist in reality.

And with the take up of digital technology from the 1990s it became no longer just a matter of shifting time or creating virtual spaces: practically all aspects of sound can now be manipulated or designed from scratch, which means on the one hand that performing, editing and composing become more or less indistinguishable, and on the other that the 'original' performance becomes irrecoverable or irrelevant. ('Recording' has in this way become a misnomer: what matters is the end product, not its antecedents.) The result is a striking disparity between the nature of production and that of reception: sounds may be manufactured rather than performed in the traditional sense, yet we hear them as performed, as human communication enacted in real time. Listening to recordings, then, involves a kind of willing suspension of disbelief, and in order to express this both Simon Trezise and Nicholas Cook borrow the concept of diegesis from film studies, where it refers to the apparent reality of a cinematically depicted scene. And it is this ability of recordings to create their own reality that is the key to how recording has transformed musical practices under the guise of merely reflecting them. This is what Zak calls an 'ontological shift' – a shift reflected in his claim that 'how music *sounds* is inseparable from what it *is*'. (Daniel Leech-Wilkinson echoes the thought: 'when music sounds different it is different'.) Self-evident as this may seem, it represents a conception of what music is quite opposed the traditional idea that music consists of works, more or less coterminous with scores, which are reproduced or translated into sound through performance.

Recording, then, is a technical process, but it is more than that: it is a complex mode of representation which generates meanings in its own right. At one level this is what Blake and Zak were saying about production and engineering. But it is also what Louise Meintjes (chapter 4) argues at a quite different level. Based on a close ethnographic study of Johannesburg recording studios in and after the final years of apartheid, Meintjes shows how sociopolitical changes are both reflected and enacted in studio practices – particularly since under apartheid sound engineers tended to be white while producers were black. Studios can be seen as metaphors of the larger reality that lies beyond them, but they are also metonyms, little bits of reality in which social change can be enacted. And recording's power to promote social change is explored on a much broader canvas in chapter 5, where Arild Bergh and Tia DeNora show how changing technologies have afforded new ways of listening, and how these new ways of listening have in turn afforded the construction and negotiation of personal and group identities. They have also reshaped experience in a more literal sense: personal stereo from the Walkman to the iPod has reconfigured the boundaries of private and public space. Often seen as emblematic of postmodernism, such reconstruction of experience is again effected by listening, and indeed listening might be seen as the underlying topic of all these first five chapters: performance, production and engineering are all forms of social interaction mediated by the ear, and the listening practices of music users as documented by Bergh and DeNora form only the final stage in an unbroken chain that links the production of recordings to their consumption.

The following group of chapters has a more overtly historical orientation, tracing the development of recording from a number of different perspectives. One of the basic drivers of this development was supplied by the recording industry, which at the beginning of the twentieth century was remarkably forward-looking in its approach (in the first years of the century the Gramophone Company was already seeking to establish offshoots throughout the world to stimulate and service local demand), which had its glory days in the decades after the Second World War, yet which by the century's end had become hopelessly embattled as a result of its failure to seize the opportunities offered by new technologies of dissemination. As David Patmore explains in chapter 6, the record industry has largely moulded our understanding of what music is, both classical and popular. It was, for example, the commercial strategies pursued between the wars that brought about the establishment of a Hollywood-like 'star' system of globe-trotting conductors, and that also established what we still see as the canon of great performers: the vast majority of CD reissues of pre-war recordings are taken from the record companies' premium labels, reserved for international stars as opposed to the now neglected yet often highly talented national artists whom they marketed on their budget labels. And it is often claimed that, in its quest for a technical perfection that would bear repeated listening, the record industry brought about a gradual homogenisation of classical performance style, a convergence on the irreproachable but bland: as will become clear, the jury is out on that one.

At the same time the record industry was itself driven by successive waves of technological innovation, summarised by Patmore but explored more thoroughly by George Brock-Nannestad in the next chapter. It is easy to think of histories of technology as a continuous evolution towards higher standards, and of course that is the broad-brush picture. But there is much light and shade in the detail. For one thing, as Simon Trezise observes, 'The assumption that progress automatically invalidates the listening habits of a previous generation … does a disservice to the many dedicated listeners who believed they had found audio perfection': electrical recordings, for example, set the standard of what recorded music should sound like – until the appearance of the LP. For another thing, industry priorities or user considerations have sometimes overridden quality of sound: the tape cassette captured much of the LP market despite its lower audio standards, because it offered recording as well as playback, while nowadays the MP3 format sacrifices sound quality in the interests of fast downloading and miniaturisation. This is as much as to say that the history of recording is to be understood in terms of the interaction between enabling technologies on the one hand, and the purposes for which individuals and institutions wish to use them on the other. In another paradox, digital technology, which at first gave the music industry a new lease of life as consumers traded in their LPs for CDs, now threatens to fatally undermine it, at least in its current form (a form that reflects the longstanding, near-monopolistic practices of a very small number of global majors): the ease of digital copying and internet dissemination renders copyright – historically the foundation of the music business – increasingly unenforceable. Whether this represents a threat or an opportunity to create new ways of disseminating music depends upon your point of view.

Trezise's own chapter has a dual role. On the one hand it offers a series of case studies in recording, arranged chronologically and illustrating in concrete form many of the issues raised in previous chapters. On the other hand it poses many of the questions that arise in making use of recordings as documents of cultural practice. Musicologists who work on scores take for granted a host of catalogues and other finding aids developed through generations of scholarship. Little of this infrastructure exists for the study of recordings, and as a result specialist knowledge is required at all stages. You need it in order to find out what records have been released, and then to locate copies of them. (The problems are in essence the same whether you are researching, say, Artur Rubinstein or Jimi Hendrix.) You also need specialist knowledge if you are to understand in what ways you can – and cannot – trust recordings as evidence for historical performance. Commercial transfers cannot be relied upon for aspects such as timbre, because they have often been remade to sound as much as possible like modern CDs, while even the original discs may be misleading because, for example, of intrusive recording techniques that may have disrupted normal performance practices, or simply because nobody knows how fast to play them. (The designation '78' is only an approximation: particularly in early recordings, speed was not standardised.) The message of Trezise's chapter, then, is that recordings do not offer a transparent window on the past. Like other documents, they are artifacts, the products of particular cultural circumstances, and as such they stand as much in need of interpretation as any other historical document.

Once you have got hold of a recording, what do you do with it? In chapter 9, Nicholas Cook explores a number of different ways of working with recordings. Perhaps the most important is the use of computer-based playback environments that provide a great deal of flexibility in navigating one or more recordings at the same time: they bring to the study of recordings some of the convenience musicologists have always taken for granted in working with scores. They also provide a range of visualisations which can help you home in on particular features of the music in which you're interested. All this means you can gain a lot of insight by working directly on the sound of the music, in contrast to older musicological approaches to performance that started with score-based analysis and then attempted to map the analysis onto the performance. Other approaches are more abstract in nature, extracting measurable information from recordings and then correlating the information across a range of contexts. Such work aims to characterise performance at a stylistic level (Hofmann as against Rubinstein, early Rubinstein as against late Rubinstein): in deflecting attention from the musical work towards performance style, it reflects a belief in the creative role of singers and instrumentalists – a belief parallel to Blake's and Zak's emphasis on the creative role of producers and engineers. Performers, producers and engineers, in short, all make music, and not just the composers who were for so long the more or less sole focus of musicology.

And performance style is the topic of chapter 10: if Trezise focuses on the documentary value of recordings and Cook on methods for analysing them, then Daniel Leech-Wilkinson illustrates how sustained historical interpretation can be built on these foundations. At one level Leech-Wilkinson's purpose is to provide an overview of stylistic developments in classical performance practice during the era of recordings. At another, however, his aim is to pose quite fundamental questions that must arise in the history of any performance practice (at least during the age of recording, for he sees any attempt to reconstruct the history of performance in the pre-audio era as essentially a lost cause): what performance style is – according to Leech-Wilkinson a set of habits, some conscious and others unconscious, some that change slowly and others rapidly – and what the principles underlying style change might be. Drawing on the 'memetic' approach originally advanced by Richard Dawkins, he draws an analogy with natural selection: only successful performers can influence other performers, and success requires a reasonable accommodation to the stylistic norms of a given time and place, coupled with a measure of novelty or idiosyncrasy. As Leech-Wilkinson puts it, 'The young performer succeeds in making a career if she is both highly competent and has something noticeably but not upsettingly new to offer.'

Finally, Simon Frith's and Georgina Born's chapters explore different aspects of the discourses around recordings. Frith documents the essentially accidental and self-appointed origins of the record critic, and identifies four overlapping types of discourse that critical writing employs: these are based on the record understood as the document of a prior performance, as something to collect and organise into a library, as a technological object with particular qualities, and as a work of art. It is in the writing of rock critics that this last discourse developed most strongly, responding to rock's more explicit recognition of the album as a constructed studio product, and the final part of Frith's chapter draws out some of the differences – and commonalities – between critical writing on classical music, jazz and rock. Frith suggests that what draws readers to record criticism is not primarily that they will learn what they should buy, or how they should listen to it, since much of what they read about they already own and know: rather, it is the stimulation and provocation elicited by this writing that is relished, what might be called the dialogics of record criticism. As Frith puts it, 'To be interested in music is to be interested in records, which is to be interested in what people write about those records.'

Styled an 'Afterword', Born's chapter draws on the previous chapters and personal takes while developing an argument about the effects of current and future technology. Situating herself squarely between Adorno's pessimism and Benjamin's optimism, Born stresses the centrality of sound reproduction within early twenty-first-century aesthetic consciousness, and traces its evolution from representation to what she calls 'remediation': a convergence of once distinct media forms in which meaning emerges from 'the *re*-presentation in novel combinations and contexts of pre-existing media content'. Remediation, Born argues, was always implicit in recording technology, but the digital revolution has brought it to stage centre. Now autonomous of any specific physical embodiment, the digital musical object is cultural through and through, and as such immanently open to re-creation. If, as a prime exemplar of commodity fetishism, analogue recording was a technology of modernism, then Born's vision of a future mediated by digital sound underlines the profound cultural processes unleashed by Edison's recitation of a nursery rhyme in 1877. Recorded music penetrates to the heart of culture even as, for more than a century, it has entertained the world.

Learning to live with recording

SUSAN TOMES

As a concert musician you gradually learn to focus on that little slice of time, typically from 7.30 to 9.30 pm, when you must be at your best. Over the years you learn how to build up towards that point, rehearsing during the day (but not wearing yourself out), eating wisely, resting at the right point, all with the aim of being at your most alert and energetic during the performance. You know you have only one chance to give your best.

Making a recording therefore comes as a shock, because in my experience it involves playing your chosen repertoire at high intensity for hours on end. Nothing in rehearsal quite prepares you for this, because in rehearsal you instinctively pace yourself, and in recording you cannot. If, like me, you work in small chamber groups or on your own, you suddenly find yourself facing unprecedented challenges. A recording session typically starts at 10 am (after an hour of warming up) and runs through until the evening, or until everyone feels too tired to go on. My groups have always wanted to record whole movements at a time, so that their shape on disc has integrity. Only when we've got the whole movement safely recorded do we go back and 'patch' mistakes. When we appear in person to play a concert somewhere, we want to be able to match up to, or do better than, our recordings. However, playing movements over and over at full stretch is something we never did before we first encountered a recording session, and something we never do at any other time.

Recording makes everyone hyper-critical of themselves and one another at a level of detail and with an intensity never sustained for so long in ordinary rehearsal. Only at recording sessions do we have the chance to listen back immediately to our own playing on state-of-the-art equipment. And when we do, we become extremely conscious not only of our playing, but of every little cough and scrape, page-turn, pedal noise and squeak of the piano stool. Then, too, there are planes, tube trains, cars, barking dogs and even birds in the rafters we didn't hear when we were playing. All this creates an acute awareness of the sound quality of each moment. Noise-free takes are at such a premium that you become all too aware that your individual slips may make a 'take' unusable. And of course your colleagues can make it unusable too. I don't know which is worse: to make a mistake while someone else is hitting their best form of the day, or to have someone else ruin yours. In a concert, such things hardly matter because the unique moment of performance, shared by the audience, means that no one has trouble understanding a minor blemish for what it is. But when it happens on a recording, the whole team knows the take is spoilt. A blemish, preserved for ever on disc to be repeated every time someone listens to it, can assume the proportions of sabotage.

In short, the process of recording has a way of isolating each person in a bell jar of self-consciousness. Instead of having a wide and free perspective, your world shrinks to the little pinpoint of light which is yourself. Instead of focusing outward on what signals you can give out and what you can add to the whole performance, you focus instead on reliability and on the surface perfection of your own part. This is closing down instead of opening up, and needless to say it's against the essential spirit of chamber music, as well as the spirit of communication.

To offset this rather negative view I should also say I've learned to be grateful for the role of recordings in my career. Whatever the rigours of recording, the finished product wings its way around the world, bringing your playing into living rooms and hopefully into hearts you could not hope to reach in person even with a campaign of non-stop touring. Also, CDs command a high level of critical attention. You can be fairly sure that even if your last three London concerts were ignored by the press, your new CD is likely to be reviewed by a galaxy of newspapers, magazines and internet sites all over the world.

However, for me a disc is never something I can whole-heartedly endorse because with the best will in the world it remains an artificial construct. The final selection of takes is generally a mosaic of the players' best attempts, the most noiseless takes, and the least error-prone versions. This choice is made not only by the producer but by the players themselves. For as they walk from the recording studio to the backstage listening room, they also leave behind their performing selves, passing through that crucial psychological gate that separates givers from takers. What seems right as you play may not seem right as you listen. But which judgement is the more important?

People have often asked me why we don't simply record live concerts and leave it at that. And indeed some live concert recordings are delightful. However, no one should be under the illusion that the recording of a concert can capture all the ingredients that make the real thing so enjoyable. I've sometimes bought the CD of a concert I attended, only to find that the special atmosphere has not been captured on disc. Yes, the sound is there, but, because of where the microphones are, it is not the sound I heard. Then, it turns out that the other elements of the concert – the visual, the spiritual, the sense of sharing the excitement of communication with other listeners – have not made it onto the disc. To some extent I can supply them from memory, but only to some extent. And if I was not at the live performance in the first place, I often wonder why a particular 'concert recording' is prized by the people who were there. At home I have dozens of my own live concert recordings on cassette. None of them evokes the precise sensations I had during the concert, and ultimately I find them one-dimensional compared with the multi-dimensional experience of being there. This is not to deny the point of making concert recordings as long as you know their limits.

Once you have accepted that recording is artificial, it makes sense to use the process constructively. Since you can expunge your worst moments and retain only your best, why not do so? The scandal that broke early in 2007 around the 'legacy' of pianist Joyce Hatto, many of whose recordings were 'borrowed' from other pianists' recordings, has made many people cynical about the manipulation that recordings may subject us to. But this is the extreme edge of such manipulation. There are many benign ways to use it. Why not leave on the cutting-room floor all the recorded moments when someone made a slip, had an uncharacteristic patch of poor concentration, or simply got weary after hours of playing? In a recording session, a player can have a break and a coffee, and try again. Very likely they will eventually succeed in playing it to everyone's satisfaction. Is it a lie to choose this version and reject the others?

I've come to feel that as long as there is no trickery – no electronic wizardry to create something you never actually played – then it's acceptable to create a patchwork of your best efforts. There are tales of players who ask the producer to speed up their playing 'at pitch' to make it sound more brilliant. Some ask for poor tuning to be corrected in post-production by digital bending of the pitch. I even heard of a pianist who changed her interpretative ideas months after the session, and sent the producer a list of passages she wanted him to mould into different shapes in the editing suite, speeding up and slowing down differently than she did in the session. These, to my mind, are examples of outright deception.

But I can't bring myself to feel that in the case of a fine musician it's wrong to use an artificial selection process to show them at their best. Human error plays a part – even a welcome part – in live music-making, but except in unusual circumstances it does not bear endless repetition on disc. So perhaps it's right to keep human frailty for the concert stage, and allow ourselves the benefits of modern recording for a product which is not exactly us, warts and all, but is us nonetheless.

A short take in praise of long takes

PETER HILL

I remember my excitement when first asked to make a commercial recording. My previous studio work had been for the BBC, where editing was frowned on and retakes permitted only in dire emergency. Now I would be able to repeat as often as I liked, subsequently editing my very best playing into a flawless whole. The theory sounded simple, and I approached the sessions with confidence, despite the difficulties of the repertoire, the piano works of Havergal Brian, a substantial footnote to the composer's thirty-two symphonies which includes the monstrously awkward *Double Fugue*. Optimism began to fade when I arrived at the venue, the concert hall of a conservatoire, to find the recording engineer gloomily assessing various sources of extraneous noise. Besides passing traffic, there was a soft but intrusive hum from the lighting and a murmured conversation of random creaks from the wooden floor, while the otherwise excellent piano had a squeaky pedal and a buzz on one of the upper strings. I learned quickly that in order to make a good recording one's best playing has to coincide with all-too-seldom moments of silence.

Another snag became apparent as soon as we began work. Neither I, nor the fledgling record company, had seen the need to engage a producer, and without an expert second pair of ears I found I would have to listen to each take, a time-consuming process that would make it impossible to establish any momentum. Fortunately, a handful of Havergal Brian enthusiasts were present out of interest, and they quickly formed themselves into a knowledgeable, if argumentative, advisory committee. After my first take, a run-through of the C Minor Fugue from 1924, a lengthy discussion produced a list of recommendations, including a new tempo, a rebalancing of the contrapuntal entries, and the addition of a grandly rhetorical final *allargando*, all of which I implemented, working for a further hour until everyone was satisfied.

The result was far from what I had expected. When a week later I received a transcript of the sessions, it was immediately striking that none of the retakes of the C Minor Fugue was useable. There was nothing wrong with the execution, but the effect was horribly false and contrived. I had to go back to my first take, which at least had the merit of being a real performance – imagined, felt, coherent; and since it was happily free from obvious blemish we were able to use it unedited.

One of the many lessons I absorbed from this near-disaster was that the first rule of studio recording is to be true to oneself. Another was the necessity of a producer in whom one could have perfect trust. An incompetent or indecisive producer is worse than none: how performers dread such remarks as 'Why not have a listen and see what *you* think?' The producer is vital to all aspects of recording, from setting the balance to (in most cases) taking charge of editing, with responsibility for vital musical decisions that must, however, remain faithful to the artist's conception. Producers need a rare combination of expertise, tact and courage, and it is no wonder that the best become celebrities in their field.

The experience of reviewing the sessions in microscopic detail taught me much about my own playing, the process of recording and how to get the best results. The most time-efficient way to record is through short takes. These enable one to focus on the immediate problem, and to play in a uniform way that enables easy editing between takes. But I have also found that the more a passage is repeated the more stilted the playing becomes. One producer told me that he always tries to use material from the earliest takes, and for preference from 'take one': later takes are more efficient, but tend to edge progressively towards self-parody. And, however expertly stitched together, the result has a sameness of atmosphere lacking the ebb and flow of natural performance. Long takes or complete performances, on the other hand, enable one to lose oneself in the music, to forget the intimidating gaze of the microphone, and (one hopes) to start to create. True, the editing is more risky and a great deal more complex, since each of these performances will have a personality of its own (often, the solution is to select a 'core' take, with inserted revisions kept as brief as possible); it also demands an absolute command of the musical structure on the part of the editor. But the bonus comes in the unexpected inspirations. Here, very fine judgement may be required to determine what is a flaw and what a valuable quirk: does a tiny hesitation need correcting? Or is it a deviation from the obvious that enables a phrase to take wing?

In one sense I was right about recording: achieving a 'clean' result *is* comparatively easy, because the whole process is geared to this end. But achieving a real performance, by whatever method, is far more elusive. Perhaps the industry is to blame, with its axiomatic belief that flaws that would go unnoticed in a concert become irritants with repeated listening. This may be so. But I would argue for a greater imperative:

recordings need to be as full of 'careless rapture' as live performances. At the same time, repeatability demands that they be more truthful, more subtle and more detailed, with a creative richness that leaves more to be discovered with each listening. Like the camera, the microphone never lies – but what it records and reveals is as much the soul of the music as its surface.

1 Performing for (and against) the microphone[*]

DONALD GREIG

The performer's view of the microphone is a unique one. Invisible to the listener and a tool of the trade for the producer or engineer, the microphone is the representative of potentially countless future audiences. As such, the microphone confronts the performer as an inhuman critic.

The following addresses the recording situation from the performer's perspective. Throughout I will make reference to my own experience and draw upon that of others who have read and commented on earlier drafts,[1] but I will also set those comments within a broader theoretical framework.

Though predominantly trained and employed in the classical field, I have corresponding experience on the lighter side of music (pop and musical theatre backing vocals, film sessions, etc.).[2] It is here that I have met and worked with performers with a different, pop background who have become more general recording artists or 'session singers'.[3] I have no direct experience, then, of working as a pop musician, but a comparison (rather than a clear-cut opposition)[4] between classical and pop musicians provides a useful methodological contrast and reveals much about different conceptions and attitudes towards recording and technology. It also underlines some of the organisational assumptions, attitudes to technology and working practices of both. Much of what I say will be true for instrumental musicians as well as for singers, but I will limit myself to specific observations about ensemble singers.

Concerts and recordings

Singers of all kinds earn their living in two distinct yet complementary ways: through performing in concerts and other live events, and making recordings. In some cases, such as when a concert is broadcast live or recorded for future use (a practice which deserves a separate essay in its own right), the two will come together, but in general they remain distinct with their own specific requirements and procedures. For some performers, recording is their primary occupation; for others, the concert hall is

[*] This chapter is dedicated to the memory of Tessa Bonner.

their natural habitat. But, in both cases, they will each have extensive experience of performing in concerts (or 'gigs') of various kinds *and* of recording. Rarely do classical musicians limit their professional lives solely to recording, Glenn Gould being the obvious exception.[5] Even rarer is the musician who can exist on concert-giving alone. Most artists work in both fields, and, whether they spend the majority of their time in the concert hall or in recording studios, all musicians agree that concerts and recordings are very different animals.

In general it is classical musicians who spend more of their professional lives giving concerts rather than making recordings. This partially explains why the sound and approach of the concert performance often determine the template for the recording experience. When classical performers arrive at a recording venue, they will know something of the pre-history of the group with which they are to perform. Even if they do not belong to or regularly perform with a group, they will at least be expected to adopt the sound and working methods favoured by that group; in other words, they must fit in. The ideal sound will have been established in concerts and rehearsals, and a preferred arrangement of the performers (in terms of physical space between themselves and towards the audience) will similarly be a part of their particular style. The performers will probably know the music; some record companies even insist that it has been performed. The group will not so much perform to the microphones as to an imaginary audience. Indeed, the larger spaces in which classical recordings take place tend to imply the space for an audience. The microphones will then be positioned by the engineers in the optimum location to 'capture' the ideal sound. This also ensures minimum disruption to the tried-and-tested *modus operandi* of the group. The recording space will mimic the kind of space in which the concerts may have occurred – thus, a hall, a large room, a church or a chapel, each with its own 'natural' acoustic (though in certain cases additional reverberation may be added later electronically; see Figure 1.1). The recording of classical repertoire, then, draws extensively upon the concert situation by adapting to the working practices of a pre-packaged physical and social entity.

By contrast, the session singer will have been booked as an individual by a 'fixer'[6] and will be expected to fit into the physical arrangement dictated by the recording studio (which often can be cramped; see Figure 1.2). The music will be unrehearsed and unseen, and contact with other singers comes as much through hearing them in the headphones provided as from physical proximity. In the unlikely event that the recording is in any way linked to a concert (this is unheard of in the case of film music, advertisements or TV themes), it will come after the recording as a supplement rather than as a precursor to it. Hence the audience and the identity

Figure 1.1 Recording renaissance polyphony: The Tallis Scholars in Temple Church, London, September 2004

Figure 1.2 A set-up for the recording of film music: Metro Voices in Air Lyndhurst Studio, North London, September 2000

of the group are both imaginary. The producer or engineer seeks the individual contribution of the performers, bound within an overall sound design, and not some pre-echo of an earlier performance or rehearsal.

In both pop and classical recording the microphone is not merely a physical manifestation of the intended audience or the (critical) ear of the producer and conductor. Whereas the absence of a real audience and the promise of retakes can reduce anxiety, the more telling demonstration of recording's attention to detail creates a distinct kind of pressure. In a recording situation performers may stretch, move, yawn, waggle their jaws, roll their shoulders – all essentially techniques for releasing tension – whereas such actions would be deemed inappropriate to the performing environment of concerts. Conversely, those things accepted on the concert stage – involuntary sounds like clearing the throat, turning pages, cough- ing, etc. – can ruin a take when recording. This has consequences for levels of anxiety in the performers according to their particular psychic disposi- tion. For some, the concert hall, which allows for fallibility (both human and technical), is the perfect medium, whereas the recording situation – in which an imperfect technique might be immediately highlighted by the unsympathetic producer – can become the more demanding situation, posing seemingly insuperable technical challenges. For others, it is the other way round. The microphone thus has a further metonymic relation- ship to technology, one that demands perfection.

The analytic dimension of recording as manifest by the cold, cruel ear of the microphone also exaggerates the importance of the physical state of the performer on the day(s) of the recording. Whereas illness is sometimes acknowledged on stage (not least by the actions cited above, including blowing one's nose and sneezing), no one has yet, I believe, ever written on a sleeve note that the performer had a bad cold or was short of sleep. Again the dimension of social interaction inherent in the concert situation – and with it an essential human context – is missing from recording. Indeed, this human context is unrecoverable other than in anecdote and reminis- cence, lost in a repressed visual domain.[7] A consequence of this is that, for the singer, the absence of the visual restricts the expression of the message (in the sense used by Jakobson).[8] Whole sets of kinesic and paralinguistic components which reinforce the acoustic content of the message – including facial expression, gesture, phatic language and rhyth- mic indicators – are no longer available.[9] Although performers continue to employ these communicative devices in the recording situation, often as an aid to themselves rather than as part of a conscious address, the listener will never directly witness them.[10] This limitation of the contrib- utory codes of expression to the purely acoustic realm places demands upon the performer different from those of the concert situation. Most obviously, onstage facial expressions reinforce human emotions such as anguish, despair and love, but they also play a part in instances of, say, dynamic variation (a physical expression of acoustic volume can suggest a greater dynamic contrast than that actually achieved). In recording, performers must compensate for this loss of secondary visual encoding by displacing some of that information into the acoustic dimension. Recording thus imposes limits on the artist's expressivity, or at least demands a different approach. It is not uncommon, for example, to hear a producer ask for more contrast – in dynamics, tempo, etc. – only to be met by the musician's response that he or she is already giving 'too much'. Restricted to the acoustic dimension (the acousmatic in Pierre Schaeffer's terms), the recording artist is made aware that musical communication is often somatic.[11]

The immediate relay of information that the producer offers, combined with instant playback, affords performers a very different and immensely valuable engagement with their own performances. The recording situation is thus a more critical and self-critical space than the concert hall.[12] Many comments made 'from the box' by the producer are accepted without further question, whereas in concerts only a limited amount of feedback is available, such as the facial expression of the conductor, a muttered comment from a colleague, and the often ambiguous responses of the audience (applause, fidgeting, etc., all of which are difficult to read with any certainty).

I will return to this theme later, after expanding upon some of the observations made above with reference to technology.

Recording and technology

Discussion of technology's mediation of sound within the classical music press focuses more upon the reception of the recording than its production. Technology is generally of secondary importance, its role recognised more in its ability faithfully to render what has been captured in the recording space than in the act of recording itself. Classical performers share this attitude, though that is not to say they lack respect for the work and contribution of the sound engineer, Tonmeister or producer. On the contrary: their respect is such that they are quite happy for producers, engineers and so on to make the important decisions in terms of balance and microphone placement. For the consumer of classical recording, however, the formula is that the better the quality of the delivery of the sound, the clearer the window onto the original performance (or rather what the consumer takes to be the original performance). This concentration on technology at the point of reception leads to the association between classical recording and high-fidelity sound most obviously manifest in magazines like *Hi-Fi and Record Review* (now defunct) and *The Gramophone*'s dedicated section on upscale audio equipment.

The eschewal of technological mediation within classical recordings contrasts sharply with recorded pop and rock music, at least since the

1960s. Production there seeks to exploit and sometimes foreground the full potential of the mixing desk, tape and digital manipulation, and other effects, so much so that they have become part of the expectation of the pop audience. Hence magazines such as *Sound on Sound* and *Music Tech Magazine* feature interviews with producers and engineers and detail the specifics of recording, including the choice of microphone, the mixing desk and various manipulations of the raw sound. Such information is rarely of interest in the classical world; instead there is an almost wilful ignorance of classical production, an attitude seemingly shared by performers.[13]

Such contrasting attitudes derive initially from the different role of technology in the concert or 'gig' where these other musics are staged. In the classical music concert, there is generally no technological mediation between the performer and the audience. Occasionally a small group in a large venue will be offered 'enhancement', which means amplification so subtle that the audience is unaware of it, and on certain occasions (for instance, at the Ozawa Hall at Tanglewood) the sound is delivered to an audience outside the concert space itself. In such cases it is an in-house arrangement whereby the sound on the stage is relayed without in any way disrupting a direct acoustic experience.

However, in pop concerts and performances of lighter music (i.e., musical theatre and popular standards), different techniques of vocal production lead to lower volumes and a less projected sound,[14] which means the voice cannot be heard above amplified electric instruments or a full orchestra. Amplification of the singer(s) is thus necessary, and a sound engineer will use either the dedicated sound system of the concert hall or an imported sound system. The aim is to achieve balance and produce an overall sound image that comes across as 'natural' and unmediated. Like its classical counterpart, the pop and light music audience is not meant to be aware of any manipulation, though in contrast to the classical context the sound engineer is closely involved in the process and will constantly adjust and re-balance according to orchestration and relative dynamics. Pop singers will be well aware of the use of technology and have a say in it. This may merely be a case of wanting more or less foldback,[15] but often they have specific demands. In addition to amplification, technology in popular concerts is sometimes present through the use of backing tracks (i.e. pre-recorded accompaniment).

Pop and classical performers' contrasting attitudes to technology in the concert hall are similarly evident in the recording studio. This is nicely illustrated in the response towards microphones and headphones ('cans') that the two different types of performers display when they find themselves working together.[16] Headphones are required because of the way the music is recorded. First comes a click track which is synchronised with the visual image. Next the orchestra record their cues 'on top' of this track. It is this mix that the singers hear through their headphones (the cue cannot be played in the room as the click and the sound of the orchestra would otherwise 'spill' onto the mikes) and with which, with the help of a conductor, they must synchronise their performance.

Pop-oriented singers will typically be accustomed to having both headphones over their ears, for they respond to the sound of their own voices as it is relayed to them through the microphone and mixing desk. Classical musicians, however, are used to responding to the sound of their own voices based solely on the unmediated acoustic cues and clues (a mix of the sound as they experience it physically, i.e. in their heads, and how it comes back to them within the room off various reflective surfaces). To the classical performer the 'cans' are a necessary evil, creating an alien experience which has no role in classical vocal training. Most singers adopt a one-headphone-on/one-headphone-off approach (indeed, some equipment is designed with this approach in mind, having a single actual headphone). This allows them to hear other voices around them, which can aid in matters of tuning and blend while also avoiding the apparent timing problems that can come from having both headphones on at once.[17] Also included in the mix of orchestra and click will be the sound of the singers' own voices, and the respective levels of these are often a subject of debate. Pop-oriented singers will often ask to hear more of themselves in the mix, whereas classical singers are less concerned with the final product and more used to determining their vocal production based on muscle memory and through acoustic cues.

Microphones provoke equally contrasting attitudes. It is not unusual for pop singers to recognise the particular model in use and to comment upon it. For them, the microphone is a tool of the trade, and many will be familiar with using a hand-mike in concerts and able to exploit the potential for dynamics that this technology affords them. A *pianissimo*, for example, can be produced in a number of ways other than by merely singing more quietly – for example, the addition of more breath than tone, singing 'off' the voice (i.e., making less use of the vocal tract), and moving the microphone away from the mouth. This is known as microphone technique, where the distance of the mike from the mouth is regulated according to the sound the singer produces: the mike will be held further away for high, loud notes, while quieter, low-register notes will be enhanced by holding the mike closer. The origins of this lie in the crooners of the 1920s to the 1950s (Rudy Vallee, Bing Crosby, Dean Martin, etc.), when microphone technology had reached a point where such singing became possible.[18] Variants of these techniques are regularly employed in the studio today, and even with large choirs it is not uncommon to see a whole section of sopranos facing away from the mike in order to achieve the (rather insensitive) request of the composer for *pianissimo* on a top C. Likewise the basses may inch forward or incline towards the microphone for maximum effect on lower notes.

The attitude of classical performers to (fixed) microphones is, unsurprisingly, casual, and they expect to have no control over them. That is the domain of the producer and sound engineer, together with the musical director (all of whom may be the singers in the case of small groups). Apart from one singer being edged forward or backward relative to the others, or in some cases raised higher by standing on boxes, virtually none of the 'tricks of the trade' characteristic of session singers will be employed, nor is there any requirement for singers to alter their preferred position. A cursory audition of the balance in the first session is often all classical singers will hear during a recording, and that is granted only when numbers allow it,[19] whereas pop or light music performers will listen to playbacks, if only through the headphones they are already using.

These contrasting observations of differing attitudes to headphones and microphones are necessarily crude, though colleagues from both camps would recognise the differences. I use them here to illustrate the differing approaches to the technology of recording. Where the classical performer regards technology as an inferior partner in the creative process, the pop performer seeks to exploit its full potential. The fact that technology in the studio – the natural home of the pop performer – is more advanced can immediately be confirmed by a quick glance at the control room, which is full of banks of monitors, mixing desks, samplers and speakers. This contrasts strongly with the mobile technology used to record classical performances, which can be reduced to a PC, an external hard drive (for backup) and a pair of stereo mikes.

In all this classical musicians draw upon earlier performances – often their own, but maybe also in reference to earlier recordings – and have in mind an essentially complete image of the musical work. To some extent this explains their attitude to editing. Though commonly used, edits and patching are regarded by many classical performers as 'cheats'.[20] Their preference is for a performance to unfold in real time rather than resulting from an accretive process in the recording studio, where tracks are layered one over the other. It is nevertheless generally accepted that the best performance of one section will be combined later in the editing suite with the best performance from another take.[21] Glenn Gould's enthusiastic embrace of the technology of recording was based primarily on the potential editing offered to produce the perfect (if sometimes unimagined) performance. Hence editing was the major focus of his writing on the subject. The manipulation of sound – the addition of effects and the possibilities of overdubbing – was of considerably less importance.

This approach remains broadly true for classical music recording today: editing is an accepted and acknowledged part of the process for performers and consumers.[22] But, however much editing is accepted, there remains the sense that the best recording would be one where no editing at all has taken place. This would be because the perfect performance had been achieved and the technology happened to be in the right place at the right time. Behind this fantasy lies a recognition that in the age of mechanical reproduction (to paraphrase Walter Benjamin) something is inevitably lost in recording. Benjamin himself would articulate this as the work of art's 'aura': the particular and unique moment of performance.[23] In addition to this there is also the recognition that editing, with its removal of errors, thereby constructs a performance which never existed. Such a practice produces an uncomfortable contradiction within an ideology where the preference is for less mediation between performer and listener.

Pop and light music, reliant upon and compliant with technology, represents an almost antithetical approach to that of classical music. This might explain the urge to reclassify as 'crossover' or 'pop' (both words used pejoratively by the classical press) any classical performance that embraces technology – for instance, Vanessa Mae using amplification for her violin, or the Kronos Quartet 'tracking' their version of Tallis's forty-part motet, *Spem in Alium*. In such instances, technology is a vital component without which the performance would not exist. Editing might also be seen in this light were it not for the lurking belief that somewhere, somehow, an ideal performance might well take place in the concert hall (and the oral history of performers is littered with memories of such magical concerts). A further determinant in the rejection of technology is the fact that the main classical canon was created before recording technology existed, and perhaps it is no accident that the more simple recording set-ups of the 1980s and 1990s were used in earlier repertoire.[24]

The seemingly 'natural', unmediated approach in classical recording that this consideration of technology has shown would suggest that the recording's subsequent documentary status is assured. However, certain qualifications need to be made, and the following discussion of performance practice and the privileged status of the work in classical recording addresses these issues.

Recording, performance practice and the work

Broadly speaking, the academic study of classical performance practice has taken two forms: historical research on the original conditions of performance at the time a given work was composed, and the study of performance practice through recordings. Although the two are not mutually exclusive, most obviously in the case of early twentieth-century recordings which are both documents of the conditions of performance coeval with composition *and* histories of interpretation, both make themselves felt in the recording situation to a surprising extent, if in different ways.

The first of these approaches was originally a sub-discipline of musicology and was developed mainly by German scholars in the early twentieth century very much in parallel with performances of early music.[25] This has led in recent years to a strain of musicologically informed performances which have been surrounded by either a quest for or expectations of the 'authentic' reproduction of an earlier performance style. Authenticity has thus become part of an almost contractual undertaking to early music audiences and individual listeners, some of whom now expect a faithful adherence to historical precepts and practices. Combined with recording's documentary function, this means that debates about *musica ficta*, proportional relations and pronunciation within the field of early music, for example, assume much greater significance. Recordings of early music, then, are a charged example of recording which takes very seriously its responsibility to history and its documentary role.

The second form of performance practice studies uses recordings as evidence. It is generally less concerned with the conditions of performance coeval with the composition of the work than with understanding individual interpretations, histories of performing styles since *c*. 1900, and current practices.[26] Such studies further demonstrate the documentary role of recordings, a perspective understood by many recording artists.[27] Again, this awareness is part of a broader responsibility that the performer may recognise in the recording situation.

Both arenas of performance practice research rest upon and make manifest a number of broad assumptions. Even if they are unfamiliar with the academic study of recordings, performers are nevertheless aware of the existence of earlier recordings and may well know a particular interpretation of a work which they themselves are recording anew. In this respect, the specific situation in the early music world is really only an amplification of a more general realisation, namely that there is a canon of recorded works ('the catalogue'), and with that comes the recognition that performers are well aware of different performance styles as well as their own distinctive approaches. Such an awareness plays a role in recording. For instance, any singer walking into a rehearsal with a small ensemble performing Dufay will know that the vocal techniques they would use for Verdi would not be appropriate. On the other hand, in certain instances the performance style of a group may become exaggerated or foregrounded in the recording venue in a way that would be impossible in a concert. It is sometimes even the case that recording a piece in smaller sections results in a performance that would be too difficult to maintain in a live context.[28] In general, though, a certain self-awareness of performance style means that performers will be cognisant of the contribution they may be making to a canon of recording, and with that comes a sense of ethical responsibility.[29]

This begs an important question, however: do recordings serve a legitimate documentary purpose, as suggested above? The disdain for 'cheating' mentioned previously, together with a common mistrust of technology, certainly suggests that performers are loath to allow misrepresentation. As for editing, it might be argued that the removal of simple errors – one of the functions of editing – potentially invalidates the documentary status of recordings. However, that is only a qualification: even if the final version presents a compilation of the 'best bits', it nevertheless represents a 'vision' (be it that of the producer, director or artists), and viewed as a montage of moments it remains a statement of a preferred performance style. The only certainty that knowledge of editing undermines is that of the ability of the performers to render such works to the same degree of accuracy in a concert situation.

However, recordings should not always be taken as evidence of *concert* performance practice. The economics of touring life often require a reduction in forces. Particularly in the 1980s, the success of the recording industry resulted in many full-scale recordings that were rarely repeated in concert performance.[30] Equally, there are examples in the early history of recordings where the inadequacy of recording technology demanded smaller forces,[31] and the latter could not serve as a guide to more general practices at the time.

With regard to so-called light music, the same point about group identity being expressed in performance style obtains. Pop performance, allied more closely to innovation and less concerned with reproduction, has its eyes firmly on the future status of the recording. But there is more to it than that. For both classical and pop music, the concert and the recording have different functions and thus bring with them differing senses of occasion, experienced in a play of tenses (as in the conjugation of verbs). In the presence of the audience, any event is firmly located in the present tense, in the 'here and now'. The event will have been anticipated and (one hopes) will be remembered, but while the event unfolds it does so in real time and in an empirically verifiable form: what is happening before the listener/viewer is what is actually happening. Recording – with the possibility of replaying, rewinding, fast-forwarding and pausing – exists in a controllable past. It is, precisely, a record of something that previously took place but which will happen again and again. Like cinema, as opposed to theatre, there is an expectation that human error will have been ironed out or at least contained, and that the event represents the best possible outcome given specific constraints. In concerts, however, the performance can be only as good as the moment allows, and thus human error and the possibility that things will go wrong is, if not desired, at least accepted. The only witness to such errors is the audience itself and, with the impossibility of conferring among themselves other than on the most local level, even errors can become subject to doubt on the part of the listener (particularly if the performer acts as if nothing has gone wrong). Error is not the central issue here, but it demonstrates that any event happens only once and is not repeatable; as such it is ephemeral, or at least considerably more fleeting than the hard evidence embodied within a recording.

For the performer, there are certain consequences of the different statuses of the two modes of music-making. With its greater emphasis upon the moment itself, the concert encourages and even invites risk-taking. Dynamic contrast, faster tempos and 'showing off' are more likely to be found in a concert situation than in the recording venue. To some extent this is because a degree of control is lost in the concert, not least on the part of a conductor. If he or she sets a faster tempo than in rehearsal, there is no way to stop and ask for a second take, or if someone is singing or playing too loudly, there is less chance of getting them to quieten down short of a few hand gestures which may be ignored. Stopping and starting is but one feature of recordings that returns the control of the rehearsal space to the conductor. Likewise, a template for the final edit will be set after the first complete, acceptable take. Tempo and pitch will thus be regulated and become a guide to any patches or retakes that need to be done. The potential for *rubato* or *accelerando*, even of local rhythmic variation (very rarely are any two bars at the same metronomic speed unless a click is used), is similarly reduced.

This suggests that bland recordings and blinding concerts are inevitable consequences, but one can also argue the opposite – namely, that a recording situation allows a greater freedom of expression, that the possibility of retakes promotes risk-taking, and that the concert situation, with its heightened sense of the present tense, dampens such overt demonstration. The truth of the matter will probably not be found in any one performer's experience.

What is nonetheless clear is that there is a a tension between two different conceptions of performance, both of which exist in recordings and concerts. These are articulated by Lydia Goehr as 'the perfect performance of music' and 'the perfect musical performance'.[32] Though these conceptions undoubtedly exist in popular and lighter music, they are categories that derive from an ideology of the work which itself is specific to classical music. This final consideration is thus limited to the field of classical music alone.

The two categories of thought or modes of assessment of music that Goehr elaborates conform roughly to what I have characterised as overt and safe forms of musical performance. The first, the perfect performance of music, foregrounds the work itself and the composer's intentions ascribed therein, and negates or effaces the contribution of the performer as the realiser of the work. This denial of the creative role of performers results in their invisibility in so far as their individuality is subsumed within a process.[33] In other words, the production of performance is effaced by the product. This can be equated with a safe form of performance in which the musician's primary aim is the accurate rendition of the score, including its dynamic or tempo indications, thus relegating the performer to the role of conduit between the composer and the audience.

The second mode of assessment is that of the perfect musical performance. This foregrounds the contribution of the performer and the process of the realisation of the work, thereby highlighting the *human* contribution involved in the process of performance and placing additional emphasis upon technique, skill and individuality. It thus invokes a transcendent notion of interpretation and musicality. As Goehr puts it, 'The perfect musical performance is conceptually broader than the perfect performance of music. It attends to the general, though elusive, dimension of musicianship inherent in a performance whether or not the performance is a performance of a work.'[34] This conforms to the second category of flamboyant or virtuosic performance, to the realm of performance that underlines the role of the performer and makes him or her visible.

Goehr's categories are by no means mutually exclusive or opposed. This becomes apparent when, as in the foregoing pages, one considers not solo but ensemble performance, wherein the individuality inherent in the notion of the perfect musical performance is already attenuated.

For all that, though, there is an undoubted tension between these two conceptions, and this is often sensed in recordings. Most obviously, it is felt in instances of first recordings of works, by which I mean those written by (dead) composers whose existence is already known and which might already be celebrated by music history. Such recordings are already allied with the notion of perfect performance of music, for the identity of the work provides a ready-made marketing angle. In such instances a sense of multivalent responsibility prevails, to the musical work, to the dead composer and to the place of the recording itself in the canon. Even if a recording of a given work is not the first to appear, a general knowledge of the recording canon will serve as a background against or within which those making the new recording may well operate. In such cases the recording and its liner notes foreground a new edition, new biographical information, new aspects of performance practice or related criteria in order to distinguish it from a previous one. The promise is of a more enlightened, elucidatory reading of the work, one which prior recordings implicitly have failed to meet.

If, however, the recording and its accompanying discourses (press releases, interviews, reviews) emphasise the predominant interpretative role of the conductor (as in the case of Solti's *Ring Cycle* or Karajan's Beethoven) or the group (for example, the Hilliard Ensemble's Gesualdo recording or the Borodin Quartet's Shostakovich cycle),[35] the dominant conception becomes that of the perfect performance of music.

In reality it can be difficult to distinguish between the two, for, as Goehr takes pains to point out, often both are present if in continual conflict. An awareness of both of these conceptions will figure in the minds of performers, though their response to them will not be easily discernible. Perhaps they may be more inclined to question the edition itself if fidelity to the score is the primary orientation of the project (the perfect performance of music). Contrarily, they may feel encouraged to suggest, either verbally or vocally, an interpretative gesture (the perfect musical performance).

What is more certain, though, is that these performers will not articulate their response in such terms, or perhaps any terms. For the professional musician, recording and concert-giving and the differences between them are experienced and lived, rather than analysed and discussed.

Producing a credible vocal

MIKE HOWLETT

To most ears, a recording of a song sounds like a reasonably accurate reproduction of the band or artist performing in front of them. Of course, most people nowadays know that many of the components of this finished product had to be played again and again until they sounded 'right' – and that what we hear all together on the recording probably wasn't all played at the same time. Nevertheless, a suspension of critical judgement is made and the song is perceived as a true representation of the artist's skills. But is there a magical 'black box' that can make anyone sound good? Since the nineties there have indeed been 'boxes' – in actuality, mostly software, but sometimes packaged up in a purpose-built box – that can adjust intonation and timing; but this wasn't always the case.

In the days before digital recording, when the hits I produced were made, the processes were more complicated. The method I used mostly was to 'comp' the vocal. This involved recording lots of takes of the vocal performance and keeping the better ones on separate tracks (we used multitrack machines usually with twenty-four tracks, but sometimes more), and then patiently sifting through each take line by line, sometimes word by word. The good ones were bounced onto another track, compiling one complete vocal track out of many. This could be an extremely tedious process at times, taking many hours to produce a three-minute vocal; but if done well, the result would be a near flawless performance that still sounded completely natural. And I have used this method even on very capable singers, because my view is that with a recording you want to hear the best version, the definitive version, one that will stand repeated listening. Even the finest singers in any genre will admit that it's very rare for a performance to be perfect.

Some people might call this 'cheating', but, by way of justification, I like to cite the example of Elvis Presley (not one of mine, unfortunately) who is reported to have recorded 'Hound Dog' forty-two times before he was happy with his performance. Of course, there weren't twenty-four tracks, or even four tracks, available in those days, so the other forty-one takes were lost to history, and who knows, perhaps the third take was actually the best he ever sang!

However, there is a curious effect that I found using this process. Sometimes, having sat at the back of the control room for hours, listening again and again to the various takes, a singer will hear the 'comped' final version and insist on singing it again. Remarkably, this later performance would often turn out to be 'the one'. The first few times it happened, it really annoyed me: all that work – a complete waste of time! But I came to realise that what had happened was that, through hearing themselves over and over again, these singers had at last defined their approach to the songs in their own minds. Something that is not often recognised about the recording process is that songs rarely arrive in the studio fully formed. The melody and the structure will have been loosely defined, but all those subtle details – the particular phrasing of a line, an emotional emphasis on a word, all the minute details that go to make a powerful rendition – these things are the stuff of great recordings. And there is a related factor, which I think is the significance of *familiarity* with a song. Even fairly poor amateur singers can knock out a fair rendition of a well-known standard, at least in the shower, because they can hear it in their mind and know where it's supposed to go. But a singer in the studio trying to record something new is starting from scratch, and all those apparently 'wasted' takes are really the singer getting to know, and hear, how that vocal should go – what it's supposed to be.

It is this process of definition, of finding the definitive version, that is the essence of good production.

'It could have happened': The evolution of music construction

STEVE SAVAGE

I was recently recording a CD for a veteran blues singer, and one of the last sessions involved a duet with a guest vocalist. The instrumental tracks had already been recorded and, as is common in pop music production, the final vocals were being added at the end of the process. The two singers were in the studio – each acoustically isolated but positioned so that they could see each other through a window. As they listened to the instrumental tracks on headphones they traded choruses, each also ad-libbing along with the other's lead vocal. At the end of the song, during the vamp, they traded ad libs by drawing from the lyrics of the previous choruses. All well and good in principle – but the reality was a bit of a mess. The first take had great spirit and enthusiasm, but also a lot of 'problems' – the vocalists were stepping on each other's lines (the ad-libbing 'comments' obscuring parts of the other singer's chorus melody) and there were a variety of nonsensical passages when a less than apt choice of phrase was used to respond to the sung lyric. The trading in the vamp was equally spirited – and equally flawed.

We made a few more complete takes of the vocals but the flaws remained, and where the singers had been loose and excited on the first take, in the subsequent takes they lacked that spontaneous enthusiasm. In the earlier, tape-based era of record production we would have had to resort to recording each section piece by piece, repeating the performance on each part until a satisfactory take was recorded. Eventually we would have got a performance that had sufficient compositional integrity to bear repeated listening, but it would surely have lacked the genuine excitement of that initial run through. Instead, I simply sent the singers to the lounge (they weren't interested in the process, only the result) and went about reconstructing that first take by rearranging the parts so that they made musical and lyrical sense. This involved moving and adjusting vocal lines so that they fitted neatly into a call and response kind of duet performance without conflicting with each other. I re-created the entire 'ad-libbed' vamp by using phrases from the first sung vamp and incorporating ad-libbed bits from earlier in the song that fitted more neatly at the end. In a few instances I actually reconstructed lyrics by taking fragments of sung lines and editing them together to create 'new' lyrical content. Once I had put something together that made musical and lyrical sense to me I called the singers back in for a listen. They were delighted.

One of the favourite parts for me of being a recordist is applying the 'it could have happened' aesthetic in making recordings. This is the process whereby musical performances are constructed using the wide-ranging capabilities of a digital audio workstation (DAW), and one of the standards used to judge the acceptability of the final recorded 'performance' is whether or not it could have happened – whether the musician might reasonably have played or sung what has been constructed. Maybe I'm stuck between the old world of making recordings of complete live performances and the new aesthetic of constructing performances that could obviously never have been performed. Maybe it's my years as a professional musician that have left me with a vestigial preference for music that sounds like it was performed at one time by one person. While I love the tools that allow me to construct performances in ways that never actually occurred in the traditional sense – done by repurposing recording elements, manipulating both pitch and rhythm, and other outright sonic inventions – I also like hewing these constructions to the 'it could have happened' standard. I've had the pleasure of living through the transition from the arduous tape splicing of performance elements to the amazing new world of digital editing and digital signal processing (DSP). The tools available now in the digital domain have exploded the 'it could have happened' options beyond anything remotely possible as little as twenty years ago.

The implication behind 'it could have happened' is, of course, that it didn't happen. That is, the recording presents a musical performance that did not happen on the specific time-line that the finished product presents. This kind of reformulation began with the earliest edited performances – and that dates all the way back to the wire recorders invented in the last decade of the nineteenth century. Tape-based systems, which provided the necessary 'plasticity' for the large-scale practice of audio editing non-contiguous musical elements, were commercially marketed in the late 1940s. In these earlier forms of editing, recordings of different live performances of the same material were pieced together to create the impression of one continuous performance. This type of editing became common for both Western art music and pop music recording, and in both cases there are elements of recomposition in the choices made. For example, the process allows the recordist to choose between one cadenza and another, or between one recording of a song's verse and another. The choices made yield a constructed piece of recorded music, though the differences from any one of the original, complete performances are usually quite small.

Generally, this type of editing retains the original progression of musical events, and preserves the essential compositional integrity of the original score or song arrangement.

But within the DAW, editing decisions can easily range far beyond simple choices about subtle variations in performance. The story of the blues duet is an example of much deeper alterations in both arrangement and composition. Intervention in compositional elements as part of the recording/editing process is prevalent in the world of pop music. For example, instrumental solos are now frequently created through a combination of improvisation and editing. Multiple improvisations over the same passage are edited together to bring a formality of structure while retaining an improvisational 'feel'. This process often involves moving elements from their original position in the musical time-line to a new location, as well as simply editing together bits from different takes. Large-scale intervention also occurs with some frequency: whole arrangements may be altered by moving, adding or deleting entire sections of the composition.

Even more intrusive intervention can occur with the use of DSP to alter the basic structure of performances. Musical passages may be rhythmically lengthened or shortened through time expansion and compression techniques (without changing pitch), or pitches fixed or reharmonised using subtle re-tuning tools that allow very fine frequency control. Passages that were sung out of tune may be 're-adjusted' to whatever extent the collaborators desire, and may still meet the 'it could have happened' criterion: the singer could have sung the line in tune (in theory): he or she just didn't happen to do so. This gets trickier when distinctly new note choices are made – could the singer actually have moved between those notes in the manner now created? Similarly, when small segments of a phrase are put together to re-create something like a guitar solo – could the guitarist actually have negotiated the passage in this particular way? This is part of the fun and the challenge of the 'it could have happened' process: I strive to construct performances that are musically and instrumentally appropriate to a single performance, and which at the same time capture as much musical interest and creative energy as possible using all the tools available.

Such activities expand the creative partnership of music-making to include recordists – not just in an advisory role (traditional for the producer) but also in the construction of the content used in the final recorded performance. 'It could have happened' performances are a key element in the transformation of music-making – in which the new paradigm of construction is replacing the old linear progression from composition through performance to master recording. Of course audio editing has allowed for all kinds of 'impossible' music as well – all the way back to *musique concrète* and before. The DAW has significantly changed our ability to make music that could never have been played as presented – and I love that stuff too – but for me, it's the hugely expanded palette of 'it could have happened' music that I enjoy the most.

2 Recording practices and the role of the producer

ANDREW BLAKE

The term 'record producer' is the greyest of grey areas. 'Producers' have had to deploy a startlingly wide range of skills. They have to play some role in pre-production (assembling the musicians and musical material to be recorded, overseeing rehearsals and sampling sessions, downloading existing tracks from bands' laptops), production (the actual recording of music) and post-production (its editing, mixing and assembly for delivery to the record company). Producers have been (and are) individual entrepreneurs, freelance operators, record label owners and record label employees. They have been people managers, whether Svengalis, artist and repertoire developers, or gifted amateur psychologists able to guide temperamental artists through a recording session. They have been events managers: the possessors of specialist legal knowledge in relation to contract and copyright law, finance and accounting (the producer will often be budget holder and administrator for the entire project of making an album). They have been musical managers: session fixers, composers, arrangers, synthesiser and drum machine programmers, and conductors. And very often they will have started as sound recording engineers, a profession dealt with in this book by Albin Zak. But most importantly they have been *listeners*, able to decode what happens in the recording and mixing studios in order to represent the eventual listening customer.

Despite this remarkable range of activities and skills, the producer has been the least visible part of the recording process. A few exemplary names such as Walter Legge or Phil Spector apart, whatever their effectiveness and in whatever genre of music they worked, their work is seldom credited, though it has more often been credited than discussed. Two examples. In the first edition of the otherwise excellent *New Grove Dictionary of Jazz*, there were only a few references to record producers but no entry for this part of the profession as such, thus denying producer-entrepreneurs such as Teo Macero, George Avakian, Creed Taylor and Ahmet Ertegun proper acknowledgement of their vital role in the very development of the music.[1] A recent and especially useful anthology, *The Popular Music Studies Reader* (2006), approaches the subject through nine subdivisions, among them 'making music', 'the music industry', and 'popular music and technology'. In each of these, record producers are referred to only in passing. Production and record producers are not indexed as such – 'producers' is a sub-category of 'recording industry'.[2] As this chapter will argue, producers have made highly significant contributions to the development of music in all its genres. Many producers have been taste-leaders whose innovations have changed the direction of both recorded and live music, and the chapter discusses examples of this creative input in the case of producers working in classical, jazz, pop, soul, rock, world, hip-hop and dance music.

Recently, in fact, there has been a growing interest in and acknowledgement of the role of the producer. Academic conferences and journals, radio programmes, and published memoirs, biographies and obituaries have all begun to register the importance of the producer in the story of recorded music.[3] As with the collecting of folk music in the early twentieth century, our new interest in the profession might be due to its perceived lack of engagement with contemporary conditions: after all, if musicians can now record, edit, mix and burn master recordings, advertise the results and/or sell them in the form of downloads on the internet, and do the band's accounts, all from a single laptop, the room for additional advisers of any sort might appear redundant. However, at least in official circles the record producer is still seen as an important part of the music business. Here is the UK government's definition, *c.* July 2007:

> Record Producer
> *What is it?*
> Creatively and financially managing the production of an album, keeping those unruly artists happy and on schedule.
> *What Higher Education qualifications help?*
> Degree or HND in Music, Commercial Music Production, Creative Music Technology, or Sound Engineering
> *What else helps?*
> Passion for music
> Being calm, patient and diplomatic
> *Pros*
> Working very closely with artists and performers
> Very rewarding job
> Great parties, free CDs
> *Cons*
> Late nights, long hours
> Stroppy artists taking it out on you[4]

But whatever the aspirations of those offering training courses might be, unlike sound engineering there is no orthodox, qualification-led route into music production. The mix of personality traits and knowledges required to succeed in this part of the music business cannot be reduced to the circular 'course aims' and 'learning outcomes' of a modular degree programme or other training scheme: through such means one might learn the rules of a specific genre of composition, or even to play the guitar, but not the multi-skilled role of record producer.

For any commercial recording project, then, the producer must ensure the following:

- adequate financing
- one or more pieces of music and/or improvising musicians
- copyright clearance for samples, and agreements with composers and publishers
- recording equipment set up in a suitable venue and with technicians to operate aspects of the equipment if the sound engineer needs such assistance
- arrangers, musicians and/or programmers
- one or more sound engineers
- an agreed schedule through which they can all participate in the recording to best advantage (this would mean, for example, not booking session singers, or trumpeters, for the morning after they have performed a demanding gig).

The producer is responsible to the record label for all this. Again, for a commercial recording the producer will need knowledge of the current state of the music business and of the market, including trends in contemporary musical taste and in the technical possibilities and sales potential of the available audio formats. It's usually agreed that the producer will also need patience (among other social and interpersonal skills) and enthusiasm. S/he will have to work with demanding musicians and engineers whose views about the use of equipment or the level of performance while recording, and the aesthetic of the mixing and editing process, are unlikely to coincide all the time.

A record producer's contract will usually, among other things, assign any rights he or she might acquire in the recording to the record company, though equally often this will be in return for 'points' – percentage points from the record's sales – an arrangement which encourages the producer to come up with the most commercially successful product.

The production of classical music: The producer as empowered listener

Classical music projects by major labels have historically tended to use the employee–producer relationship (though recently, typically of capitalism's tendency to outsource risk, the freelance classical producer has become routine). The employee usually doesn't have to engage with the same range of functions and relationships as the freelance producer, and the relationship does not involve the same contractual driver of sales points. In the end, though, the *musical* fundamentals are the same: the producer is the privileged listener, mediating the relationship between the score, the performing artists and the technologies. (Less often the classical producer has also mediated with the composer.) The task seemed to revolve around the correction of mistakes, which sometimes required aesthetic decisions and also asking the engineer to produce various types of sound, in particular what Colin Symes has called the 'best seat in the house' approach to sonic values (see below).[5]

Through most of the twentieth century classical recordings were sold as the expected companion of prestige domestic equipment for their reproduction: hi-fi. The target consumer of these expensive goods was affluent, male and middle-aged. Alongside the hardware of conspicuous consumption and precision-engineered response came the software – the music itself – sold as well-packaged and expensive high art for the amateur enthusiast. EMI had exploited the relative profitability of classical recordings during the first fifty years of recorded music by building Abbey Road studios, which were opened in 1931.[6] After the Second World War and the establishment of the LP, this profitability declined somewhat, but, whatever was made from actual sales, the artists signed to these labels were amply rewarded. Singers and conductors could make half a million pounds annually from recording royalties in the late 1950s/early 1960s.[7] The best-known classical record producers were, perhaps unsurprisingly, the same sort of person as the target consumer: middle-class men who knew what they liked and who bestowed, in collaboration with journalists and consumers alike, the discourses of superior technical ability, taste and even genius on the performers they recorded and listened to.

In other words, the classical record industry worked from the 1930s to the 1960s with an autodidact as producer and an engineer to do the actual recording. Producers such as Walter Legge at EMI and John Culshaw at Decca had no formal degree-level musical training (Culshaw's memoirs register somewhat disapprovingly the arrival from the 1960s onwards of music graduates as producers, and university-trained 'Tonmeister' sound engineers).[8] Legge and Culshaw had been 'trained' not in performance or composition but in music appreciation, of an already existing repertoire. What emerged in consequence, in commercial classical music recording, was a star system in which the 'stars' were mostly performers, not composers – stars who operated within a museum-repertoire of a relatively small number of recognised 'masterpieces' from the eighteenth and nineteenth centuries. Associated with EMI, for example, were a number of technically gifted aesthetic perfectionists with relatively limited musical ambition that matched fairly precisely the tastes and ambitions of those recording them and selling the results. The entire conducting repertoire of the Italian conductor Carlo Maria Giulini comprises an incandescent recording of the Verdi Requiem in 1964 – which is still available – and a handful of other relatively successful recordings; he seems to have known very little music, or about music, apart from these few pieces. No producer seems to have tried to persuade him into a more adventurous *modus operandi*, despite the ready audience for his recordings.

While radio music production in the UK could at times be defiantly modernist,[9] classical record production started and largely remained conservative in outlook, with conservative producers working for conservative label heads. John Culshaw notes Decca's reluctance to record Benjamin Britten's *Peter Grimes*. Culshaw had argued against his employers – successfully, in the end – that 'if we were to abandon so relatively conservative a modern composer we should rule out contemporary music altogether'.[10] The 1960s rehabilitation of Mahler's music, which is often seen as a by-product of stereo, is also an aspect of this anti-modernism: in jumping on the Mahler bandwagon, the record labels could record *twentieth-century music* which in the early 1960s was unfamiliar but which was not dissonant, and therefore might be expected to sell reasonably well.[11]

Many producers lacked even Culshaw's concern for the state of composition. Take as an example of this conservatism Suvi Raj Grubb, a South Indian Christian who was born in Madras in 1917 and socialised into the Anglican music repertoire (while still working in India he was a church organist and choirmaster).[12] From 1949 to 1953 he had a career in All-India Radio, ending as a producer, and on emigration to England in 1953 he worked as a freelance producer with the BBC. Grubb became a member of the Philharmonia Chorus, which was first set up for Otto Klemperer's recording of Beethoven's Ninth Symphony with the Philharmonia Orchestra. This led to a meeting with the founder of the Philharmonia Orchestra, Walter Legge. Grubb became Legge's assistant at EMI in 1960, then a full producer in 1964, with responsibility for a roster of international artists including Daniel Barenboim and Itzhak Perlman, and a key early role in the remastering of existing recordings. He retired in 1985.

The production of those conservative values can be seen from Grubb's first encounter with Legge, who saw Richard Strauss and Sibelius as the great twentieth-century composers. Before Legge offered him the assistant's job Grubb had to answer twenty questions on standard Austro-German repertoire and the minutiae of opus and Köchel numbers, ending with the questions 'How many minor key piano concertos are there by Mozart?', and 'What are the instruments in Schubert's octet?'[13] He got them all right. None of the questions was on *twentieth-century music* (whether classical or otherwise) or on pre-eighteenth-century music, or for that matter on Indian music.

Grubb's inheritance of Legge's values is clear: talking of working with Pierre Boulez on a recording of Bartók's piano concertos with Daniel Barenboim, he remarks, 'I confessed to him at one point that I found very modern music a tough proposition.'[14] Such tastes are directly reflected in Grubb's recording career. The 240 gramophone recordings produced for EMI that are mentioned in the appendix to Grubb's memoir (though this list is not claimed to be a complete discography) contain approximately 1,000 individual pieces of music. Only sixty-one of these are twentieth-century works, most of them tonal pieces by composers such as Strauss, Sibelius, Debussy, Ravel, Rachmaninoff, Shostakovich and Falla. There's a smattering of Stravinsky and Bartók; one piece each by Schoenberg and Berg, each of whom was safely dead by the time of recording; but nothing by any post-war modernist composer. The few important first recordings of *twentieth-century music* supervised by Grubb were Shostakovich's opera *Lady Macbeth of Mtsensk* and the more or less complete version of Falla's opera *Atlantida*, plus John Ogdon's 1967 recording of the fearsomely long and eccentric piano concerto by Busoni.

Whatever the adventurousness or otherwise of the repertoire recorded by Grubb, his sonic ambition remained the same: attempting to simulate the experience of the listener in the expensive seats of the concert hall or opera house. Recording equipment was used as a register but not as a conditioner or manipulator of sound, so the recording environment was considered vital. Decca, for example, would tend to use the Kingsway Hall but not the lightweight Royal Festival Hall, which produced an unsatisfactory bass. Grubb imagined himself as that ideal listener – someone sitting in the 'best seat in the house', dead centre a dozen rows back. This isn't to say that he just let the engineer set up the microphones and then looked at the score and listened for wrong notes and intonation errors. He occasionally allowed himself to bring out details of the music that might be lost in some concert halls, and the extra clarity possible in this respect meant that his comments on stereo were positive. More adventurously, his aesthetic sometimes accommodated changes in balance and equalisation during a recording session, to match his assessment of the temper of the different works being recorded.[15] But about the quadraphonic experiment of the mid-1970s Grubb was uniformly negative, explaining that when he mixed for quad he just replicated the stereo mix for the front channels at the back, with a little extra reverb.[16] He also had a lifelong suspicion of multitrack recording techniques, arguing that they gave too much power to the producer.[17]

This, then, is the relatively unambitious soundworld of would-be high-fidelity, the attempt to be faithful to the concert performance as perceived by the listener sitting in row twelve. It is the fundamental aesthetic position which still apparently drives the production of classical recordings (for instance, very few classical recordings in the SACD and DVD-Audio formats, which offer surround-sound capabilities, actually challenge the row-twelve ideal). Despite this, recordings were never in danger of being any such thing: recurrent throughout Grubb's memoir is the acknowledgement that recordings should never, unlike actual concert performances, contain poor intonation, wrong notes or distorted sound, and he and his engineers would always edit the various takes to produce an 'ideal' performance. He would doubtless have employed to the full the current digital editing software that allows music to be cut and pasted with microtonal and micro-temporal accuracy way beyond the dreams of Grubb's tape-splicing world. Cumulatively, classical recording had arrived by the late 1950s at a point where it is not a copy of a live performance, but a simulacrum produced by the micro-editing of 'repeated takes', in the apt title of Michael Chanan's book: a copy of a performance of which there is no original.[18]

But Suvi Raj Grubb did not always merely try to reproduce what he was given. The aesthetics of restoration provide interesting variations on the conservative theme. Older recordings, especially those made before stereo, were often remastered and repackaged as the music business grew in confidence during the 1960s (a procedure that was repeated *ad nauseam* in the CD era twenty years later). The object was as often to enhance as to restore an original recording. Many of these older recordings had favoured the named artist's voice or solo instrument at the expense of the orchestra or accompanist, and in his remastering work for EMI Grubb changed the balance and often produced pseudo-stereo, in another simulation of the ideal listening position in the concert hall or opera house. For example, when in 1964 he remastered Wilhelm Furtwängler's 1950 version of Wagner's *Tristan und Isolde*, which had been produced by Legge, he tried to restore the balance between orchestra and singers, using a fairly crude form of equalisation:

> All I had to do to give the orchestra greater prominence was, judiciously, to emphasise electronically the frequencies above and below the range of the voices – and considering that a tuba starts from about 43 cycles per second and a piccolo can play notes of up to 4,000 cycles per second ... a wide field was available.[19]

In doing this re-balancing, Grubb may well have been critiquing the musicality of Walter Legge's work. His refurbishment of acknowledged highlights of Legge's contribution to the history of recording such as that *Tristan*, the 1953 Dennis Brain/Herbert von Karajan recording of the Mozart horn concertos which was re-released in 1972, or the 1963 rendition of Mozart's *Così fan tutte* conducted by Karl Böhm, which was re-released in 1973, all involved such changes in the relationship of soloist and ensemble. (In any event, well before Legge's death in 1979 the two were no longer on speaking terms; Legge's published writings make no mention of Grubb or of any aspect of their long professional and personal relationship.[20])

1950s jazz to 1960s rock: The producer as midwife

Like classical music, most recorded jazz in the 1950s remained largely in the world of the simulation; indeed, it grew into it. The emerging album format – the vinyl record, twelve inches in diameter, revolving at 33⅓ rpm, which could hold about twenty minutes of music per side – meant that the producer could emulate not just the position of the listener, but the structure of the jazz concert itself. The liner notes for the 1956 album *April in Paris* by the Count Basie Band, produced by Norman Granz for his new Verve label, begin thus:

> One night in Birdland the Count Basie Band was playing a new arrangement by William 'Wild Bill' Davis of an old song by Vernon Duke, 'April in Paris' … Finally there's the ending, which is a delightful fooler, as all jazz followers will be aware by now. Well, on this night in Birdland it seemed natural for Basie to give his orders verbally. 'One more time', he ordered. Then, 'One more once'.[21]

And so does the album itself, opening with that arrangement of 'April in Paris' complete with Basie's repeated orders to replay the final section, before moving through a typical concert sequence featuring mid-concert down-tempo numbers 'Shiny Stockings' and 'What Am I Here For?', and then finishing with the high-tempo Latin of 'Mambo Inn' and swing of 'Dinner with Friends', notable for their show-stopping drum breaks and high trumpet notes.

But album-based jazz in the 1950s was also in an emergent state of experimentation. The new vinyl album was not necessarily a direct reflection of events in the concert hall, but a format which like its 78 rpm shellac predecessors could instigate new ways of making music. In the later 1940s, bebop recordings by Charlie Parker and Dizzie Gillespie had set new musical standards worldwide, and the evolution of the genre and the subsequent hard bop, funk and free-form developments in jazz were based at least as much on the recording session ensemble as the live-performance band. The length of the album meant that *ad hoc* session groups could be together for longer and therefore experiment more fruitfully; and meanwhile the new technologies of tape recording and, from the 1960s, multitracking meant that the producer's influence could grow. Musicians were booked for album sessions, not just tours, and, though most jazz was still based on the controlled spontaneity of soloists' improvisations around agreed structures, some of the resulting music experimented with the new technologies of tape recording and editing, and with longer stretches of recorded music, in creative use of the vinyl album format. Albums such as Miles Davis's *Birth of the Cool* (whose sessions first appeared on three ten-inch albums, released 1949–50) and *Kind of Blue* (1959), or Ornette Coleman's *Free Jazz* (1960), took the music in radically different directions in the studio before such music was toured live, and each album's producer was important to the aesthetic choices. Rock music was to learn from this experimentalism with the album form, and rock in turn encouraged other genres to experiment.

Miles Davis was among the learners. Davis had worked with producer Teo Macero for his recordings on the Columbia label during the 1950s, including *Kind of Blue*. Though the practice of actually naming record producers on record covers – which began in the early 1960s – annoyed Davis somewhat (as did credits to arranger Gil Evans), Macero became more of a collaborator as the opportunities for the creative use of the studio widened. *In a Silent Way* (1969) was an epoch-making album in which the music finally encoded in vinyl grooves had been manufactured from many performances, rather than being a register of any one of them, and the 'manufacturer' of that final product was as much Macero as Davis. For 'It's About That Time', for example, 'Teo edited pieces together to create this section, moving a short solo by Miles to the front of the piece to form a beginning, then repeating the same solo for an ending';[22] ultimately only thirty-three minutes of recorded music were used to make a forty-minute album, to the confusion and anger of many jazz critics, some of whom accused the producer of faulty editing, and the label of selling a mistake. But those thirty-three minutes had themselves been selected by Davis and Macero, listening to the many hours of music they had recorded and then discussing ways in which to edit, splice and cut to produce a final album-length offering (if that: the first proposed edit was only eighteen minutes long). Increasingly after this album Miles left the final edit to Macero and his engineers, so it can be argued that the equally influential double album *Bitches Brew* which followed *In a Silent Way* is conceptually and compositionally as much Macero's work as the trumpeter's – and Macero certainly defended it as such.[23] From then on this was the way Miles Davis and Teo

Macero worked: assemble a group of musicians, enter the studio with them, briefly discuss what to do, then play for several hours at a stretch with tape running all the time. Davis and Macero then listen to the resulting performances, edit and, finally, assemble – which might mean moving solos or riffs around, or even using tape loops to repeat short stretches of material. The making of any new album, in other words, could now include post-production.

Copying nothing: The pop single and the rock album

This was the way pop and rock had always sought to work. With no concert tradition to guide it or dictate its terms, rock 'n' roll was a blank canvas, and the pop of the early 1960s which followed it was about the making of records that would sound good on the small record players and radios used by teenagers. Producers, engineers and songwriters were therefore free to experiment with formal structures, orchestration, balance, non-naturalistic reverb and other sound effects, and the use of session musicians to replace inexperienced or incompetent band members or vocalists. Phil Spector's 'wall of sound' for singles by the Crystals, the Righteous Brothers, the Ronettes and others, and Joe Meek's use of home-made electronic sound effects for the Tornadoes, are among the best known of those early-1960s experiments. Each of these producers helped to shape the sounds of others: Spector's symphonic use of massed unison guitars and layered percussion behind reverb-rich vocals led directly to his work for the Beatles and the post-Beatles solo work of George Harrison and John Lennon, and indirectly to African-American soul–pop sub-genres such as the symphonic soul of the O'Jays and other representatives of the Philly Sound.[24] Meek's sci-fi experimentalism, using compression, tape editing and overdubbing, influenced among many others the early, experimental work of Pink Floyd, in which Meek's work is echoed both in Syd Barrett's whimsical and melancholic songs, such as the mono single 'Arnold Layne', produced in 1967 by Joe Boyd, and in the exuberant stereo playfulness of the band's first album (produced by former Beatles engineer Norman Smith), *The Piper at the Gates of Dawn*.[25]

That first Pink Floyd album was being recorded at Abbey Road Studios while the Beatles were also at Abbey Road, recording *Sergeant Pepper's Lonely Hearts Club Band*, under the inspired production of George Martin. Their partnership had started in the early 1960s when the object of a session was to make singles as quickly as possible; at this point, Martin – an EMI employee who had started his career in the company's classical division – was fixer, arranger and listener, very much in the 'traditional' producer mould. In this way he also produced successful singles for Billy J. Kramer and the Dakotas, Gerry and the Pacemakers, Cilla Black and many others from the heroic moment of early-1960s British pop. But as the technologies of recording developed alongside the confidence of the Lennon–McCartney song-writing partnership, Martin's collaborative role increased. The innovative use on 'Eleanor Rigby' of a double string quartet – four violins, two violas and two cellos – and the swirling orchestral spiral that features twice on 'A Day in the Life', as much as the varispeed editing, multitracking and assembly-editing of tracks such as 'Being for the Benefit of Mr Kite' and 'Revolution no. 9', all marked Martin out as an arranger-producer able to remake music while bringing out commercially successful records. His success with the Beatles then enabled him to leave EMI and set up AIR (Associated Independent Recording) studios and enjoy a freelance career.

Martin's work helped to establish the viability of the rock album and swing the music industry's attention away from pop singles; album-based rock (and jazz offerings such as *In a Silent Way* and *Bitches Brew*) became highly profitable, as well as the object of critical attention by the growing popular music press. African-American pop and soul was also moving in this direction, with Marvin Gaye, Stevie Wonder and the Temptations among the artists who defied the Motown hit-factory formula, and Norman Whitfield among the producers who helped to redefine the album. Like Martin, Whitfield forged a creative partnership with one particular group, the Temptations, and, again like Martin's with the Beatles, this began with relatively orthodox pop singles such as '(I know) I'm Losing You' (1966) and progressed through the aggressive acid funk of 'Psychedelic Shack' (1970) to long tracks made not for single but for album release, such as 'Papa Was a Rolling Stone' (1972), in which wha-wha guitars snaked and crackled across repeated riffs which are played as often by full string orchestra in unison as by the bass guitar, keyboards and percussion of the orthodox rhythm section. This became Whitfield's trademark, as effective on Rose Royce's melancholic disco classic 'Is It Love You're After' (1976) as on Temptations albums such as *Masterpiece* (1973).

In turn, the expansive Whitfield sound was mutated by Nile Rogers and Bernard Edwards into the trademark sound of the Chic organisation: ultratight drums and percussion, a mobile and melodic but very precise bass guitar line, and chopping rhythm guitar support the vocals, with supplementary licks by keyboard, orchestra or brass section. The results are then edited into long tracks with breakdown sections dominated by solid, explicit bass drum beats, all the better for dancing at this, the height of the disco era. Rodgers and Edwards produced their own records because, they claimed, they had to: no one else understood the way they wanted records to sound.[26] As soon as the world had gauged the success of the first Chic single, 'Le Freak' (1978), the two became a hard-working production team, making similar-sounding vehicles (using themselves and the Chic team of musicians to play the backing tracks) for Sister Sledge, Debbie Harry, Diana Ross and Carly Simon among others. Rodgers then went on to produce two albums that kept dance music alive in the brief era between the height of disco and the post-rave dance music of the later 1980s and after: David Bowie's 1983 *Let's Dance* and Madonna's 1984 *Like a Virgin*. Meanwhile the Sugarhill Gang used the Chic single 'Good Times' as the basis for their 'Rapper's Delight' (1979), which helped launch hip-hop to an eager world.[27]

1980s pop: Producer as composer, computer as musician

In the early 1980s the confluence of record company investment strategies and new recording technologies saw the pop producer's power and independence wax greatly. Record companies were (sometimes hesitantly) investing in CD pressing plants and digital recording equipment, while beginning to cut back on their rosters of artists in favour of concentrated spending on records most likely to be hits. One aspect of this strategy was the hiring of producers with track records in hit-making. The early years of the decade were dominated by producer, arranger and composer Quincy Jones, whose work with Michael Jackson and others produced a new wall of sound. Jones had trained as a classical composer, studying with Nadia Boulanger in Paris; he had played jazz trumpet, and worked as arranger with the Count Basie Band and Frank Sinatra during the 1960s, then spending a decade on solo albums and music for film (*The Italian Job*) and television (*Ironside*) as well as producing records for pop, soul and jazz artists. In the early 1980s he started to work with Michael Jackson, balancing his light voice by extending the backing tracks' bass frequencies downwards (using synthesisers rather than bass guitars) and compressing most of the recorded instruments. He and engineer Bruce Swedien recorded and mixed using several multitrack tape decks slaved together, recording and choosing from forty-eight or sixty-four rather than twenty-four tracks for the final mixdown. The results – *Off the Wall* (1982), *Thriller* (1984) and *Bad* (1986) – sold in all about 150 million albums worldwide.

By this time multitrack recording was being supplemented by sampling and computer-based sequencing, and among the producers who first capitalised on the opportunities presented by the new technologies was

Trevor Horn, who had been part of the Buggles and Yes. Horn started producing in 1981. ABC's 1982 *Lexicon of Love* was his first hit album, for which he assembled a production team including composer/keyboardist Anne Dudley, and J. J. Jeczalik as programmer of the new Fairlight Computer Musical Instrument (CMI), an early, and very expensive, sampling and sequencing device. They set up a record label, ZTT, and Dudley and Jeczalik led the studio band Art of Noise. 1983 saw the label's most successful record, Frankie Goes to Hollywood's 'Relax', which was controversial because of its sexually explicit lyrics as well as Horn's later claim that he had assembled the whole thing, using the Fairlight CMI to sample lead singer Holly Johnson's voice rather than allowing him actually to sing anything, and with no other band input.

Whether or not this was the case, the success of 'Relax' (in the context of similar success for *Thriller*, the Bowie/Rodgers and Madonna/Rodgers combinations, and the emergent pop genius of self-producer Prince) led to a wave of producer-led pop, dominated in the UK by the Stock, Aitken and Waterman production team.[28] Sampling sounds such as the bass drum from the Bowie/Rodgers track 'Let's Dance', and sequencing bass lines in imitation of Quincy Jones, the trio made formulaic hit singles for a roster of artists such as Mel and Kim, Kylie Minogue, Rick Astley and Bananarama.

Alongside such mass production, however, were producers whose input was anything but formulaic; the most notable was Brian Eno, sometime art student, synthesiser player for Roxy Music, artist, label owner, musical innovator, and collaborator with David Bowie and David Byrne among many others. Eno has produced albums for Talking Heads, Ultravox, Laurie Anderson, Paul Simon and Coldplay, but his best-known production work has been for U2. With the band's active collaboration he turned them, in the early 1980s, from yet another reasonably successful stadium rock band into one of the world's best-known bands (and highest earners). Recorded in Dublin and engineered by Daniel Lanois, the first U2–Eno project, *The Unforgettable Fire* (1984), launched the band as world-beaters. Lanois and Eno warmed the sound and decreased its definition, making the whole album sound more orchestral and less like a few musicians playing in a fairly small space with the tape running. Working with Eno, the band was encouraged not simply to record and polish existing songs, but to use the studio as an instrument, improvising in the creation of new songs and overdubbing parts to add to the richness of the final mix. The result changed the way U2 worked live. To replicate the complexity achieved in the studio, they started to use pre-programmed sequencers to back their stage performances. Subsequent Eno–U2 albums, including the band's bestseller, *The Joshua Tree* (1987), *Achtung Baby* (1991) and *Zooropa* (1993), explored further aspects of the producer's and the band's musicalities, often –

particularly in the recording of *Achtung Baby* – using the tension of aesthetic differences within the band, or between the band and Eno, to create a distinctive sound for a particular album and its subsequent promotional tour (e.g., 'Zoo TV' in the case of *Zooropa*). Eno thrives on such differences, responding to new challenges with psycho-musical techniques such as establishing a project's cultural placement by, for example, asking the musicians what books and films they would like the album to 'sound like'. Here the work of the producer has helped to change the way live music, as well as recorded music, sounds.[29]

Producing 'world music': Integration and difference

The same was happening in many parts of the world, even in musics whose claims lay with the authenticity of tradition. Värttinä had started in the early 1980s as a group of school friends in a small town in Northern Karelia, Finland. Mixing traditional songs and instrumental music from the area, the band reformed in 1990 in Helsinki, where they released a break-through album, *Oi Dai*, in 1991, just as the new sales category 'world music' was becoming established throughout Western Europe. *Oi Dai*'s energetic renditions of traditional songs and dances were supplemented on the next album, *Seleniko* (1992), by original compositions in traditional styles played and sung – it was now obvious – by people who had listened to jazz, rock and pop. To help cement these changes the band then turned to Hijaz Mustapha (Ben Mandelson), the English label owner and former leader of the pioneering world-music band Three Mustaphas Three. Hijaz Mustapha's production altered the balance between the musicians and singers, and among the singers themselves, while making the recording sound more like an album as an aesthetic whole than a collection of songs, and bringing it slightly closer to orthodox Western popular music. The differences are subtle. More of the songs start with the instrumental ensemble rather than one or more vocalists, while there are fewer pure instrumentals; the songs are longer, with structures that often go beyond verse–chorus, and therefore feel more like album tracks. The third track, 'Kyla Vuotti Uuta Kuuta', for example, features solo voices as much as the ensemble, and, with its slow build-up of voices and accompaniment and prominent string bass part, the whole has the feeling of a rock ballad. Hijaz Mustapha's production helped move the band beyond 'folk' and into the globalised transactional currency of world music, which as well as earning the band fans from across the world led among other things to their collaboration with Bollywood composer A.R. Rahman on the musical version of J.R.R. Tolkien's *The Lord of the Rings*, staged in London in 2007.

1990s hip-hop: The producer-performer

The 1990s were good for producers; as Suvi Raj Grubb had predicted, new technologies meant that the producer could exert increasing control at every stage of the recording process. Nowhere is this more true than in hip-hop and R&B, where the named producer is often responsible for the recording, sampling, sequencing and/or assembly of every part of a musical track apart from the lead vocals. Dr Dre (Andre Young), for example, produced NWA's groundbreaking album *Straight Outta Compton* (1988) from within the band. Over the following decade after leaving NWA he built up his own pre- and post-production style known as G-funk, favouring slow beats and programmed sequences played by synthesisers rather than samples (he often hires session musicians to re-create the feel of samples he likes, in order to avoid synchronisation and intonation problems). This more controlled style, along with the confrontationally aggressive delivery of lyrics, helped to shift most commercially released rap away from good-time music, with words yelled good-naturedly over repetitive beats (M.C. Hammer, the Beastie Boys), or political songs using samples from the history of African-American music (Grandmaster Flash and the Furious Five, Public Enemy). The result was 'gangsta rap', an almost self-parodic form in which the braggadocio performance of the rapper, delivered with more time and intensity because of the space allowed by Dre's beats, could all too easily mirror the gangland clashes that formed the subject of much of the lyrics. From this musical and ideological base Dr Dre began in the later 1990s to work with rappers such as Snoop Dogg, Eminem, and 50 Cent, to make a 'post-gangsta rap' music which is far more lyrical, often recorded using live instruments, and structured around sung choruses and rapped verses.

Taking rap back towards the relative orthodoxy of song structures, Dr Dre is moving in the opposite direction to Rick Rubin, who started as a hip-hop producer and helped to give birth to the unlikely hybrid of 'rapcore'. Rubin started producing hip-hop records in 1983, when he co-founded the Def Jam label. Rubin was responsible for the collaboration of hip-hoppers Run-DMC with stadium rockers Aerosmith on the 1986 single 'Walk This Way'. Such collaborations helped the emergence of the 'nu-metal' of Linkin Park, Limp Bizkit and Korn (which features hip-hop elements such as rapped vocals and/or DJs with turntables as band members), and the angry political rap-rock of Rage Against the Machine. Rubin went on to produce albums for artists from a variety of genres – including the Dixie Chicks, Red Hot Chili Peppers, Mick Jagger and Donovan – as well as rappers Geto Boys and Jay-Z, and heavy metal bands such as Slayer, Linkin Park, and notably the Armenian-American metal band System of a Down's influential 2005 albums *Hypnotise* and *Mesmerise* (on which the band's politically forthright writer, guitarist and backup vocalist Daron Malakian is listed as co-producer).

The sound signature as the producer's choice

As we saw even in the case of Suvi Raj Grubb's too-perfect recordings, the producer has played a key part in the making of recorded music as a separate entity from musics that rely on the moment: recordings are usually copies of an event that did not, precisely, happen. The French philosopher Jean Baudrillard has claimed that we are now in what he calls the third age of simulacra, in which we are surrounded by 'copies' without originals. It is certainly easy to agree that we share a diminished sense of the importance of origin. As he sees it, we have lost our ability to differentiate between the natural and the artificial. In the contemporary world, Baudrillard claims, we are confronted with what he calls 'precession' of simulacra; in other words, the representation precedes and determines our understanding of the real.[30] The 'perfection' attainable by recording has changed our expectations of the sounds of music, and this has impacted on ways in which classical and jazz artists perform live, while rock 'tribute bands' such as Let Zeppelin or the Bootleg Beatles copy all aspects of a successful band's recorded and live performance practices. It is easy to see that, to the panic of legislators and lobbyists alike, most music is indeed approaching a state of perpetual copying without reference to an original, and that for many makers and users of music this has become the cultural norm. This is especially so in the dance music that emerged during the later 1980s, where the collation of samples and high-technology instruments controlled by computers, and the profusion of remixes and mashups, further blurred the distinctions of creativity and ownership, as well as the roles of composer, performer and producer.

In 1992 *MCMXC A.D.* was released on the Virgin label. Under the band name Enigma, the album featured the Romanian musician Michael Cretu as composer and performer, with a production team that included Frank Peterson. 'Sadeness', the first single taken from the album, became a global hit. This track featured a distinctive sound signature: breakbeat rhythm loops, long-sustained synthesiser chords slowly changing in timbre, a melody line played by a sampled shakuhachi (a Japanese wooden flute with a breathy and wistful quality), female spoken voice and lead vocals, and – most strikingly – a male voice choir, synchronised to the rhythm track, singing Gregorian chant in Latin. The German choir that had been sampled then fought for and won financial reward for its unwitting contribution to Enigma's success.[31]

The Enigma album's producer went on to produce pop music using the same soundworld. Frank Peterson avoided further legal difficulties by hiring a male voice choir, consisting of men schooled in opera and/or the Anglican choral tradition, to sing Gregorian-chant-style arrangements (with lyrics sung in English, not Latin) of classic pop songs from the Anglo-American repertoire. The arrangements also featured a sound signature that any fan of Enigma would have found familiar: breakbeats, synthesised bass lines, gently washing synthesiser chords, solo female lead vocals, and at times sampled melody lines that apparently use the exact shakuhachi sample featured on 'Sadeness'.[32] The first album under the name 'Gregorian', *Masters of Chant*, released in 1999, achieved gold status in sixteen countries. Gregorian has at the time of writing produced five CD albums, a greatest hits collection, and a live concert DVD. Peterson had turned a slightly edgy – if very commercially successful – dance music experiment into a pop formula.

Epilogue: So, what do producers actually *do*?

One answer is that it helps if you own the label. Manfred Eicher set up Editions of Contemporary Music (ECM) in 1979, and since then has produced the vast majority of its jazz, folk, early music and new classical recordings. Eicher was a bass player whose chief influences in recorded sound were the Deutsche Grammophon Archiv recordings of the pre-classical tradition, and in jazz the work of Miles Davis and Teo Macero, and Bill Evans and producer Orrin Keepnews. ECM recordings quickly gained a reputation for a set of sonic values: a nuanced clarity, with tasteful resonance sometimes added by the natural acoustic, sometimes by electronic aids, in performances that are usually edited to sound 'live'. At the heart of the label's choices, Manfred Eicher has assembled bands, introduced collaborators, commissioned pieces and produced the result:

> The natural ambience of an acoustically neutral recording studio needs some help if instruments are to sing … he vividly conveys his requirements to his engineers. Sometimes, too, in the mixing process, he plays the faders of the studio console like a keyboard, outstretched fingers making minute level adjustments. He has a poetic grasp of the parameters of Lexicon's reverb machines, a good sense of the character of diverse microphones … and an intuitive feeling for microphone placement. Does this add up to the 'ECM sound'?[33]

But the real trick is in the detail, for like Brian Eno Eicher has a feel for 'the grain of the voice',[34] and in the end this allows him to act as the inspired mediator between artist and listener, to help the artist make music, and along the way to make distinctive recordings. Listening to Meredith Monk as she describes her first experience of recording for ECM, we realise that there is indeed more to the ECM sound, and far more to the role of the record producer, than mere microphone placement.

> I completed the take and went to the control room. Manfred was beaming and dancing round the room. I said, 'didn't you hear my voice crack on that phrase; didn't you hear an intonation problem on that one?' Manfred looked at me and said, 'that was magic, but if you want to do another one, go ahead. I'm going out to have a cup of coffee'. I proceeded to record another take, which I thought was perfect technically. When Manfred returned, we listened to both takes and sure enough, the first one had a raw mystery and power that was missing from the second. There was simply more life in it.[35]

Producers, too, make music.

Still small voices

JONATHAN FREEMAN-ATTWOOD

Increasingly, listening to 'historic' performances on record presents exciting challenges to those making new recordings in the studio. Among their many purposes, recordings enable us to plot lineages of musical accomplishment and also to observe where musicians in the last century or so have sought to break away from established traditions. Histories of interpretation can now be traced compellingly through a judicious synthesis of biography and the source-evidence on record. Wrongly imagined histories can be righted. And yet the recent surge of musicological interest in recordings and the resulting scholarly output has barely registered on the radar of performers (as distinct from those who study performance), as a catalyst either to pursue models of enquiry into past interpretative values or to measure what these achievements count for in their own creative lives. The study of recordings by academics is rarely motivated by how it can inspire performers. Therefore the study of recordings by performers needs to be built on its own practical and cultural foundations where a close intertextual relationship can be established between the recording studios of yesterday and today.

If the post-war recording studio is deemed partly responsible for a perceived erosion of the 'commitment at risk' of the performer's 'enactment of chosen meanings and values' (as George Steiner ennobled the interpreter),[1] the solution I offer below provides a chance for atonement: performers properly equipped with a broad and discriminating musical vocabulary from the past (as observers and possible re-activators of specific rhetorics, means of characterisation, hierarchies of elocution and nuance, etc.) can re-invent the 'studio' as a critical workshop for evaluating the ideals of previous generations and stimulating a practical re-appraisal of modern musical interpretative values. For history to impact creatively in this way, performers must conquer fears of past 'greats' as a yoke that stifles individuality and then wrestle with those elements which, however remotely, already inspire them.

The old studio

A composer's voice is matured, nurtured and developed by valuing or rejecting the work of 'past masters', sometimes even both at the same time. The performer heightens awareness of working in his or her own tradition by adopting a similar approach. A recording of a baroque concerto grosso made in 1929 may therefore serve as 'conscience', even for the most self-contained and informed performer of today.

Ernest Ansermet offers particular challenges in the opening movement of Handel's Concerto Grosso in A Minor, Op. 6 No. 4, recorded eighty years ago.[2] The performance of this short Larghetto is neither especially conventional nor iconoclastic for its period, but it establishes a coherent set of values that fundamentally reflect the imaginative world of the executants. The background of its personality is underpinned by Ansermet as a pioneer for 'antique' music, while still immersed in the prevailing performing traditions of mainstream nineteenth-century repertories. Immediately striking is a keen delight in balanced textures, supple timing and the delicately guided appoggiaturas of a re-elevated baroque – a canvas that allows Handel's vocalised lines to be shaped luminously, alongside the recognisable rhetorical signposts widely applicable to all musical performance in the 1920s.

On the one hand, a palpable neo-classical clarity is derived from both the evolving tastes and the knowledge of the time (notably Ansermet's interest in Stravinsky and a prophetically stylish use of a 'period' harpsichord – a 1790 Broadwood played by Leslie Heward), while, on the other, we discern in this 'old studio' a staged evolution, part pre-ordained and part bubbling out of an arsenal of spontaneity. Ansermet harnesses important points of reference: some are especially pronounced, while other details of elocution are (like speech) less articulated and act as a form of grammatical necessity towards the next peak which, in this case, concerns the manipulation of a recurring hallmark phrase. Through a combination of rubatos, accentuated placement, cool and unvibrated tone colour, 'local' hesitations and minute dislocations, leading to a series of assuaging portamentos and a single dramatic point of arrival, this is a journey that discriminates between what should be spelt out and what should not. No single technical or musical device can, on its own, offer a rounded explanation; no phrase of music can say the same thing twice.

To value an example in a musical territory whose parameters of acceptable execution have become so demarcated in the last thirty years requires us to expunge the notion of appropriate 'style', either as guiding principle or *sine qua non*, as we grapple with these old – but new – artistic visions. Must the modern listener or practitioner abandon modern ideals of rhythmic steadiness, ensemble, tuning and homogeneity to accept this old vocabulary as potentially enriching? Surely no more than he or she accepts, uncritically, the portamentos and rubatos witnessed here. Indeed, is there not a case today for a form of expressive sliding in a Handel movement at a moment of marked intensity in the music? As a time-honoured expressive vehicle, can this ubiquitous 'historicism' not be re-fashioned to mean something genuine in a current musical vernacular? Do we sacrifice integrity by changing practice habits through a degree of copy and pastiche? Should we not question whether its disappearance is retrospectively or historically justified?

There is every reason – on this evidence and, for example, in the plethora of recordings of Bach and Handel from 1900 to 1930 – to search out models for both practical and philosophical outlooks on how to counter expressive limitations and inhibitions and, certainly in trends established in the 1970s, to challenge conventions which have been built on less than solid foundations. We *invigorate* our creativity by isolating musical decisions and comparing them with models from all periods. 'Performance practice' cannot be the primary catalyst for creativity. In any case, 'practice' would have meant as little to early-recorded musicians as the concept of 'performer' (revealingly, the Germans would say *'musizieren'* – someone who 'musics'). Players or singers were simply musicians whose calling obviated advocacy of a particular 'practice'; they lived their lives and played music as one, largely within the traditions in which they found themselves. The implications of this are considerable if we accept performance as an artistic endeavour with its own internal coherence, set apart from the external sets of values we liberally apply in the name of historical rectitude or convenience.

The new studio

How can we generate 'commitment at risk' in our new studio and acquire a state of mind where these 'still small voices' become re-animated, assembled consciously and transformed for the here and now? Whether perusing special artists, geographical traits, specific performances or general characteristics, we need to capture something of that 'authentic' spontaneity through a growing confidence to draw readily from examples that enlighten each of us personally. Each unique dialect expands its expressive vocabulary, almost as an artistic reflex. Musicians can then critique what is 'responsible' for them – in the Steiner sense – and 'invest their own being' in an interpretation.

With our tools at the ready, we toy afresh with Glenn Gould's ideal of studio recording: 'an art form with its own laws … an environment where the magnetic compulsion of time is suspended, though warped at the very least. It is a vacuum, in a sense a place where one can properly feel the most horrendously constricting force of nature. The inexorable linearity of time has been, to a remarkable extent, circumvented.'[3] Gould's vacuum is what makes the studio a terrifying place for many musicians, especially those whose model of projection falls predominantly within the scope of the athletic. For them, the studio is not live but a restricting and lonely place where adrenaline is elusive without the audience. Such performers do not adapt well to studio 'liveness': they cannot enter into dialogue with themselves as part of an evolving creative act or generate musical ideas deliberately not so formed as to restrict the 'liveness' we know can emerge in Gould's 'inexorable linearity of time'. Here, a reflective, incremental assembly of 'live' performances is the means to an end that is not yet fully imagined as a formed musical statement.

The ideal conditions for our new studio require a dynamic convergence between artist, producer and the artwork. The performers rely on the ears of the producer to oversee the project, willing the artists to do their best every time, identifying with their aspirations, questioning them and then gathering the fruits of their work with each 'take' rather than toeing a company line. Producers should spot the moment of keenest musical perception and energy in the session and then let the performers take wing. They may pause to correct a repeated misreading or to question a conceit that succeeds in concert but may pall on repeated listening. All the time they are collecting their wares but, as yet, cannot predetermine how the stall will eventually be set out. The producer thinks, 'Will that luminous tone in the violins match the restless cello counterpoint at that recapitulation point (as we know is desired) or shall we record some alternatives for later consideration?'

Further consideration occurs when the artists have left the studio. The producer holds all these 'voices', de-contextualised in a litany of seemingly incoherent takes. The one person who has not created the music must now sing for the artists and the work. The performers may challenge the producer's will in the studio, but in the cutting-room they must trust that the latter's first 'edit' or 'proof' will recognisably evince each layer of session in memory, hope and expectation. In an environment where as many artistic decisions are made after the event(s) as during the sessions, editing can only contribute to the creative process *if there is the quality and range of possibilities behind the decision to choose one take above another.*

New patterns of musical possibilities emerge as the producer (with or without an attentive artist) alights on creative solutions, juxtaposing and connecting paragraphs of sound, incorporating a gesture emboldened by a particular edit, engendered by an artistic whim drawn, perhaps, from our Ansermet-inspired palette. Is it really too idealistic to suggest that the intuitive interpreter can emerge from within a legacy of continuity and thus define his or her own inventiveness? These connected studios – old and new – can at least allow musicians to be explicit with themselves, as recordings become objects of perception (to be responded to) and renewal (to respond to). Not so still, these small voices from the past can resonate with fresh meanings.

Broadening horizons: 'Performance' in the studio

MICHAEL HAAS

The past thirty or so years that I've worked as a recording producer have certainly formed my view on the relationship between music, recording and interpretation. Perhaps most of all, I have come to see how important it is for producers – themselves a form of musical catalyst – actively to engage with repertoire rather than contenting themselves only with performance. The longer I work in recording, the more convinced I become that *composers* rather than performers provide our music. The crisis the 'business' is now experiencing is due to the lack of platforms available to composers who have something to say to an intelligent, receptive, *paying* public. In a world where audiences have the freedom to choose what they wish to hear, it cannot be enough to rely on tax-payers to provide whatever meagre exposure composers have as their only means of dissemination. All my observations on performance and interpretation must therefore be taken in the context of an environment offering a surfeit of different musical views on a relatively static number of works. Indeed, discussing whether the studio adds or detracts to someone's performance of a Beethoven sonata recorded hundreds of times already is akin to calculating the number of angels dancing on the head of a pin during the Grand Inquisition. Pop music has stolen the initiative, told us what people are prepared to buy and left intelligent music lovers with less choice than before. If we were dealing with the written word, we would be living in a world of comic books with literature inhabiting the margins and virtually nothing in between except ungratifying verses by some worthy, publicly financed poets.

Yet decades of studio work have resulted in more than just grumpy ruminations on the sorry state of new music. As awkward as it is, I must accept the fact that the music business is based on the success of interpretive rather than what I see as the truly creative artists. As a recording producer, I am compelled to help the performer maximise his or her potential. So I should emphasise that the studio is a *creative* tool. A musician who announces he cannot work in one because his performance 'magic' is lost is in fact missing a far more crucial point: no studio can capture *any* performance – even a live performance ceases to be 'live' the moment it's heard a second time. Capturing a *performance* is like trying to hold on to the breeze: its nature is transitory and its effect ephemeral. The moment it's recorded, it ceases to animate and becomes only a reproduction. Nevertheless, the studio remains the only tool we have by which we may maximise the *effect* of animation within musical reproductions.

I wish I could find another word – but as I can't, let's call these reproductions 'performances' too, while recognising their fundamentally different nature. The best way to illustrate this is by addressing a question about another interpretive art: would one prefer a performance of a script as a play, a film or a television series? Most people would probably feel that an appropriate treatment would work with any of the above. If a play is removed from the theatre to a studio, we may lose the momentary and ephemeral while gaining an opportunity of experiencing the narrative in a different, more layered way. Obviously, a play when turned into a movie or TV drama undergoes a change of fundamental text, while a Beethoven sonata, once moved from a concert hall to a studio, undergoes a change of fundamental *context*.

The advent of recordings brought about a conflation of two relatively new phenomena that have now become inalterable. The first of these was the manner in which a listener perceived music, and the second, growing from the first, was the manner in which a musician performed it. One cannot emphasise enough the fact that, prior to recording and broadcasting, music was an *experience* and not a *thing*. The 'thing' was the score. Enthusiasts forced themselves to develop an inner ear capable of hearing works from the printed page. Schoenberg tried to persuade radio-addicted Americans that teaching composition was the best means of developing this ability. People went to concerts tuned to catching a work's every note, perhaps heard only once in a lifetime. If one missed anything, it was gone for ever. Music lovers were *active* listeners.

Recording took these ephemeral experiences and turned them into tangibles. Once the experience could be repeated at will, music lovers became *passive*. Passive listening was never an option in a pre-recording age. As I wrote above, this phenomenon is not alterable. It is here to stay, so musicians should take note and consider something quite fundamental: passive listening does not mean less dynamic listening. The passive listening of today is absolutely not to be confused with Adorno's views of a complacent bourgeoisie's delight in hearing pretty music. On the contrary, it means that the music lover's experience has shifted and even become more subtle. The moment something intangible is made tangible it must bear scrutiny, and scrutiny demands detail. Details do not kill a performance but provide additional layers of expression that engage the listener far more complexly. To provide another thespian example: Bette Davis was never the success on stage that she was on film. The reasons are obvious: a cocked eyebrow, the twitch of a lip or the roll of an eye were too detailed to be registered in the theatre. Yet these same minutiae managed to chill spines with repeated viewing in the cinema.

More than one performer has mentioned that the studio is the key to becoming a better musician. The oft-cited 'great arc' that mysteriously disappears in takes, sapping all life from once-animated performances, is a lazy misconception that misses the central reality of today's listener. They hear music while answering emails, ironing shirts or cleaning their cat-trays. All of these are no doubt reprehensible activities to undertake in the presence of masterpieces. But there is an important compensating factor: the same recording will be played repeatedly, thus demanding a type of *active* listening unfamiliar to the pre-recording age. This type of listening instinctively seeks out even the tiniest differences with each repeated hearing. If this element of scrutiny is demanded, details need to be subtle and ever shifting. Such subtlety means that the concept, indeed the very pulse of the work itself changes. But a change in pulse should not mean a lack of pulse!

A producer should be able to help the performer find these different interpretive layers. They often whistle past on a preliminary take, allowing the performer to winkle them out during the course of the recording. The most common mistake made by musicians is to see the studio as a microscope that can explode cosmetic irregularities into near-nuclear genocide. Indeed, the studio's means of removing minor blemishes nor-mally liberates the creative performer and allows risks never taken in concert. I personally do not see an inconsistency between taking technical or interpretive risks in a studio that are not attempted in live perfor-mances. Certain exposed passages may simply work better in solitude than in front of an audience. In the past thirty years, I can recall no more galvanising studio experience than Radu Lupu's extraordinary dynamic control and especially the scrupulousness with which he voiced every harmony in a single chord. These are moments that thrill with repeated listening. The fact that he stopped making recordings only underlined the bewilderment of a gifted musician frustrated by the interpretive abyss between live performance and the endless possibilities of the studio. For him, the studio became the microscope, emphasising too many interpre-tive gradations. Glenn Gould's recognition of the same situation led him in the other direction, giving up concerts altogether. Obviously, it's ideal to master both, though we should not despair of Gould, who never left the studio, nor of Lupu, who never returned to one. Both recognised that their individual artistic sanity demanded the cultivation of one and only one musical platform. Generations of great actors and actresses who have concentrated on theatre at the expense of film or vice versa are no different. Yet would anyone seriously ask whether works created in a film studio are dead compared with those of the theatre? Is music so very different? The environment created by recordings means that today's music enthusiast is more *passive* when listening to live performances (perhaps unconsciously comparing events on stage with familiar CDs at home), while remaining more *active* when listening to recordings, eking out more and more subtleties with repeated playing. The studio broadens musical horizons and by no means inhibits the interpretive options of the receptive performer.

3 Getting sounds: The art of sound engineering

ALBIN ZAK

You, as the engineer, have to share in the painting with the artist. PHIL RAMONE*

In transforming musical thought and action into sound recordings, sounds are converted into electric current and sent along a signal path to a storage medium from which they can be reconstituted at the push of a button. This bit of technological magic has introduced a new figure into the music-making process – not a musician, nor a composer, arranger or songwriter, but one who nonetheless exerts a measure of influence over a listener's musical experience: the recording engineer. The tasks performed by engineers, while practical, have an aesthetic dimension as well, which amounts to an expressive voice in the sound-recording project, an example of what Hans-Joachim Braun calls the 'technologization of musical aesthetics'.[1] The voices of recording engineers, always present though historically 'silent', have long influenced the ways in which we perceive musical sound. Indeed, their accumulated work has shaped essential contours of our recorded musical landscape. Sound recordings are renderings of sound events and, like any rendering, they embody the attitudes, skills, habits and aesthetic stances of those who make them. Some renderings aspire to acoustic realism, others to fantasy, but whatever the case, the sound of a recording has much to do with the technical abilities and aesthetic choices of those whose hands control the signal path.

In sound recording's early decades, when engineers were referred to as recordists and mixers, there was a general developmental trend toward accurate transcription, conceived as fidelity to the music's source. Because sound recording forces music and the artifacts of the transcription process into competition within the space of the same inscribed line, achieving fidelity is an ongoing challenge. In the days of acoustic recording, technical vagaries were such that, as music became transformed from ephemeral event to durable thing, the task confronting a recordist was convincingly to weight the scale on the side of music. When electrical recording was introduced in the mid-1920s, it was embraced for its potential, through

* H. Massey, *Behind the Glass: Top Record Producers Tell How They Craft the Hits*, San Francisco, Backbeat Books, 2000, p. 50

amplification, to offer a more detailed representation than the acoustic recording it sought to supplant, a more realistic portrayal of musical events. If 'the object of all reproduction was to simulate the real thing – to create the illusion of reality', as one critic put it in 1929, then the new technology made significant strides in that direction.[2]

But sonic realism remained a slippery notion. There was no doubt that microphones allowed for more precise control than acoustic recording horns, but how should the control be exercised? The sound-gathering process still involved the translation of musical expression from one medium to another – from fluctuating air pressure to oscillating electric current – which, in turn, required feats of aural interpretation. Engineers were given a freer hand to refine their sonic images, but what criteria should guide their interpretive decisions? Perhaps close-miking in a relatively dead, or dry, space, free from the capricious artifacts of reverberation, might provide a cleaner, more precise representation of an instrument's timbre. Yet wouldn't the natural distortion provided by acoustic 'liveness' make for a more accurate representation of real-world listening? If so, how should the reverberation be mixed with the music, and in what proportion? And what of the other noises intrinsic to music-making – a guitarist's finger squeaks or a violinist's scraping bow? These are part of real-world musical perception, and a realist approach would capture them as faithfully as possible. In the enduring form of a recording, however, they may become wearing with repeated listening. Are they to be minimised by some kind of sonic air-brush? Is the primary goal of a recording project to make an aesthetic object of delight or to strive towards some sort of truthful account?

Opinions have always varied, and debates have been ongoing more or less from the beginning, rehearsed in such periodicals as *The Gramophone, Phonograph Monthly Review, Saturday Review of Recordings, Audio* and *High Fidelity*. In an introduction to the first issue of *High Fidelity*, which rolled off the presses in the summer of 1951, Milton B. Sleeper acknowledged the broad range of views concerning qualitative criteria for recorded sound and its reproduction. 'One of the most intriguing aspects of undertaking to publish *High Fidelity*', he wrote, 'is the number of widely divergent opinions held by the devotees of the field this magazine will serve.'[3] The magazine focused on sound reproduction topics for the home audiophile, but a significant portion of each issue was devoted to reviews of recordings focusing on musical expression and its sonic realisation 'from every standpoint', as one review put it – 'performance, spirit, balance, acoustics, recording'.[4]

Faced with a new medium of musical perception and only real-world musical experience for comparison, recordists sought guidance from a musical idiom's historical traditions. There was a general, if tacit, sense that recording ought to be as true as possible to an idiom's historical sonic context. (Interestingly, unlike film, sound recording would not be regarded as an art form for several decades.) So electronic manipulation was more appropriate for music of recent vintage than for music of venerable tradition. While dry close-miking, for example, might be suitable for a popular music combo playing in a radio station studio – and indeed, the singers relied on it – a symphony orchestra required a more encompassing microphone technique where the sounds of different instruments and the sound of the recording space were blended together, as they had done historically for live audiences. Carson Taylor, who engineered sessions for performers ranging from Nat Cole and Stan Kenton to George Szell and Carlo Maria Giulini, claimed that, in contrast to a pop record, a recording of classical music should bear 'no intrusion that is apparent on the part of the engineer. He has to be a truly transparent entity.'[5]

But transparency in the signal path is elusive, and aesthetic questions remain ever in play. Is it best to use many mikes to control the ensemble balance electronically? Or to minimise that artifice, and the problems that come with it, in favor of fewer mikes – perhaps only one? Having settled these questions, what types and models of mikes should be used? Where should they be placed for the most realistic effect? And realistic, that is, from which, or whose, perspective? Because the answers to such questions result in widely varying sonic effects, there are no absolutes, only aesthetic choices commingling the behaviour of electronic devices and architectural spaces with musical expression, taste and traditional conventions. As Thomas Porcello has put it, because microphones 'do not "hear" in the same way as ears, the sound engineer must … mediate between the interpretive and performance habits of the conductor and the musicians on the one hand, and the acoustic properties of microphones and the (psycho)acoustics of the ear on the other'.[6] Add to this formulation the acoustic properties of the architectural spaces and a picture emerges of a complex set of elements ever in motion. Indeed, the 'original' version of an acoustic event changes its form depending on what sort of microphone is used and where it is placed. The question, then, is more properly framed in terms not of transparency or realism but of suitability. What will suit the aesthetic stance and aim of the project at hand? Making such decisions regarding the colour, shape and texture of the sonic rendering (elements, ultimately, of a recording's affective impact) fall to the recording team, of which there may be many members. But turning the concept into actual recorded sound is the job of the project's engineer.

At the beginning of his radio career in 1929, Leopold Stokowski realised immediately the importance of the sound engineer when he saw one setting balances among microphones. 'He's the conductor and I'm not,' Stokowski insisted, adding that the performance should not be broadcast under his name unless he was 'controlling the *pianissimo*, the *mezzo forte*, and the *fortissimo*'.[7] Stokowski recognised that the engineer's job of microphone placement and balancing included, necessarily, an element of interpretation. The man playing no instrument and wielding no baton nevertheless had a significant influence on how the music sounded on record. Indeed, as engineers 'rode gain', moving volume controls in the course of a performance, they participated in real-time music-making. Such control could be contentious: drummer Johnny Blowers remembered Frank Sinatra, during his stormy collaboration with Mitch Miller at Columbia in the early 1950s, becoming enraged at such tampering. 'With Frank and Axel [Stordahl, arranger] … you made your own dynamics. Frank didn't want [the engineer] turning dials.'[8] Although engineers had routinely made inconspicuous use of the 'dials' to control problematic levels, Sinatra was reacting to a change in record production that saw the process moving away from the documentary and towards Miller's more activist style of production, characterised disapprovingly, yet accurately, by one critic as a focus on 'sound *per se*'.[9] Over the coming decades, this trend would grow as electronic mediation became increasingly integrated in the musical process in ever more complex ways.

Devices such as equalisers and compressors would provide the means for more refined shaping of timbre and loudness contour. Tape allowed for unprecedented ease and flexibility of editing. And electronic enhancements such as reverb, delay, and their many special-effects offspring made for an extensive palette of resources with which to craft a recording's unique sonic world. With the expanded responsibility and skill set, the mixer's role would evolve into that of the recording engineer.

Representation

Recorded representation involves both craft and art which, in the end, are facets of a single process. The craft side involves the techniques for realising a sonic conception; the art lies in the conception itself. In miking the double string quartet for the Beatles's 'Eleanor Rigby', for example, Geoff Emerick placed the microphones 'very very close to the strings, almost touching them'.[10] Emerick chose the unusual technique in order to realise a conception formed in response to Paul McCartney's desire for an unconventional representation of George Martin's arrangement. The pop context and the general climate of experimentation at this point in the Beatles's career made such a representation plausible, though unconventional. 'The [classical] musicians were in horror,' Emerick recalled, for they were used to the more airy representation achieved by placing microphones further away from the instruments, whereby the strings' blend, along with the extra room ambience, would make for a warm, rounded sound akin to what a listener in the room might perceive. Emerick's choice made the sound more incisive and sharply focused. Such a sound might grate in the course of a thirty-minute classical piece, but in a two-and-a-half-minute pop song it provided an appropriately edgy quality.

While a particular idea for a sonic representation may be influenced in some way by any member of a recording team, the ear and skill of the engineer are usually responsible for its materialisation. The engineer is the member of the recording team best acquainted with not only the technical possibilities and limitations of electronics and acoustics, but also the nuances of rhetorical and stylistic uses of electronic mediation as a component of musical expression. The point is borne out repeatedly that the engineer is a 'subtle sub-producer', as Cosimo Matassa puts it.[11] That is, the engineer–producer relationship is cooperative. The producer Alfred Lion, owner of Blue Note records, was in charge of the sessions that, in the 1950s, produced a heralded new sound in jazz records. According to engineer Rudy Van Gelder, 'Alfred Lion knew exactly what he wanted to hear. He communicated it to me and I got it for him technically. The Blue Note sound was really his sound.'[12] But Lion, admitting his lack of technical knowledge, disagrees: 'He's very modest. It wasn't just the Alfred Lion sound, it was the combination of the two of us.'[13] Blue Note artist Horace Silver, too, recalls Van Gelder and Lion 'getting their heads together to get the Blue Note sound'. Each man 'had a great deal to do' with the final product.[14]

Redefining the sound of jazz records is clearly more than a simple matter of electronic know-how. It requires a nuanced integration of skill and sensibility both technical and musical, pragmatic and aesthetic, whose fusion amounts to an artistic discipline in its own right. Engineers are often said to 'play' the medium much as a musician plays an instrument. In claiming to 'play the console', Kevin Killen (engineer for Peter Gabriel, U2, Sam Phillips) uses his combination of musical and technological skill to 'interpret the ideas and get them to tape'.[15] In a 1957 interview, Van Gelder, who also engineered sessions for many other jazz labels, described some of his working philosophy. 'I think learning the sounds a mic can give is of first importance. Then it should be utilised to fit the music, with the same care a photographer employs in selecting a lens.' He stressed that recording tools 'must be used creatively', to serve a particular stylistic end.

> Thelonious Monk, Horace Silver, and Mal Waldron all come under the general classification of modern pianists. Yet each has an individual touch, a different sense of dynamics and distinct ideas as to the use of a piano in a group ... I try to give their separate styles full value, according to the framework of the music. I may also vary my set-up from track to track.[16]

Van Gelder's conception of microphony is hardly separable from his musical sensibility. It was his ability to discern the unique elements of a performer's musical persona, and then enlist his tools to translate those elements, that made him so sought after and celebrated.

The craft of sonic representation involves an array of tools and skills whose number and complexity has increased generally over time, with occasional milestones marked by especially notable innovations like magnetic tape or digital recording. This trend has tended to give engineers an increasingly specialised knowledge and central aesthetic place. As Edward Kealy noted over thirty years ago, the advent of magnetic tape in music recording brought not only convenience and superior sound quality, but 'a whole new range of aesthetic decision points [in which] the sound mixer was directly involved'.[17] Kealy cites, for example, the new range of editing and overdubbing techniques that tape offered; given the ability, as never before, to intrude into the musical line, the recording process took on a decidedly analytic quality that demanded skills not previously associated with music-making. In a similar vein, Susan Schmidt Horning points out that, in response to the availability of a newly expanded range of microphones following the Second World War, engineers learned to adapt the mikes' particular characteristics to specific musical needs. In an interview she conducted with the engineer Al Schmitt, he explained the process of choosing mikes in terms of timbral criteria: 'I learned to *get* my sounds. If I wanted a brighter vocal sound, I used a brighter mike. If I wanted a warmer bass sound, warmer piano sound, I used maybe a ribbon mike.'[18] Such timbral considerations complement the timbres of instruments and voices and the timbral control of musicians in collaborative ways. Schmitt's detailed knowledge of the characteristics of various microphones provided, as for Van Gelder, a guide to matching electronic devices and recording techniques to musical aims. And while timbral coloration is a perennial concern with any electronic mediation, there are any number of other criteria that may influence the musical result. Ultimately, both experience and creativity, deliberation and intuition, inform the engineer's manipulation of a matrix comprising interactive acoustic and electronic forces.

Electronic devices and ambient spaces provide engineers with the resources to accomplish both their technical and artistic aims. Indeed, many advances in recording technology that have shaped the sounds and influenced the musical styles of recorded culture were fostered by engineers. These include the tape recorders that Jack Mullin (among others) brought home from Germany in 1945 and introduced to Bing Crosby, thrusting the magnificent machine onto popular music's biggest stage; Bill Putnam's Universal Audio 1176 Peak Limiter, first manufactured in 1967

and still used widely; the ambient chambers at Gold Star studio in Los
Angeles – Dave Gold's contribution, along with the studio console, to Phil
Spector's wall of sound; Ken Townsend's automatic double tracking
innovation that the Beatles put to extensive use, beginning with
Revolver, as they expanded pop's stylistic bounds. The use of all such
resources is determined by a mix of pragmatism and aesthetic sensibility.
Engineer Shelley Yakus is reported to have taped cardboard over the VU
meters of his compressors, eliminating their visual input and focusing
exclusively on his hearing. ''Til it sounds right,' was his answer to how
much compression to use. 'You'll know when it's wrong.'[19] Equalisers,
another basic resource, are commonly used to shape timbre and to
enhance complementarity of multiple timbres within a given texture.
But sensing the suitability of such pragmatic sonic refinements requires
a degree of aesthetic engagement informed by the language of recorded
sound. In forming their preferences for this or that piece of gear, engineers
blend a concern for efficiency and rhetorical effect. Tom Tucker, engineer
for such artists as Tuck and Patti, Prince, and Sergio Mendes, describes
his assessment of various brands of equalisers in vividly affective terms:

> If I want something to be crunchy, I use SSL EQs, like for drums. However,
> I use a couple of different EQs for the bottom. I will use the SSL EQ in the
> 80 to 150 Hz range, because it's kind of punchy, and then for the deeper stuff,
> where I really want the subs to be pure, I will go to an Avalon or Pultec. The
> API is very clean and pristine. It can get harsh, though. If something is
> already a little harsh, I might opt to add the Neve for the additive EQ, or
> a Pultec, which has a very soft top.[20]

The machines, then, are chosen not only for what they do, but how they
feel according to this engineer's assessment of their sonic personalities and
their suitability to a given musical goal.

The widespread arrival of digital sound technology in the 1980s made
for new sound-shaping devices – most notably reverb simulators and
digital delays – that integrated technology and music as never before.
Ambient space, a key affective component of musical sound, could be
tailored in all kinds of fascinating and fanciful ways simply by manipulating the controls on a reverb simulator such as the Lexicon 224. While
artfully shaping ambience was not a new practice, the digital realm made
far more permutations not only possible but easily available.[21] The most
famous single example is the gated reverb applied to snare drums on pop
records of all sorts, which presented listeners with an insistent artifice
running the course of the track. Each explosive onset of reverb suggests
a large space, but as the anticipated long decay (a sort of ambient shadow)
is truncated artificially, or 'gated', the impression is formed of repeated

interruption. Because a short decay time is associated with a small space, the cavernous sonic explosion followed by an abrupt decay presents listeners with a paradoxical ambient architecture. The repeated morphing of space gives the ambience a dynamic temporality, that is, an essentially musical character. Such a space could only exist electronically, and its architect was the recording engineer. Indeed, it was just this sound that brought Hugh Padgham a public acclaim rarely accorded engineers. With such work as *Peter Gabriel* (third album), Phil Collins's *Face Value*, and XTC's *English Settlement*, Padgham 'developed a sound that has become an industry standard in pop, rock, and dance music', trumpeted a 1996 retrospective profile in *Billboard*.[22]

Equally enmeshed with the musical syntax and performances on modern recordings are the myriad effects created by digital delay (echo), many of which have become common in the current lexicon of record making.[23] Electronic echo is a relatively old technique in sound recording, and its increasing use mirrored the growth of recorded artifice in post-war pop recording.[24] The effect, however, requires capturing sound, and prior to digital recording it was cumbersome to produce (requiring a second tape machine) and relatively limited in its applications. Digital technology made high-quality replication a simple matter and provided precise control over the relationship between source sounds and their replicas, allowing effects to be 'tuned' for a specific circumstance. While many uses of delay involve some sort of rhythmic effect, others are far less apparent, manipulating the music from somewhere behind the scenes to thicken or elongate sounds. Delay may also produce dramatic timbral transformation in the form of flanging and chorusing. With such new technologies, as well as new uses for existing ones, the array of electronic artifice expanded in the 1980s as pop record production became increasingly complex – more tracks, more treatments. As engineers became associated with distinctive stylistic habits that proved successful in the crowded sonic economy, their sonic signatures became sought after, leading many to assume the mantle of producer.

The increased blurring of lines between engineering and producing in pop music over the last twenty-five years is the by-product of a process that began in the late 1940s, most notably (based on record sales) with the work of Mitch Miller. The practice of making records whose sounds distinguished them from real-world music-making fostered a gradual change in the nature of sonic representation. Contemporary pop records are most often made not simply to represent a performance, a performer, or a performing tradition, but to evince in themselves a distinctive reality. So, as sounds are gathered through the recording process, though they represent the process itself (the series of steps leading toward the finished piece), they accumulate to form not a representation but a new work. The only real-world analogue would be one fashioned after the fact as a copy of the recording, in which case the performance turns out to be the representation. This ontological shift accounts for the broad array of varying sonic conceptions to be found among contemporary pop records. Tchad Blake's calculatedly lo-fi renderings – his proud use of 'really rotten compressors', for example – are as plausible as the crystalline clarity of George Massenburg's clean, burnished textures.[25] The rhetorical field of pop recordings has moved far from the criterion of emulating natural sound, with records situating themselves in consciousness not by analogy with real-world events but through interactive association with other records.

Analytic listening

Sound recording has drastically altered two historical fundamentals of musical perception: impermanence and physical presence. The transient nature of sound, and the impossibility of exact repetition, meant that each musical iteration was unique and heard only once. And the auditory experience was usually accompanied by the sight of music-making. The sound and the sight commingled in a listener's consciousness to form a fleeting impression, never to be duplicated. Recording overturned these axioms, forcing listeners to confront a new reality of repeatability and the absence of visual stimulus. For recordists, listening became work. 'That's the whole thing,' says Chick Plotkin, Bruce Springsteen's long-time engineer. 'That's what you do: You put some music down and you listen to it … Listen hard.'[26] Such intent listening has a fundamentally analytic quality, assessing disembodied sonic impressions with an ear to their aesthetic durability as well as their immediate appeal. As technologies and the craft of their use became more complex, sounds were increasingly deconstructed; that is, sounds were removed from their narrative and textural contexts in order to examine and refine their most subtle details. This is illustrated most clearly by the near-universal adoption of multi-track recording, which places each component of musical texture in its own discrete place, to be addressed individually at the push of a 'solo' button. Such analytic listening involves shifting perspectives. The critical focus, for example, may shift from a relatively atomic level of detail – refining individual sounds, specific areas of the frequency spectrum, or discrete moments in a performance – to a broader perspective taking in larger swatches of musical texture or narrative.

Along with the changes in perspective are changing criteria, which must adapt to context defined not only by the level of sonic detail but by the differing nature of practical and stylistic needs. A practical example would be the shift from highlighting an instrument's full-bodied sound, in a solo or sparsely populated texture, to thinning the sound, removing some of its character, to give it a subsidiary, complementary role in a more complex texture. Stylistic concerns are a matter of language and rhetoric, shaping sounds in relation to a broad field of existing recordings. The complexity of the overall formulation – granular/gestural, pragmatic/rhetorical – is neatly summarised by Massenburg in his characterisation of mixing: 'I mix like I'm decorating a four-dimensional "space". Starting with some essential structural elements, I craft artifact and gesture, all of which say something about themselves and often refer to other elements in the "space".'[27] In other words, the individual (artifact) and the composite (gesture) are continually in interaction. The physical natures of the individual sounds combine to form the timbral character of the composite while, at the same time, articulating an identity (saying 'something about themselves') and entering into a broader dialogue (referring 'to other elements'). Furthermore, the rhetorical aspects of Massenburg's formulation reach beyond the boundaries of any given track. The full significance of the artifacts and gestures emerges only in relation to other tracks, and it is in this sense that one can speak of engineers' work as a language.

Further insight into the nature of analytic listening can be glimpsed in engineers' discriminating preferences among electronic resources and in their characterisation of particular pieces of gear as being particularly 'musical'. Comparing a range of similarly well-made mike preamps – for many, the most important piece of equipment after the microphone – is an exercise in the subtleties and vagaries of sonic representation. None can be said objectively to sound bad, yet most professional engineers are keen about their preferences, which amount to a stylistic perspective on representation that is fundamentally aesthetic and highly refined. The differences among preamps – as well as equalisers, compressors, gates, reverb and delay devices, consoles, monitors, amplifiers, recording media, and so forth – cannot be assessed in any meaningful way without an extensive reservoir of experience in sonic rhetoric, requiring knowledge of both recorded sonic language and methods of sonic 'argument'. Which tools, for instance, have been used in which ways to produce what sorts of musical results which have had what kind of market impact? The ability to answer such questions depends on accumulated knowledge gained through specialised modes of detailed listening and an experienced understanding that disembodiment and permanence are everyday features of recorded musical utterance.

Mediation techniques that flow from analytic listening are often directed at achieving musical results in fairly inconspicuous ways, shaping things from inside the sonic texture to vivify the track through highly artificial means. Importing Charles Keil's conceptual language into the recording studio, Thomas Porcello notes how engineers develop what he calls 'textural participatory discrepancies' by 'subtly shifting frequency information to provide microvariations in pitch and tuning (and temporal variation as well)'.[28] Keil's participatory discrepancies – small variations in tuning and timing – are functions of live performance.[29] The convincing *construction* of such textural 'microvariations' is a good example not only of the subtlety of the analytic process but also of the degree to which musical and electronic techniques are integrated in the engineer's craft.

A couple of specific techniques further illustrate Porcello's point. So-called multi-band compression treats particular segments of the frequency spectrum in different ways. The technique originated in radio, where it was used to craft a station's distinctive sound. But it is also used by recording engineers as a technique of timbral manipulation that shapes discrete portions of a sound's frequency content not through filtering (EQ) but through compression, emphasising selected frequency bands by partitioning the frequency spectrum and assigning each segment its own dynamic envelope. Another technique, multing, takes a duplicate signal, processes it in some way, and combines it with the original signal in some desired proportion, affecting the overall texture while often leaving the processed signal itself with little or no individual presence. These sorts of more or less arcane, or 'hidden', techniques are among the many in the engineer's bag of tricks from which he or she conjures sounds whose distinctive qualities routinely astonish even experienced professionals. As producer Jack Douglas, with a background himself as an engineer, puts it:

> I'll take the tracks to where I think they should be, and then when I'm out in the studio running it down with the band that super class of engineer has taken it to twice what I heard while I was in [the control room]. I'll come back in and get a great big surprise. Engineering is really an art, and there are some real good artists out there.[30]

Partnership and teamwork

Formulating a concept for a given project is most often a collaborative matter. While 'engineer' describes a specific category of participation, to 'engineer' a representation may involve many voices expressing many sonic and musical sensibilities. That is, while engineers are responsible for a project's technical challenges, the conceptual dimensions of such matters as tone colour and balance are subjects of a dialogue. While the discussion may include any member of a recording team, its central figures are the producer and engineer (bearing in mind that performers are often co-producers as well). Producers are ultimately in charge of a recording project and many, like Padgham, are engineers themselves. The relationship between engineer and producer is roughly analogous to that of a film's cinematographer (and editor) and its director. The former is charged with the actualisation of the latter's imagined visions, ideas and speculations, which explains Killen's claim that 'certain producers … choose their engineers very carefully, because the producers know that those engineers are going to bring certain aspects to the record'.[31] When successful, collaborations between engineers, producers and performers may become enduring partnerships. Producer Mitchell Froom's and engineer Tchad Blake's 'creative partnership', as Froom calls it, has produced many distinctive records, from Los Lobos and Suzanne Vega to Ron Sexsmith and Cibo Matto, over the past two decades.[32] Larry Levine worked on all of Phil Spector's wall of sound records. Andrew Kazdin served as Glenn Gould's engineer/producer for twenty years. Rudy Van Gelder and Alfred Lion's partnership lasted from its inception in 1953 until Lion sold the company in 1966.

Among the requirements for such partnerships is an aesthetic kinship fuelling the collaboration. Lion, for example, attributed much of his successful partnership with Van Gelder to the latter's 'good feeling for jazz'. Lion's communication with his engineer did not involve specific technical advice of which Lion was, by his own admission, ignorant. It was Van Gelder's job to translate the producer's directives and the musicians' utterances into convincing realisations of the team's aesthetic intentions. 'When the guys played out there, he knew what to do with them,' Lion explained. 'Sometimes he'd make the guy sound better than he actually did in person. He gave them a little extra, which you can do in the studio. The musicians learned from him, too … Rudy's a very knowledgeable and soulful person.' Lion's portrait of the engineer's role is one of empathy and understanding forging intuitive connections with the team's other members. The importance of such connections is underscored by the contrast Lion offers: those engineers who 'just look at that needle on the meter'.[33]

Translation is at the heart of an engineer's endeavours, whether translating sound into electric current, or ideas – sometimes vague impressions – into concrete results. Andrew Kazdin, in his role as Glenn Gould's producer, also performed engineering tasks, particularly on recordings made in Canada (which were free from the union rules in the US mandating an engineer other than the producer). At a session in the auditorium of Toronto's Eaton's department store, Kazdin made a series of preliminary test recordings (to determine the placement of the piano and the microphones), whose sound Gould found somehow lacking. Kazdin thought the sound was 'basically good', and it was only through 'long periods' of discussion that he deduced that the reason for Gould's complaint was a subtle smear detracting from the pianist's sense of clarity in the individual musical lines. Gould, though an experienced recording musician, was 'not conversant with the technical terms that define sound quality', and thus unable 'to describe definitively his subjective impression when listening to a recording'.[34] It fell to Kazdin first to unpack Gould's complaint, and then to solve the problem, which he accomplished by removing the piano's lid, something they had never needed to do before, and configuring a different plan of mike placement and balance. The result so suited Gould's ear that the procedure was strictly adhered to for the next nine years.

In interpreting the ideas, complaints and aural fantasies of the recording team, engineers serve as facilitators of both performance and creativity in the recording studio. Tchad Blake was a natural fit for Los Lobos on an exploratory record such as *Colossal Head*. Band members were struck at how he managed to turn barely articulated whims into sounds that resonated with their creative sensibilities. They were impressed as well by his ability to adapt to whatever path seemed to fit the creative flow, rather than insisting on any particular logistical plan. The band's saxophonist, Steve Berlin, puts it this way: 'Tchad's artistry is that he starts in a place that's very, very colorful, and he frees you to think abstractly. It's not like you have to get from A to B to C to D. If you want to start at Y with him, you can see a whole range of possibilities.'[35] Berlin's description suggests a situation where the engineer works in seamless creative sync with the band, the project driven by a collective imagination unfettered by technological orthodoxy. Engineering is a complex technical job, which may easily take on the sort of stultifying dogmatism the Beatles encountered among the lab-coated staff at Abbey Road. Their partnership with Geoff Emerick flourished, in part, because he resisted the longstanding house rules governing microphone techniques and recording levels. Like the other members of the recording team, the creative engineer, having mastered or at least made peace with his technical array (Emerick does not consider himself much of a technician), transcends technique to enter the creative flow of the artistic process unhampered by the necessary mundanities of technical execution.

Conclusion

Perhaps the clearest indication of the aesthetic nature of engineering is to be seen in the development of the so-called project studio. Over the past twenty-five years, growing numbers of performers, songwriters and composers have set up small studios of their own and taken up engineering to realise their musical expression in recorded form. This inclination has its historical precursors. For Les Paul, pushing the bounds of technological possibility seems to have been nearly as important as creating arrangements and playing the guitar. On his 1950s records with Mary Ford, Paul blended all three activities in a comprehensive production process. As soon as he had the means, Buddy Holly acquired his own recording equipment to materialise his ideas and sketches. He had come to appreciate the creative nature of the recording process while working with Norman Petty, himself a musician/engineer. Over the next couple of decades, many commercially successful artists involved themselves ever more deeply in the intricacies of recording, working in close collaboration with their engineers and often assembling their own collections of equipment.

Prohibitive costs, however, limited the practice in the 1960s and 1970s to those with substantial means. In the 1980s, affordable recording and sound processing equipment began coming onto the market, and the last two decades have seen quality increase and prices decrease to the point that almost anyone so inclined can make their own recordings. And while few non-professional engineers possess the skills to rival the pro's ability to tackle whatever problem presents itself, an increasing number of self-produced recordings are remarkably effective. With their own personal music as their sole concern, recordists learn to engineer their sounds as part of a comprehensive compositional practice that includes writing and performing. The impulse to work with 'sound *per se*', to integrate musical expression of all sorts with the technologies of sound recording and processing, is evident on a global scale. As Paul Greene has reminded us recently, 'a new ... means of music making has emerged within and among the world's musical cultures. It is driven not so much by the vibrations of membranes, chords, hard surfaces, or molecules of air but rather primarily by the manipulation of electrical impulses.'[36] For such music-making, engineering is a necessary, often central, component. Technology has permeated musical life such that electricity has become a crucial enabler for anyone whose conception of musical expression includes its enduring materialisation, anyone who believes that how music *sounds* is inseparable from what it *is*.

Limitations and creativity in recording and performance

MARTYN WARE

I was involved with the Human League for the period from 1978, when we formed the band from various precursors, until that version of the band split in late 1980; and that whole time was fundamentally about a new form of recording technique. What we were doing evolved from previous approaches, of course, but it was the limitations of what was available to us then, compared to today's technology, that was the key point – and actually made for a more spicy creative environment. It was about physical limitations as well as the limitations of recording and musical instrument technology. We were in the Devonshire quarter of Sheffield,[1] where there were Little Mesters's shops that had fallen into disrepair, which you could pick up for rehearsal purposes for almost nothing – like five pounds a week.[2] They were basically ruins, and it kind of appealed to us because all that was needed was a lick of paint, and then you'd got a studio. Things were so basic for us when we started out that we didn't have a mixing desk, we didn't have equalisation, we didn't even have stereo at that point: we were just bouncing material from track to track on a Revox. But those limitations led us to all kinds of interesting creative solutions – things that we wouldn't otherwise have stumbled upon.

An analogy might be the comparison with an artist like Yves Klein, and the idea of confining yourself to an extremely limited palette: the idea of having a deliberately very limited resource. I'm doing a new British Electric Foundation (BEF) album,[3] and I've decided to do this current one specifically just with two virtual synthesisers, and one drum machine, and voices.[4] And that's it: it's like a mad scientist's experiment, you know, to see what happens when you have such tight limitations. Even that's cheating, really, because the flexibility and potential of these new virtual synthesisers is incredible: I can have twenty instances of a Moog modular on my laptop, which would have cost me in the region of three or four hundred thousand pounds if I'd had to go out and actually buy the things. I've been through the entire gamut of recording possibilities over the last thirty years or more, from the most meagre resources back at the start, through to eighty-piece orchestras – and although I absolutely love what you can do with those massive resources, I do genuinely believe that if you have a limited palette you end up with something that is more focused and more direct. The Beatles, for instance, originally had a limited palette, and their collaboration with George Martin expanded it dramatically. Now I like their expanded palette stuff, but there's also something special about the earlier material, when it's just those specific instruments that they've got, and the challenge to do something new with them.

It's something that I feel really passionate about trying to get over, especially to people who are starting out now. If you go to a music college now, how many instruments – virtual instruments, presets – do you have at your disposal? I went to the music department of a college of technology recently where they had a room with thirty workstations in it all equipped with a standard piece of current commercial sequencer/synthesiser software – and there are probably something like five thousand preset instruments or virtual synthesisers there; and that's before you've even started buying anything extra. Now in lots of ways this is fantastic – so many possibilities, such incredible resources. But the danger is that you get option paralysis: you look at all these banks and banks of possibilities, wonder what on earth they all do, realise that you just don't have time to find out, and end up sticking to the ones that you already know. And so ironically you can end up narrowing your options – not in a creative way, but just through lack of time and a kind of bewilderment.

With the infinitely more limited resources that we had back in the seventies and eighties everything had to be made by hand – totally bespoke sounds for every instrument. So if we wanted a kick drum we had to make it by hand from scratch, like an electronic version of the potter's wheel. We just had to create everything from the bits and pieces and raw materials of these much more primitive sound-making devices. Even if you just wanted something simple like a repeated hi-hat pattern, for example, you had to set up the hardware sequencer, turn on the white noise generator, filter it in a particular way, put it through the ring modulator to make it sound a bit electronic. And that gave you a unique sound – whether it was really like a true hi-hat or not. If you want a hi-hat sound now, you can just type 'hi-hat' into a search engine, and you've got millions of them available in a fraction of a second. But the crucial thing is that if you download or select a preset, it's very unlikely that you're going to come up with any-thing unexpected, while if you're designing and making something your-self, it's almost inevitable that you'll have some interesting accidents, and get led in directions that you would never have imagined.

All this hard and detailed work on the sounds meant that the studio was really our natural habitat, and even before we did our first gig, we realised that we were going to look boring. Something had to be happening on stage, apart from us. So for the first gig, we actually begged, borrowed or stole about six or seven televisions, and just de-tuned them and had them showing visual static. That was the best that we could do, but in the audience at that first gig was Adrian Wright, and he became our projectionist – probably the first and possibly the only, ever, fully paid-up member of a pop group who didn't actually play a musical instrument. His job was to create a visual accompaniment, a kind of early VJ-ing, I suppose – except that it wasn't responsive live. It was based on slides and carousel projectors, which became more sophisticated over the years, until Adrian had kind of a show control system, so that you could do much more flexible and interesting combinations and overlays. I'm sure that played a definite part in our success, because the whole live act was like a science fiction film: not just because of the technology, but also because the content of the lyrics was strongly influenced by science fiction books. Phil Oakey and I were obsessed with science fiction at that time, and as a result the entire ambience was about as different as you could imagine from a normal rock'n'roll band singing about the usual themes of sex and romance. We were doing this really geeky stuff, but in a creative way – not geeky in the sense of singing about diodes, not techno geeky. It was rather that the sonic landscape we were working with had a kind of affinity with a certain kind of futuristic narrative, so that a lot of the songs ended up being about that kind of world. The music just seemed to lend itself to that type of subject matter.

Records and recordings in post-punk England, 1978–80[1]

RICHARD WITTS

In 1978 if you played in a Manchester 'new wave' band, like I did, you recorded in two ways. You spent eight hours in an antiseptic radio studio taping four songs for what were called 'Peel sessions' (whether or not they were for use by John Peel, the kingpin BBC Radio 1 DJ, on his nightly orgy of the aural 'other'). Otherwise you made records, mainly seven-inch vinyl 45 rpm singles or 'extended play' (EP) discs, often packaged in a picture-cover sleeve designed with either little thought (New Hormones label) or too much (Factory Records). Compilation discs, where groups shared track space with others, were an accepted way of gaining attention and they showed the inclination at that time for collective action.[2] Live 'gigs' built up a local audience, the radio sessions a national one, but the records brought you local, national and international attention in one bound.

However, bands like ours – which sought to be 'creative' in the recording studio – soon encountered an unexpected problem. One night we played in a Munich club where a fan asked for a certain song from one of our records. We obliged. Afterwards she complained that we hadn't met her request. We insisted we had. 'No,' she said, 'I didn't hear it. You know, the one with the bells.' Ah, the bells, on the record: 'Sadly we didn't bring our tubular bells to Bavaria.' To her mind the song was what she heard on the disc, not what we, who made it, played before her ears and eyes. So much for authenticity.

We hadn't always dug a trench between our live performances and the recorded ones, even though our first single was recorded in Manchester's plush 24-track Arrow studio. A punkish entrepreneur planned to make enough money out of records to finance his (now her) sex-change operation, and we were one of four bands who were each given thirty minutes of studio time to tape two tracks for his 'independent' label, an approach to provisional record production pioneered by Manchester punk band the Buzzcocks.[3] There was just enough time to lug the equipment into the studio, play it in ensemble as we would at a gig, and haul it out again for the next band to take over.

That a recording business such as Arrow – used often by Granada Television to make voice-overs and trails for its programmes – should end up in 1978 operating like a spit-and-sawdust Memphis studio of thirty years before was a consequence of larger economic and stylistic factors. Facilities like this were often resourced from the financial credit swimming around the international rock music scene between 1967 and 1973, when hi-tech developments enabled musicians to indulge in technical experimentation connected with prog rock and the elaborate productions of Manchester bands like Barclay James Harvest, 10cc and Sad Café. But the oil crisis inflation – of 25 per cent by 1975[4] – and the first stirrings of mass unemployment as new technology impacted on the labour market, forced an end to that phase of expansion.[5]

In tandem, a stylistic shift took hold in favour of the 'ecstatic', 'unfinished' or 'un-sound' performance. This was manifested in different ways by, say, a vibrant revival of free improvisation, pub rock, and punk. In this climate many bands wanted to record, but live or 'as-live'.[6] Swish studios found themselves hosts to clients with little time for effects and 'toys'. What we had done in Arrow, the Buzzcocks had begun in its sister Indigo in December 1976, recording there its debut *Spiral Scratch* EP, of which a thousand copies were pressed, though it rapidly sold sixteen times that number. *Spiral Scratch* is a dry account of that band's aural energy. It's a record rather than a recording.

Several studio engineers of the prog rock tendency had invested in four-track Tascam or Fostex recording machines for home use in order to explore and trial-record their pet projects.[7] Thus, as they looked to survive while the larger studio work withered, they turned their homes into microstudios to meet the need for a new breed of musicians inspired by the punk do-it-yourself aesthetic but who wanted to make an alternative pop music in the era (1978–84) that became known as 'post-punk'. There was Andy Mac's Revolution Studio in Cheadle Hulme where the Buzzcocks first recorded, and Graveyard (it was near one) in Prestwich, where Joy Division, A Certain Ratio and ourselves recorded material for albums. In the centre of Liverpool, the publicly subsidised Open Eye video project set up a four-track studio where bands with fabulous names first got taped, like Pink Military Stand Alone, Dalek I Love You and The Teardrop Explodes. Four-track (later eight-track) studios like these were cheapish and you would book them by the day rather than the hour.

At domestic studio outfits you might record in the lounge, mix-down in the attic, and play the result on tiny Audax 5-inch speakers in the kitchen in order to check how it would sound on portable radios. The studio's owner would sway you into using the FX units and electronic techniques for transforming the 'dry' recorded tracks.[8] At that point prog rock experimentation met the post-punk aesthetic and fashioned some of the most singular recordings in the history of popular music. They are unusual – and now somewhat influential – because they used mainly analogue equipment but also brought in the proto-digital 'toys' and worked in a mongrel manner with both formats.

By the early 1980s analogue sound synthesis was being challenged by digital sampling technology. But, as analogue and early digital equipment in these maverick circumstances had their idiosyncrasies and contradictions, the unpredictable was always just a noodling of a knob away. We still edited by slicing magnetic tape with razor blades, and standard analogue techniques included echo plates, reverberation units, double-tracking using varispeed, flanging, direct-injecting (often to get a clean signal on the bass guitar), equalisation (EQ) effects, chorusing, bouncing-down, and tape loops. Through constructs of spatial location and motion these FX produced a sense of distance or depth, of flows, 'other-worldness' or alienation.[9] And by then domestic analogue synthesisers had been developed alongside analogue drum machines such as the programmable Roland CR-78. Bands like the Human League and Cabaret Voltaire in Sheffield or Orchestral Manoeuvres in the Dark from Merseyside – influenced by 1970s German electro pioneers (Kraftwerk, Can, Giorgio Moroder) or British art school glam (David Bowie, Roxy Music) – designed fabricated 'acousmatic' sonorities that they could replicate on stage. When digital technology became affordable it tended to be used by post-punks in its most synthetic modes, like a meta-analogue machine, to foreground its artificiality. Overall, what had been enhanced, sculptured and seductive in prog rock was now turned into a sheen, or exposed, made 'dirty' and provocative. To grasp the range, one might listen to 'Pictures on My Wall' by Liverpool's Echo and the Bunnymen,[10] then 'Nag, Nag, Nag' by Sheffield's Cabaret Voltaire or *The Dignity of Labour* by the Human League (also from Sheffield), all of which were recorded in 1979 using cheap analogue drum machines.

Different technological tendencies characterised distinctions between Liverpool and Manchester – the former (like Sheffield) more likely to employ machines, while the latter explored treatments at the mixing desk. In terms of breadth, the scale of studio use – from the 'direct' end (just a reverbed voice track) to the 'processed' one – may be charted as in Table 3.1.

Most extreme were the productions of Martin Hannett for Joy Division. Hannett emulated the 'heavy dub' sound pioneered in the early 1970s by Jamaican producers like Lee 'Scratch' Perry – radical, druggy studio mutations of reggae instrumentals by means of reverb, echo and sound effects. Hannett translated this style using a prototype digital delay unit, the AMS 15–80, which he hired from the Advance Music Systems (AMS) works in nearby Burnley and carried around with him under his arm like a much-loved pet. Hannett would dump the drum kit and

Table 3.1

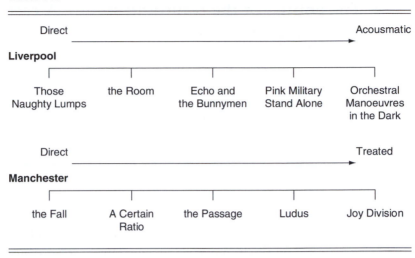

Direct				Acousmatic
Liverpool				
Those Naughty Lumps	the Room	Echo and the Bunnymen	Pink Military Stand Alone	Orchestral Manoeuvres in the Dark

Direct				Treated
Manchester				
the Fall	A Certain Ratio	the Passage	Ludus	Joy Division

drummer in the stairwell of Stockport's 24-track Strawberry Studio (founded by 10cc) or Rochdale's 16-track Cargo, record each component separately – to Steve the drummer's immense irritation – and route the microphoned sound through the 15–80 with two short delays on the outputs which he mixed with the original. He used the 15–80 with analogue FX too, and employed it on instruments and Ian Curtis's doleful voice. The result was exceptional, and can be heard in varied ways throughout Joy Division's debut album *Unknown Pleasures* (1979), most clearly at the opening of 'Disorder', or in 'New Dawn Fades' (after the reversed-tape intro) where the drums sound as if they've been tossed down a mineshaft.

Ultimately, the recorded soundworld of the post-punk scene in the North-West and in Yorkshire (Sheffield, Leeds) may have been a thrifty reaction to glitzy settings elsewhere. At the London headquarters of Virgin Records, the label we eventually signed to, we were invited to use its chic Manor Studios in rural Oxfordshire, a place replete with diversions. While we discussed this in the foyer, a London band overheard us. 'Oi mate, don't go to Manor. The go-karts don't work.' So we didn't.

4 The politics of the recording studio: A case study from South Africa

LOUISE MEINTJES

In 1985 Paul Simon called the South African producer Koloi Lebona into the studio. He needed to borrow Lebona's ears, for Simon wanted to reproduce the quality of the accordion that he had heard on an inspiring production by Lebona before coming to South Africa.[1] Lebona sat in the control room in a Johannesburg studio. He sat there for days, listening and advising, while South African musicians played and the tape rolled and rolled, and Simon laid down backing tracks for the *Graceland* album. He gave Simon the sound of his own mix. Lebona didn't care about basking in Simon's glory, though he admires him, but he sat there for days, listening intently. For him the hook was Simon's engineer, the famous Roy Halee. For producer Lebona, Halee held the secret to production success: the more he could learn from this expert sound engineer, the more control he could have in the studio as a producer, especially as a black producer in apartheid South Africa's recording studios.[2]

In the ideal studio, the producer, as the studio's client, directs studio sessions and has final authority over the sound, so that the engineer serves his or her client. But in practice, in South African studios during the apartheid era, this was not always the case. The engineer, usually white, middle-class and male, wielded significantly more power working the controls of the console than would probably be the case elsewhere, especially in major studios in the metropoles of the global North. In the 1970s and 1980s, during years of increasing political repression and the concomitant mobilisation of resistance out in the streets, Lebona and his then assistant, Monty Bogatsu, recount being marked as radical inside the studio. They argued for what they believed were their rights to quality sound and insisted on their entitlement to use whatever technological facilities they needed. As Lebona put it: 'Some producers were afraid of telling a white engineer "but this is not right, I don't want this". Now because we were doing that, we came across as "the people who need to be watched because they are so militant." ... But it's not that I was being militant – I know what I want and we should actually try my way before the engineer imposes.'[3]

The producer, usually black, male, and representing an upwardly mobile class fraction with a thoroughly urban lifestyle, may have been at a disadvantage in the control room of the studio, but he was a powerful figure in another way. A white-controlled industry whose executives and white employees lacked the necessary knowledge about local black music styles, languages, audiences, locations, practices, and so forth, and who increasingly lacked access to black-designated areas as state repression increased, had to rely on their black employees to scout for talent, negotiate with musicians, and promote their product. Producers became critical mediating figures and influential gatekeepers in the industry.[4]

In some studio sessions, the engineer could lay down dozens of songs in a day, if the producer arrived with his group rehearsed and ready to go and didn't intervene in the recording process, and if the engineer recorded the songs using only the basic techniques.[5] But, as engineer Peter Ceronio recalled, other sessions in the 1970s used to cause all kinds of aggravation: when producers argued, changed their arrangements during recording, and tried out new ideas – when, from Peter's point of view, producers lacked discipline, he got much less laid to tape and out to the factory for pressing. Struggles for producers who had musical ideas that they wanted to realise were at once struggles for engineers who wanted to be efficient and were responsible to the studio and the record companies it served. Producers and engineers felt their reputations to be at stake in sometimes conflicting ways.

In the early 1990s, the years of negotiated transition to a democratic South Africa, recording sessions bore strong traces of apartheid studio practices. The demographics of producing and engineering remained largely unchanged, though on the whole those working in studios enjoyed more open relationships than they had in earlier years. While a diversity of musical styles was recorded, 'traditional' and *mbaqanga* music (a South African form of Afropop) enjoyed some resurgence in the industry, providing the studios with some of their bread-and-butter earnings.[6] Performing artists in 'traditional' and *mbaqanga* styles were generally working-class men and women. Some lived in the decrepit inner city or in satellite townships around Johannesburg, while others were rurally based, migrating between town and countryside. Most of these musicians were only employed in temporary or part-time positions, or were seeking work.

For all these artists, the early 1990s were a time of promise for new forms of empowerment, and for better race relations. It was a time of intense political debate, of celebration about pending equal citizenship, of anxiety and struggle, leading up to the first democratic elections in 1994. At national political negotiating tables, politicians thrashed out a settlement and an interim constitution for a new South Africa, while in the streets anxieties and struggles for empowerment spilled out into some of the worst violence the country had experienced over the past few decades. 'That was an Uzi, not an AK [47],' Downtown Studio's then only black engineer, Humphrey Mabote, quipped nonchalantly during informal conversation with me when he heard a shot fired somewhere outside the studios in a Johannesburg street. He explained the difference in the envelope and timbre of the sound to me, as though he was describing the difference between a trumpet and a clarinet. Concomitant with the political changes, markets shifted for South African musics. With South Africa no longer the pariah nation, its cultural production enjoyed renewed international interest, while local markets were reshaped in part by domestic political dynamics: a rise in Zulu ethnic nationalism, for example, reinforced a Zulu-identified market, which lay regionally in the province of what was then Natal (now KwaZulu-Natal). At this time, Zulu recordings were virtually only marketed in Natal and around Johannesburg, the city destination of Zulu migrants.

To talk of the politics of a recording studio, then, is to attend to two intersecting political planes. First, the micro-politics of studio interaction determine what sounds are recorded for commercial distribution. How do artists collectively produce an album, when they are differentially invested in the outcome of the recording, when they are differently positioned in terms of the division of labour in the studio, when they hold potentially competing fantasies about how it should sound, and in some cases when they only partially share modes of communication? Second, the micro-politics of studio interaction are a prism for the political dynamics of the historically specific moment and place. How do social practices and values about race, ethnicity, class and gender, as articulated in the political moment in which studio artists find themselves, impinge upon the recording process and affect the creative outcome? How does the studio process in turn come to bear upon political struggles in civic and national arenas?

Race, class and divisions of labour

30 March 1992, Downtown Studios, Johannesburg.[7] Engineer Neil Kuny and producer West Nkosi have just triple-tracked the backing male vocals on the first chorus of a song for a *mbaqanga* group named Isigqi sesiManje. Some singers and musicians in the band hang around the control room, listening. West decides to check the newly recorded section. They listen through the huge speakers up on the wall.

Singer Joana Thango enthuses in Zulu: 'Can you hear how nicely they sing it? It's nice!'[8]

West and Neil discuss how they will sequence this chorus of male voices to insert wherever it is needed in the song, rather than recording it anew each time.

Joana chats on to her musician friends, standing alongside the MIDI rack. 'Eyi! This thing,' she remarks, pointing at the MIDI clock on the top deck, 'small as it is, it is carrying all different types of things within it, which are going to be recorded. Now we are on this choir.'[9]

With the choir triple tracked, nine men's voices are captured in that small machine. But Joana implies more than this: nine men's voices, plus twelve women's voices (the verses triple tracked), a solo voice and all the instrumental backing already recorded now reside in that small machine.

Neil and West move on with the session. They turn to work on the weak programmed bass drum sound. They extract it from the small box to change its frequency profile and perhaps to add effects.

The MIDI clock does not actually house the sounds to which Joana refers. Rather, it is a central node for entering information into the MIDI (Musical Instrument Digital Interface) system. It synchronises the digitally processed sounds with the sounds recorded on tape. However, its positioning for quick and easy access right next to the console at Neil's right hand and its constant use readily give it the appearance of being the central housing unit for the recorded sound, from Joana's point of view. For her, there is a whole sonic world packed into that sleek machine, which only registers the presence of its precious contents as digitised figures in a tiny control window, and as a steady red 'power on' light the size of a pinhead. It is a world to which Joana can point, but that she cannot enter herself. This sonic world encoded in complex electronics is sensed to be of enormous proportions. The digital processes that encode it are as sophisticated as the face of their component's casing is simple. This phenomenon – the extensive and ephemeral residing in the complex and digital, yet presented as the small, intact, and simple – imbues the technology with an affecting presence.[10] Its presence is further enhanced by the complex user interface that surrounds it: the multiple steps required for its operation (and these steps are far from transparent), and the elaborate lexicon that accompanies them, inhibits contact with the sound enclosed within it by all but the specialist. Technical lexicons enshroud inscrutable objects and already opaque processes in mystery. 'Eyi, these are white people's things!' exclaims keyboardist Tefo Sikhale in admiration when the engineer electronically renders a pleasing sound for the musicians.

18 November 1991. Coordinating the guitar, bass, organ and keyboard entries on the introduction of an *mbaqanga* song is proving difficult. Engineer Peter Pearlson starts recording but cuts whenever an entry is sloppy. They rehearse. They record it again. It's not clean. They retake it. Rehearse again. The stopping and starting is confusing. Keyboardist Tefo stands behind the outboard gear. His fingers are poised anxiously on the Yamaha DX7 keyboard that rests on the top of the outboard console.

'We don't see the blinking (of the controls),' he mumbles in Zulu to his friends, 'they are the ones who can see the blinking.'[11] Tefo can't tell for sure when Peter is recording him and when he's not. Tefo's Zulu language mumble passes by unnoticed.

Once the voice of Joana (and those of her co-singers) has been recorded into that 'small machine', it takes on a life of its own. Though delighted by the sound she hears and awed by the machine encapsulating it, she is now separated from this instance of her voice, and distanced from the controls over it. Drawing on their experience and knowledge, Neil and West could conceivably manipulate her recorded voice electronically until it is no longer recognisably hers – a play sanctioned by the roles they hold in the studio. Though her voice is there (somewhere inside the small machine) it is no longer accessible to her without the assistance of that machine's technician, the engineer.

The status of the studio's technicians, and admiration for the studio's technological capacity, is measured differentially according to the training and experience of the music-makers and the division of labour during production. Those most awed and alienated by the studio environment are the musicians, particularly those with less recording experience and no expertise with electronic music technology. Tefo, paid as a session musician, criticises his producer and engineer from the bottom of the labour hierarchy, while from a distance he admires the studio's technological facility. Joana, a vocalist rather than an engineer, has none of the knowledge nor the authority required to manipulate the electronic controls to play back her voice of her own accord, let alone to further shape its timbral form.

Direct access to technology is determined by the division of labour and experience within the studio. But these professional asymmetries are magnified by other social divisions. As with many of his fellow musicians, Tefo's English-language abilities are poor though he is multilingual. He would be able to confirm his understanding of Peter's instructions if he were able to watch the blinking lights, which would also help him to perform better and deliver the requested riff faster in the studio. While the engineers didn't have the linguistic resources to override the use of English as the *lingua franca* of the studio, the musicians rarely stepped out of their own linguistically exclusive domain to include the white engineers, none of whom spoke African languages.

18 November 1991. West, Peter and the musicians of the *mbaqanga* group Isigqi sesiManje are working on a song that came to be titled 'South Africa'.[12] They are laying down a keyboard track, a sequenced synth bass riff which Peter programs on the Yamaha DX7 keyboard and then tweaks at the console.

'OK, let's try one more time,' Peter instructs Makhosini, who is playing the riff on the keyboard. Peter starts the click track and counts the keyboard entry for Makhosini, who then plays along with the rhythm tracks. The synth bass sound vibrates the studio with its deep and gritty repeated sixteenths. Sixteen pulses on the first tone (tonic) are followed by sixteen on the second (dominant), repeated throughout the song.

'Heyi!' exclaims Tefo in township Zulu. 'Peter is putting down hot stuff!'[13] This is one of the few times during the production that a musician refers to Peter by his name. Singer Janet Dlamini agrees with Tefo about Peter's raspy synth bass sound. 'He's really hit it!' she cheers, using the same Zulu verb she would use to describe a dynamic performer.[14] In response musician Michael Mpholofolo pronounces triumphantly (in Sotho): 'The sound of Africa! Africa!'[15]

At the moment when Peter gets the sound programmed right, Tefo refers to him by his first name. Janet recognises him as an artist instead of a mere technician when she describes his action with the Zulu verb she would use for a good performer. Having delivered 'the sound of Africa, Africa!' for the band, he is acknowledged as a team participant, and from their point of view Peter momentarily shares their artistic status, for he has constructed an African sound. But the musicians don't think to inform him of their sentiment. In fact, during the entire production Tefo and Janet never directly address Peter and rarely express themselves in a language that he could understand and participate in.

Lack of technical knowledge and technical lexicons, as well as the absence of shared language competencies, places additional barriers between some recording participants and their informed use of the studio gear, between experts and labourers, and between technicians and artists. On the one hand, the layering of technological mystification onto the linguistic matrix empowers white men in the *mbaqanga* studio. It propagates the idea that technology and technological expertise are differentially accessible to music-makers on the basis of their class and colour. Musicians who are black, working-class and – though multilingual – not necessarily well versed in English, experience the studio from the least empowered position of all studio music-makers.[16] On the other hand, musicians retain as their own the cultural and aesthetic domain and do not share it linguistically with their white and Anglophone sound engineers. They might not have technological expertise, but they do have culture, itself a precious commodity in the domestic and world music markets.[17] Even if it is Peter who engineers a sound of 'Africa' with purely electronic means, it is the musicians who claim it as theirs by naming it as African.

November 1991.[18] The engineer, producer and singers are getting ready for a take in the studio. It is the engineer's usual duty to announce the name of the band and song number onto the tape as an identifying measure before recording a song.

'Well – you can say it this time,' Peter tells West. The band's name is Isigqi sesiManje. Correct Zulu pronunciation of 'Isigqi' requires the sounding of a voiced alveolar-palatal 'click' (represented by 'q').

West responds authoritatively: 'You must say that, Peter.'

Silence.

'I'm teaching you now. Isigqi, cut one,' West says to Peter, who is meant to repeat the phrase after him. Silence. 'Isigqi,' says West. 'Say it,' he demands, playfully acting out his authority as producer over his engineer.

West repeats it till Peter reluctantly has to try.

He sounds 'isi-ke,' hesitating mid-word to get his tongue in place. No good, no resounding 'click'.

West leans forward, looks him in the face, and prompts him syllable by syllable with perfect deliberation.

Everyone in the studio laughs.

West jostles with him. 'Ah, come on, Peter, you must improve, man!'

At this point Peter pulls out his professional card: 'We've taken two hours to set up, we're going to spend another two hours trying to start the first song.'

West relents.

Peter checks the console. 'OK, standby!' he calls to the musicians in the recording booth, his fingers poised on the record and play buttons.

West pronounces 'Isigqi, cut one' onto the tape as it rolls and the recording begins.[19]

A struggle that arose out of recording procedure was waged playfully over a discrepancy in linguistic skills. Bringing attention to an inadequacy of the engineer that limits his ability to perform his standard studio role provides the producer with an opportunity to reassert his authority by drawing on a marked feature of Zulu culture, the 'click' as consonant. West is in fact not Zulu himself, but he demonstrates his multilingual virtuosity. In urban South Africa multilingualism is a prized value that these musicians view as a quality that African South Africans have mastered, and which they imagine white South Africans to lack. That West chooses the Zulu 'click' to make this point here does additional work for him, a person with a staunchly Africa-centred sensibility. For these musicians, traditional Zuluness is often upheld as the epitome of Africanness. To demonstrate mastery over Zulu expression in this studio setting is to make a claim to be deeply African – to embody cultural knowledge. These dynamics, grounded in apartheid practices and ideology, superimpose South African social differences onto the professional divisions of labour within the studio, cultivating a studio practice that produces moments of distanced wonder and desired entry, intensifying an already heightened system of social inclusion and exclusion.

Playing in the interstices

In this social and professional environment, how do those who feel less empowered get their preferred processes of recording enacted? How do they ensure that their own aesthetic choices are laid to tape? How do they assert their own rights as co-workers, creative participants, and as people?

21 November 1991. Isigqi sesiManje are recording the vocal overdubs on their wedding song. Joana, lead singer on this song, and West are to insert spoken interjections between some of the sung verses. They stand side by side in front of a mike in the recording booth. For once, the musicians can hear everything since they are listening in the control room while West, cooped up in the recording booth, has to gesticulate through the control-room window at Peter when he wants to commu-nicate if the mike lines are not open. Peter has control over piping music and talk into West's puffy headphones.

West improvises the words and corrects Joana's impromptu responses. Joana and others in the group suggest details back to West. Peter works the console.

'*Mkhaliseleni ibell, akwazi ukuvuka!* [Ring the bell, she just won't wake up!]' he bellows, as if he is the patriarch of a rural homestead, appropriate to the narrative in the lyrics.

Peter rolls the tape, West has to insert his interjection. He misses. Peter stops the tape.

'*Vuka!* [Wake up!]' calls out Tefo playfully at West, as if he were the producer now, and picking up on West's inserted interjection. (Tefo's exclamation is not audible to West in the booth.)

West rehearses the line, and they try to put it down again. One more time. He's having trouble finding the correct moment of entry and metering out the line to fit with the backing. He asks Peter to repeat it once again.

He practises cold a few times. It doesn't fit. Distracted, he plays around with the wording. For fun he invents an onomatopoeic alternative to *ibell*. He sings:

Mshayeleni *ibell* -
Mshayeleni *iting ting* akwaz'ukuvuka, bo.

West's playfulness offers an opening to the musicians to voice their ideas. Joana corrects his township wording by substituting the Zulu word for an iron bell into his line – the word for a school or church bell.

'Mshayeleni *insimbi*,' she directs him.

No problem, West switches to 'Mshayeleni *insimbi*' without missing a beat while rehearsing the line with the backing tracks.

He laughs, and improvises a groaned exclamation to precede the line:

Wo! Mshayeleni *insimbi* akwaz'ukuvuka, bo.

Joana voices agreement. Peter rolls the tape again. They start and stop, because the timing is still not accurate. Tefo leaps into a moment of silence:

'Yini yicilongo? Insimbi yicilongo, angithi?' he asks in Zulu ('Why not *icilongo*, *insimbi* is *icilongo*, isn't it?'), *icilongo* referring to the bugle played at festive events in rural communities. It has replaced the animal horn trumpet.

No one answers. Peter starts the tape again. West enters in the right place, but this time he reverts to the original word *ibell*:

Wo! Mshayeleni *ibell* akwaz'ukuvuka, bo.

Wrong again, so he practises, changing back to use *insimbi*:

Wo! Mshayeleni *insimbi* akwaz'ukuvuka, bo.

'It's *icilongo*!' insists musician Michael.

'Hey?' asks West.

'It's *icilongo*!' he repeats.

West can be stubborn, authoritarian, provocative. He exacerbates the distance between his and the musicians' positions by replacing the anglicised *ibell* with an Afrikaans version, *iklok*,[20] instead.

'It's *icilongo* – in Zulu it's *icilongo*!' Michael asserts again.

'I can't hear you,' replies West from the recording booth.

A chorus of voices in the control room tells him, 'It's *icilongo*!'

'Hey?' he asks again. 'Just put through those voices, Peter.'

Tefo explains to him that it's *icilongo* they want.

'Oh!' replies West, and then he practises his part inserting the right word.

After some joking around, West practises singing his lines the Zulu way, and he gets the timing right. 'OK,' he says. They're ready for a take. Peter rolls the tape.

From West's perspective, this substitution was principally a technical one. He was trying to find a word with the right number of syllables to fit the metre of the line. The musicians wanted some authority in the shaping of their song – the temporary inversion of their and West's studio roles and spatial positioning made this possible. That West has momentarily set aside his authority as producer in order to stand behind a microphone opens the possibility for the musicians to renegotiate their professional positions and concerns, which they do by arguing over the poetics that they felt were appropriate for their song. They also vie with West – and among themselves – to best represent Zuluness. Their alteration in the interjection is a Zuluising substitution in both language (from *ibell* to *icilongo*) and in the object to which it refers (from an iron school/mission bell to the rural bugle), a shift from the colonial closer to the pre-colonial and deep Zulu equivalent.

12 February 1991. Zulu traditional guitarist Nogabisela Xaba is warming up in his booth. He has set a stinging sound on the amp alongside him, just the way he likes it. Dumisani Ngqobo is slapping and pounding on his bass in the adjoining booth. Msawetshitshi Zakwe warms up his breathy, rolling concertina on the other side of the sound board. Thembinkosi Ntuli is getting settled in the control room. He is to produce the session. Engineer Lee Short is trekking in and out of the recording booths moving microphones. In passing he cuts Nogabisela's amp settings to zero – dry. Then he returns to the control room to set initial sound levels and EQs on his console, isolating each of their warm-up runs to get the sounds just right.

While Lee is preoccupied, Nogabisela turns his mix back up on his amp.

'What's going on?' puzzles Lee as he listens to his guitar settings. He asks Nogabisela not to tamper with the amp so they can maintain a consistent sound.

When the tape is rolling and the song is beginning to groove, Ntuli hears a mistake. He stops the musicians. 'You're touching two strings near the end of the intro,' he points out to Nogabisela in Zulu; 'let's do it again.'[21] Take. Erase. Take. No, listen nicely. Cut, rewind to try again. Nogabisela sneaks in a little change on his amp.

'Sorry, give me a second. There's something going on,' puzzles Lee again. He listens, isolating the guitar.

While Lee fiddles about on the controls to finesse the guitar sound, Ntuli reassures Nogabisela from the control room. 'I heard you touching [your amp controls] where I don't want you to. I'm looking after your interests.'[22]

Msawetshitshi calls for another take.

'Stand by!' announces Ntuli.

'How're their headphones? Can they hear everything?' intercedes Lee, getting ready to roll the tape again.

Music-makers constantly intervene in the recording process to look after their own interests, interrupting those studio practices that reinstantiate apartheid's systemic pathologies. Some artists work at improving their own technological skills and acquiring their own electronic equipment. Koloi Lebona learns intently from Roy Halee. Others argue against the authority of technology and its exponents, and do so in multiple ways. First, the musicians can undermine the kinds of knowledge valorised on the production side of the glass simply by brilliant performance. Peter especially likes recording traditional Sotho music, despite the difficulties that arise when working with musicians with little understanding of studio technology or practice. He simply likes Sotho rhythms. He wants to record music that 'kicks ass', and he wants to record it well.[23] Second, the musicians can argue against the authority of the control room more explicitly by bringing into the studio's hallowed arenas other discourses over which they themselves claim mastery – a cultural authority or a multilingual virtuosity for example. Peter can't pronounce the Zulu 'click'. The lyric in a wedding song should be 'icilongo', not 'ibell', or 'iklok' or 'insimbi': it should be the Zulu word appropriate to a rural setting in Zululand, insist the musicians.

They also play with the linguistic inequalities of the studio, exploiting the engineer's inability to understand local languages for the exclusive discursive space it opens up, and using their own incompetence at communicating verbally with the engineer in English as a pretext for taking action without consultation: Nogabisela resets his own amp; the musicians claim Peter's sound of 'Africa' without having to include him. These local dynamics unsettle the conventional social and professional hierarchies of studio practice, at times causing breakdowns in communication, social disintegration of sessions, or creative failure. At other times, these local dynamics open a space for empowering moves and creative innovation: the musicians assert control over the lyrics of their song; Nogabisela gets a sound closer to his preference, and by tweaking his own sound alerts his producer to be vigilant about representing the musicians' aesthetic interests in the control room.

These various asymmetries in studio relations are produced by different histories of learning about languages, technologies, and local African culture. Studio participants recognise these asymmetries as symptoms of a South African race and class history and interpret the contemporary limitations on their own creative power in this light. 'Know the desk, man!' exclaims engineer Darryl Heilbrunn to me in frustration. '[African American producers] could talk to you in technical terms, they were thoroughbred, qualified producers. Our guys just aren't educated in that manner. Yes, blame apartheid, blame the white man – whatever – but it's a fact, you know.'[24] Alton Ngubane who leads and co-produces Special Five, a struggling low-budget *mbaqanga*/soul/pop group, advises me one day in informal conversation that I should set up my own studio. 'Just a small studio,' Ngubane reassures me. 'You could get money from the government. It's easy for you,' he says, 'aren't you even from Pretoria, *nê*?'[25] While he is mistaken about my personal finances and political contacts, he rightly recognises that in the past my race, class and ethnicity might have granted me a privileged entry into the domains of the apartheid state power that he knows to be fundamentally tied to capital. He imagines that this privileged access would still be possible in 1992 for someone with an Afrikaner background, who grew up in Pretoria, the bosom city of the apartheid state apparatus. He identifies some of the creative limitations he experiences in South African studio practice as produced by the nation's troubled history, and aspires after a studio released from this history. What Ngubane has instead is a studio practice inextricably saturated with the political.

Negotiations for the control over electronic manipulation of the sound is at once a struggle over the shaping of musical styles and a means by which South Africans articulate political ideas, reassess their values, and rework social relations. When Peter Ceronio looks back at the 1970s from the 1990s, he reassesses his earlier racialised perspective. 'In those days it used to aggravate us sometimes … But in actual fact, if you think about it today, they [argumentative producers] were right, basically, because they were creating and that's what it's all about.' By thinking through the abstract principles of the creative process, Peter comes to a more humane understanding of his former co-workers, and implies that he recognises that apartheid values had undergirded his studio working practices (and those of others) and their negative evaluations of their musical colleagues. He thinks differently now. When West insists that Peter Pearlson says 'Isigqi' and subsequently relents, he critiques and teaches Peter. He reminds those present that there are still differences in privilege while cultivating jovial goodwill at the console. When Tefo retorts 'Wake up!' to West's mistakes at the microphone, he empowers himself as a working-class musician by claiming the right to criticise those socially and profes-sionally above him while simultaneously seizing an opportunity for the musicians to collectively re-work the lyrics that West sings on their song. '*Ungumnguni lona!*'exclaims a musician about engineer Neil when he delivers a backing track with a groove. When the praise is translated for once – 'That man is a Zulu!' – the joking tricksters acknowledge Neil's presence and the aesthetic sensibility they have in common with him, at the same time that their joke marks social differences between him and them. (Neil is white.)

These examples of language use in the studio – language about tech-nology, sound and aesthetics[26] – stand in for explicit talk about race, class and apartheid history. Language choice, code-switching, chosen silences, ideas and feelings articulated in gestures or in moments of musical expres-sion all perform political struggles that are as much about being personally enabled within the studio as they are about being collectively recognised or empowered within civic and national arenas. In the effort to control the details of the recording procedure and the electronic manipulation of sound – to have some say over style and sound quality – South African politics is revealed and addressed in the studio.

Animating politics

The studio represents a microcosm of South Africa. The prospect of a South African-led African 'renaissance' in the world of continental politics certainly fuelled musicians' interests in sounding 'African' in the early 1990s.[27] Africa-focused sentiment had market potential and expressed some musicians' deeply felt subject positions, but, at the same time, other dynamics also came to the fore in the world in which these musicians found themselves. Most notably the rise in Zulu nationalism prompted hot debate at the national negotiating table around questions of ethnicity, especially Zulu ethnicity. When the musicians celebrate Neil as 'Zulu', they loosen ethnicity from its constraining referent, and implicitly critique ethnic nationalist essentialisms that are being played out violently in the streets. This studio concern echoes the talk in more explicitly political arenas: when the musicians call for a rural bugle rather than an iron mission/school bell in their lyrics, they foreground the Zuluness of their recording in a way that they probably would not have cared to do in the 1970s, when Zuluness carried neither the same commodity potential nor the political cachet it had for some in the early 1990s.[28] When Nogabisela strives to keep the sound of his Zulu traditional guitar strident, he makes an aesthetic choice that also identifies him for his Zulu fans as a Zulu musician. As that of a migrant then living in a Zulu-identified men's hostel in the Johannesburg area, his sound marked a covert allegiance to Zulu nationalist politics for many of his fans. In this volatile transition period, artists' production choices shape the reception of their music in relation to values of Zuluness (and Africanness more broadly), and help to determine their market. They open up some Zulu-identified spaces that are safe to perform in, and limit others, recirculating ideas and feelings about Zuluness back into an arena of public discussion. All of which does not mean that these musicians regarded themselves as political ideologues or as activists: on the contrary, they were working as artists with aesthetic ideals and market hopes. But, as commercially distributed products, their sounds were available to be retrieved as 'Zulu' (or, in other moments, as 'South African' or 'African'), by those for whom 'Zulu' mattered. The studio process comes to bear upon political struggles with which it is contemporaneous.

A decade later, post apartheid, in the 'new South Africa', 24 July 2002, Shirimani Studios, Johannesburg. Zulu traditional musician Siyazi Zulu, having formerly recorded at Downtown Studios, then the biggest studios in town, now chooses to record a CD at Shirimani Studios. Tucked away on the eighth floor of a decrepit office block on a crumbling edge of downtown, the studio is owned by Joe Shirimani who has ploughed the returns from his hits as an artist into an independent business. Siyazi's three sessions are long boisterous ones. All the musicians arrange, rearrange, improvise their parts, co-conceive of the backing tracks, and dance to their creations in the control room of the studio. Zulu is the *lingua franca*. Siyazi wants aesthetic control. He wants, at last, to do his own project his own way. He picks a co-producer, his musicians, and the studio.

Pakie Mohale, the young African house engineer, learned his trade as an active fan of *kwaito* music, South Africa's youth music of the later 1990s through to the present. He taught himself how to use sound-processing computer programs in order to create *kwaito* music, a blend of house and hip-hop overlaid with lyrics in local languages.[29] When he discusses components of the recording process with the co-producer for the session, he gestures to the computer's screen that has become a focus of visual attention in the studio.[30] His hand and finger movements mirror the moving bars of the graphs of the sound being recorded. He works visually, using the computer graphics to identify the detailed make-up of the sounds, more than he uses his ears. He has yet to develop an engineer's hearing acuity and the skills to translate the musicians' poetic lexicon into the language of acoustic and electronic science. His dream is to apprentice himself to Quincy Jones.

Siyazi is struggling with the intonation of a line of his lead vocals. They take, erase, retake, erase. 'Please practise,' suggests the young engineer, holding down the talk-back button so he can be heard by Siyazi in the recording booth. He uses a polite form of request to his elder. This is the only time during the production that I hear him criticising the performance of the musicians, all Zulu men and all his seniors.

'Ah, I don't want to practise!' retorts Siyazi. 'It is you who is causing me to go astray!'

The control room and Siyazi erupt in laughter. The engineer records Siyazi repeatedly until he has a good take.

The production quality is poor. The CD is yet to be released.[31]

August 2007. For Zulu concertina player Lahl'Umlenze, there are now four prized sound engineers in Johannesburg who can get the Zulu sound: Mzamo Mavudla, Bazooka, David Molwelwe and Jan Smit. Three are Africans; three own independent studios; all have recorded hits. Jan Smit has apprenticed Betty Ndlovu. She sits there for days, listening intently.

From Lanza to Lassus

TULLY POTTER

My serious involvement with recordings, which has already lasted fifty-five years, has given me much of my musical education as well as endless inspiration. Growing up in the South African countryside, I was largely dependent for entertainment on what we had in the house. The Broadwood baby grand piano was vital: my father played by ear (hence my predilection for James P. Johnson and the Harlem stride style) but my mother played only from printed music – we regularly sang songs round the piano to her accompaniment. I do not recall that we listened to the radio much but we had two cupboards full of 78 rpm discs. Among the twelve-inch records, housed in strong cardboard boxes, were classic sets: Toscanini's 1936 NYPSO Beethoven Seventh; Stokowski's Philadelphia *Petrushka*; the Grieg Concerto with Moiseiwitsch; *Faust* with Marcel Journet; Fritz Busch's Glyndebourne *Don Giovanni*; *Lucia di Lammermoor* with Pagliughi; the plum label *Rigoletto* with Piazza, Pagliughi and Folgar; and, perhaps most important for my early development, *La traviata* with Guerrini, Infantino and Silveri.[1] Our ten-inch discs were often not even dignified with paper covers but stood in convenient piles from which eight would be selected at random to be placed on the 'record changer' in the radiogram. We always had background music at dinner and it might be anything from Roberto Inglez or Amalia Rodriguez to Sir George Henschel or Richard Tauber or, at the lighter extreme, Layton and Johnstone, Bing Crosby, Danny Kaye or the Andrews Sisters.

I went to my first opera aged seven, a matinee of *La traviata*, and even then I made the connection between what I saw on the stage and what I knew from the records, because the same tenor – cruelly called Elefantino by Johannesburg opera-goers – was involved. But the decisive turning point came four years later, when I heard my elders talking about 'The Great Caruso'. Was this something to do with Robinson Crusoe? They explained that it was a film about a famous singer and told me a little about him. I did not see the movie starring Mario Lanza at the time (and I have never been able to sit through the whole thing, as it is so risible) but my curiosity was piqued – and I found two Caruso records among our ten-inch stock. No doubt I had already heard them, as I knew the coupling of 'La donna è mobile' and 'O sole mio' (one of those monstrosities onto which a modern orchestra had been grafted). As soon as I started listening attentively to Caruso, I was riveted by the singing, especially the two arias from *Tosca*.[2] I was already something of a collector, and when my twelfth birthday came I asked for the two-LP Caruso album that was available locally. I can still remember the thrill of walking into my bedroom and seeing it on my bed: my eldest brother had bought it for me in Johannesburg. I played it and played it; eventually I acquired the three-disc German box from which my set had been excerpted, and little by little I expanded my knowledge of the great singers. We already had records of Galli-Curci, Gigli and De Luca, including the famous white label *Rigoletto* Quartet and *Lucia* Sextet,[3] as well as fine examples of Cernay, Widdop, Dawson, Radford, Martinelli and de Gogorza, but I unearthed Schipa, Schorr, Schumann, Leider, Dal Monte, Pertile and many others for myself. The visit of the Piccola Scala company for the 1956 Johannesburg Festival disclosed the delights of Italian comic opera – I vividly recall the two Nicolas, Monti and Rossi-Lemeni, in *L'elisir d'amore* – and through records I discovered Sesto Bruscantini, who led me first to *Le nozze di Figaro*, then to *Così fan tutte*.[4] I cultivated the habit of listening to a recording of an opera at my boarding school if I knew I was to hear a performance in the holidays: that was how I became familiar with every vocal inflection of the Callas *Tosca*.[5] The first three orchestral LPs I bought were all conducted by Ferenc Fricsay, which suited my collector's mentality: the most exciting was Tchaikovsky's 'Pathétique'.[6]

Various mentors in the Johannesburg and Cape Town collectors' clubs widened my horizons, and Prof. C. G. S. de Villiers of Stellenbosch taught me to listen properly on many Sunday afternoon visits to his apartment during my spell in the Cape. The first lesson was delivered via an early Richard Crooks disc. Who was singing? 'John McCormack?' I hazarded, to be told that I was not focusing on the timbre of the voice. One of the Johannesburg record shops was owned by a jolly, fat, bald man, Mr Merritt. He did not have a good LP selection and would annoy my sister's friend Eileen, who ran The Long Player, by constantly borrowing from her stock to supply his customers; but at the back of his premises were shelves of 78 rpm discs. He gave me the run of the place and I found all manner of things, including a beautiful pressing of Isobel Baillie singing 'I know that my redeemer liveth'.[7] I haunted the classical basement of Recordia, the superb shop in Eloff Street, and from friends who also gathered there, as well as the helpful staff (especially Brian Amor), I garnered recommendations for LPs which were seminal in my appreciation of music. Mozart's *Sinfonia concertante*, K. 364, played by Menuhin and Barshai, led to a lifelong love of the viola and other string instruments.[8] Four 'Great Recordings of the Century' LPs won me over to the best of all German musicians, Adolf Busch, especially Schubert's E-flat Trio. Klemperer's Beethoven Fifth seemed the very essence of drama. Haydn's Piano Sonata in C Minor introduced me to Emil Gilels, who in turn brought me to many concertos. Aksel Schiøtz and Gerald Moore revealed *Die schöne Müllerin* and *Dichterliebe*. Teresa Stich-Randall and Dagmar Hermann duetting in Bach's BWV78 initiated me into another rich vein; I still listen to a cantata every Sunday morning.[9]

Returning in 1966 to Britain, which I had left as a child of five, I could bring only about 100 LPs in a big wooden box – no 78 rpm discs, as the cost of shipping them was prohibitive. I therefore became a habitué of the London record shops as I steadily rebuilt my collection. From Michael Letchford at HMV, Cranbourn Street, I bought Schumann's *Humoreske*, played by Sviatoslav Richter, and Beethoven's 'Archduke' with Gilels, Kogan and Rostropovich.[10] There was an excellent shop in Romford, where I lived: in its classical basement Edward Dowdall – more recently at The Collector's Room, Salisbury – held sway, and from him I acquired Mozart's C Major Quintet, with the Budapest Quartet and Milton Katims, and my first Beethoven quartets, played by the Smetana Quartet.[11] Through that wonderful group's concerts and records I was to discover Czech music: a particular ear-opener would be their stereo Janáček quartets. The Smetana's Shostakovich Third would also usher in Russian chamber music.[12] Meanwhile I had heard that Beethoven's late quartets were the ultimate summit, but from all accounts rather forbidding. I bought all three LPs then available by the Busch Quartet, including Opp. 131 and 132, and found that all I had to do was concentrate my attention on them. I would stay up far into the night, absorbing these other-worldly sounds.[13] My mother had always stopped me listening to the few pieces by English composers to which I had access – she thought Elgar wrote 'brass band music' – and so I was well into my twenties before I realised Elgar's greatness: the key was one of Boult's versions of the Second Symphony.[14] From there it was a natural step to Vaughan Williams; and through BBC Radio 3 I discovered Wilfred Brown's definitive *Dies Natalis*.[15]

Although I am still finding both old and new pieces, the last major building block in my education through recordings was put in place by the early music movement. I attended David Munrow's concerts but the revelation was encountering Bruno Turner's records with Pro Cantione Antiqua. Their version of Ockeghem's *Requiem* was a gateway to the Middle Ages;[16] and I moved on to Josquin Desprez, Lassus, Victoria and Palestrina. King's College Choir and David Willcocks took me to Tallis and Gibbons, especially their performance of 'Glorious and powerful God' with Thurston Dart leading the viol consort.[17]

I would never suggest records as substitutes for concerts but they can be a powerful supplement; and through them I have discovered composers who are never heard in our stereotyped concert programmes, such as Reger. In my teens I kept a book in which I entered each Caruso recording as I acquired it. Some were on LPs but many more came on heavy, bulky 78 rpm discs. Today I have all the great tenor's records on a set of CDs that I can hold in one hand. Perhaps there are tracks that I have not yet got round to hearing, but I am in no hurry …

5 From wind-up to iPod: Techno-cultures of listening

ARILD BERGH AND TIA DENORA

At 7.18 pm on 30 November 2006 three hundred people began to dance in a London railway station. Conga lines formed, some danced together while others were engrossed in their own dance steps on the concourse: not a single strain of music was heard by the bemused onlookers.[1]

What took place was a flash mob, a happening organised via mobile phone text messages and email sent from person to person. In this case it was devoted to people dancing to different, individually chosen music that only they could hear on their personal MP3 players. In this brief moment many of the themes of this chapter are encapsulated: the centrality of listening to recordings in our modern relationship to music; how technological innovations have encouraged this; the increasing atomisation of the musical experience coupled, paradoxically, with a yearning for (musical) community; and, most of all, the idea that listening is far from being a passive, receive-only mode of interacting with music. In what follows we provide a sketch of how listening became institutionalised as the prevalent and normative mode of musical appreciation in industrialised locations; how the activity of listening has been variously configured over time and place (in interaction with technology); and how listening needs to be theorised as a form of social practice, even when it takes place in solitude. We set these themes in the context of what listening, as a social activity, has enabled listeners to do, and we examine the symbiosis between recorded music, related industries and the listener.

Listening situated in history

Although the advent of recorded music is often thought to mark the start of focused music listening, listening as an exclusive way of appreciating music was a well-established practice long before Thomas Edison supposedly played a recording of 'Mary had a little lamb' to his assistant.[2] In Indian classical music, focused listening as a technique for achieving certain mental states goes back hundreds of years.[3] In Europe and North America, where listening without participating is comparatively young, it was still institutionalised more than a hundred years prior to Edison's

Figure 5.1 A flash mob event at a London railway station

invention, linked to the development of purpose-built concert halls and paraphernalia such as programme notes. It was also linked to social codes of appropriation that varied over time, from hot paroxysms of emotional rapture to cooler and more contemplative modes of connois-seurship.[4] As various historians of listening have observed, the history of focused musical attention, as opposed to more functional appropriation of music (as entertainment, for instance, or as accompaniment to dance, or to enhance sacred ritual) is simultaneously the history of cultural entrepreneurship and social difference. Listening, in other words, was initially a public activity and a signal of status. Even after Beethoven reportedly uttered the words 'I will not play for such swine' and stormed out of the room when a nobleman was disrespectfully conversing at one of his salons, music, in the West at least, was perhaps more often ignored than pursued intently.[5]

Arguably the phonograph and the recording technologies that followed afforded a democratisation of listening that increased with time, making the purportedly 'genuine' sound of music available through cheaper reproduction.[6] While it was by no means the first form of mechanical reproduction (previous examples included organs and pianos driven by simple cylinder mechanisms at the courts of the Caliph of Baghdad and automatons at European courts), the player piano and the phonograph (in the generic sense) were the first technologies to use reproducible software and to allow the 'accurate' repetition of a sonic event (an issue later to be a topic in its own right within the high-fidelity movement).[7]

Unlike piano rolls, which were dependent upon the instrument technology to which they were coupled, the phonograph's ability to record sound could make available virtually any previous performance – and any combination of timbres – through the simple exchange of a cylinder or later a disc or tape. This change was at first admired mainly for its technological novelty. But, as we suggest below, it also afforded a critical shift in the human relations that formed around music consumption: a shift that coincided with the rise of individualism, urbanism and the growth of consumption, and that nurtured the relativism associated with postmodernism and its challenges to aesthetic canons. The development of recorded music thus crystallised the role of the listener, rather than creating it. It opened up the possibility for increased numbers of people to become listeners in their own time and space, a trend enhanced through mass-copied recording media, then through radio and TV, and finally through electronic means, such as internet distribution. In short, developments in the eighteenth century paved the way for listening to emerge, in the twentieth, as a desirable social activity and a means for the acquisition (and diversification) of cultural capital. At the same time, the sound of music slowly became ubiquitous without requiring participation on any other level than (often subliminal) awareness.

The rise of listening in 'the West'

Listening as a recognisable and focused activity, rather than a by-product of being near music, had a slow start in the West. The rise of interest in music over and above its use within rituals was fomented by cultural entrepreneurs who tried to place music centre-stage, partly through a broad and long-lasting programme,[8] and partly through the various spectacles which Richard Leppert has described as 'the sight of sound'.[9] This was helped by the fact that strong physical participation in music was suppressed and even became suspect during the seventeenth and eighteenth centuries, with a move from music's association with practical magic to a focus on the internally emotional and outwardly inert mode of reception.[10] Simultaneously, as music improved the cultural and economic capital of entrepreneurs, those forms of music that were freely and easily available, such as folk music or the music employed as an adjunct to ritual, were relegated to secondary status. This reallocation was achieved through various forms of boundary work that distinguished between 'serious' music, usually Western classical music, and 'lighter music' such as folk and popular music. That work simultaneously delineated a hierarchy of listening types, alive and well in Adorno's discussion of listeners.[11] Thus, from the late eighteenth century onward, rituals *with* music were replaced – at least in elite culture – by rituals *around* music.[12] The flash mob in Paddington, discussed above, is an example of a ritual around music and one that simultaneously demonstrates the curious nature of modern ritual experience: co-presence and an indication of collective obeisance coupled with inner differentiation.[13] Throughout the nineteenth century, these rituals provided new scripts for participants in musical events, enacted by individuals in social settings. During this time the structures these scripts delineated were authoritarian; they sketched the rudiments of subsequent 'star' systems through the figure of the composer-hero and charismatic performer to whom a devotional listening audience literally 'looked up', a system echoed in popular music with its fans and stars.[14] Even today the same process takes place in societies that go from communally involved music-making to separate presentations of music.[15] Where they differed from prior worshipful forms (perhaps most notably in religion) was in the enfranchisement of the listener: for the first time she was placed in the curious position of willingly submitting to the 'authority' of an aesthetic (musical) experience while remaining in the position of paymaster of that authority, having the power to withdraw support without sanction and seemingly at will as a matter of 'taste'. This modern form of aesthetic reflexivity was directly linked to a changing concept of the individual.[16] No longer part of a group that may or may not have been engaged in casual musicking,[17] she became a clearly defined entity, someone whose identity shifted according to group affiliation and whose identity was signalled through individual activities and consumption, with music slowly becoming one of the most important arenas in which this identity work was done.

Thus, even before the phonograph, the objectification of music was established initially through live performance. The market for listening via the commercial dissemination of recordings was, in other words, primed for Fred Gaisberg's globe-trotting record-producing career for the Gramophone Company (later EMI) at the beginning of the twentieth century and the subsequent rise of the global record industry. [18]

Passive listening or active musicking?

The history of recorded music is very much the story of how one of many possible ways of interacting with music has become the normative structure for most people in industrialised societies. But what is 'listening'? As a practical social activity what does it consist of? And how does consideration of this question help to shed some light on the problem of artistic value; in particular, how does it facilitate a sidestepping of the relativist/absolutist dichotomy that characterises so many (too many) debates about musical value today?[19]

Listening is frequently mistaken for, or more deliberately brushed off as, a passive activity. But recent studies of the minutiae of listening document listeners as not only active but also reflexive as they develop their tastes in music.[20] Even when we outwardly desire to be passive we always bring something with us, if only our own heartbeat and breathing, as John Cage observed.[21] But beyond this very basic and unavoidable baggage, most listening situations will involve the listener as she interprets and deduces or adds meaning to the music. Even when we seek relative passivity music frequently evokes and invokes emotions, embodied memories and altered somatic states.[22] It is in this sense, then, that listening is active. Listening is an activity that not only provides aesthetic pleasure, but also affords the listener opportunities for 'work', the creation, consolidation and elaboration of meaning systems alone or in interaction with other listeners, be it in real time or retrospectively. In this sense, the listener is indeed also a composer/performer; she is like the craftsperson who 'finishes off' an object, or a picture framer/hanger or arts curator who situates a musical item.[23] This takes place on the level of the immediate and intimate as well as within a larger perspective. For instance, music may be chosen to fit with the physical environment in which listening occurs, or to fit in with activities taking place before, during and after listening. Or, more symbolically, the listening may situate the piece within the social topology of affiliated works, genres or sound qualities, or chronologically within a timescape of other works the music might be addressing or acknowledging. Finally, it may act as a container of various furnishings, soft and more durable, such as memories, connotations, or conventional practices associated with music. Through a rich range of often idiosyncratic practices learned and developed informally, through happenstance, and linked to personal biography, listeners come to empower the musics that in turn come to have power 'over' them. The cases of DeNora's 'Lucy',[24] who chose the time of day, room and even chair for listening to Schumann's *Impromptus*, and Gomart and Hennion's listeners, who craft particular listening environments so as to achieve ecstatic heights when experiencing their favourite musical moments, highlight listening as minute and richly textured practice.[25] This set of practices, and the conjoining of music and other things, generates value(s) that are embedded in and arise from the current situation and the biography of those involved, rather than the value(s) being autonomous and external to the place and situation from which they emerge.

Understood in this way, listening as activity illuminates key debates around the issue of music's value, its aesthetic, emotional or intellectual impact, and thus its proposed location within a hierarchy of other musics. Value is, in other words, yet another collective achievement, produced by the ways people are able to establish links between music, other people, practices and things. This drawing together ('assemblage') is what 'finishes off' the music. In other words, the love of music, its impact and its perceived value are all accomplished by drawing music into relation with other things, such as memories or evaluative dialogues with other listeners. From within this new ontology of music, which implies an 'extended mind' model of creativity,[26] critiques of musical works or forms (for example Adorno on popular music)[27] are always nothing more nor less than assemblages; there is no privileged critique that can stand outside assembly work. By this logic, negative assessments of works are those that omit certain links in the assembly process and add others, thus recontextualising (recomposing) works in less flattering ways. They remove, in other words, some features of the 'composition' that would otherwise allow works/forms to be perceived from more laudable angles. Like a potentially functional light bulb severed from a source of electricity, to borrow a metaphor from Edison, works that fail to 'shine' do not do so because the connection between these works and complex networks and infrastructures of other processes are not made. The system has not been assembled in the way that would generate light. Such misconnections often take institutional forms where they may be made so routine that, for all practical purposes, a fault may seem quite 'naturally' to lie in a part of a system rather than in the system's assemblage. Although this is critically naive and thus wasteful, the controversy that surrounds so many new developments in music exemplifies this (*The Rite of Spring*, Cage's *4'33"*, Hendrix's 'Star Spangled Banner', punk music), either because critics fail to understand the full network involved in valuing the work/musician or because they dislike the ethics and modes of conduct implied in the network that makes latent value manifest.[28]

Listening and recording technology

Before looking at how listening and recording technology have interacted, it is worth noting that the software (in other words, the music) has had, and still has, a shifting role here. When recordings were first marketed on a large scale in the early twentieth century, they were only an accessory to selling gramophones and radio cabinets. Later the music itself became the main focus, financially and emotionally, but in recent years the emphasis has again shifted, with Apple using the online iTunes music shop as a way of selling more iPods, and Nokia recently having announced a similar shop partly to increase the number of mobile handsets they can sell.[29] Today, then, we have to some extent gone full circle and music has for many been removed from its exalted position to become once again part of a more fluid entertainment landscape.

Two key changes in the psycho-culture of listening were enabled by the invention of the phonograph, both of which have been further enhanced by later technological developments, mirroring development in other areas of life where technology has made products cheaper to produce and distribute and more individual. First has been listeners' increasing ability to isolate themselves, both from other listeners and from the performers, something taken to new heights with the invention of the Sony Walkman and later media players such as the iPod, which were put to such innovative use by the flash mob at Paddington. This isolation turned the communal circle of traditional music performances into a worshipping half circle around gramophone cabinets and later hi-fi systems, or one-on-one forms of real-time or time-shifted communication.

Second, music quite literally became an object. In his book *Noise*, Jacques Attali discusses the progression from individual exchanges (for example, the musician being paid for his work) to a situation in which music, through copyright on compositions and presentation, is traded as a commodity with added value for the individual or group that controls it.[30] In her study of recording technology in the 1920s and 1930s, Sophie Maisonneuve shows how a confluence of agents helped to cement the idea of 'great music' as a worthwhile object to own.[31] This object was easy to exchange, easy to reproduce and, most importantly for the music lovers, gave exactly the same performance on every listening occasion.[32] Added to this aesthetic reliability, the plethora of versions of classical works facilitated minute discrimination and the possibility to affiliate with micro-features of performance, such as the interpretation of double-dotted rhythms, tempo, tone colour or the rendering of a phrase, and to associate these micro-features with forms and imageries of identity.[33] This was paralleled in other music forms, with bootlegs of rock bands' live performances eliciting similar comparisons among the 'aficionados'. The phonograph thus paved the way for the possibility of aesthetic reliability and with it the features of rehearing, a new form of listening experience involving anticipation, premeditation in choosing music for listening, and the fulfilment of expectation on re-experiencing the 'same' musical event. It thus allowed the listener to focus on music in separation from other activities and so readily lent itself to an ever-increasing devotion to music, whatever the genre. In this respect, and like the social distribution of mirrors in earlier times,[34] the phonograph facilitated new ways of articulating self-identity, permitting listeners to reflect upon their own subjective responses as reliable ('objective') phenomena – the ability to watch oneself responding as a subject to a musical object. In this sense, the phonograph was an important medium for music's role as a technology of the self.[35] It afforded a new configuration of what Maisonneuve terms the 'musical patrimony' (heritage and consumer produce) as a personal experience; and, *as* a personal experience, the hierarchy of forms, works and musicians came to be deregulated, instigating a backlash against the initial canonic ideology that hitherto underwrote the inception of listening as a social activity.[36] As these new allegiances to different music forms were voluntary they tended to be stronger and more difficult for individuals to shift, as artists like Bob Dylan found to their cost.[37]

Backlash

Just as recordings afforded new listening stances, the decreasing cost of recording, listening and distribution equipment allowed different strata of society access to an ever-widening range of music. The difference between serious and non-serious listening, and by extension serious and non-serious music, often flowed in channels that demarcated social status. So at the same time as lavish recordings were made of entire symphonies for expensive gramophone sets there were cheaply available records made of folk-ditties played free on the radio, and while in the 1970s progressive rock bands spent several years on making one album that would require attentive listening, punk bands would record a three-minute single in one take for listeners to pogo to in their bedrooms.

Adorno saw this affordable and accessible music as demeaning the musical experience, offering only false happiness.[38] Later, critiques would be voiced by those concerned about local musical styles being overrun by international pop music.[39] Even today these debates engage those concerned with music listening, despite thorough-going attempts to articulate alternative canons and to theorise the pop/high-culture musical divide.[40] At the time of writing, a two-page article in the *Independent* worries about the disappearance of the 'album' as downloading individual tracks is becoming the norm: 'Sales shouldn't affect anyone because [the album is] an art form.'[41] Similar worries have been echoed by others: 'The accessibility of music has meant that it is taken for granted and does not require a deep emotional commitment once associated with music appreciation.'[42] It is more than a little ironic that these worries centre on the loss of a musical format that only forty years ago was looked down upon as lacking in value and as being a commodity itself.

What is 'finished off' through listening? The reflexivity of listening

Much research on recorded music and listeners has focused on the fan – the specialist listener – and music therefore often appears to be more central in people's lives than it necessarily is, as Christina Williams discovered in her work with teenagers and pop music.[43] At the same time, writings on music listening often have a penchant for the fascinating and romantic subject of the musical catharsis, or peak experience, self-reported and often sought out by listeners.[44] Both those streams clearly echo the ideals of early listening habits, and although interesting in themselves do not necessarily reflect how most people encounter and use music and music (distribution) technologies in everyday life, which is our focus in this section.

As we have suggested, listening to recordings is active and passive at the same time, and the use of music by listeners similarly wavers in and out of focus. For instance, music may be used to make the workday more bearable, in which case it takes on the active role of enhancing daily life.[45] But at the same time it is relegated to a background position without any active listening. And the choice to use music is likewise one over which we sometimes have total control, for instance when someone chooses to play music for an intimate encounter; sometimes have partial control, as when music occurs in the background in shops to encourage certain purchasing patterns; or it may be forced upon us as it has been in situations of torture and humiliation.[46]

In all these situations, music listening occurs as an activity that simultaneously helps create the prerequisites of other activities and thus space for social manoeuvring. We believe that this dynamic relationship between listening activity and other social activities is what makes listening activity such a useful and at times powerful ally for social agents. These social situations, involving the formation or reinforcement of social groups and spaces for individual agents to act within, include identity and boundary maintenance, the creation of culture, memory work and the setting up of social parameters for certain situations. Most of this, as we describe in the next section, is achieved through the development of collective canons of accepted music, personal 'catalogues' of music filed according to use and/or occasion, and embodied techniques of (often transformative) music listening.

How does listening get done?

The key to most listeners' music use is often their collections of recordings, which in turn provide clues to their own personal canons. Through the development of these collections, people create an available resource that they can control and that provides them with further resources for the work that listening enables, whether alone or with others. In earlier times, these collections could occupy considerable space. Evan Eisenberg describes one of his interviewees who owned three-quarters of a million records while living on benefits.[47] These days a life's worth of music can fit on a small MP3 player, allowing for random access to any track within seconds.

These personal collections may be a reflection of a larger canon, 'approved' by experts in the field, or by the listeners' peer group(s). But however the criteria are determined, and regardless of their reference points, most people are highly reflexive about the way they access their collection, as Hennion has demonstrated.[48] Most ethnographies of music listening show, moreover, that people are often able to tell in great detail why they have chosen a particular piece or, even when it is chosen randomly (via radio for instance), why and how it affected them.[49]

Listening to music in purpose-built locations may be organisationally constrained (as Ola Stockfelt points out, dancing in a concert hall would be frowned upon),[50] but, once outside these designated settings, listening is configured in various and idiosyncratic ways determined by use – dancing, crying, sleeping, making love. And in these uses music listening emerges as a reflexive, embodied praxis.[51]

What gets done?

Despite Williams's caveat that music is not necessarily important to all people all of the time, music listening is frequently used to develop, display and maintain our identities.[52] In particular, music allows for real-time shared group identities to be built. It may provide the aesthetic base for concerted activity. In this sense, music may provide cultural anchors and cues for future collaborative action, acting as a tacit orientational medium which structures or prepares action along particular trajectories.[53] To show, for example, that we are sophisticated and well off we may establish a record collection of smooth jazz, whereas a large number of world-music records would indicate leftist politics and openness, both these examples in effect being a subset of a publicly defined canon. Over time, of course, what records mean will change: in the 1960s owning a Martin Denny record would indicate middle-class and indeed 'square' affiliation; now it is more likely to signal 'hip and ironic'.

However, individuals are by no means musical free agents. They are, as it were, 'chosen' by music at least some of the time, for example when music provides emblematic materials (exemplars) for social movement activity.[54] Also, identities are frequently assigned by others in positive and negative ways, as Richard Jenkins has shown: hence certain types of musics are currently associated with 'chavs', the derogatory term for a certain group in British society in the early 2000s.[55] So we have three types of identity work here, accomplished through listening activity: that which is deliberately done by individuals, that done by groups internally, and that assigned by outsiders. And these three types can either be those that revolve around music (like the mods or punks in the UK) or those where music is simply implicit, for instance among immigrant communities around the world.[56]

Recent studies of applied music listening consider occasions where music is consciously deployed as an everyday health strategy or as an aid to conflict resolution, where shared musical experiences may provide resources for discovering common ground or for transforming the emotional dynamic of adversarial groups.[57] Moving beyond the issues of identity and boundaries, but linked to the notion that music listening is an 'anchoring practice', a common semi-automatic act around which other practices are organised or towards which they are orientated, recorded music is frequently used to 'set the scene', to provide parameters within which social actors can perform everyday social work from mourning to dating, and act upon shared visions and collective memory, as seen for instance in movements that used music recordings to protest against apartheid in South Africa or the dictatorship in the Philippines.[58]

Again, the music is empowered in ways that in turn imbue its 'passive' recipients with forms of empowerment – or transubstantiation. Some recent research on this topic has been conducted by Kari Batt-Rawden, who describes how music is, in the terms we have developed here, 'finished off' in ways that include somatic alterations in the listener (palliative and allopathic interventions). As one respondent, 'Veronica', described this experience:

> I have to tell you a strange story about something that happened to me just a few weeks ago. I listened to a piece of music called Venice Aqua, well, even if this was a quiet melody, it has also a very dramatic flavour to it, and I sat and listened to it very intensely, well, I am an extremely romantic kind of person and while I sat there listening to it, suddenly some strong forces

lifted me up and do you know what I did, well this is a month ago, I have
stopped smoking (laughs) and I have not smoked since, it was just like
I managed to fetch something in me and my legs are not as swollen and my
breathing has improved and I sleep better during the night.[59]

Making recordings and doing listening – new inter-changeability?

Over the past century a dialogue has taken place between the listener and
consumer of music on the one hand and playback technologies on the
other. Here the enabling (and constraining) features of different technologies have resulted in new social interactions around music, such as the
silent disco in our opening, as well as in new ways for people to understand
and experience themselves and society. At the same time the hegemony of
listening to recorded music has affected both the technology of recording
and playback and the way in which musicians relate to recording and
performing music.

One of the key results of recording and distribution technologies is that
they have potentially democratised the field of aesthetic music experiences. Without recording technology, only the richest and most powerful
in a society can afford to pay musicians to perform specially for them. For
instance, in recent fieldwork in the Sudan one interviewee lamented the
fact that he was not rich, because if he were he would fly to Wau (a city in
western Sudan) and attend the concerts that take place there every
Friday.[60] Though there was plenty of music in his own village, he felt the
bands in Wau were better. Since the bands did not record, access to this
'superior' music was limited.

Inexpensive technology has also erased the line between listener/fan and
record producer/patron. Today that line is fairly easy to cross; for example,
fans who feel that 'their' music has not got enough attention have started their
own record companies catering for a small band of like-minded listeners.[61]
This has been seen in the history of Afro-American music in the USA, and
later in the so-called cassette music scene that was widespread around the
world in the 1980s; here musicians would reach a new market through mail-
order cassettes.[62] And outside Western subcultures, cheap technology like
cassettes gave many local musical traditions a new lease of life; for instance in
India in the 1970s and 1980s local record companies started recording tapes
of different local musics that had generally been ignored in favour of 'serious'
Indian classical music or populist Hindi film music.[63]

The ever-decreasing cost of recording and distributing music has had
another side-effect: it affords the preservation of many musics that might

otherwise have been forgotten, allowing them to thrive via geographically dispersed audiences. Progressive rock music, for instance, which to a large extent 'died' in the late 1970s, still exists through reissues on CDs and through fan-clubs and internet websites.[64] In earlier times, a subgenre such as this would probably never have been seen again. At the same time, new genres can find an audience that sustains them across time and place. In this way there is no doubt that recording technologies and distribution have enriched the music world.

However, recorded music has also been spread through more subliminal means. The Muzak company, which specialised in 'canned music' for factories and shops, was started early in the twentieth century, initially piping music through telephone lines to houses; later it supplied a wide range of musics meant to control or augment people's productivity.[65] In the latter part of the century a range of artists worked in the field of ambient music, music that was not meant to be the focal point of listening.[66] We see similar attitudes in the use of music in cars, at the same time a private and a public space, where music is used to keep one awake or cheer one up on the way to work without being given one's main attention.[67] Currently new developments in information technology are being prototyped in public spaces to democratise access to public (background) music.[68]

A final location for such subconscious music listening is in film, an area where music has acted as a great mood enhancer, to the extent that it has its own practices such as 'scary' violin parts to indicate suspense and tension.[69] This brings us to the present day where music can be obtained within seconds via the internet, where people connect via Last.FM to automatically form communities of the like-minded, and where no recording musician is without a MySpace page. Here we have communities of people who are emphatic about music and may connect together from different continents. This is for now the culmination of a process that was started by Edison and his phonograph: our musical ties have less to do with geographical proximity (though music may still be used to signify 'place' – often for 'displaced' peoples),[70] and more to do with individual aesthetic 'tastes' through which we project ourselves and our relationships with fellow listeners around the world.

Conclusion: Listening as social order

Listening to recordings, we hope to have shown, is an active process, one that has assumed a variety of modes both across cultures and over time. Since the invention of the phonograph and the devices that followed, listening has had a symbiotic relationship with such innovations; and the relative importance of the music itself in this relationship has been, and is, a matter of occasional and rapid change. Listening to recorded music was not predestined for the central place it eventually attained in modern life; but, in combination with cultural entrepreneurship, the increased reflexivity of modern life, and innovations in technology and distribution, it ended up being the normative mode of music enjoyment in industrialised societies.

This dominance has enabled not only more intense and personal forms of musical experiences but also the democratisation of intent listening and deregulated canonic musical tastes, opening up the possibility of multiple and contending canons, and diverse audience groups decoupled from geographical proximity but united through taste. At the same time as music has configured social events and interactions, individuals and groups have also configured music to their needs, thus developing a plethora of forms of listening, from the formal enjoyment of classical music on radio, to the informal happening of the flash mob dancing to their iPods. As new technologies and ways of listening have developed we have always seen them augmenting existing modes rather than replacing them wholesale, to the extent that today we can easily be a listener, fan and distributor of music at the same time, thus fulfilling the evangelical zeal that many feel for 'their' music.

In recent years, focused music listening has taken a less central place in many people's everyday lives, requiring us to understand music use not only among the 'connoisseurs' but also among casual 'users'. Despite not being so central, listening (or subconscious listening) is today a ubiquitous activity to the extent that it is possible to speak of music 'choosing' listeners as well as the opposite. The metaphor of the flash mob with which we began this chapter stands as a metaphor for social life today more broadly – outwardly observed rituals combined with an ever-widening diversity of inward experience. Music listening, and the 'work' that is done through it and with it, therefore remains an area where we can learn more about society as a whole.

A matter of circumstance: On experiencing recordings

MARTIN ELSTE

My first experience with the gramophone was a total failure. It must have been around 1960, when I was seven or eight years of age. My father had given me a second-hand radio set with an integrated record player, and I happily went to a second-hand dealer and bought one of those seven-inch discs for just a Mark – a single with Harry Belafonte singing his 'Banana Boat Song' of 1957.[1] The battle of the speeds, which had been waged in a country unknown to me at the time, now reached me, and I became one of its casualties. I owned a record player and I owned a disc, but the two did not go together as my record player had only one speed – 78 rpm – for which no records were still made. Instead, the characteristic Belafonte sonority was transformed into a flickering castrato each time I put the disc onto the turntable. To an artist like Paul Hindemith, this might have been a stimulus for experimenting with sounds formerly unknown and unheard of.[2] To me, it was a frustrating experience which led me to neglect the gramophone altogether for some years. Instead, I looked at the back of the radio case through the little ventilation holes to search for *Heinzelmännchen* (munchkins) making music inside the box.[3]

Later, when I was thirteen or fourteen, I wanted to buy my first classical record. We still had no proper record player: in fact, the old one had been disposed of by then. But I was eager to get a recording of Schubert's beautiful and haunting Piano Trio Op. 100, even before I had a record player to play it on. I had grown to love the Trio's slow movement because it was practised by older pupils at my school during a week in a holiday camp devoted to music-making. But the local shop did not have a record in stock; the sales assistant looked it up in a catalogue – it must have been the *Bielefelder* – and informed me that there were two recordings for 25 DM and 21 DM respectively. Appreciating a bargain even in my tender years, I opted for the cheaper issue, and several days later I bought my first twelve-inch record, an Electrola disc,[4] namely Vol. 188 of the series *Unvergänglich – Unvergessen*. Strangely, only on one side of the disc did the label read 'Schubert, Piano Trio': on the other side it had 'Nicolai, Die lustigen Weiber von Windsor – Querschnitt'. It seemed highly peculiar to me that highlights from a German opera should appear on the reverse side of a chamber music disc. I did not quite believe it, as nothing about Nicolai was stated on the cover. I did not dare consider the possibility that the wrong stamper had been used – or perhaps the wrong label affixed. I could not check for myself, as I had no record player as yet, and to go back to the record shop to discover the truth was impossible. What would the lady have thought about a customer buying a record without the equipment to play it?

Months later I had saved enough pocket money to buy my first record player, a Dual record changer with integrated amplifier and a loudspeaker in the lid. Now I found that Electrola had simply confused the labels but not the stampers: my Schubert Trio was complete and filled both sides. And as it turned out, the cheaper disc happened to contain one of the most treasured interpretations of this work: the famous recording by the Busch Trio. I had been very lucky. On the other hand, even as an adolescent I had experienced entirely typical problems of sound archivism and of discology and discography: establishing the appropriate playback speed, having the proper playback equipment available, and cataloguing by listening and not just visually from the source document.

One day my mother was given a Mozart disc by her boss, quite obviously only because Mozart was not his cup of tea and this very disc was 'Record of the Month' of the record club to which he subscribed. My mother passed it on to her sister who had a record player and a few classical recordings, among them the 1962 set of the Beethoven symphonies conducted by Herbert von Karajan, and one or two recital discs with Rudolf Schock, the most famous German tenor in the early 1960s. While I cannot remember listening to any of the Beethoven symphonies, I am still aware of the trashy sentimentality of Schock singing 'Vater, Mutter, Schwestern, Brüder hab' ich auf der Welt nicht mehr' from Lortzing's *Undine,* and 'Ich bin nur ein armer Wandergesell' from *Der Vetter aus Dingsda,* arias which no one within the family seemed to care for. And I also remember that one day my aunt put on the Mozart disc – only to find the music uninteresting. Some time later during my adolescence, I deliberately scratched this Mozart disc. For some reason I found it interesting to experiment with the extent to which one could scratch a disc without actually destroying it. Later I put it on my own record player and experienced some truly fascinating improvisations. Needless to say, the pianist was Friedrich Gulda, who improvised in the solo sections and who also played a sort of continuo during the tutti sections. This recording has become one of the Mozart recordings that most fascinates me: Piano Concertos K. 467 and K. 595 with the Orchestra of the Vienna State Opera conducted by Hans Swarowsky, originally released on Concert Hall.[5]

When I was a pupil at school, I saved most of my pocket money for discs. And every other month I was able to buy a full-price disc, but

I preferred to shop for budget releases, which typically were distinctly poorer in sound as they were often reissues of recordings from the 1950s, a time when sound recording could still be pretty bad. So I also looked for special offers, and one of them was Bach's B Minor Mass on Telefunken.[6] It was a special offer as the Mass filled only five sides, the sixth side being left blank and thus, at the time of fixed retail prices, costing half a record less than any of the competing issues, all of which were on three full discs. This made me buy the set as soon as it was released, although I did not know the composition at all. But at least I liked Bach's music, or what I then knew of it. I still remember when I played the first side. What strange music it was to my ears then – almost incomprehensible – and I had paid the price of two and a half discs for it! I listened over and over again, however, and finally I grasped it. Is it surprising that this Mass has become one of my most treasured musical masterpieces?

Of course the influence of record criticism on my tastes and listening habits cannot be denied. The reason I bought Béla Bartók's *Divertimento for Strings* with the Zimbler Sinfonietta under Lucas Foss[7] was a splendid review published in the German record magazine *HiFi-Stereophonie*, which assigned marks to each of the discs under review.[8] This one received the highest possible mark on four counts – 10/10/10/10 – which meant that not only was the performance top notch, but so were the recording, the value of the repertoire recorded, and the actual surface of the disc. (The last of these was not to be taken for granted in the days of the LP, especially in the case of US pressings. A record dealer once told me, 'Germans listen to scratches, Americans listen to the music,' and there was truth in this!) No doubt one of the reasons why I had to get this disc as a young music lover was that Turnabout was sold at an affordable price. I do understand why the reviewer attributed a '10' to the performance, but neither the surface of my disc nor the sound quality was perfect. In fact the sound was rather bad, and I soon realised that this was an electronically 'enhanced' mono recording that only simulated stereophonic sound. A glimpse into Kurtz Myers's *Index to Record Reviews* would have told me more about the true age of this recording,[9] but at that time I didn't know anything about this useful section in *Notes*, the American music librarians' journal. Nevertheless, I am still more than grateful to the reviewer who, by rather carelessly giving top marks to this disc, made me encounter one of the most passionate and affective performances of Bartók's *Divertimento*. It has an urgency that is unique. The players give the impression of having to play each note out of sheer musical need. It is a most moving performance, so different from all those middle-of-the-road performances that end up trivialising Bartók's composition. About forty years later, I wonder how many recorded performances of this and all other works I have since

heard – some fascinating ones, to be sure, but more usually dull interpretations with little individuality, urgency or impact.

Undoubtedly, gramophone records are more than sound documents
or 'sound carriers', to use the literal translation of a useful German term
for them (*Tonträger*). That we appreciate some of them more highly than
others often happens only by chance. This makes record collecting a
highly personal matter, all the more so as the number of alternative
interpretations available on the market increases. We should keep this
in mind whenever we read hymns of praise or less enthusiastic verdicts
about given releases. Thanks to sound recording, we can describe a given
performance in fairly objective terms to do with timing, balance and
dynamics, but its evaluation will always remain subjective, depending
on individual musical circumstances and experiences as much as the
supposed quality of the recording itself.

6 Selling sounds: Recordings and the record business

DAVID PATMORE

Introduction

In 1998 the distinguished economic and social historian Cyril Ehrlich suggested that the history of the record industry could be divided into five phases.[1] Each of these has been driven by new sound-recording technologies. They are: the recording horn and the cylinder (1877– *c.* 1907); the acoustic disc (*c.* 1907–*c.* 1925); the microphone and electrical recording (*c.* 1925–*c.* 1948); tape recording and the vinyl long-playing record (*c.* 1948–*c.* 1983); and digital sound and the compact disc (*c.* 1983– *c.* 1998). To the last phase may now be added the computer file, such as the MP3 format (*c.* 1998–). This chapter will examine each of these periods. It will outline the dominant technologies of each phase, their commercial exploitation and related artistic developments, principally in the fields of musical repertoire.

1877–*c.* 1907

The inventor of the phonograph, Thomas Edison, saw its future as an office machine for dictation. Its mechanical basis was simple: a metal stylus inscribed sounds transmitted through a speaking tube onto the surface of a revolving cylinder, in this instance covered with silver foil, which could then be played back to the listener using the same stylus.[2] Edison patented his invention in 1878, the year after its first presentation, and set up the Edison Speaking Phonograph Company to exploit it commercially. Both public and inventor soon lost interest. Three years later, another major inventor, Alexander Graham Bell, together with colleagues, set up the Volta Laboratories to study sound recording and reproduction. In 1887 they unveiled their new machine, called the graphophone, which used wax as the recording medium in place of foil. Edison responded with a similar machine and the rights to both were purchased by Jesse Lippincott, who created the North American Phonograph Company to market them. Lippincott franchised the exploitation rights on geographical lines to companies such as the Columbia Phonograph Company, which operated in Washington DC.

By 1890 franchise holders were selling machines to fairgrounds and amusement arcades, where for a nickel interested listeners could hear recordings of, for instance, minstrel songs and marches played by Sousa's band, thus establishing early on the principle of 'pay per play', as well as two of the primary musical genres of the acoustic era of recording: popular songs and music for military and brass bands. A key weakness of the early phonograph machines was that the cylinders they used could not be easily duplicated. Thus, as demand grew, copies could only be made by performers repeating their act many times, although devices based on the pantograph were developed which could handle simultaneous recording on linked batteries of machines.

Also in 1887, Emile Berliner had patented his own system, recording onto a zinc disc covered with beeswax and benzene. When the disc was placed in acid, a groove was etched onto the zinc. From this a reverse matrix could be made, with raised grooves; this in turn could be used to stamp out duplicates of the original. At a stroke Berliner had created a process that overcame the critical commercial weakness of the phonograph, of not being easy to duplicate. With the invention of this process, he laid the foundations for the gramophone and the global recording industry of the twentieth century.

At first the gramophone and its discs were seen as toys: Berliner's first licensee, from 1889, was the German toy manufacturer Kammerer & Reinhardt, which had limited success with his invention. In 1895 the Philadelphia Syndicate was formed to manufacture both discs and players, initially for sale in the USA, under the name of the Berliner Company. Once (from 1896) Eldridge Johnson's clockwork motors were installed in Berliner's originally hand-cranked gramophones to provide regular speed for their turntables, sales started to grow rapidly. In the financial year 1897/8 the Berliner Company sold 11,211 gramophones and 408,195 records.[3] A series of lawsuits then halted growth until the two principal parties involved, the Berliner and Columbia companies, were merged by Johnson into the Victor Talking Machine Company. By 1903 this company was selling approximately 2 million discs and accounted for approximately a third of the total American record sales of 6 million units.[4]

In 1897 Berliner sent William Barry Owen to England to sell the European rights for the gramophone processes. Initially Owen meet with little interest until he, with Berliner in America, was able to persuade a young lawyer, Trevor Williams, of the gramophone's potential. Williams and a small group of investors formed the Gramophone Company in 1898. Gramophones were assembled from parts manufactured in the USA, but recordings were made locally – a shrewd move on which Williams insisted. In charge of recording was Fred Gaisberg, who had known and worked with Berliner since the creation of the gramophone. Gaisberg commenced recording in the United Kingdom in mid-1898. Demand for the company's products proved to be huge. In order to satisfy the international markets which quickly opened up, and which were exploited through a system of affiliated branches of the Gramophone Company,[5] an extensive programme of recording was initiated. Gaisberg visited the major European cities to record in 1899; the following year he covered Northern Europe and Scandinavia; 1900 saw him in Russia, and during 1902 and 1903 he travelled to the Far East. Following initial reluctance from established opera singers to record for the new process – 'They just laughed at us,' Fred reported in 1900 – the recruitment of the persuasive young pianist, coach and conductor Landon Ronald as musical adviser to the company in 1900, combined with the phenomenal success of the records that the tenor Enrico Caruso made for Gaisberg in Milan two years later, meant that by 1905 the last major star in the operatic firmament to resist making records, Adelina Patti, had succumbed to the Gramophone Company's entreaties to record for it. The gramophone was certainly no longer a toy but the basis of a major international business, as well as becoming socially acceptable.

Acoustic recording favoured sound sources with plenty of aural 'attack', such as brass and plucked instruments and the human voice. Softer-edged sounds such as those of the piano and stringed instruments were less clearly captured by the early recording horn. Thus the repertoire recorded for this period was largely dictated by what would record well for the process then in use. Demand for records was such that most items would achieve some level of sales, but the catalogues featured predominantly recordings by military bands, music-hall artists who were used to projecting in the rowdy conditions of the Victorian and Edwardian theatres and halls, and opera singers, also fully experienced in vocal projection in similar if more elite premises. Edison's phonograph was also used by ethnographers, such as Bartók in Hungary in 1906, for capturing local folk music (and continued to be until about 1940), as well as by enthusiasts such as the librarian of the Metropolitan Opera, New York, Lionel Mapleson, who between 1900 and 1904 recorded short extracts from the company's performances, precariously located above the stage with his recording machine.

C. 1907–c. 1925

In 1907 Alfred Clark, aged thirty-two and a former employee of both Berliner and Edison, had earned enough money from setting up and running a

French subsidiary of the Gramophone Company from 1899 onwards to retire to a château in the Loire. This act neatly symbolises the end of the first phase of the growth of the recording industry, just as Clark's acceptance a year later of the post of Managing Director of the Gramophone Company in England may be taken as the start of the second phase. Before Clark took up his new position, another American, Louis Sterling, had left the phonograph business, which he believed had little future (although companies such as Pathé in France were selling large quantities of cylinders and players), and had taken over the British branch of the American Columbia company, which had unsuccessfully been trying to sell American recordings on disc to the English. Sterling was a most effective salesman and manager, and suddenly the Gramophone Company was faced with aggressive competition from Columbia (UK). To increase its dominant position, the Gramophone Company agreed with the Victor Talking Machine Company to divide the world into two territories in each of which one of the companies would sell both its own and its partner's recordings. Victor took control of the USA, Canada and South America, while the Gramophone Company appropriated Europe, Africa, India, Russia and Australasia. To meet continuously growing demand, the Gramophone Company ceased importing its pressings from Hanover in Germany and opened a large factory at Hayes, Middlesex, initially equipped with twenty-eight record presses.

While in the USA Victor and Columbia (USA) were able in the short term to maintain some control of the record industry as a duopoly, in Europe competitors to the main concerns started to spring up. In Germany the Carl Lindström conglomerate published records on labels such as Odeon, Parlophon and Fonotipia, and grew into a serious international rival to both the Victor and Gramophone companies. In Argentina, for instance, where sales of records of largely indigenous music manufactured abroad had approximately doubled between 1909 and 1910 to 1.75 million discs,[6] Lindström set up its own factory in 1913 to speed up production and distribution, and to reduce costs. In the same year 2.7 million records were sold there.[7] At the time of the outbreak of the First World War Lindström was planning to open a factory in the United States. In the years immediately before 1914, world sales were estimated at approximately 50 million discs per annum, with Germany, Russia and the United Kingdom accounting for approximately 10 million units each.

The outbreak of war had a major negative effect upon the European side of the record business. The Gramophone Company's new factory at Hayes was partly given over to armaments manufacture, and although patriotic fervour gave an initial boost to record sales, this did not last. In Germany the company's matrices (master recordings) housed at Hanover were seized by the German government. In the face of the German advance, the Gramophone Company's factory at Riga, which had served the whole of Northern Europe and Russia, was abandoned. Production was resumed on a much smaller scale in Moscow, but this again was to cease in 1917 with the outbreak of the Russian Revolution.

In America, however, no such negative effects were felt: in 1915 record sales were estimated to have reached 18.6 million units. The American market was to experience further growth after 1919 when the Supreme Court ruled that the cartel operated by the Victor and Columbia (USA) companies was illegal. New companies sprang up and 100 million records were estimated to have been sold in the USA in 1920,[8] with a figure of 106 million being achieved in the following year.[9] Bankruptcy ensued for several companies during 1922 and 1923, threatening even Columbia (USA), but by the middle of the decade, despite the perceived threat of the new technology of radio broadcasting, record sales were extremely buoyant, totalling 70 million units in both 1926 and 1927.

In Europe it took longer for the industry to re-establish itself. In 1920 the Gramophone Company's American partner, the Victor Company, bought half the English company's ordinary shares, thus providing a welcome injection of capital. The German element of the Gramophone Company, now independent and renamed Deutsche Grammophon, released its recordings predominantly on the Polydor label. To regain a presence in the important German market, the Gramophone Company established a new German label, Electrola. Not to be outdone, during the 1920s the fiercely competitive Sterling engineered a management buyout of the British branch of Columbia (UK). The previously important Russian market had by now, however, vanished, with the advent of the Communist government. The European market for both recordings and gramophones was thus effectively dominated by two organisations, Gramophone and Columbia (UK), generating competition that pushed sales to new heights for much of the remainder of the decade.

The competitive nature of the record industry, which began to come more sharply into focus with Sterling's acquisition of Columbia (UK) in 1923, had a discernible effect upon the repertoire offered to the public. For instance, following the great success of Lehár's operetta *The Merry Widow* in London in 1907, excerpts from which Columbia (UK) recorded with the original cast, the label sought to corner the market in original-cast recordings of popular musical comedies. Similarly, songs popularised through summer resort shows were recorded, to be available to returning holiday-makers in the major metropolitan areas. With the Gramophone Company having cornered the market in opera singers, Columbia (UK) looked elsewhere for distinctiveness in the field of classical music and saw it in conductors. In 1915 it signed up both Sir Henry Wood and Sir Thomas

Beecham, artists with whom it was to be closely associated for many years. Despite the exigencies of acoustic recording techniques, the recording of orchestral music developed significantly after the advent of peace in 1918. Both Columbia (UK) and Gramophone added other currently distinguished conductors to their lists, as well as major contemporary composers conducting their own works. In Germany, with the need to re-establish a new catalogue now that it was independent, Deutsche Grammophon embarked upon a programme of recording complete works, as did Lindström's Parlophon label. From 1923 the two major English labels followed suit, preparing the ground for an expansion of activity following the introduction of electrical recording.

While the First World War had a dampening effect upon innovation in Europe, this was not the case across the Atlantic. The first recording of a white jazz band, the Dixieland Jazz Band, was made by Victor in 1917. The growth of small labels following the break-up of the Victor–Columbia (USA) cartel also saw the introduction of 'race records', by labels such as the Okeh marque and the short-lived Black Swan, featuring black musicians and intended solely for the black market. Their records included the earliest recordings of the jazz and blues genre. In the field of jazz, the first black New Orleans band to be recorded was Kid Ory's Sunshine Band, in 1922; by 1925 the American market was flooded with jazz records. At the same time location visits for recording purposes to rural areas in the United States, which captured many of the contemporary blues performers, also yielded the first recordings of white 'hillbilly' music, which later grew into the repertoire category 'country and western'.

In England recordings of dance bands, or 'rhythm' records, found a large and ready market after the end of the First World War. Following the lead of the American Paul Whiteman in performing orchestrated jazz, the Gramophone Company started to release similar repertoire in 1921. Hotels, restaurants and night clubs fed this genre: dance bands brought in customers and added prestige, while regular location broadcasts by the new British Broadcasting Company from 1923 effectively added to the marketing mix, although few recognised this initially. The two most popular bands of the period, the Savoy Havana Band and the Savoy Orpheans, made over 300 titles between 1922 and 1927,[10] setting a trend that was to grow even further with the advent of electrical recording.

C. 1925–c. 1948

A major change, both technological and commercial, took place at the beginning of 1925, when Sterling, having heard some test records of the new electrical recording process developed by the Western Electric Company, travelled to the USA, bought a controlling interest in Columbia (UK)'s parent company, Columbia (USA) (as the latter would not invest in the new recording system and Western Electric would not sell the rights to European companies), and signed a licence agreement for this new process, which had also been adopted by Victor. This new technology, known as electrical recording, ushered in a new phase in the growth of the industry. Electrical recording, through the use of the microphone in place of the acoustic horn, captured a greater sound range, and so yielded noticeably improved fidelity of sound in reproduction. In addition it generally permitted musicians to maintain their usual platform positions, unlike the acoustic system of recording which required close proximity to the recording devices. Sterling went on to acquire controlling interests in the Okeh label, Lindström, the Dutch company Transoceanic (also active in South America), the Japanese company Nipponophone and the French company Pathé, thus intensifying competition with the Gramophone Company throughout the latter half of the 1920s.

This third phase in the history of the recording industry witnessed significant social and political changes, all of which had major impacts upon the development of the industry. Initially the return to prosperity during the 1920s triggered increasing consumer spending in both Europe and the USA. For the recording industry, demand was further stimulated by the improved sound quality of electrical recording, by extensions of the repertoires recorded, and by commercial competition driven by several labels seeking to exploit this beneficent environment. In the USA sales totalled 150 million discs in 1929, a level that was not be to be reached again for many years.[11] Of these records 34 million were sold by RCA-Victor (as the Victor Company had become following its acquisition by the Radio Corporation of America). In Europe, sales in the same year in the United Kingdom and Germany totalled 60 million units, split equally across both countries.[12] The Wall Street Crash of October 1929, and the ensuing Great Depression, stopped this growth in its tracks. In the USA Edison ceased production altogether while labels such as Columbia (USA), Brunswick and Okeh contracted significantly, and RCA-Victor concentrated its efforts on wireless set manufacture. By 1933 total sales were a mere 10 million units, of which RCA-Victor accounted for only 3.6 million units.[13]

In the USA recovery began to take place as the 1930s progressed. The election of Franklin D. Roosevelt as President in 1932 and the institution of the New Deal gradually brought the economy round. By 1935 record sales were starting to climb again: total sales for 1936 were in excess of 20 million units,[14] and by 1938 had reached 33 million units.[15] In the same year, Edward Wallerstein persuaded the head of the Columbia Broadcasting System (CBS), William Paley, to buy Consolidated Film Laboratories' record-company holdings. Control of Columbia (USA) had passed back to the USA when Consolidated had acquired it, along with the Pathé, Brunswick and Vocalion labels among others, as the deleterious effects of the Depression had been felt earlier in the decade. Once installed as head of Columbia (USA), Wallerstein in 1940 dramatically reduced the price of its records. RCA-Victor, owner of the National Broadcasting Company (NBC) network and so CBS's broadcasting as well as record-industry rival, and controlled by another commercial titan, David Sarnoff, was compelled to follow suit. Consumers reacted positively, with the result that by 1942 record sales had risen dramatically to 127 million units. With a war to fight and win the American economy went into overdrive, and by 1946, the year after peace was finally declared, record sales had reached 218 million units,[16] despite two major trade disputes, with ASCAP, one of the two American copyright agencies, and with the American Federation of Musicians, both of which had earlier put a brake on record sales.

In Europe, the logic for a merger of the Gramophone Company and Columbia (UK) proved irresistible, although the 'fusion' of the two companies had already been discussed before the Crash occurred.[17] In 1931 EMI (Electric and Music Industries) was formed with Alfred Clark as Chairman and Louis Sterling as Managing Director. Apart from Deutsche Grammophon in Germany, EMI effectively now held a monopoly in all the territories in which it operated. As was the custom in this period with holding companies, the individual component parts of EMI, identified by its different labels, operated in competition with each other while sharing manufacturing facilities. The only competitor to EMI's dominance during the 1930s was the young Decca label, created in 1929 when the stockbroker Edward Lewis purchased the Decca Gramophone Company and branched out into record manufacture as well as making players.

The rise of National Socialism in Germany and the assumption of power by Hitler in 1933 had a highly deleterious effect upon that country's musical life. Leading Jewish musicians, among many others, left the country, many settling in America; those who remained were not permitted to work. The restrictions upon the publication, recording and performance of music written by Jewish composers severely restricted catalogue development. By 1936 annual record sales in Germany were hovering around 5 million units.[18] With a sluggish economy throughout the continent, the presence of a monopoly in France and Great Britain, and a dictatorship in Germany, the pre-conditions for growth within the record industry did not exist in Europe during the 1930s. The situation deteriorated even further with the outbreak of the Second World War in 1939. Supplies of shellac (imported from the Far East) were limited and, as in the First World War, factories were partly turned over to armaments manufacture. Wartime economies did not allow for either the significant production or the purchase of gramophone records. As had been the case in 1919, by 1945 the industry in Europe was a hollow shell of what it once had been.

The intense competition of the later 1920s drove considerable expansion of the gramophone record catalogue, especially for classical music. The centenary of Beethoven's death in 1927 was marked by the issue of many of the composer's major works by both Columbia (UK) and HMV, the Gramophone Company's foremost label. This was followed by similar celebrations for Schubert in 1928, when the scene for rivalry moved to La Scala, Milan, with both companies recording the core operatic repertoire using this company's forces. Once the most popular works had been committed to disc across all labels, rivalry then took the form of each company building similar tranches of what might be termed the 'music appreciation' catalogue, drawing upon the traditional symphonic repertoire, but distinguished by the participation of rival musicians. This process in turn gave rise to the concept of the 'star' or 'celebrity' conductor, with each company proclaiming the definitive character of their particular champion's interpretations. The most vigorously promoted example of this tendency during this period was Arturo Toscanini, for whom Sarnoff formed the NBC Symphony Orchestra in 1937.[19] In Europe the need for international sales favoured those musicians with international concert careers, to the detriment of the present and future reputation of many local musicians.

In the field of popular music, in the USA recording executives recognised different demographic markets for emerging musical niches, such as jazz, blues and country music. In the mid-1930s it was big band swing that captured the public's imagination and assisted the restoration of financial health to the industry. In Europe the enthusiasm for dance band music, often with saccharine vocals, persisted throughout the period to the end of the Second World War. With the advent in 1927 of films with sound, initially known as 'talkies', the relationship between the film and recording industries became closer: singing stars such as Gracie Fields and George Formby built upon the success of their recordings by appearing in hugely popular locally produced films. This period also saw the rise of the record producer. In the United Kingdom Fred Gaisberg was the dominant figure in determining what was recorded by EMI.[20] The success of the 'Society' concept, whereby prospective purchasers subscribed to records in advance of their production, thus minimising any financial risk for EMI, was developed by Walter Legge to maintain freshness of repertoire – an early step in a distinguished career.[21] In the USA Charles O'Connell was given charge of RCA-Victor's Red Label catalogue of classical music and developed both friends and foes as a result.[22] John Hammond used recording to defy the social taboo on mixed-race jazz bands, and in the process became one of America's most distinguished producers of jazz, folk and popular music.[23]

This period also witnessed several technological innovations that together were to play significant roles in the later growth of the industry. Alan Blumlein, working at EMI's Central Research Laboratories, devised a system for recording stereophonically during 1930, and two years later Bell Telephone Company engineers made several experimental stereophonic recordings with Leopold Stokowski and the Philadelphia Orchestra. The cumbersome playback systems of the period prevented the adoption of either system. In Germany in 1935 AEG displayed its 'Magnetophon', which recorded sound onto magnetic tape. The 'Magnetophon' was to be extensively used during the Second World War to record performances for delayed broadcasting in order to boost morale by giving a semblance of normality. At the same time Decca engineers were developing their company's 'full frequency range recording' system through work for the British War Office. This extended the range of sound that could be recorded from approximately 10,000 to 15,000 kilocycles. The application of this technology to the recording of orchestral music in particular would greatly improve the quality of sound available to the consumer. The final, and perhaps most significant, innovation of the period was the use of plastic vinyl for the manufacture of gramophone records themselves. Originally developed in the USA to overcome the difficulties presented by the shortage of shellac, and to allow for the easy transportation (generally by post) of recordings, vinyl was the essential ingredient for the long-playing record, revolving at 33⅓ rpm. When Edward Wallerstein launched Columbia (USA)'s innovation in the summer of 1948 the music contained in a two-metre pile of 78s was duplicated by a forty-centimetre stack of LPs.[24]

C. 1948–c. 1983

The two major innovations of magnetic tape recording and the vinyl long-playing record that entered the commercial chain at the end of the 1940s had major consequences for the record industry. The use of tape for recording allowed for longer recording time, and did away with the need for perfection of performance during a single take. With editing it became possible to cut out an error and replace it with a correction. Furthermore the creative possibilities of working with tape paved the way for the adoption of different philosophies of recording in both the commercial and creative spheres. Tape-recording machines were also relatively portable and so opened up the possibility of recording, for both private and public uses, in many more locations than had been used in the past.

The double-sided long-playing vinyl record (colloquially known as the LP) allowed for the recording of many new repertoires by permitting between 20 and 25 minutes of uninterrupted playing time per side, without the physical degradation that had been experienced with the materials used earlier for long playback. Columbia (USA) astutely also offered to press records for any company that wished to make use of the new long-playing process. The combination of a buoyant commercial environment in the USA, tape-recording equipment, excellent musicians in Europe eager to work for limited pay, and easier access to methods of production resulted in the growth of many smaller labels, serving various different niche markets. These might be dedicated, for instance, to a single composer or to a specific musical genre. Effectively the independent label movement took root at this time. These technological innovations also marked the beginning of the shift of power away from the producer to the consumer, although it was to be some time before the tipping-point of change was reached.

By the end of the 1940s, approximately half the global output of records was manufactured and sold in the USA. Sales of recordings in the USA in 1948 were estimated to be worth $189 million.[25] They dipped slightly the following year, as RCA-Victor and Columbia (USA) fought the 'speed wars', with RCA-Victor bringing out the seven-inch 45 rpm disc to spite Columbia (USA)'s LP, before both companies agreed to use the former predominantly for popular music and the latter initially for classical music. Between 1950, when sales returned to the level of 1948, and 1957, the year before the introduction of stereophonic discs, sales in the USA grew steadily to $460 million. Bearing in mind the differences in currency valuation (in 1950 $1 was worth slightly less than 40 pence), in 1950 global sales excluding the USA were estimated to be worth approximately £29 million, with sales in the United Kingdom, France and Germany accounting for about £2.5 million each. By 1955 these figures were estimated to have grown by about 45 per cent.[26]

At the start of this period 90 per cent of American records were devoted to different forms of popular music: commercial songs and dance band music accounted for the majority, followed by country music, jazz, and rhythm and blues. This mix did not change dramatically during the first half of the 1950s. Significant change in published repertoire began to take place from the middle of the decade onwards, fuelled by the advent of the post-war 'baby boom', and the desire of youth to align itself to musical forms different from those favoured by its progenitors. The object of attention was rock 'n' roll, essentially a white spin-off from rhythm and blues. Greater air-play of recordings on radio assisted the consequent dramatic growth of this genre, as did the increasing presence of many smaller, independent labels. Whereas, between 1946 and 1952, 158 of the 163 recordings that sold more than 1 million units were produced by the major record companies,[27] between 1955 and 1959, of the 147 'Top Ten' records produced, forty-six emanated from the majors and 101 from the independent labels.[28]

The introduction of stereo discs in 1958 acted as a further spur to growth. Recording in stereophonic sound had been developing since the early 1950s, and commercial stereo tapes had been on the American market since 1954, when the major companies also began to record classical repertoire in this new medium, thus creating a bank of recordings ready for later release. Intense domestic interest in stereo in the USA fuelled the development of the stereo disc, and above all a uniform specification for creating it which was rapidly adopted by the whole of the record industry. Stereo discs had the colossal advantage of reverse compatibility. Older mono LPs could be played on new stereo reproducers to often enhanced effect, while stereo discs could be played, if not to best effect, on older mono gramophones. Stereo also allowed for the possibility of further significant creative interventions in the process of record production. In the field of classical music these possibilities were recognised and articulated only by the producer John Culshaw and the pianist Glenn Gould, whereas in popular music they featured strongly in global successes such as the Beatles's *Sergeant Pepper's Lonely Hearts Club Band*, produced by George Martin, and became a commonplace in popular music record production.[29] The impact that stereo had on the record market, together with continuing years of peace, as well as of protest against the Vietnam War, all of which in different ways stimulated record sales, may be seen in the supercharged growth that took place in both America and Europe between 1960 and 1970 (Table 6.1).

By 1970 the corporate terrain had changed significantly. In the early 1950s EMI suffered from poor leadership: the Columbia (USA) label broke

Table 6.1[30]

	US: sales ($)	UK: sales (units)	France: sales (units)
1960	600 mil	72 mil	28 mil
1970	1,660 mil (+177%)	114 mil (+58%)	62 mil (+121%)

its longstanding reciprocal agreement with EMI for record production and distribution, and for its European operations went into partnership with a new entrant, the Dutch electrical company Philips. A short time later, RCA-Victor did likewise and vested its English pressing, marketing and distribution functions with Decca, an arrangement that was reputed to be more valuable to Decca in financial terms than all of its own recording activities. Urgently needing an outlet for its productions in the USA, EMI in turn purchased the Capitol label, just as a few years later Philips purchased Mercury. In 1962 Philips and Deutsche Grammophon formed an alliance under the banner Polygram, formally merging in 1972. In the USA, CBS, the owner of the Columbia (USA) label, and RCA, the parent of the RCA-Victor label, had been joined as major companies by Warner Records, initially a subsidiary company of the film studio of the same name, which had grown by acquiring several independent labels, such as Atlantic and Reprise. Thus by the start of the 1980s there were five multinational record companies operating globally, three of which were American and two European in ownership: CBS, RCA, Warner, EMI and Polygram. Between them these companies were responsible for approximately 50 per cent of global record production.[31] Each sought to maintain competitive advantage by buying independent companies which in effect acted as 'off-shore' research and development operations.

Further growth was fuelled by the introduction of the compact cassette at the end of the 1960s. While this technology had the benefit of low duplication and so production costs, it also contained within it the seeds of the destruction of the record industry as it was then constituted, by offering the possibility of easy duplication of published recordings. This facet only became obvious with the production of 'music centres' intended for the home market and which combined turntable, radio and cassette recorder, thus offering the opportunity of painless domestic recording. The cassette also allowed for rampant piracy in second-world countries where copyright control mechanisms were weak. In India, for instance, vinyl records had virtually disappeared by 1982.[32] Nonetheless in the West for most of the 1970s growth continued, as may be seen in Table 6.2 (percentage increases measured from similar figures for 1970).

By the end of the decade it was clear, as sales stabilised at around this level, that a new sound-carrier which initially defied easy duplication

Table 6.2[33]

	US sales ($)	US sales (units)	UK sales (units)	France (units)
1978	4,131 mil (+149%)	762.2 mil	196 mil (+72%)	157 mil (+ 153%)

was urgently needed if further growth was to be achieved by the record industry. The answer lay in digital sound recording and reproduction, and its domestic carrier, the compact disc, which was introduced into Europe in 1983.

C. 1983–c. 1998

The introduction of the compact disc to the world market initially allowed the record industry once again to achieve high rates of growth. The digital format, which is based upon the conversion of sound into binary units and which is also the language of information technology and specifically computers, was not at first easily duplicated in the form of the CD, and so saw off the threat from cassette players, which had effectively destroyed the vinyl disc as a sound-carrier. At the same time the new format allowed for higher retail prices to be charged, and for greater profits to be earned. Furthermore, once the initial flurry of excitement about new digital recordings had died down, record companies realised that the re-packaging of old recordings as reissues in the new format allowed for both higher income and lower costs.

Adoption of the compact disc across the world followed a pattern not dissimilar to that experienced with the replacement of the 78 rpm record by the long-playing disc. Introduced into the USA during the summer of 1983, by 1986 the CD had captured there a tenth of recorded music sales; within the next two years the CD overtook the LP in sales, and by 1990 LP production was being phased out.[34] A similar pattern of development was experienced in the other major territories for commercial recorded sound, such as Japan, the United Kingdom and Germany. The impact of the CD on consumption may be seen in Table 6.3, which compares sales figures for 1981, at the end of the LP era, with those for 1995, by which time the CD was well established: the International Federation of Phonographic Industries (IFPI) reported that in 1995 annual global sales of recorded music had achieved an unprecedented level of 3.8 billion units, with a value of $40 billion.[35]

Table 6.3

	1981 (units)	1995 (units)
USA	593 mil	1,100.5 mil (+86%)
Japan	202.5 mil	416.6 mil (+106%)
UK	170.2 mil	266.9 mil (+57%)
Germany (FRG)	202 mil	252.8 mil (+25%)

The corporate terrain during this period underwent a significant shift, with foreign companies buying two major labels. In 1986 RCA sold RCA-Victor, the oldest and most senior of American record companies, to the German book and magazine publisher Bertelsmann. The following year CBS followed suit, selling its Columbia (USA) label to the Japanese hardware manufacturer Sony. In 1989 Warner Records merged with another publisher: the Time Incorporated magazine organisation. Polygram, which had acquired the English Decca label in 1980, was acquired in 1998 by Universal Music, which in turn became part of the Vivendi conglomerate in 2000. EMI remained independent – the only multinational record company remaining whose main purpose was the production and selling of records.

These changes had a profound impact upon the recording of classical music in particular. Whereas in the days of the dedicated record company classical music sales had been permitted extended periods of time for the return on capital employed to be achieved, in general at least two years but in some cases considerably more, the advent of corporate accounting policies, which frequently demanded faster rates of return, allied to very high sales achieved by particular releases that were substantially aided by television exposure, resulted in classical music releases being expected to cover their costs within periods of a year or even less. As a result classical divisions moved away from the traditional repertoire and into areas such as 'crossover', which mixed popular music with classical procedures, and in addition abandoned previously innovative avenues of catalogue development, such as period performance. Such areas were left to the numerous independent labels, which in classical music at least moved into many of the repertoire fields previously dominated by the major companies. In addition several orchestras and individual musicians, acknowledging the enormous power of the publication of recordings as a marketing medium, developed their own labels, often using (less expensive) concert rather than studio recordings as a basis for such releases.

C. 1998–

The digital nature of compact discs proved to be an Achilles heel for the record industry, as a result of the international adoption of computers for both business and domestic applications, the rapid spread of usage of the internet, and the creation of the MP3 file format. Once CD-ROM and writing drives became standard, personal computers could copy CDs while MP3 and similar file formats allowed sound to be held as a computer file and hence easily transported through the world wide web. Thus the control of sound-recording carriers rapidly passed away from commercial organisations and to the consumer. The record industry spent much of its energies from the turn of the millennium onwards in defending its right to control the distribution and use of its publications, but with limited effect. The introduction into the market of simple-to-use music-file carriers such as the iPod, manufactured by the hardware company Apple Computer and launched in 2001, marked a decisive shift away from sound recordings as concrete objects and towards their general adoption as dematerialised artifacts. The impact of these developments on the established supply chain for recordings continues to evolve. One noticeable victim has been the mass retail chains, which have seen themselves squeezed by high-volume suppliers to the public such as supermarkets on the one hand, and on the other by individuals accessing what they want when they want (ironically Alfred Clark's initial justification for the commercial vitality of gramophone records) through the internet, as either discs, often purchased at lower costs than the high street can offer, or as sound files, from either formal or informal providers. Sales of CDs have effectively collapsed: in the USA between 2000 and 2005 they fell by 25 per cent in volume and by 20 per cent in value.[36] In 2007 one major United Kingdom retailer, HMV, forecast a reduction on sales of compact discs by 26 per cent, or a quarter of total sales, within the two-year period to 2009. On present evidence of past changes in the record industry, this estimate looks to be conservative and the future life of the CD to be limited.

In this environment the supply of music to the public is likely to take two forms.[37] On the one hand it may develop in the same way that public utilities such as water have done: it will become generally available to consumers in return for a subscription that is paid regularly to the supplier. The cost-per-time unit of consumption in this scenario is likely to be much lower than previously experienced (in fact the history of the recording industry is one of the progressive reduction of the cost to the consumer per unit of recorded time). At the same time, and as part of this development, recorded music will be consumed through an increasing number of devices, such as mobile phones and personal organisers, and through social networks powered by the internet: it will become truly ubiquitous as a mass medium. On the other hand specialist publishers and retailers are likely to cater for those consumers with specific requirements, and who are prepared to pay for the satisfaction of these, with specialised products, similar to designer bottled waters. At this end of the scale costs to the consumer could actually increase: in-depth knowledge and understanding both of catalogues and of customer requirements, and exceptional customer care, are likely to be critical success factors.

Industrially the major record companies are likely to become primarily sound archives, seeking to spin out the use of their copyright holdings in music for as long as they can. Independent production, which in the post-war era has progressively developed as an important source of supply to the major companies, either through absorption or licensing, will become a principal avenue to publication and distribution. The process of further fragmentation which this implies may mean that the income previously attained from the sale of recordings by musicians could fall. The progression of the gradual loss of the monopolistic control of production, which has been a leitmotif in the first century of the record industry, is likely to be completed unless a major new proprietary technology for the domestic consumption of sound and image is brought to the international market. The irony here is that, while the disc as a tangible object may be dead, humankind's insatiable desire to listen to music is likely to result in an ever-greater variety of musical genres being created and made available to the public through an ever-increasing variety of technological channels.

Significant movements in ownership of major record companies

1888	North American Phonograph Company formed from Edison and Tainter and Bell patents to exploit commercial applications of cylinders.
1889	Columbia Phonograph Company formed, as agent of North American Phonograph Company in the District of Washington (DC).
1889	Berliner licenses Kämmerer and Reinhardt in Germany to produce gramophones and discs as toys.
1892	Berliner forms the United States Gramophone Company.
1892	Columbia severs links with Edison and North American Phonograph Company and henceforth sells only its own products.
1893	Carl Lindström Company formed, initially to manufacture gramophones and later discs. The company's numerous labels included: Bekka, Fonotipia, Jumbo, Odeon, Parlophon. Active in Europe and South America.
1897	Gramophone Company formed in United Kingdom with exclusive rights from Berliner to sell gramophones and discs in Europe (from 1900 to 1907 named the Gramophone and Typewriter Company).
1898	Berliner forms Deutsche Grammophon Gesellschaft to press records for the Gramophone Company.
1900	Columbia label introduced into Europe.

1901	Victor Talking Machine Company formed in USA to produce gramophones and discs from Berliner's inventions. Together with the Columbia Company (Columbia (USA)), which in the same year starts to sell discs, maintains US monopoly until 1910.
1905	Pathé Company, already formed in France and manufacturing phonographs and cylinders, starts to manufacture and sell discs, but with vertically cut grooves and played from centre to edge.
1909	Gramophone Company starts to use the 'His Master's Voice' image.
1914	Deutsche Grammophon separates from parent company, moves into German hands, and releases records on the Polydor and Polyphon labels.
1919	Victor and Columbia (USA) cartel declared illegal by US Supreme Court. Many small labels created as a result, e.g. Black Swan, Cameo, Gennett, Grey Gull, Paramount, Perfect, Plaza.
1920	Victor buys significant interest in the Gramophone Company to assist the re-capitalisation of the company after the First World War.
1920	Brunswick Records starts to sell lateral cut records and soon establishes itself as a rival to Victor and Columbia in the USA.
1923	Lindström establishes the British branch of the Parlophon / Parlophone label.
1923	Columbia (UK)'s British management buys Columbia (UK) from Columbia (USA).
1925	Columbia (UK) buys Columbia (USA), to exploit electrical recording patents available only to American companies.
1925	Gramophone Company creates Electrola label to market records in Germany.
1926	Columbia (UK) buys the American Okeh label.
1920s	Columbia (UK) buys controlling interests in Lindström (1926); Transoceanic Trading (a Dutch company formed to exploit Lindström's overseas assets); Nipponophone and Pathé.
1927	Consortium of US banks buys controlling interest in Victor.
1929	Radio Corporation of America (RCA) buys Victor from banks and creates the RCA-Victor label.
1929	Decca Record Company formed in UK to manufacture discs. Decca Gramophone Company already in existence as manufacturer of gramophones, notably during the First World War.
1930	Consolidated Film Laboratories buys Cameo and Plaza labels and the American branch of Pathé.

1931	Consolidated Film Laboratories buys the Brunswick and Vocalion labels.
1931	Gramophone Company and Columbia (UK) merge to form Electric and Musical Industries (EMI).
1931	Columbia (UK) sells Columbia (USA) to Grigsby-Gronow Corporation.
1932	Decca buys the UK branch of Brunswick Records.
1934	Consolidated Film Laboratories (through its American Record Corporation operation) buys Columbia (USA) from the Grigsby-Gronow Corporation.
1934	Decca Record Company establishes an American subsidiary of the same name, and buys Gennett's recordings.
1930s	Record labels under the Nazi regime: EMI: Electrola; EMI–Lindström: Columbia, Odeon; Siemens: Deutsche Grammophon, Telefunken.
1938	Columbia Broadcasting System (CBS) buys entire Consolidated Films' record concern, including Columbia (USA) label.
1939–45	Decca has to dispose of Decca label in the USA, after which the American label functions separately.
1939	Blue Note label formed.
1941	Siemens buys Deutsche Grammophon.
1942	Capitol label formed, the first major label to be based on the west coast of America.
1943	King Records label formed.
1945	Mercury label formed.
1946	MGM records label founded by the Metro-Goldwyn-Mayer film studio to release soundtrack albums.
1947	Atlantic label formed.
1948	Columbia (USA) releases the first long-playing (LP) records.
1948	Folkways label formed.
1949	Prestige and Westminster labels formed.
1950	Chess and Philips labels formed.
1951	Deutsche Grammophon releases its first LP.
1952	Columbia (USA) switches its European distribution from EMI (which markets the Columbia (UK) label) to Philips.
1955	EMI buys Capitol label and initiates the Angel label in the USA.
1957	RCA-Victor switches its European distribution from EMI to Decca.
1958	Warner Bros. Records formed.
1959	Tamla Records formed, later known as Motown.
1960s	CBS and RCA establish subsidiary companies in the UK.
1961	Philips acquires the Mercury label.

1962	Deutsche Grammophon and Philips begin to collaborate through a 50 per cent share swap, and the creation of the Phonogram company.
1962	Music Corporation of America (MCA) buys the American Decca label.
1960s/70s	Warner label grows by acquiring middle-level labels: Reprise (1963), Atlantic (1967), Elektra (1972), Nonesuch (1972), Asylum (1972), and Erato (1992).
1972	Phonogram merges with Polydor to form Polygram, which acquires *inter alia* MGM (1972), Decca (1980), Island (1989), Motown (1994).
1972	EMI Records label created, absorbing the HMV and Columbia (UK) labels.
1970s	Major dedicated international record companies: CBS/EMI/Polygram/RCA/Warner.
1977	Thorn Electronics buys EMI to form Thorn-EMI.
1979	EMI buys record division of United Artists.
1983	Philips releases the first compact discs in Europe.
1986	Bertellsmann Music Group (BMG) buys record division of RCA.
1987	Siemens sells its interest in Polygram to Philips, which becomes the majority shareholder in the company.
1987	Sony buys record division of CBS.
1987	Naxos label founded.
1990	Warner merges with Time-Life Corporation to form Time Warner.
1992	Thorn-EMI acquires Virgin Records.
1995	Seagram Company of Canada, led by Edgar Bronfman Jr, acquires 80 per cent of MCA, and renames it Universal Music in 1996.
1996	Naxos best-selling classical music label in the UK.
1996	EMI demerged from Thorn-EMI to become EMI Group.
1998	Seagram buys Polygram labels and folds them into Universal Music.
2000	Time Warner merges with AOL to form AOL Time Warner.
2000	Vivendi acquires Universal Music from Seagram which ceases to exist.
2002	Electrola merged with the German branch of Virgin Records to form EMI Music Germany.
2004	Edgar Bronfman Jr buys Warner Music Group from AOL Time Warner.
2004	Sony forms a joint venture with BMG.
2007	The venture capital company Terra Firma acquires EMI Group.
2008	Sony acquires BMG.

Revisiting concert life in the mid-century: The survival of acetate discs

LEWIS FOREMAN

It is remarkable that we are still seeing the release on compact disc of newly discovered off-air recordings of live performances from the thirty or more years after the mid-1930s, which many assumed had not survived. It reminds us how important was the emergence at this time of direct-cut disc recording. Its development in the UK by Cecil Watts in 1928–32 is vividly recounted by Agnes Watts in her 1972 biography of her husband.[1]

The use in Germany of disc pressings of broadcast material to disseminate programmes between German radio stations meant that such recordings (a few of which survive) were of remarkable fidelity from 1931. From 1935 they began using tape coated with iron oxide, with increasingly high quality as a result, though this Magnetophon sound recording and reproducing technology was not generally available outside Germany before the end of the Second World War, when it was disseminated by the celebrated British Intelligence Objectives Sub-Committee report in 1946.[2] While as early as 1927 Reith had told the BBC Board that close touch was being kept with developments in the recording field, even in the 1930s recording was not a mainstream activity of British broadcasters. In the UK a succession of clumsy, crude recording systems came and went, but the mindset of broadcasters and musicians was not to preserve concerts. Even repeats of concerts on the BBC were achieved by booking the performers twice, and as late as the mid-1950s the major concert series on the Third Programme were always played on Friday evenings and again on Sunday afternoons, and were preserved only if the composers, artists or private individuals had them recorded off-air.

In the UK, the demand for a robust recording system was driven by an imperative to send programmes to the Empire in high quality rather than broadcasting by shortwave through the night to distant time-zones. During the Second World War this was developed by the need to record actuality material for subsequent use at home and overseas, and also to represent Britain, British performers and British music through the BBC's Special Music Recordings catalogue, and later via the Transcription Service. In her wonderful novel *Human Voices*, Penelope Fitzgerald evokes the BBC during the war and the department processing wartime recordings into the archives, referring to 'aluminium discs coated on one side with acetate whose pungent rankness was the true smell of the BBC's war'.[3]

Using equipment supplied by Cecil Watts, the BBC also started a direct recording service in April 1934, although throughout the 1930s it tended to be dependent on the less flexible Blattnerphone. The veteran BBC television announcer Robert Dougall remembered it as 'a clumsy process of recording on steel tapes, requiring large, cumbersome machines'.[4] Indeed, cutting acetate discs suddenly became possible in the home, though only for the rich and technically minded. For most people with an inclination to record off-air, a much more practical solution emerged when commercial direct recording studios appeared in London and elsewhere, particularly in the USA. Better-off composers and artists were thus able to have their performances privately recorded off-air; and while radio stations in the USA and Europe have been the prime sources for live reissues from that time, in the UK it is very often these private recordings that have survived and become available.

At that time most composers were not interested in such activity. One who did have recordings made was Josef Holbrooke, who had not only discs cut – by the Sphinx Studios at 131 Wigmore Street – but also duplicates from them which he used to promote his music. (See Figure PT1.[5]) Holbrooke persuaded his friend Granville Bantock to do the same, and Bantock patronised Watts's M. S. S. Recording Co. Ltd (later called New Marguerite Sound Studios), first at 99a Charing Cross Road and from 1937 as Disc Recording Ltd at Kew. (See Figure PT2.) I was fortunate in being able to include examples of these historical recordings on Dutton Laboratories' Bantock historical CD (CDLX 7043). Indeed, the first track, the 'Shulamite's Monologue' from Bantock's romantic setting of *The Song of Songs*, is remarkable not only for being a BBC Symphony Orchestra broadcast conducted by the composer from 30 March 1936, but also for allowing us to hear the soprano Laelia Finneberg, who is revealed as a considerable artist but whose art does not otherwise survive.[6]

In the 1930s, in addition to HMV cutting waxes for commercial release from Queen's Hall concerts, notably of Toscanini and Koussevitsky, the BBC used a succession of systems, at first with aluminium discs, then the Blattnerphone – huge and heavy reels of steel tape being recorded at high speed. There were also methods using film, including the Philips-Miller system. None of these was particularly convenient to use, and all were certainly outside the remit of the amateur. I am not aware of any Blattnerphone recordings that have survived. Perhaps the most celebrated Philips-Miller recordings are of the BBC's 1942 production of the MacNeice/ Walton *Christopher Columbus*, which has not been issued commercially, and Mengelberg's 1939 Amsterdam performance of the *St Matthew*

Figure PT1 M. S. S. Recording Co. Ltd at 99a Charing Cross Road, receiving station at Hendon. Copy acetate of Holbrooke's own copy of his piano concerto *The Song of Gwyn ap Nudd*, broadcast on 6 May 1936 (Frank Merrick (piano)/LSO/Sir Dan Godfrey) and used for promotional purposes

Passion, which has been re-released, most recently on Naxos 8.110880-2. The disc recorder used by Cecil Watts and the similar equipment in studios across the USA provided the medium for most of the recordings that have survived from the 1930s and 1940s. The first Watts machine was installed at the BBC in April 1934.

In the very early 1930s there was a brief craze for home recording systems.[7] At first they were little more than acoustic dictaphones, such as the Mivoice Speakeasie and Fay Acoustic Home Recorder, though playable on a conventional gramophone. Electrical home systems were not really serious equipment, and the one with such pretensions – the Parmeko – cost twice the price of a car. I know of a single surviving recording of such material, though that is of Henry Wood at Queen's Hall, reissued in 2000 on Symposium 1253. The unique value of such home recordings, and the quality that could be achieved using Permarec discs, have been brought into focus by the presentation to the British Library of the collection of Kenneth Leech. Leech was an engineer and amateur composer of professional training who died as recently as 1995 at the amazing age of 103, leaving his off-air home disc recordings made between 1934 and 1955.[8] There are 1,700 sides. The Elgar Society has issued a remarkable three-CD set (EECD 003-5) taken from this vivid

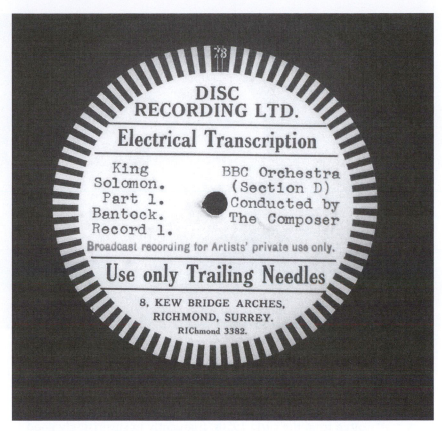

Figure PT2 Disc Recording Ltd at 8 Kew Bridge Arches. Sir Granville Bantock's own recording of his *King Solomon*, broadcast on 6 May 1937 (London Select Choir/BBC Symphony Orchestra/Sir Granville Bantock)

material, all performances that otherwise would never have been heard again. One wonders what else may still be out there in the attics of former enthusiasts' families.

Unique recordings are still turning up. Acetates from the 1930s and 1940s have survived far longer than anyone predicted, but those from before the Second World War are unlikely to last for much longer. In another twenty years most will probably have self-destructed, the victims of chemical change and decomposition in the layer of cellulose acetate holding the recording. So it is vital that records of historical value are copied into a more permanent medium.

Inevitably when one is dealing with collections of recordings once owned by musicians who flourished in the period from the 1930s onward, one comes across examples cut by local recording studios, sometimes of off-air performances, sometimes of private or public performances not otherwise recorded. Usually such collections also include tape recordings,

Figure PT3 Private recording by Levy's. Geoffrey Bush's Concerto for Oboe and Strings, broadcast on 27 August 1956 from The Proms at the Royal Albert Hall (Evelyn Rothwell/Hallé Orchestra/George Weldon)

often from the early 1950s, frequently in surprisingly good sound. Labels from studios cutting 78 rpm discs include the British Recording Service (Bristol), Modern Recording Co. (Piccadilly Arcade, London SW1), Levy's Sound Studios (Bond Street, London; see Figure PT3[9]), Snelson (Swansea), Mercury Sound Recordings (London) and Star Sound Studios (17 Cavendish Square, London W1; see Figure PT4). Undoubtedly the most frequently seen of these from the 1930s was Watts's own M. S. S. Recording Co. Ltd, and later the most widely used was Levy's Sound Studios, the 1931 opening of which was announced in the September issue of *The Gramophone* ('at last a really first-class private recording studio has been opened').

The quality achieved before the days of VHF broadcasts must have depended on the physical location of the receiver, the transmitter it was taking its signal from, and also how close such an operation was to the BBC. Watts's company, although having retail premises on Charing Cross Road, actually recorded at Hendon. Bearing in mind the high quality he achieved, this suggests that he possibly had a landline feed from the BBC Hendon transmitter, though I have been unable to document this.

Microgroove LP transcriptions at 33 rpm started very early; the equipment used was either custom built or, presumably, imported from the USA, where custom recording had been the backbone of the radio industry

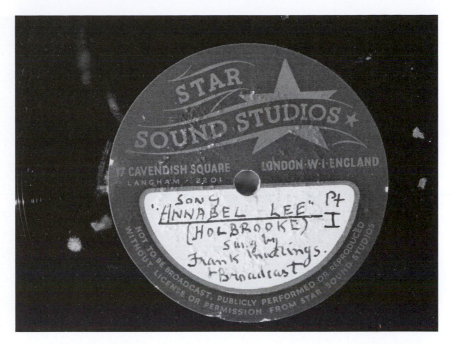

Figure PT4 Star Sound Studios. Holbrooke's orchestral song *Annabel Lee* (Frank Mullings (tenor)/BBC Orchestra (Section C)/Sir Granville Bantock), broadcast in the BBC Regional Programme, 14 September 1936

since before the war. However, discs found in private collections generally were recorded at 78 rpm, most likely because until the early 1950s few had equipment on which to play microgroove records.

Many of these studios offered services that continued well into the 1970s and beyond, by when most such recordings had migrated to tape. Familiar names include John Hassell Recordings and Recorded Productions (London) Ltd, 'Deroy' Sound Service (Ormskirk, Lancashire) and Isis Records Ltd (Oxford). (See Figures PT5 and PT6.) But the most often seen and widely used was W. H. Troutbeck, whose familiar green labels, recorded on Emidisc blanks, almost always designate consistent high quality.

I was introduced to the disc-cutting engineer W. H. Troutbeck by the pianist Harriet Cohen in 1966. He lived at Twickenham where his studio was in his home. In March 1967, with Harriet's permission and encouragement, I ordered a custom-cut recording of her 1954 BBC performance of Arnold Bax's *Winter Legends*. Once I knew him it was like being in Aladdin's cave. I soon learned that he cut off-air and custom recorded discs for most of the leading names on the British music scene at that time. Examples constantly turn up: I have discs of music by Geoffrey Bush, Hubert Clifford, Harriet Cohen, Peter Crossley-Holland (see Figure PT7),

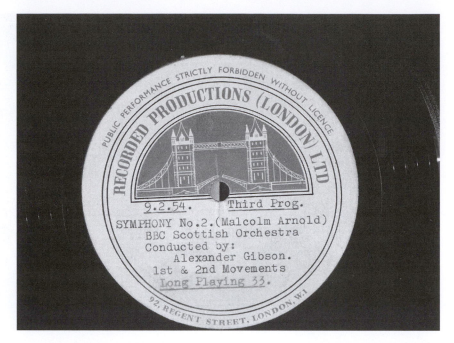

Figure PT5 Recorded Productions (London) Ltd 10-inch acetate. First broadcast performance of Malcolm Arnold's Second Symphony, 9 February 1954 (BBC Scottish Orchestra/Alexander Gibson)

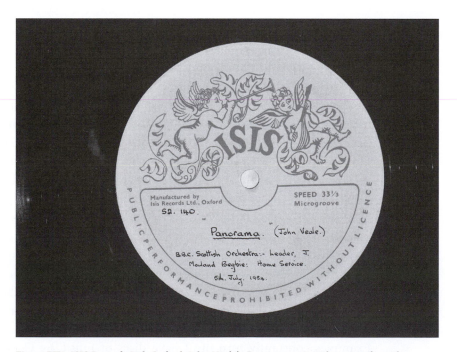

Figure PT6 ISIS Records Ltd, Oxford. John Veale's *Panorama*. 10-inch acetate from the composer's collection, broadcast on 5 July 1954. (BBC Scottish Orchestra/Alexander Gibson)

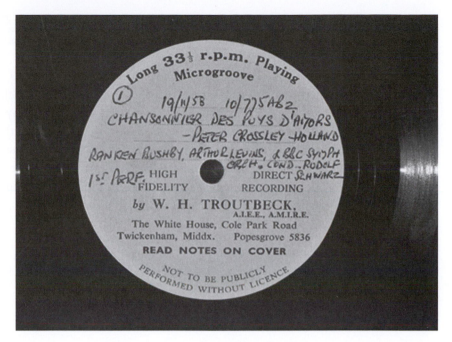

Figure PT7 W. H. Troutbeck, 10-inch acetate from his original address at Twickenham. First performance of Peter Crossley-Holland's *Chansonnier des Puys d'Amors* for baritone, violin and strings (with harp) (Ranken Bushby (bass), Arthur Levins (violin), BBC Symphony Orchestra/ Rudolf Schwarz), broadcast on 19 November 1958

Julius Harrison, Patrick Piggott, Edmund Rubbra and John Veale. A search of Cadensa, the catalogue of the British Library Sound Archive, finds forty-three hits under 'W.H. Troutbeck'. In response to my enquiry in 1967, Troutbeck promised to ask Rubbra, Michael Tippett and Sir Adrian Boult if he could copy their recordings for me, and all agreed. Eventually, in the mid-1970s, he left Twickenham and moved to Robin Hill near Reigate, continuing to cut discs until it was no longer possible to get his equipment serviced, when he changed to tape before his eventual retirement.

Troutbeck was personally acquainted with a substantial cross-section of British musicians for over twenty-five years. On one occasion in the late 1960s he was cutting a disc for a leading British composer who was present, listening on the monitor and supervising how he wanted his discs cut. The composer was smoking and flicked cigarette ash into a waste bin into which, unknown to him, the engineer had deposited the swarf cut from the discs. The room (which had recently been decorated) was instantly filled with choking black smoke.

Troutbeck also produced high-quality reel-to-reel recordings in the early 1950s. One of his customers was the composer William Alwyn, whose collection of recordings is now in the Cambridge University Library. The earliest that I have seen dates from July 1953 and is of Sir John Barbirolli's performance of his First Symphony, now reissued on a Dutton Vocalion historical CD (CDSJB 1029).

Acetate discs, whether used by broadcasting organisations or cut for individual musicians, were largely intended as a current playback mechanism. While they have been widely tapped as a source for many historical recordings from the United States, the extent of their use in the UK has tended to be forgotten. But as the libraries of the generation active in the mid-century become available for research, more acetates are still being found. The prospects for preserving more of the past seem increasingly auspicious, though time is at a premium.

7 The development of recording technologies

GEORGE BROCK-NANNESTAD

Introduction

When we consider the use of sound recordings for the transport and presentation of performance, the history of sound-recording technology must be taken into account, but in doing so we need to concentrate on those types of sound recording that have provided an important influence or contribution. Short-lived systems, esoteric systems, and discussions of who invented what are not particularly interesting in this context. This presentation of the historical development will concentrate rather on the performance of the systems *then*, while they influenced contemporary appreciation and further development, and *now*, when we have a possibility of providing better signal extraction than ever before. The first is related to the reception history of sound recording, the second to realising the correctable parameters of historical recording.

Readers will have noted the somewhat clumsy expression 'transport and presentation of performance'. This broadness of purpose is necessary because, seventy years into the development of sound recording, most records being produced began to be *edited* on a microscopic level into a coherent whole, presenting the performer as he or she would have played in almost ideal circumstances. From that point, performance as a specific sonic event is not created until an edited recording, perhaps in conjunction with a recording of a synthesised sound, is played. Traditional thinking about sound recording and reproduction was that it was a 'naive' recording, an image of sorts of a live performance, the later reproduction of an event in time that had really taken place earlier. To a large degree the general public is still under this illusion.

If we want to compare the various systems for sound recording and their usefulness for our purpose we have to understand some fundamental concepts, apart from the historical development. This requires a few definitions that should not cloud the historical presentation.

Sound recording and sound reproduction are entirely separate activities, and they each have their separate uses, but for a time they may be joined in the recording–reproduction chain that is colloquially called 'sound recording'.

If we are in the business of listening to sounds, obviously the actual provider of sound must be the focus of our primary interest. All providers (except when the sound is transmitted via bone conduction) set up local pressure variations in air that travel with the speed of sound to the receiving ear. There was a time when the only providers were the human voice, the wind and other natural sound generators, and musical instruments. Nowadays, most of the meaningful sound we hear comes via the intermediary of a loudspeaker, which is capable of reproducing any sound.

Musical instruments when sounded, and other well-known sources of sound, provide characteristic pressure variations that may be classified, and so identify the instrument, whereas a loudspeaker must be able to provide *any* characteristic of pressure variation, and that information must be fed to it in some form. Loudspeakers are controlled by signals fed to them, and the source of the signals may be a store, habitually called a *recording*. Another source – very much in modern use – is a microphone in order to create a *public address system*. The loudspeaker should not modify the sound it is intended to provide.

If the signals generate characteristic pressure variations that correspond to some of the classifications that we know from musical instruments and other well-known sounds, then we recognise the sound of the loudspeaker as if it came from the original. If the right signals are delivered, then any natural source of sound as well as any artificial sound may be simulated. The spatial placement of the loudspeaker does have an influence on the illusion. An earphone is merely a loudspeaker that is very close to the ear and avoids the influence from the room acoustics.

Basic principles

Sound as we hear it has a development in time, and when sound is reproduced it will be faithfully represented only if the regenerated sound has the same development in time. And a sound obtained via any other process must equally have a recognisable development in time for it to appear as an image of an event. This is really all that we require from a recording and reproduction system. The manner in which the system handles all the information that constitutes the sound need only concern us to the degree that errors or manipulations may influence the end result. During the history of sound recording various physical phenomena have been used to represent the sound, in its storage as a recording on a carrier.

The phenomena that have been used are:

(1) the disturbance of the smoothness of a surface – termed *mechanical recording*;
(2) the change in local magnetisation of a layer – termed *magnetic recording*;
(3) the change in transparency of a layer – termed *optical recording*;

(4) the storage of timing and intensity information for a particular key of a keyboard instrument – termed *piano roll* (and nowadays in a completely generalised form called MIDI);

(5) the storage of a table of timing and desired positions of a loudspeaker membrane – termed *digital recording.*

For each of the above there are carriers for a surface, for a layer, for perforations, or for tabular information, each carrier relying on a suitable phenomenon. The signal used in the phenomenon does not need to have any resemblance to the actual sound heard before and after, as long as the apparatus involved is able to interpret it and create a sound. The essential condition for a repetition of a recorded event is that the reproducing apparatus is able to interpret the carrier correctly. That is putting our reliance on the system as originally conceived. Certainly, the reproducing apparatus may be instructed to provide a different interpretation for obtaining special effects, in accordance with the wish of a producer and with artistic or scientific intent. For instance, just changing the speed of reproduction will influence the result noticeably.

How the above phenomena overlapped in time is shown in Figure 7.1. For instance the piano roll, which only stored instructions, overlapped considerably with the pre-electric or acoustic recording method, because it was a better-sounding alternative. In the present chapter it will be found outside the mainstream of the development of recording and reproduction and is treated separately.

Mainstream historical development

General scientific awareness in the Western world rose sharply around 1850, and scientific approaches were made to analyse and structure the fields of music, language, and many other subject areas related to the arts and humanities. Acoustics and music were related by sound, and the scientific explanation that sound is in reality a time function of pressure variations became manifest and the basis for measurements with a time axis. One piece of equipment that became very useful was the phonautograph, invented and patented in France in 1857 by Edouard-Léon Scott de Martinville. One hundred and fifty years after the filing of the patent application it was finally translated into English.[1] His tracings occurred on a sooted surface, and later on sooted sheets of paper wound round a cylinder rotated at a uniform speed on a threaded rod, so that it was gradually shifted sideways, permitting a very long time axis. Scott's manufacturer was Rudolph Koenig in Paris who became the premier scientific acoustical equipment manufacturer for the latter part of the 1800s. The

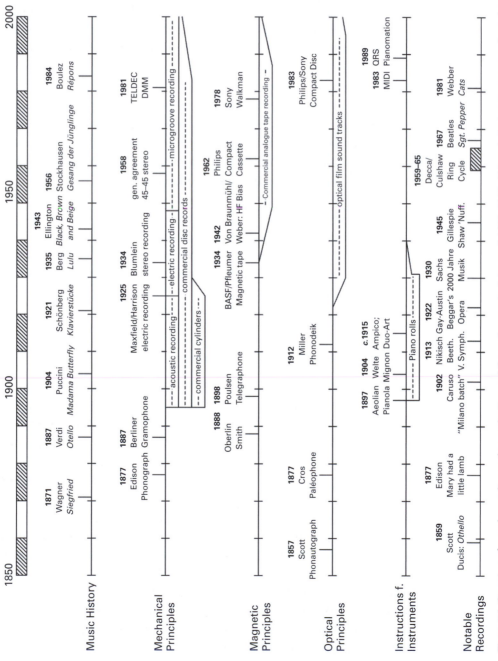

Figure 7.1 Overview of sound recording and reproduction and the analogue principles used, 1850–2000. Although the last twenty years have shown digital technologies and much change in distribution, most existing content still has an analogue origin.

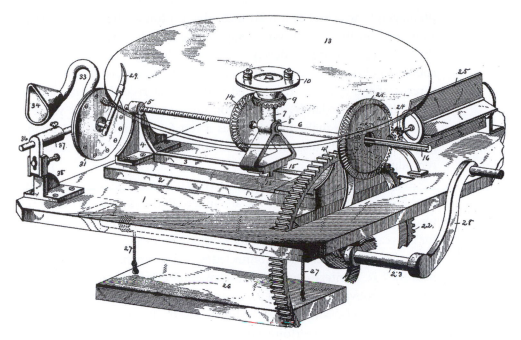

Figure 7.2 Emile Berliner's first two-step recording method, 1887, emulating Charles Cros's method from 1877: tracing on a blackened glass plate, with subsequent contact copying to a surface that was etched to obtain grooves

tracings were distorted but were still able to tell scientists very much about arbitrary sounds and their time functions. Scott's method was only intended as a *recording* method, permitting observation and graphical analysis.

In 1877 two methods of *reproduction* were conceived, one directly inspired by the tracings, the other independent, via telephone research. Charles Cros deposited his idea of the use of tracings in a sealed letter to the Academy of Sciences in Paris in 1877, but it did not materialise until Emile Berliner devised practical means ten years later (see Figure 7.2). The idea was based on photo-engraving. The tracings were transferred photographically by contact printing to a zinc surface that was subsequently etched in order to obtain an undulating groove corresponding to the tracings.

Thomas A. Edison was a more or less self-taught telegraph engineer with a large capacity for systematic experimentation. Combining work on re-transmission of telegraph signals with work on telephones and the action of diaphragms, he realised in 1877 that if his microphone diaphragm could make a direct impression in a moving medium, then that impression could make a diaphragm move in the same manner when the medium was moved to drive it, and the sound *recorded* as impressions would be directly listenable – *reproduction*. This was the basis for his phonograph, which at first used malleable tin foil as the medium, freely supported on threads cut into a supporting cylinder. Again there was a threaded rod providing sideways movement during rotation, so that the rounded point of the diaphragm would always be precisely between the threads of the cylinder. It is stated that his first recorded sentence was 'Mary had a little lamb', but the continuation 'its fleece was white as snow' would be equally important as a test for telephones and phonographs alike – the treble content in the sibilants and fricatives needed to be reproduced faithfully.

According to Edison's intentions, his instrument's greatest use should have been in office dictation work, and indeed that was always a minor role for it up to the early 1960s. Yet although he did not improve it himself for ten years, the scientific world took eagerly to the phonograph as it was. In the meantime researchers connected with a competing telephone business (Bell & Tainter) developed fundamental principles in recording by cutting a groove directly into a wax surface, and they eventually became competitors to Edison. The wax cylinder was the beginning of the recording industry, with a repertoire consisting of monologues, songs and bands.

Emile Berliner performed Cros's method in practice in 1887, but later realised that it was possible to trace directly to the zinc surface, avoiding the photo-engraving. He also realised that it would be possible to obtain a negative impression from the etched master and use that to press disc records in a thermoplastic material. Berliner founded his entertainment business based, again, on recording monologues, songs and bands, and pressing records for reproduction on gramophones, which he also developed.

Steps in the development of the cylinder recording system

Although cylinder recording did not survive as long as the disc record, sufficient recordings of culturally important material were created that it is essential to put it into its proper perspective. The most important feature of cylinder recording is that it was essentially a system of relatively high fidelity, although the background noise was sometimes a drawback. The more expensive models of cylinder machine were designed to record as well as reproduce, and they enabled both the first commercial recordings and also the first home recordings. The recording occurred by means of variation of depth of recording on equipment that was very lathe-like: a cutting tool moved along the cylinder and generated swarf that was removed while the cylinder rotated.

The first commercial cylinders were all originals: a number of cylinders of a performance, recorded by several recording machines simultaneously.

Later a pantographic method of copying from an original appeared, and still later Edison developed a process that permitted making galvanotypic negative matrices in which commercial cylinders could be cast in any number. The material for commercial distribution was more durable than the material used for recording. In 1912 Edison introduced the use of a plastic, Blue Amberol, which was in reality celluloid, and this became known to be the most durable material for cylinder records. The layer of celluloid was very thin, like sausage skin, and while made flexible it was given the impression from a negative of the recording; after hardening it was provided with a support of cast plaster of Paris.

The fact that cylinder recording was completely self-contained meant that it was uniquely suited for field recordings in remote places without electrical supply. Indeed, ethnomusicological recordings were made on cylinders from 1887 to 1940, and the only drawbacks were the cylindrical shape that contained a lot of empty space and the fragility of original cylinders – breakage and mould were the major problems. Once the cylinders had been carried safely home to the archive, a matrixing process was used to create copper negatives, in which the recording was now sitting as a spiral track like a mountain ridge on the inside of a copper cylinder matrix. The original wax-like substance was melted away, and as many copies as was desired could be cast in the matrix. The process was somewhat cruder than commercial cylinder manufacture, but the results formed the basis of innumerable ethnomusicological analyses. The major problem with the surviving recordings is that the documentation is in many cases very scanty, so that, while the original cylinders may well benefit from modern reproduction technology, it is to some extent unknown what is now available.

Steps in the development of the disc record

Berliner's etching method of transforming a tracing to a groove was basically a good one, and the complication that a chromic acid solution had to be carried along on a recording trip did not offset the fact that, once the original zinc record had been etched, a very sturdy master recording was available. However, the reproduction by means of a needle and soundbox was not able to cope with the heavy modulation, and the graininess of the original etched surface created background noise. That noise was mixed with the noise from the thermoplastic record material, which industry-wide eventually became a mixture of shellac as a binder material (*c.* 20 per cent) and slate dust as a filler (*c.* 80 per cent), with a small amount of carbon black to avoid a grey, concrete-like look for the finished record.

In 1900 Berliner's successors, Victor Talking Machine Co. and the Gramophone Co. were no longer worried about Bell & Tainter's patents and now recorded by cutting the groove into a wax surface. This way the groove shape was decided by the cutting stylus and not by etching, making a smoother surface. The effort in cutting the wax was much larger than in tracing in the thin protective layer for the zinc, and hence the modulation was generally less. The wax surface with the grooves was metallised with copper using galvanotypic methods, and when the copper was removed from the wax a negative mould was available for pressing records in the heated shellac compound. One type of recording wax was obtained by melting down commercial Pathé cylinders,[2] which was a fairly hard wax; this may account for the fact that it was apparently possible to make several consecutive galvanotypic negatives from one and the same original wax.[3] These records were easier to reproduce on early gramophones because the modulation was less. The copper mould when used as a *stamper* was rather quickly worn by the combination of hydraulic power and the abrasive quality of the compound, and the last records of a print run were muffled and noisy and not saleable.[4] A process was invented for creating identical and high-quality secondary masters so that production could continue almost indefinitely. Eventually, the process became entirely galvanotypic, and it remained so from *c.* 1910 until a simplified alternative, Direct Metal Mastering (DMM), was developed during the late 1970s.

In the beginning, content information was a spoken announcement with minimal indication engraved in the master record to be copied during the manufacture. Later, heat-resistant labels were fixed to the records, containing a description of the contents, the catalogue number, and trade marks.

Further steps in the development of recording technology

All collecting of the sound for recording occurred by means of one or more recording horns suitably connected into one conduit leading to the recording soundbox. Many experiments were made to make recording more predictable, since this meant that a record did not have to be discarded because of a recording fault but only because of unsatisfactory artistic performance. The distances from performers to the horn were critical if a suitable blend was to be heard on replay. The only other criterion, and indeed the only objective measuring method available to early record manufacture, was durability on contemporary machinery. If a record was recorded with a modulation that was too heavy, the pressed record would not last long (Adelina Patti's *La Calasera* was withdrawn within a month of its appearance in 1907, because it could only last three replays). Durability was paramount as a business philosophy, in particular for the Victor Talking Machine Co. During the experiments to record consistently and to obtain durability, use was made of micro-photographed grooves, and it was discovered in 1911 that one particular groove shape held up longer than any other, and this became the in-house standard for both Victor and Gramophone Company. Victor also initiated the use of nickel stampers, which were much stronger than copper. Irrespective of these developments, there was a tendency that Gramophone Company would record more brilliant-sounding records than Victor, but with reduced durability.[5] The placing of the instruments for recording at Victor is shown in Figure 7.3.

After the First World War Victor developed a recording soundbox that enabled very good sound quality (in some respects it applied principles that had been used ten years previously by Columbia), in particular for orchestras and that very difficult instrument the grand piano.

Durability: Re-recording, groove modification

Some early recordings did not have the proper groove shape for the durability requirements, and two solutions were used by the two large companies, Victor and Gramphone Company. One was re-recording much more slowly than real-time, using the correct profile for cutting the copy groove: this was the original meaning of the word 'dubbing'. The other was making a galva-notypic positive copy that was very thin and malleable, and running a spherical sapphire stylus through the groove with a polishing agent, thereby re-shaping the groove. Both methods created a distortion of the signal, but the durability of the records was much increased. Unfortunately, the original negatives were not always preserved, though the more production-friendly but distorted versions were.

An interlude on loudspeakers

The first phonographs could only be heard by means of listening tubes ending in earpieces; however, for entertainment purposes and for dancing a reasonable volume was required. A horn fitted to the soundbox was an efficient means to increase volume, with the power supplied by the spring of the phonograph or gramophone. However, this also had its limits, and methods of controlling outside power sources were found. David Higham constructed a friction amplifier, in which the vibrating stylus controlled

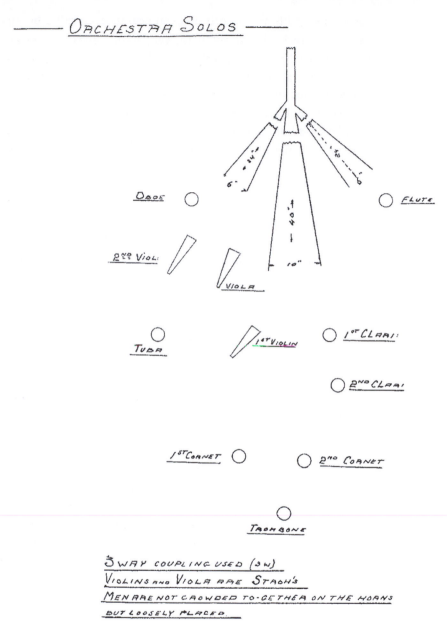

Figure 7.3 Acoustic recording by means of horns for collecting the sound from the instruments. From Fred Gaisberg's 1907 report to the Gramophone Company on a study tour to the Victor Talking Machine Company in Camden, New Jersey, USA. Adapted from a drawing in the EMI Music Archives

the coupling to a small continuously rotating amber cylinder, so that a larger diaphragm could be set in motion. Sir Charles Parsons, who knew about compressors (and turbines), created a smoothly operating valve controlled by the vibrating stylus, so that compressed air could make a huge horn create a sound sufficient for a bandstand in a park – the Auxetophone. When electronic amplification in the form of valves became common *c.* 1920, various types of electromagnetic drives for loudspeaker cones were devised. The two most useful were the 'balanced armature' and the 'moving coil', both of which had a reasonable efficiency. They were obviously introduced in broadcast receivers that were already operating by means of valves. However, the highest efficiency and the least distortion was still obtained by means of horns, and they became dominant in the movie theatre field.

Electrical recording = central level control

The increasing availability of valve amplifiers and their use in telephone transmission demonstrated their usefulness for sound signals, and it was realised by several record companies that using electronic amplification, with the possibility of controlling the volume at will by means of a knob, would simplify recording in two ways: a level of recording suitable for the task might be used, creating some independence of the placement of performers, and, second, it would be possible to reduce amplification somewhat if part of a performance was very strong in itself. In this way, a greater dynamic range would be possible. However, only the telephone giant Western Electric and its Bell Telephone Laboratory had sufficient experience of, and theoretical insight into, electrical transmission of sound. It had considered that there would be a need in the professional market for sound recording, namely for moving images with dialogue. In 1924–5 Western Electric came up with a practical system for doing these things. The system consisted of electronically amplified disc recording, and for the commercial market it was combined with a very much improved acoustic reproduction device that avoided the use of amplifying valves in every gramophone (see Figure 7.4). A microphone provided an input to an amplifier and the output fed a cutter-head that was transported across a master disc by suitable gearing means. The cutter-head construction was reminiscent of a telephone relay and it meant that considerable mechanical force was available for the cutting. A number of record companies were quick to license these inventions, and a licence fee was paid until in-house alternative systems had been developed by some of them. The fact that the sound signal was now represented by an electrical signal enabled routing to several cutting lathes simultaneously, enabling safety backup copies.

As broadcasting branched out from radio communication from 1922, more and more homes obtained valve-equipped wireless sets, in which

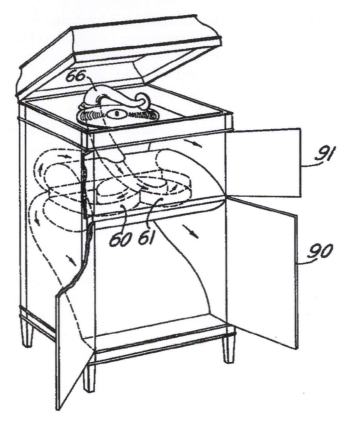

Figure 7.4 Maxfield and Harrison of the Bell Telephone Laboratories in 1925 invented an electrical recording system and a matched-impedance mechanical reproducing system with a huge, folded horn

there was a separation of the task of the radio frequency valves and the audio frequency valves; each set actually contained an audio amplifier for the loudspeaker. The industry was quick to realise that an electrical pickup might be plugged into the set in order to obtain electrical reproduction of gramophone records. The pickup was a heavy construction (see Figure 7.5), using a horseshoe magnet and a rubber-damped pivotable armature that held the steel needle.[6] In order to obtain reproducibility in recording, precise placement of the instruments was still a requirement, as shown in Figure 7.6.

Recording longer works

When longer works were to be recorded, they had to be broken up into pieces that could fit on the sides of shellac records played consecutively

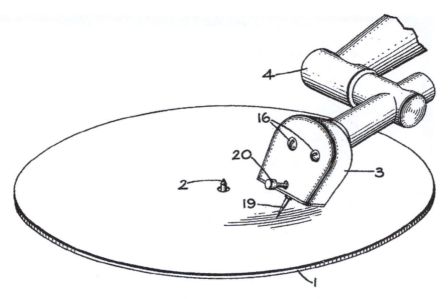

Figure 7.5 Edward Kellogg invented an electrical pickup in 1925 that was the prototype for all pickups and many cutter-heads until *c.* 1940

while not being too obtrusively edited. Sometimes, for example in German Lieder cycles, the original order was deviated from. For all other works, the sequence was not broken, and deciding on the placement of the side-breaks was an artistic matter. The essential atmosphere of the work was to be retained as much as possible, and the interruption for the change of record was made as gentle as possible by, for example, slowing down more than if the music just continued, or even adding a cadence to the score at the end of the side.

For uniformity of sound, record sides making up a set ought to be recorded consecutively in a brief span of time. However, the wear test might indicate that some sides had to be re-recorded on a later occasion, and this happened to a number of early 'complete' works. When the record changer became popular in the 1930s a subsequent side was placed on the next record and not as 'side B' (a so-called 'auto-coupled' set). The record changer could play through all the 'A' sides of a pile of records and, when the end of the top record was reached, the whole pile was turned over and all the 'B' sides were played. This reduced the interruption, some clonking of falling records remaining, and RCA-Victor, for example, 'improved' on this by editing the record sides so that each side began with a fade-in and ended with a fade-out.

Editing was a rare occurrence, because copying to a new wax increased the background noise, and other approaches were rare.[7]

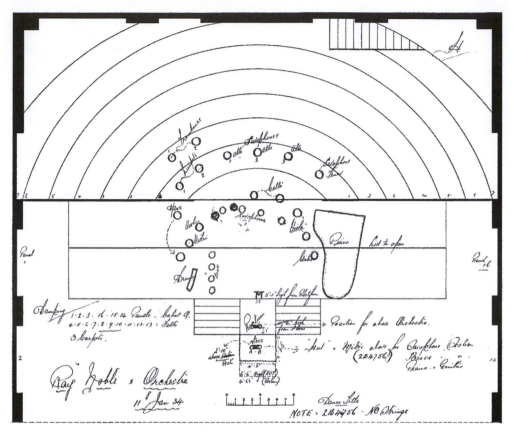

Figure 7.6 Ray Noble and dance orchestra (making records under the name New Mayfair Orchestra) used this layout on 11 January 1934 at the Abbey Road Studios. The occasion was also used by Alan D. Blumlein to make experimental stereo recordings. Adapted from a drawing in the EMI Music Archives

Lacquer records for home and professional use

As electrical pickups became more common towards the end of the 1920s, a further use was found for the audio amplifier part of the wireless set. A microphone was used as the input and, instead of providing the output to the loudspeaker, a cutter-head, somewhat more primitive than the professional heads, was connected. The master disc was mainly of two kinds, one a nitro-cellulose lacquer bonded to a very flat aluminium disc, the other a gelatine formulation, either bonded to flimsier aluminium discs or solid. Some lacquers were more like varnishes and had to harden by chemical treatment after recording. The reproduction needles prescribed to consumers for these records were devised to 'trail' in the groove, because of the heavy soundboxes and pickups in which they were used. Lacquer records were used for private recording in Germany and in the US from *c.* 1930 and in the UK from *c.* 1937, and a hobby not unlike home film-making sprang up.

Lacquer recording slowly penetrated the professional recording field, in particular in broadcasting,[8] but did not really enter commercial recording until the late 1930s, when it was in particular used for recording locally for the colonial market. The reason was that the ease of use outweighed the slightly but audibly higher background noise. This improved with the development of the heated cutting stylus (Columbia Records, 1948), and the lacquer (sometimes erroneously termed 'acetate') is still used as the recording material in the manufacture of vinyl records. An improvement in performance was obtained by the introduction of Direct Metal Mastering, a development from Teldec which was commercialised by Neumann from 1981. The (nowadays) stereo signal is cut directly into a very fine-grained copper layer, which becomes an instant 'mother' and so avoids a step in the galvanotypic process.

Magnetic sound recording

Magnetic recording was thought about almost at the same time as the other recording methods, but it did not materialise until 1898 when Valdemar Poulsen demonstrated practical electromagnetic recording and reproduction. The development took off quite quickly, but the technology was limited to use in a telephone environment, because no practical amplifiers existed for reproduction of the weak electrical signals obtained from the magnetic head. Also the distortion levels were very similar to the distortion in telephones of that period. Analogue magnetic recording is a very non-linear process, but with suitable electronic circuitry that was developed from *c.* 1930 the medium eventually became eminently transparent. Recording occurred first on carbon steel strip (Marconi-Stille), which was available in a reliable quality only from Sweden. In particular in the US the wire recorder used steel and later stainless wires, which did not corrode. Paper and polymer tape coated or impregnated with magnetisable iron oxide was developed in Germany from 1935, and in 1941 German radio serendipitously made use of a phenomenon from a laboratory experiment and obtained a vast improvement by the use of 'high frequency bias'; the result was widely publicised but neglected outside Germany. Tape recording also had little difficulty in accommodating two or more channels, and AEG and BASF built and demonstrated stereophonic tape recording in 1942, using principles that remained to the end of analogue tape recording.[9]

German equipment confiscated after the Second World War taught US manufacturers, in particular, how to manufacture reel-to-reel tape

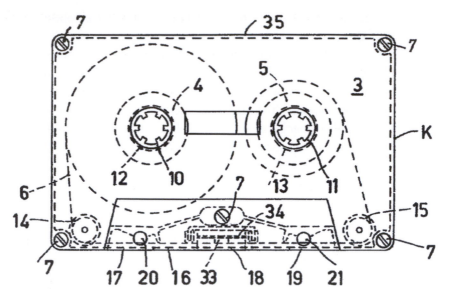

Figure 7.7 Philips of the Netherlands introduced this type of cassette for magnetic recording in 1962. Its usefulness rested on strict adherence to the precise construction and the dimensions involved

recorders, which quickly replaced the wire recorders that from 1946 had become quite widespread, mostly for home use and monitoring purposes. The wire recorder replaced the lacquer disc, and the tape recorder replaced the wire recorder. Because of the need for very much electronic compensation many important industry standards were developed in the 1950s in order to ensure compatibility between makes. This paved the way for miniaturisation, which was driven by Philips in the Netherlands in the form of their compact cassette which appeared in 1962 (see Figure 7.7). Philips freely licensed their cassette technology which was covered by patents, but part of the licence agreement was a requirement to adhere meticulously to the mechanical and electrical specifications. This created a very strong *de facto* standard, and the cassette is still a very useful medium, in particular in regions that are not interesting to the large international recording organisations. In the industrialised world the compact cassette became a very important distribution medium for the music that had been offered on LP records from 1950, not least because of the adoption of another licensed technology, Dolby-B noise reduction, and the fact that the cassette mechanism was well suited to automotive use. The semi-professional field was catered for by the use of cassettes at double speed (TASCAM).

Analogue tape reel-to-reel recording was an almost ideal medium for editing (only surpassed by modern digital editing, in which the original is always available for further attempts), because it could be done either by splicing the desired parts together in the precise order desired, or by copying. In the beginning performances might be constructed by subsequent adding of instruments while copying to the mix already recorded, but once multitrack using very wide magnetic tapes became available the several tracks were mixed down quite late in the process to the few channels needed for distribution, for instance as a vinyl record.

The professional and consumer tape recorder from the 1950s

The German professional literature regarding magnetic recording had been freely available, but the worldwide distribution of the knowledge of how to construct a machine occurred via Allied investigating teams reporting in English on German technology in 1945–6.[10] In the USA the development was aided by an almost free licence to all Axis-owned patents (via the Office of the Alien Property Custodian), which had given US manufacturers a head start when the patents were finally restituted to their German owners in 1949.

Each country had several radio-set manufacturers about 1950, and a number in each country decided to manufacture tape recorders. Between 1950 and 1965 a bewildering number of makes was available as well as a huge selection of tapes, which were all ¼ inch in width, with more and more sophisticated track layout: full track (mono), half track (stereo in one direction, or, if turned upside down, double-duration mono), quarter track (bi-directional stereo, quadruple-duration mono). A certain selection of pre-recorded tape was available in the beginning, in particular before the advent of the stereo vinyl record (1958). Towards 1970 a huge concentration to only a few manufacturers worldwide took place, partly driven by the new compact cassette medium that fulfilled most consumer needs.

The professional field had few manufacturers that supplied the recording and broadcast industries. Tapes were developed to high and uniform standards, but in the late 1970s types of exceptional dynamic range were developed that unfortunately did not have a very long storage life. The professional Dolby noise reduction systems prolonged the useful life of this analogue technology but, because of the developments in the digital field, analogue tape recording was phased out, and production of equipment petered out during the 1990s, to the great detriment of sound archives in all areas, whose holdings of magnetic tape are at risk of being unplayable due to lack of equipment.

Commercialisation of 33⅓ rpm and 45 rpm – silent surfaces, stereo

In US broadcasting, 33⅓ rpm vertical recording on 16-inch lacquer discs became the norm during the 1930s, as air-checks and for re-transmission. These specifications were originally derived from simple gearing using 60 Hz mains to supply a synchronous motor, and from an optimisation described by Joseph Maxfield in US patent 1,637,082 (published 1927), which specified a record that would contain sound to be reproduced along with a standard roll of film (sound-on-disc). A maximum of 15 minutes could be accommodated on each side using the normal coarse grooves.

Shellac was the binder material in most record manufacture, and as it became an expensive ingredient replacements were sought and found in cellulose acetate. It was both strong and gave a silent surface, because the material was itself so inexpensive that there was no need for a mineral filler. However, it was very hygroscopic and in practice unsuitable as a record material. Polyvinyl chloride was found to be much better in all respects except cost. Thus the stage was set to create a consumer record that would have a large capacity (to reduce the amount of material) and low noise (due to the good material) and was based on technologies not too far removed from professional use. Such a record, the long-playing vinyl record, was developed by Columbia Records and CBS Laboratories and presented to the world in 1948. It had 33⅓ rpm, 10- or 12-inch diameter, and using c. 260 revolutions per radial inch it had a maximum playing time of 22½ minutes per side, five times that of a standard 78 rpm record. The signal-to-noise ratio eventually rose to 55 dB (compared to 40 dB in a shellac record). New speed and the new groove dimensions required new equipment, but that was an advantage to post-war industry requiring products to replace war production.

The 33⅓ rpm vinyl record from Columbia was followed in 1949 by the 45 rpm vinyl record (the 'single') from RCA-Victor, which was a 7-inch record only (since c. 1980 a 12-inch version is known as a 'disco single'). It was in most respects a replacement for the 10-inch shellac record and eventually concentrated on entertainment music, but in the beginning it was issued with a record changer that could change to the next record in a pile in one second, so that longer works could be accommodated without the irritating pauses known from 78 rpm record changers. Jukebox manufacturers welcomed this format, because it enabled very sturdy changer mechanisms, and the consumer had to get used to having a gramophone with three speeds. In USA the 78 speed was phased out before 1955, but in England the last commercial 78 rpm records (featuring royal speeches) were pressed in 1962. In India, the Beatles were available in this format until the mid-1960s.

The development of fine-groove records meant that all development of equipment suitable for reproducing coarse-groove records, in particular pickups, was halted, to the detriment of good reproduction of early discs. If their reproduction had experienced a similar refinement as that afforded the fine-groove format, they would not have been the focus of the excuse 'It is only an old record', and many reissues would not have been subjected to various forms of noise-reducing treatment that also corrodes the contents.

Stereo records

About 1930, when commercial recording and reproduction had become electronic and the result not dissimilar to the sound obtained in broadcasting, there was no pressure to increase the quality of the illusion by providing a sense of space. However, in film sound there was a continuous development, partly caused by the need to obtain leverage in the complex patent and licensing situation. So, while the fundamental principles of stereophonic mechanical recording were first publicly described by Alan Blumlein (UK patent 394,325, published 14 June 1933) and later developed for optical recording, Arthur Keller in the Bell Telephone Laboratories developed the same principles as a part of the general development of film sound in particular (US patent 2,114,471 published 19 April 1938).

Stereophonic recording needs two independent channels, and the output of headphones or loudspeakers combines in the listener's head to create a sense of left and right in the soundscape. The sense of depth in the soundscape will exist even in monophonic recordings, for instance if only one omnidirectional microphone is used. The two channels require two tracks on the sound-carrier, and the first experiments with mechanical records used either two lateral recorders (one closer to the centre of the record) or a combination of vertical ('hill-and-dale') and lateral in the same groove. Later, it was determined that a greater similarity between the characteristics of the two channels might be obtained if each groove flank were individually modulated 'hill-and-dale' with respect to its local surface, which is at 45 degrees to the surface of the record. This principle was finally commercialised in 1958.[11]

To understand how a modern stereo recording works it is actually quite relevant to quote verbatim from the lucid presentation in Blumlein's 1933 patent:

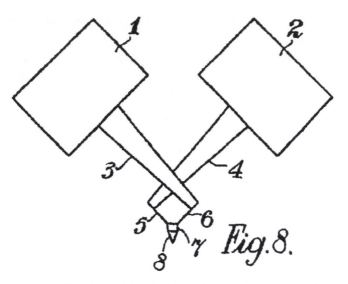

Figure 7.8 Alan D. Blumlein's fundamental patent from 1933 described all the principles that could be applied to mechanical records in order to record and reproduce stereo

The recorder whereby both channels may be cut by a single tool on the same groove may take various forms, the underlying feature being that a light stylus is pulled in two directions at right angles to one another and each preferably at 45° to the wax surface. Figure 8 [reproduced here as Figure 7.8] shows schematically a recorder of this kind suitable for producing records having complex cuts. 1 and 2 represent the driving elements of two recorders normally adapted for cutting lateral cut records. These driving elements drive arms 3 and 4 about axes at right angles to the plane of the paper within 1 and 2. The ends of these arms are connected by ligaments 5 and 6 to the end of a reed 7 which extends backwards along an axis perpendicular to the paper to supports not shown. This reed carries a cutting sapphire 8. Movements of the recording arms 3 and 4 produce movements in the end of the reed 7. Thus, currents in movement 1 will cause the reed 7 to move along an axis approximately 45° to the vertical rising from left to right across the figure. Similarly, currents in movement 2 will produce movement of the reed 7 in an axis at right angles to the former axis, while currents in both movements will of course result in vertical movement of the reed.[12]

It is inherent in fine-groove stereo records that there is noticeable distortion due to the groove being traced by a finite-size replay stylus after having been cut by a chisel edge: the details of the sound are fuzzier. However, now it had become possible to do electronically what had been done mechanically in the 1910s: pre-distortion of the groove to accommodate the replay stylus. The geometrical mechanism that created the distortion due to the replay stylus was analysed mathematically, and electronic filters were built that distorted the signal sent to the cutter-head in precisely such a way that the tracing replay stylus re-created the desired audio waveform when it played the record. This was before the advent of elliptical and line-contact styli, which sadly perform less well on those pre-distorted records. RCA Records developed this procedure as part of their Dynagroove system (1964) and the similar 'Tracing Simulator' was marketed by the German cutting-equipment manufacturer Neumann from 1966.

Film sound

The term 'silent movies' was really a misnomer, because a film show always had musical accompaniment. But the accompaniment was mostly live, and what was really missing to make the illusion complete was synchronous dialogue, possibly singing. The dialogue had to be presented as inter-titles, requiring the audience to read. For this reason many attempts were made to record and reproduce sound synchronously, but in general this was a very complex undertaking in the acoustic period. With improved control over the sound-recording process because of electrical recording the attempts were renewed, and several competing systems were developed. One was sound on disc (Western Electric Vitaphone, 1926), from which commercial disc recording was really a spin-off. The other systems – from *c.* 1930 – used an optical soundtrack that was placed on the film strip itself outside the row of images (see Figure 7.9). We now had 'talkies'. The purpose of the optical soundtrack was to modulate the amount of light that passed through the film to the photosensor in accordance with the audio signal that it was desired to reproduce. The recording was photographic, that is, the amount of light used to expose the film was continuously modulated. This could be done either by adjusting the intensity of light that created the exposure, or by using full intensity at all times but varying the width of a shadow cast by a vibrating vane. Noise-reducing systems ensured that no light was let through when there was no relevant signal.

Image recording, requiring the film to be completely still during the exposure of a frame, and sound recording, requiring the film to move with absolute constancy, were opposing requirements, and for this reason a sound from an event was further along the film than the corresponding image. The vibrations in the film strip were tamed by a flywheel connected to the transport drum that was part of the sound system. The same time shift was used in screening. This created problems when a film had torn

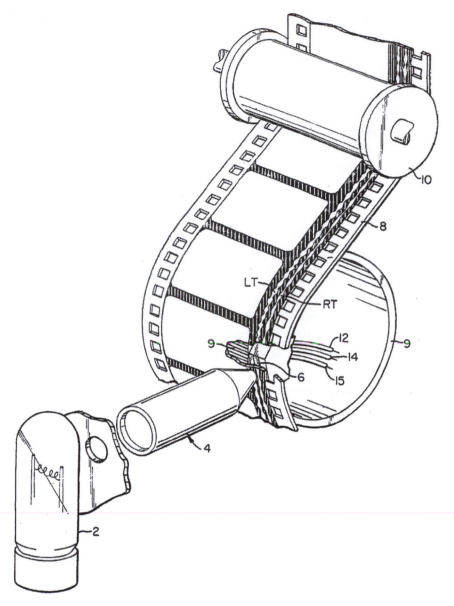

Figure 7.9 An analogue film soundtrack was placed just outside the row of images, and it was read by a narrow beam of light. Since *c.* 1995 it is also possible for this space to be used for digital address information, and the sound is stored on an accompanying CD

and had to be spliced, because real synchronism was not re-established until the splice had passed the sound reproducer.

Based on an American invention, Philips in the Netherlands developed (1936) the Philips–Miller system of mechanical vertical recording on a blackened film, which could subsequently be reproduced by a film sound reproducing system. This system had a reasonably broad professional acceptance in the broadcast field, because it could make long recordings and the result was instantly available for playback, and permitted infinite repetition because there was no wear.

The principle of optical soundtracks for film was quite amenable to two channels and even more: *Fantasia* (Disney, 1940, Philadelphia Orchestra, Leopold Stokowski) used eight channels ('Fantasound').

The piano roll

We need to mention a completely different way of providing a performance: that of telling an instrument what to do. Carillons and musical boxes had for centuries used pegs fitted in the right places on a cylinder to activate bells and other vibrators, but *c.* 1900 several musical-instrument manufacturers began using coded paper strips to activate individual keys of a piano or an organ. The coding was in the form of a perforation that permitted air to pass to activate a sounding mechanism when the perforation opened an air passage. The recording took place either by rote punching according to the sheet music, strictly observing the note values, or by recording a live performance, during which a pressed key on a piano worthy of the artist would make a line on a wide strip of paper corresponding to the individual key. The strength of the key pressure could be detected or annotated on a score by the recording technician. This formed the basis for the generation of a master perforated roll of paper strip – with corrections where needed – which then controlled automatic punches in the manufacture of the distributed product, the piano roll.

The rolls were placed into a mechanism that was able to use the perforations to activate the keys as needed, either built into a piano or placed before it, with small leather-covered levers placed above each key on the piano keyboard (the 'Vorsetzer'). Due to the natural timbre of the result, this manner of reproducing great pianism was in vogue until *c.* 1930, but it was restricted to wealthy customers. Later studies have indicated that at least some of the interpretations thus obtained are valid representations of a number of the elements of the performer's art.

In the digital age, synthesisers may be controlled not only by keyboards, but also by signals presented electronically, and the instructions of what and when may be given in coded form in the Musical Instrument Digital Interface standard (MIDI).

From analogue to digital

From the establishment in the 1920s of the fundamental physical principles regarding the structure of sound and how to generate signals that were suitable for impressing on storage media, the representation of the signal was always in the form of a phenomenon with a time function that was an analogue of the original sound's time function. For professional audio all that had to be observed was the signal level and the impedance of the interconnections.[13]

The development of audio technology was to a large degree linked to the development of communications technology, in which two parallel lines were pursued: signalling technology, in which codes were sent over wires (cable telegraphy was the earliest), and telephone technology. Both were dependent on reconstituting the signal after it had degraded in the transmission channel. At one stage, telegraph technology became so fast and the reconstitution so efficient that it became feasible to treat telephone (audio) signals by the same kind of apparatus. Two kinds of apparatus were essential to this development: the A/D (analogue-to-digital) converter at the input and the D/A (digital-to-analogue) converter at the output. The very fast signals were in their nature very high-frequency signals, and the digital equipment provided repeatability and reliability.

In parallel to this development, various analogue systems were developed for recording video, also requiring very high-frequency signals and a high data density. The technology eventually surviving in the market was based on a rotating head drum, with a slow-moving tape wrapped around a fast-rotating head drum that created the necessary relative velocity.

These digital and pulse technologies converged when Sony Corp designed a converter, the Sony F1, that would convert a stereo sound signal into a pulse code modulation (PCM) in a format that resembled video signals that could be recorded on a Sony Betamax video cassette recorder (1979).[14] The apparatus would also take a PCM signal received from the recorder and convert it back to audio. Originally a proprietary consumer product was contemplated; however, the professional industry found the repeatability of performance very useful and this paved the way for professional digital technology that had greater sophistication. A similar fate befell the Rotating (Head) Digital Audio Tape (R-DAT, 1986),[15] which was a system very much supported by standardisation work: it only half-heartedly entered the market as a consumer format but became used in professional installations and broadcasting. One reason that the intense work by the manufacturers resulted in relatively little turnover was that the holders of content were very worried that high-quality copying of vinyl records and especially CDs would occur uncontrollably.

Many coding schemes and formats were used for both consumer and professional formats, but as with various now defunct videotape formats it is difficult to find books in print that define the respective properties and standards, and the task of archives to access recordings on defunct formats will be huge and potentially impossible.

In parallel with the major efforts described above, Philips and Sony concluded a long line of development that drew upon optical video disc formats, and relied on data streams protected by advanced error-correcting codes, by presenting the compact disc in 1982. The principle was licensed to many manufacturers and record companies under strict adherence to 'Red Book' standards (for audio CDs), 'Yellow Book' standards (for data CDs, also called CD-ROMs (Read-Only-Memories)), and 'Orange Book' standards for blank CDs (CD-R, 1990) that could be inscribed with any high-level data structure, the fine structure on the disc itself still very much controlled by various error-correcting schemes. Further coloured binders for the Philips-controlled standards for other uses exist.[16]

While audio was mainly a real-time event, the amount of data based on the digitisation standards developed in connection with R-DAT and CD was such that interfacing to personal computers was difficult, even in the late 1980s. However, the speed of computer hardware increased, fast memory and hard disc capacity increased exponentially, and from the latter half of the 1990s it became feasible for consumers to enter the digital audio field in a recording and editing capacity. The output format became that of CD-R with audio CD compatible coding.[17] Eventually the recording of a CD-R became an operation at multiples of real-time speed, which meant that eighty minutes of stereo sound could be stored in ten minutes or less, in a quality identical to commercial CDs. This created a high-quality home studio to a much larger degree than had been the case with compact cassettes 15–20 years earlier. The difference between professional studio equipment and consumer equipment that had existed for 100 years suddenly disappeared.

The industry decided that the population needed surround sound in their home entertainment centres, and so various coding schemes for distributing sound information with a suitable frequency-dependent time delay to a number of loudspeakers were devised. Based on hearing research and digital signal processing, this became feasible and could be synthesised based on a two-channel recording. This was a renewed attempt on a market that had failed in the early 1970s when it was tried by means of encoded four-channel vinyl records. Simultaneously, personal, portable sound systems became fashionable, building on a market that had been generated by Sony's Walkman (a portable cassette reproducer) in 1978. First the consumer format the Minidisc was introduced (1992) and duly taken over by the recording industry, although the coding was proprietary, based on psychoacoustic criteria and not at all an industry standard. Then, based on further psychoacoustic research fuelled by the desire to obtain a Digital Audio Broadcast (DAB) standard, and data reduction in general, one of the coding schemes suddenly enabled the fastest growing distribution means ever: data files encoded according to MPEG Layer III, abbreviated MP3. MPEG is a strict and well-constructed set of standards for video and audio, the aim being to save on transmission bandwidth and storage needs. MP3 discards 90 per cent of the audio information and creates an ear stimulus that to a surprising degree appears to represent acceptable sound. The digital files are so small that only small memory units are required, and hours of music may be stored in equipment the size of a fat pencil. The loading of the memory unit occurs from a computer at a very high speed. MP3 has also enabled transmission of sound over the internet to a degree that enables uncontrolled exchange of copyrighted material to an unprecedented degree and to some worry for the rights holders. However, it is still only 10 per cent of the original sound.

Breaking the system: Modern reproduction of early recordings

Early sound recording and reproduction was described as a system, a sort of mirroring in which certain deficiencies of sound recording were compensated on reproduction. The actual signal on the carrier, in terms of being analogous to the sound pressure variations, was immaterial as long as the pre-determined system was used. However, even though the development of coarse groove reproduction was halted commercially, some of the equipment designed for LP use, for example, may still be usefully adapted.[18]

But because of the change in access to the actual signal on the carrier, it suddenly becomes important to know in considerable detail what the original recording equipment did to the signal. Phenomena like 'pre-emphasis' become important subjects for research.[19] Calibration of the modern reproducing equipment becomes equally important, because only the researched influences may be compensated by applying the knowledge obtained about the original recording equipment; the modern equipment must be transparent.

Noise reduction in reproduction

The development in sound recording and reproduction technology has always aimed for the least background noise in a given system, and the general trend has been to push the noise down and increase the dynamic level that can faithfully be reproduced. However, it was always recognised that earlier mechanical recordings had content of immense cultural value, and various schemes were developed from the 1940s on to reduce the apparent background noise when early recordings were reproduced. The simplest scheme was an electronic filter that removed the high frequencies where most of the noise usually resides, but it also attacked the content. The next scheme, from 1947, was a dynamic filter that only acted when the signal level was low (and the noise most irritating) and provided full bandwidth at high levels.[20] This was the first, primitive attempt to invoke the masking effect that is part of the mechanism of hearing (described by the discipline called psychoacoustics).[21] A major step forward was taken in 1977 when Thomas Packard and Richard Burns (e.g., US patent 4,155,041) introduced simple analysis of the high-frequency content of both groove walls and were able to select the one that was instantaneously the more silent (the 'Switcher'). Until digital signal processing appeared, such approaches were the only ones available.[22] Digital signal processing enabled better distinguishing between content and background as well as suitable interpolation schemes to replace the parts of a signal that were noisy. In the beginning such schemes were computer bulk operations because of the huge amounts of data and filtering, but since *c.* 2000 (CEDAR) they have effectively become real-time operations.[23] The latest developments apply more sophisticated psychoacoustic methods, but for some reason refrain from applying precise knowledge about the generation of the background noise in the first place.[24]

Conclusion

What started out in the commercial field as a non-ideal medium, with analysable and partly correctable deficiencies, has become the total illusion it was intended to be. Certainly most performances, even by solo artists, are now collaborative efforts. And the fastest-growing medium only provides a semblance of sound. The deficiencies deliberately introduced to increase throughput can no longer be subsequently corrected. This is to the advantage of the holders of content rights, because they will be the sole owners of high-quality audio. The development to higher and higher standards of quality that was seen for 110 years has changed into a race to provide as much material as possible in a quality that is objectively the minimum that the consumers will tolerate. And a decision to handle recordings carefully in order to conserve them has no longer any bearing on their useful life – that is only a matter of how long a system is permitted to survive.

Raiders of the lost archive

ROGER BEARDSLEY

Every collector, whether of rare porcelain, jade or Old Masters, dreams of that one find that will astonish their peers and bring fame everlasting: their name will be spoken with bated breath for as long as there is interest in their field. Collectors of gramophone records are no different. For the instrumental enthusiast it might be a previously unknown recording of Johanna Martzy; the vocal collector may dream of finding the two fabled Fonotipia sides of the nineteenth-century tenor, Jean de Reszke. Whatever it may be, each and every collector has the belief that once in their lifetime he, or sometimes she (and it does seem that collecting is a male feature, or problem, depending on your point of view!), will make 'the great discovery' that will place them at the forefront of the craft.

At this juncture I must confess to being a 'record collector' – there, I've said it! My excuse is that I am a second-generation collector and my father inspired me with stories of his visits to Covent Garden to hear Supervia and Chaliapine (that's how it was spelt then): my earliest memories are of thorn needles being sharpened prior to wonderful sounds coming from an elaborate radio-gramophone. I still remember my first records when I can have been no more than five years old: a job-lot box from Morphet's sale room in Harrogate that included, oh joy of joys, Charles Penrose's 'The Laughing Policeman'. That's probably why my professional life has revolved around records and recording for more years than I care to think. Love of the artists, and their performances, has been why I am in this strange business of ours. But although I had been on the receiving end of luck in finding interesting and sometimes rare records, I still awaited The Great Discovery.

Among the various roles I perform, I have the privilege to be a member of the Historic Masters Committee. We work with the EMI Archive to produce limited editions of important 78 rpm records pressed directly from the original metal parts in the Archive, many of which were unpublished during the 78 era or are exceptionally rare as originals. In 2005, while we were planning a complete Adelina Patti edition, I became aware that Deutsche Grammophon had some HMV masters from before the First World War, when DG was still part of the Gramophone Company (HMV and later EMI). In fact DG pressed all the Gramophone Company's

records up until 1907, when the Hayes plant opened. This new information was despite enquiries over the last fifty years being met with the reply
that almost no metal masters from pre-1914 had survived the two world wars.

My contact at DG checked some numbers, and there in the vaults was
an almost complete set of first shells (metal masters taken from the
original waxes) of the Patti recordings. DG could not identify most of
them, however, and this I offered to do, also for any more they might have.
In due course an old handwritten list in an obviously German script
arrived. As soon as I started work, it became obvious that, as well as the
Patti masters, there was a group of unpublished recordings from 1903,
long thought destroyed.

The artist was Francesco Tamagno, the tenor chosen by Verdi for the
role of the Moor in arguably his greatest opera, *Otello*. Tamagno did make
published records, but they were mostly ten inch and the masters soon
wore badly. He also made a batch of the then new twelve-inch records – a
dozen in all. Only three were published, and they were soon superseded by
remakes. A fourth was discovered at Hayes, and we published it a few years
ago. But there on this list were all twelve, including four made for the
private use of Tamagno only. You can imagine that I needed a very stiff
drink shortly after. If I tell you that a battered test copy of one of these
changed hands for over £7,000 some years ago, you'll get some idea why!
Many of the others had never been found, although the titles were known
and were repeated when he made them as ten-inch published sides.

I requested the loan of these metals so that stampers could be made,
and a few weeks later they arrived. I made transfers while checking them
and was bowled over by the immediacy of the sound on these unworn
masters. Looking at them it was obvious that they were the original
masters made from the waxes. That in itself would have been enough –
to hold in my hand the masters for all those unpublished recordings
by one of the super-tenors of Verdi's generation was quite overwhelming –
but there was a further twist. Two of the private recordings were always
understood to be different takes of the same aria from *Messalina* by
Tamagno's friend, Isadore de Lara. These were the last two metals I was
to play and transfer. What I thought was the second take was the same as
the test pressing found some years ago, but of course in so much better
sound than had been heard before. For some reason I left its companion
until later that evening.

Returning to the turntable, I sat the metal on the platter, clamped it in
place (metals are not as flat as pressings) and lowered the pickup onto
the first grooves. The music I heard was not *Messalina*, and momentarily
I cursed, thinking that the matrix had been wrongly identified, but then
I realised that it was the opening to that great *Otello* duet, 'Sì, pel Ciel'. Of

course it had to be someone else: after all, Tamagno's records had been the subject of intensive study for over seventy years and he had never recorded that duet, so who would the Otello turn out to be, and also the baritone? Seconds later, I really was in a state of complete amazement: the tenor was so definitely Francesco, and soaring in the upper registers as only he could.

To say I was speechless would be putting it mildly. I played it again, and no mistake, it really was what I thought: I had not imagined it. Here it was in master form that we could press to make records for the world to hear. Perhaps the greatest vocal record discovery of the last 100 years – something I could never even have dreamed of. An unknown recording by the creator of the Moor, personally chosen and coached by the composer, and I was the first person to hear it in over a century.

The next thing I did was to pour that stiff drink and telephone my dear friend, Richard Bebb (then Historic Masters's chairman), who in my estimation was the world's foremost collector of vocal 78s. Like me he was lost for words: as he said, a Holy Grail, but one not known despite so much research. Sadly Richard died only a few months later, in April 2006, although he did hear the transfer I made for him. I wish he could be with us to see the special set of all these Tamagno sides that Historic Masters are issuing: rightly the set will be dedicated to him. It was through Richard that I learned so much about records, singers and the music, spurring me to go to the lengths that resulted in the discovery of these long-forgotten masters. He is as much responsible for their discovery as anyone.

Ave atque vale.

Discography

Matrix numbers of the Tamagno records referred to above were all in the Gramophone and Typewriter Company's 'C' series and were recorded at Tamagno's villa in Ospedaletti, Susa, Italy in February 1903. They are:

10 W	*Otello* (Verdi): 'Esultate!' (published as Gramophone and Typewriter issue number 052101)
11 W	*Otello* (Verdi): 'Esultate!' (unpublished)
12 W	*Otello* (Verdi): 'Ora e per sempre addio' (published as Gramophone and Typewriter issue number 052102)
13 R	*Otello* (Verdi): 'Ora e per sempre addio' (unpublished)
14 R	*Otello* (Verdi): 'Niun mi tema' (unpublished except as HM 36)
15 R	*Otello* (Verdi): 'Niun mi tema' (unpublished)

16 W   *Andrea Chénier* (Giordano): 'Un dì all'azzuro spazio'
(unpublished)

17 R   *Guglielmo Tell* (Rossini): 'O muto asil'
(published as Gramophone and Typewriter issue number 052103)

18 R   *Roi de Lahore* (Massenet): 'O casto fior' (Promesse de mon
avenir)
(private recording and unpublished; sung by an unnamed
baritone – see also 19 W)

19 W   *Otello* (Verdi): 'Sì, pel Ciel marmoreo giuro'
(with unnamed baritone; private recording and unpublished)

20 R   *Messalina* (De Lara): 'Dei del patria suol'
(private recording and unpublished)

21 R   *Ave Maria* (Mapelli)
(private recording and unpublished)

The 'R' suffix indicates Belford Royal, and the 'W' indicates Will Gaisberg –
the two engineers who made the recordings.

   As of March 2007 the identity of the unnamed baritone remained unknown.
A plausible theory is that it is Tamagno's brother, who was also a singer, if of
rather less repute.

   All published as direct pressings from the original masters in 2007 by
Historic Masters Ltd, www.historicmasters.org

The original cast recording of *West Side Story*

As historical documents, Broadway cast recordings preserve the performances of the original singers fresh from the stage, but as record albums
they were conceived to be satisfying in purely aural terms. So, while a cast
recording may be known to a far larger audience than ever experienced the
show in the theatre, what listeners actually hear is, in the vast majority of
cases, a paradoxical kind of authenticity: the original cast performing an
abridged version of the music, with little or no dialogue, and with numbers
sometimes presented in a different order (in the days of long-playing
records, a strong ending to side one and beginning to side two were further
conditioning factors). Since it is usually the cast album that provides the
most lasting and most widely known documentation of a show in its
'original' form, it is worth considering the musical alterations made to
transform it into a successful recording, and the case of *West Side Story*
provides an unusually well documented 'personal take' on a famous
example of the genre. Composers of shows are almost always present at
recording sessions, but in this case Leonard Bernstein had to be away in
Israel, and the happy consequence for later historians is that Stephen
Sondheim, who wrote the lyrics, provided him with an unusually detailed
report of the sessions. Goddard Lieberson – the producer of the album –
also wrote to Bernstein, giving his first reactions to the musical before its
Broadway opening.

    West Side Story opened on Thursday, 26 September 1957, and the
original cast recording was made by Columbia at the 30th Street Studio
three days later, on Sunday 29 September. (The custom was to record a
show, usually at the end of its first or second week, in one long session on
the 'rest' day for Broadway theatres, invariably a Sunday at the time.) This
one-day session involved recording all the music and also preparing a
complete edited mastertape, since production of the record began at
Columbia's Bridgeport CT pressing plant the next day – as reported in
the *New York Times* on 2 October 1957, which declared that 'by Monday
[7 October] the advertising and marketing program for the album will be
in full swing, and disks will be in the hands of music stores'.[1]

    The guiding force behind Columbia's cast albums from the 1940s to the
1970s was Goddard Lieberson (1911–77), who had worked for Columbia

Masterworks (the firm's classical division) since 1939 and became its president in 1956. Lieberson saw the potential of the long-playing record – with its playing time of about fifty minutes – as the ideal medium for cast recordings. As cast albums were made under great time pressure, meticulous preparation was essential. In his article 'The non-visual theatre' Lieberson described the preliminary work as well as describing what he set out to achieve in the 1949 cast recording of *South Pacific*:

> The recording procedure of *South Pacific* started long before its New York opening. Counting rehearsals, Boston and New York performances, I saw *South Pacific* fourteen times before we went into the recording studios. I also had out-of-theatre conferences with Dick Rodgers, Oscar Hammerstein, Joshua Logan, Mary Martin and Ezio Pinza. Despite all this, the most important moments are those in the studio itself. It's there that it becomes perfectly clear what is aural and what is not. It is there that ingenuity must substitute heightened musical effects for the action and scenery of the theatre. The elusive quality of atmosphere is all-important to the recordings ... I suppose it is obvious to say that one could collect together the best possible musicians, singers and conductor and still not convey the excitement of an opening night. Yet this should be the sought-for ideal in recording a complete show. Some of this excitement can be achieved technically, which is to say by the use of microphone placement. But yet more can be done by editing of the material and careful building of climaxes, just as they are carefully built in the theatre.[2]

Gary Marmorstein's definitive account of Columbia Records reveals that Lieberson was initially unenthusiastic about recording *West Side Story*. He quotes the recollections of Columbia executive Peter Munves: 'The story I heard was that Lieberson didn't want to sign *West Side Story* ... he heard it and didn't like it. And [David] Oppenheim, who was very close to Bernstein, probably prevailed on him to sign. Lieberson told me to go down and see it in tryouts in Philadelphia ... and I was *bowled over* by the first act!'[3] William Paley, President of CBS, was certainly unimpressed when Bernstein and Sondheim played the show through to him. Bernstein's datebook includes an appointment on 26 February 1957 – '3.00: Steve here. 5.00: William Paley coming to Studio to hear *Romeo* score.'[4] It was evidently a dismal occasion, as Bernstein later recalled:

> I remember Steve and I, poor bastards that we were, trying by ourselves at a piano to audition the score for Columbia Records, my record company. They said no, there's nothing in it anybody could sing, too depressing, too many tritones, too many words in the lyrics, too rangy – 'Ma-ri-a' – nobody could sing notes like that, impossible. They turned it down. Later they changed their minds, but that was an afternoon Steve and I will never forget ... There was tremendous animosity to the whole idea.[5]

If Lieberson shared any of Paley's doubts, these soon vanished when he experienced the show in the theatre. On 30 August 1957 he wrote to Bernstein giving his first impressions, after seeing a tryout in Washington:

> I've never known anything in musical theater to do me in the way *West Side Story* did. I'm usually a pain in the neck about those things – thinking all the while, officiously, how it ought to be better done and what I'd see thrown out. But Saturday it just threw me around and that's about the end of it ... I haven't ever seen a production which held together the way yours does ...[6]

Stephen Sondheim – whose Broadway debut was as the author of the lyrics for *West Side Story* – emphasised two aspects of Lieberson's decision-making during the sessions.[7] First, there was his thinking on tempo: that 'dance and other instrumental music needed to be played significantly faster on a recording than in the theatre'. Sondheim mentioned this as a general trait of Lieberson's cast albums, but with specific reference to *West Side Story* he recalled Lieberson's view that this was needed 'to approach on record the kind of excitement generated by Jerome Robbins's choreography on stage'. Second, Sondheim remembered that Lieberson deliberately aimed to capture something of the show's theatricality, and its raw energy: 'Goddard liked the rough moments, as they were closer to theatre.'

On 23 October 1957, Sondheim wrote to Bernstein,[8] reporting on the sessions that had taken place a few weeks earlier, while Bernstein was in Israel (he had flown there straight after the opening night). Sondheim began with his thoughts on the album as a whole, then moved on to the specific problem of the Balcony Scene:

> I was amazed at Goddard's efficiency and dispatch, as well as his efforts at maintaining quality. You will probably be displeased with the record for reasons stated below as well as dozens of others, but on the whole I think it's pretty good – at least, by show album standards. It was recorded simultaneously for stereophonic tape (to be released in November as the first show so recorded[9]) and sounds much better than the record. Some of the balancing isn't all it could be, but most of the trouble we had was due to lack of time – time on the record and time in the recording studio. As we had suspected, the amount of music was way overlong. Someone had goofed on the pre-recording timing, claiming that the balcony scene (starting with the singing) was 2:40, whereas it turned out to be 5:10. I don't have time to go into all the suggestions for remedying this, but the only one that worked was to cut out the best part – namely, the dialogue. Consequently, to our ears, the scene has been emasculated, going straight from the second chorus to the sung 'Goodnight's, with four hurried lines spoken over the bridge between. Thus the first 'goodnight' has to start on the fifth instead of the second, which ruins it, because the second doesn't fit in with the harmony. It's too

bad, but I assure you there was no other way out – at least, none that occurred to us.

This cut in the Balcony Scene excised bars 121–44,[10] with the 'hurried lines of dialogue' spoken over bars 118–20, ending with Tony's 'I love you' (taken from the middle of the original passage of dialogue), substituted for his final 'Te adoro, Maria'. Sondheim went on to prepare Bernstein for more possible disappointments, mostly the consequence of limited time in the studio:

> Drawbacks in the recording, cont'd: A very fast tempo for the prologue, not so much to save time as to make it more interesting. Without the accompanying action, it tended toward monotony.[11] Incidentally, we included street noises and shouts throughout the album, which works very well for the most part, though they tend to drown out the music in The Rumble. (2) Larry's[12] voice on 'Something's Coming' gets a little froggy in a few places and he sang the wrong rhythm for 'come on, deliver', but it was by far the best of the takes, because the feeling was right. Unfortunately, it was the next to last song recorded and he was very tired, having been at the session for nine hours. His best is 'Maria,' which was the first number he recorded. (3) Frank Green[13] took Larry's part in The Rumble (shouting 'Riff, don't!') and came in about ten bars too late – just before the stabbing – but the orchestra played it so well, that we didn't try another take (it was already the third). Also, they forgot to blow the police whistle at the climax. (By the way, the orchestra was increased to 37 men for the recording.)[14] (4) 'America' and 'I Feel Pretty' don't sound any better on the record than they do on the stage. (5) A trumpet player goofed badly on the change of key in the final procession. Oddly enough, nobody heard it until it was too late. I was out getting five minutes' sleep during it (I also slept during 'America', since the session lasted from 10am to 1am). There will be a hundred other subtle and unsubtle goofs that will probably anger you, but the general reaction to the record so far (it came out last Friday – first order being 46,000 copies – is that good?) has been wonderful. *Variety* raved, and Douglas Watt in the *News* gave it a good notice (where he objected to anything, it was to the material, not the recording). The singers were not at their best, Lenny, but they were tired.

Finally, Sondheim mentioned two decisions taken on the spot during the sessions, the first of which was a telling intervention on Lieberson's part:

> One thing you ought to like: Goddard insisted that the final chorus of 'Krupke' be played very slow with a heavy vaudeville beat. Jerry must have had conniptions.[15] Another sidelight: Irv and Sid[16] put a major cadence at the end of 'I Have A Love'. I had conniptions, so it was changed back to the relative minor. I presume you didn't want it changed. I certainly didn't.

Sondheim makes no mention of the far-reaching changes made to the ending, so presumably this had been agreed in advance. The Finale of the show (full score p. 471) begins with Maria and Tony singing a halting fragment of 'Somewhere', unaccompanied, starting with 'Hold my hand and we're halfway there'. Tony dies as Maria sings 'Someday', she 'falters and stops', then the orchestra enters for the first time in the scene, playing a tender recollection of 'Somewhere' for seven bars. The music is interrupted by Maria's final monologue ('Stay back! … Te adoro Anton'), and a fourteen-bar orchestral epilogue brings *West Side Story* to a close.

On the cast recording this scene is handled quite differently. There's no attempt to replicate in sound the stage experience of Tony's death and Maria's reaction – neither is even hinted at on the record. Instead, the finale begins with two bars of rocking piano accompaniment taken from the original 'Somewhere' (p. 372, bars 147–8), followed by a choral arrangement of the song, which leads directly to the fourteen-bar epilogue. There's also a change to the last bar as it appears in the published full score and revised piano–vocal score: the final low F sharp (timpani, cellos and basses) is omitted, so the last chord we hear is a quiet, unclouded C major triad.

8 The recorded document: Interpretation and discography

SIMON TREZISE

To understand what we hear from recordings we must first understand them as sources of evidence. Although initially the usefulness of recording was unclear, in the twentieth century the industry became profitable through focusing on entertainment. Providing consumers were entertained they were content not to enquire too closely into the distortions and illusions that recording created, especially as sound quality improved and relative prices decreased. Thus throughout the past 110 years records have been widely if naively accepted as surrogate accounts of live performance. Nevertheless, reading through the medium reveals the extent to which recording transmutes music-making. Even when production and record seem at one, as in much rock music from the 1960s when albums were created over long periods in the studio, records contain secrets that challenge preconceptions. Outlining the most significant is one purpose of this chapter. First, though, we need to know how to find recordings, and how to date and place them: then we shall be in a better position to ask about the sounds they encode.

Discographies and information trails

There are many discographies and other useful materials available via the internet, but it is often impossible to estimate how accurate the information is for there is less obvious editorial control or review than in printed publications.[1] Nevertheless, a comprehensive online discography for a single performer, Eugene Ormandy for example,[2] is often reliable, and when an institution like the London Symphony Orchestra puts up discographical information one has good reason to trust it.[3] Digging into the frustratingly awkward catalogues of the great sound archives, such as those at the British Library, Library of Congress and Bibliothèque nationale, can often yield useful information, but each is riddled with quirks and uncertainties.[4]

Much helpful information is given by internet retailers, such as the vast American store ArkivMusic.com. Their excellent search engine enables one to search by composer, performer, conductor, ensemble and label, so for example if one wishes to know how many performances conducted by Thomas Beecham are available from the store, one has only to drill through the list of conductors to his name; then one has detailed information by composer, orchestra and label. Unfortunately, Naxos's excellent historical series is not included, so there are gaps. More unpredictable but staggeringly numerous results can be obtained by doing artist and composer searches at allmusic.com. A search under the Beatles, for example, yields much historical and biographical information, an extensive discography, a list of some of the bootleg CDs, DVDs, videos and more. There are pictures and a peculiar but possibly helpful list of moods encompassed in the songs.[5]

Even with so much online, the primary source of discographical information is the library, and it takes time and practice to find what one needs (plus a well-funded music section). There are two essential publications, which are often the first place to look for information on classical music on record during the 78 and early LP eras. One is *WERM, The World's Encyclopedia of Record Music*, which first appeared in 1952 and was followed by supplements; it sought to list all available recordings of 'permanent music' (which in practice meant broadly canonical classical music), plus selected 'historical' issues, by composer.[6] Similar in structure is *The Gramophone Shop Encyclopaedia of Recorded Music*, first published in 1932 and revised in 1936 and 1948.[7] Jazz collectors find extensive information in three seminal works: Rust, Jepsen and Bruyninckx.[8] Hundreds of discographies have been published since then, all falling into one of three main categories, namely subject, performer and label. Some appear separately as books; others appear in journals, as appendices in books, and elsewhere.[9] The last bibliography of discographies able to satisfy a wide range of questions appeared in 1988: Michael Gray, *Classical Music Discographies, 1976–88*, which formed a supplement to Gray's *Bibliography of Discographies* of 1977.[10] Various information resources can help to locate discographies, such as RILM, IIMP and Google Scholar, as can some library catalogues, but some queries take a great deal of work. Finding 78s and early LPs should become easier with the publication of the CHARM online discography in 2009. Failing all these, in desperate straits one can consult the annual catalogues issued by each record company, many of which are available in the British Library.

The format and quality of discographies varies immensely, as does their reliability. For example, a 'subject' who has fared well is Mahler, culminating in the splendid *Mahler Discography* by Péter Fülöp.[11] As well as detail on sources and background, coverage is by work, with recordings given in chronological order; there are performer indexes. In a summary list of recordings of each work, timings for every movement and song are given. In addition to details of ensemble and conductor, recording dates and location are provided; there is a list of first releases on LP in various countries, each with release date, the first CD release, the author of insert notes, and reviews in journals such as *Records and Recording*. Entries are stacked: the discography 'presents each entry in a uniform stack of lines, with each piece of information always appearing on the same line'.[12]

The 'performer' discography is the most common form, especially in the documentation of singers. An example shows some of the pitfalls. John Hunt has privately produced numerous discographies, many of them indispensable. However, *Giants of the Keyboard: Kempf, Gieseking, Fischer, Haskil, Backhaus, Schnabel* is problematic.[13] Entries are arranged by composer, but work order is inconsistent. Month and year are given but not the day, which is usually known. The locale is given, typically the city but not the venue although it is also known in many instances. Matrix numbers (of which more shortly) are not given. The author fails to distinguish between live and studio recordings. Concerning Gieseking, for example, Donald Manildi writes:

> Gieseking recorded Debussy's *Preludes*, *Children's Corner*, and *Suite bergamesque* twice in the early 1950s … [As they] appeared in the US on Columbia and Angel some collectors have assumed them to be identical, but they are not. Hunt lumps them together … and makes no distinction between them.[14]

Other recordings are omitted altogether.

'Label' discographies are the workhorses of discography. Once they have been tackled much else becomes possible. *His Master's Voice: The German Catalogue: A Complete Numerical Catalogue of German Gramophone Recordings Made from 1898 to 1929 in Germany, Austria, and Elsewhere by the Gramophone Company Ltd = Die Stimme seines Herrn*, compiled by Alan Kelly with the cooperation of the EMI Music Archive, London is a prime example.[15] The volume provides detailed history and explanation of often highly complex matrix and catalogue-number sequences. Orchestral records were given catalogue numbers 40500 to 40999, so the listing can be done by type of recording, orchestra records for example, and catalogue numbers. Entries are in columnar format with the information reading from left to right, thus: catalogue number, matrix number, performers, work and section details, other issues and couplings. Discographies of this quality and extent are formidable and generous acts of scholarship.

What the discs tell us

Surface markings and surrounding documentation can tell us a great deal about a recording. Most shellac-disc labels identify the composer, work, performers, and sometimes even the venue. To take an example at random, DB 1555 is the second record in a three-disc HMV set of Borodin's Second Symphony. The following information is displayed on the label:

Company of origin:	Gramophone Company, His Master's Voice
Composer:	Borodin
Work and movement(s):	Symphony No. 2 in B Minor, third movement – Andante (first record)
Orchestra and conductor:	London Symphony Orchestra, conducted by Albert Coates

Figure 8.1a HMV DB 1555, Matrix Cc17857-IIA, label, with warning sticker added by the BBC Gramophone Library

Figure 8.1b HMV DB 1555, Matrix Cc17857-IIA, detail of matrix number

The catalogue number was assigned according to the area of distribution, so a sister company might issue the same recording under its own catalogue number. This potentially confusing situation is resolved by the most important number (or sequence of letters and numbers), which is preserved in the area between the grooved area and the label, usually at 6.00 o'clock (under the label). This is the matrix number, which is the number of the master record. It is a unique identifier which can, when the company's records have survived (or there is an alternative source of information), yield the date and place of the recording, often more. Early matrix numbers identify the 'expert' responsible for the recording, such as Fred Gaisberg, who is identified by a G or FG.[16] RCA-Victor also printed the matrix number on the label. Here the matrix number is Cc17857 IIA Δ. HMV matrix numbers in the Bb and Cc series were mostly recorded in London, Bb being used for ten-inch discs and Cc for twelve-inch. They have been catalogued and dated by Alan Kelly,[17] and so we know that Cc17857 was recorded in the Kingsway Hall on 6 November 1929. The roman-numeral II indicates that the side issued was of the second useable take, and the A shows that this matrix was cut on the second of at least two lathes simultaneously recording the same performance: in this case the A lathe presumably produced the better-sounding disc, and take II the better-sounding performance (not necessarily the most musical). The triangle was a symbol used by HMV to designate electrical recordings made by the American Westrex system.[18]

In contrast, the English Decca recording of extracts from Mendelssohn's *A Midsummer Night's Dream*, catalogue number K. 1769, is documented on the CHARM website in one of several discographies by Michael Gray, this one being of the British Decca 78 catalogue.[19] In addition to the label information, which gives the performers as the Concertgebouw Orchestra of Amsterdam conducted by Eduard van Beinum, Gray gives the following:

Date and place of recording:	12 September 1946, Grote Zaal, Concertgebouw
Producer:	[Victor] Olof
Engineer:	[Ken] Wilkinson

Apart from the matrix number, other surface markings are of less historical interest, but typically refer to 'the development of negative and positive metal parts from the wax or acetate session disc and to the sequence of those transfers'.[20]

The diligence of companies in marking take numbers and, on some sequences but not others, the use of a second transcription lathe at the recording session (by a suffix A on HMV 78s) yields fascinating insights into the practices of recording companies. With popular issues in particular, the matrices used for manufacture might eventually wear out and the company would resort to substitution with an alternative take from the original session. Rachmaninov's Piano Concerto No. 2 in C Minor was recorded on 10 and 13 April 1929 by the composer with the Philadelphia Orchestra conducted by Leopold Stokowski. It appeared on Victor 8148-52 with the matrices CVE 48963-72. The original takes used were:

Original issue
I: 3, 1, 1
II: 1, 3, 2, 1
III: 2, 2, 1

The substitutions were made in the Second World War and affected nine sides.

Substitutions
I: 2, 2, 2
II: 1, 1, 3, 2
III: 1, 3, 3

The original artists' file session sheet was amended to indicate that the 'the substitute takes were the ones which had always been chosen for mastering'. This mistake was perpetuated in the official release of the original takes on CD: the booklet accompanying the CD wrongly lists the substitute sides even though the originals were used.[21] There are musically significant differences between takes.

When a matrix number is not provided, as in the instance of Caruso's two recordings of 'Celeste Aïda' of 1908 and 1911, confusion may arise, for both recordings were issued under the same Victor catalogue number 88127. One only discovers this through listening or visual identification: the 1911 version has a shorter run-out area.[22]

Compared with 78s, LPs, EPs and many CDs are uninformative, especially in the early days of LP. Columbia ML 4092 is an early twelve-inch LP of Stravinsky conducting the Philharmonic Symphony Orchestra of New York in *Le sacre du printemps*. The performers and work are clearly labelled, and it was standard practice even in the early days of LP to give a programme note, which 78s often lacked. There is, however, no indication that this is the 1940 recording originally on Columbia 78s 11367–70. Another Michael Gray discography on the CHARM website gives further details, including the location of the recording, Carnegie Hall, the 78 matrix numbers, and an early CD transfer by Pearl.[23]

It later became customary for LPs to provide copyright information, in the form of the publication date, but this is at best only a rough guide to the date of the recording and may be many years after. The number engraved on the surface between the grooves and the label refers to 'an edited session tape cut onto an LP record' and is of no interest to the historian, though some collectors find it useful in differentiating between issues.[24]

With the advent of CD the recording process and its potential interest to the consumer was sometimes taken more seriously. One of the first Decca releases, for example, was of Janáček's Sinfonietta and *Taras Bulba* with Charles Mackerras conducting the Vienna Philharmonic Orchestra (410 138–2). In addition to the publication date of 1983 (which applies only to the CD, not the LP that preceded it), the location and approximate date of the recording were also given: Sofiensaal, Vienna, March 1980.

Finding discs

Having established that a record was indeed made one has to find ways to get hold of it. The largest collections are national and other major archives, though many of them are unlikely to give the user access to the original disc. Some will play the recording from a remote point in the building, often with a microphone link to the engineer at the other end. Depending upon local copyright laws, archives may make copies (for a price); in the UK this usually means that anything recorded more than fifty years ago is potentially in the public domain, though this may change. If access to the original is required, there are a small number of collections that will allow this, such as the sound archive at King's College London. Otherwise one may be able to pick up original copies from specialist dealers, including Princeton Record Exchange, Academy Records in New York, Jerry's Records in Pittsburgh, Raymond Glaspole in Oxford, Mikrokosmos, Norbeck and Peters, Nauck's, and Larry Holdridge;[25] eBay can be an excellent source as well, though one should be aware of the extremely optimistic terms used to describe the condition of records on eBay and elsewhere (G, 'good', denoting a record that is only just playable, if that). If on the other hand one is able to work from commercial transfers (see later in the chapter for the significant limitations this imposes), then a great deal of material is available and one can search for it in the catalogues of the transfer labels or on retailers' websites like Amazon. Amazon is useful since many reissues are no longer available and Amazon resellers may have them second hand (remember also to try different national Amazon sites: the French and Japanese ones can be very productive). Transfer labels include the originating companies, such as DG and EMI, though their level of activity is modest compared with the 'independents', including Andante, Archipel, Avid, Biddulph, Brilliant Classics, Doremi, Dutton, Dynamic, Guild, Hardy Classic, Lys, Membran, Music & Arts, Myto, Naxos, Nimbus, Opera d'oro, Pearl, Regis, Tahra and Testament.

Diminutions and distortions

Having found a recording, and as much as we can about its origins, our next challenge is to understand the respects in which the technology that produced it imposes restrictions on the presentation of music. The following are some of the major constraints.

Frequency response

The human ear in optimum, youthful condition can detect frequencies from *c*. 20 to 20,000 Hz. Until after the Second World War technology could reproduce a small part of this spectrum, so a great deal of information heard at a live performance was lost. In the acoustic period this meant that tinkling, sibilance, the natural brightness of a soprano voice, the bass notes of a piano, and much more could neither be recorded nor reproduced. After the introduction of electrical recording in 1925 a steady stream of innovations raised the ceiling from around 5,000 cycles to 15,000 by 1944.

Dynamic response

Until recently recording struggled with the extremes of loudness that the ear can effortlessly disentangle, so experts (as producers or engineers were called in the early days) sought to contain the dynamics. In the acoustic period this could not be done on the recording equipment, so the performer had either to modify her position relative to the receiving horn or modify her performance so that it used less dynamic contrast than it would at a concert. Pianists were encouraged to play loudly, often on upright instruments with hardened hammers and missing backs; violins were often replaced by instruments with metal sound boxes (Stroh violins); and (for example) Adelina Patti was placed on a 'small movable platform' so that she could be pulled away from the horn when a loud note approached and towards it for a quiet one.[26] With the advent of microphones 'gain riding' was applied by an engineer guided by a score-reading assistant: an anticipated peak was curtailed and the level reinstated when the music returned to, say, *mezzo forte*; quiet passages were amplified to bring them over the level of the surface noise. Later, electronic compressors and limiters would be used together with manual gain riding, for it was often impossible for an engineer to react to sudden changes in dynamic. Magnetic tapes used for recording in the LP era encompassed a dynamic range of around 60 dB before distortion set in (the human ear can accommodate around 120 dB). Compact disc went further (around 94 dB); new formats, such as DVD-Audio and SACD, match the human ear. In many recording situations it is hard to know the extent to which the musician performed as he or she was accustomed to do live, because the recording process intervenes stealthily and sometimes with considerable skill to retain a sense of a 'real' performance; on the other hand, some gain riding is crude and immediately identifiable.

Spatial information

In the acoustic period performers were confined within a small space and the recordings often lack a sense of depth, though this aspect should not be overstated: great sophistication evolved in the use of horns and many recordings give the impression of a soundstage. As the electrical era dawned some music was recorded in a realistic way with orchestras set out on the stages of concert halls, but many spatial anomalies have remained, such as the use of recording booths for soloists, especially in popular song. Unfamiliar spatial arrangements even in quite modern recordings can interfere with sightlines and in other ways disrupt musicians' accustomed performing arrangements.

Timbral realism

The timbral quality of an instrument or voice in a recording is dependent upon a multitude of factors. If the upper frequencies are missing, as they are above around 3,500 Hz in an acoustic recording, this will affect the realism of the sound. Other factors, such as the quality of a horn or microphone, its placement, unsteadiness in the cutter or tape, the condition of the commercial 78 after many playings, and the equipment used by the purchaser, will determine the quality of the sound. If one is working from a commercial transfer of a 78, for example, some aspects of the timbre are the product of undocumented decisions by the transfer engineer.

Duration

At first compact discs played for up to *c.* sixty minutes and have now been extended to over eighty; high-definition formats (DVD-Audio and video, SACD) play for longer. The earliest recordings lasted less than two minutes. Until the late 1940s performers and listeners usually had to make music in three- or four-minute units, depending on record diameter. There is occasional evidence to suggest that performers accelerated their performances to suit the restricted playing time, but a more common consequence of it is extensive cutting of the musical text, which diminished over the years. Twelve-inch LPs, first issued in 1948, increased each side's playing time to around twenty minutes at first, and commercial tapes, first issued in the 1950s, extended this still further.

Commercial, political, racial, social, and other agendas

Race, society, commercial pressure, and other ideologies and agendas have affected the production and distribution of gramophone records. Racism in America explains why the early propagation of jazz on record came late and mostly with white musicians. Commercial concerns (and differences in practice between England and America) forced Sergei Rachmaninov to record short works; he was not given the opportunity to record major examples of his core repertoire such as Beethoven's last piano sonata.

Expediency

Expediency plays a revelatory role in the history of recording. For example, in the early part of its existence RCA and companies in Europe found they could record in concert-like acoustics with credible results. That they chose not to must be partly explained by the effort and expenditure entailed: if Lionel Mapleson was able to make sometimes quite convincing recordings of live Metropolitan Opera performances on an amateur cylinder set-up in the period 1901–4, major companies might surely have done likewise had not the small, cramped, acoustically dead studio been more expedient.

In addition to factors restricting the recording of music, once the recorded document entered the market place it was subject to the whims and vicissitudes of its many differently disposed owners. Records were themselves the subject of performance. Rituals were enacted; finely engineered products were treated with a obsessive, quasi-religious concern for their faithful reproduction by some and with a carelessness boarding on crassness by others. These extremes are already discernible in the early days of 78s and peaked in the age of the LP.

Playback curves

Early recordings were recorded at many speeds around 78 rpm, but working out what they were in each case is based on knowledge, judgement, taste and guesswork, so that is another constraint. Pre-war and many post-war electrical 78s were recorded with a system of equalisation that attenuated the mid to bass frequencies (and in some cases boosted the treble as well), as were LPs. In order to achieve optimum playback one seeks a near-exact reciprocal of the original 'curve' so that the mid-to-low frequencies are amplified and thereby reproduced at the strength heard in the studio. Electrical gramophones, which started to appear in the late 1920s, could do this to an extent, and from the 1950s amplifiers were appearing that could be adjusted for the various curves used by LPs (standardised to the LP curve in the mid-1950s).

Contingencies of playback

There is no limit to the capacity of consumers to affect playback in their homes. Anyone old enough to remember 78s and LPs will recall discs warped by electric fires, LPs with soup spilt on them, scratches on the playing surface, and so on. Some record players were almost infinitely adjustable for the enthusiast, so great variations in playback could be achieved, including, on most machines, speed adjustment for 78s.

Case studies of recording

The following examples examine recordings that are characteristic of their time. Under critical scrutiny they emerge as complex documents that demand interpretation in the same way that written texts do. The studies include consideration of the crucial role of the remastering engineer.

Patti

Adelina Patti was the most acclaimed soprano of the second half of the nineteenth century. She made a number of recordings over two extended sessions in 1905 and 1906 at her home in Craig-Y-Nos (South Wales). For many they represent the epitome of golden-age singing, albeit diminished by the singer's age and the limitations of the acoustic gramophone. The recording scaled her voice down chiefly by reducing the amplitude – hence the need to roll her away from the horn at climaxes – and by removing the upper harmonics of her voice above *c.* 3,500 cycles. The acoustic properties of the horn added a complex series of frequency distortions. We cannot say how bright or mellow her voice was, not just because the high frequencies are missing, but because we cannot be sure what pitch the records should be played at. It is widely accepted that she transposed Zerlina's 'Batti, batti, O bel Masetto' down from F to E♭. Played back at 74 rpm we hear the song at this pitch, but the A is set to 440: the likelihood is that her piano was tuned to a lower pitch, so some transfers are possibly too fast. Played in F at 440, 'Batti, batti' sounds bright, very impressive in the runs, despite a certain shrillness in her voice (age and wear). But if we take the speed down below 74 rpm, her voice is gentler, less brilliant, and the runs now seem more realistic for a singer in the twilight of her career.

Boston Symphony Orchestra

The Boston Symphony Orchestra made its first recordings in 1917 under the direction of Karl Muck. It was not the first time an American orchestra had been placed in front of a horn, but it was still a major event subject to much planning and promotion. The conductor hoped to record movements of symphonies, including the finales of Tchaikovsky's Fourth and Beethoven's Seventh, but RCA officials also brought a stash of short popular works, such as the Act III Prelude from *Lohengrin*, which formed the basis of most of the takes. The orchestra of 100 men travelled down to Philadelphia from Boston in an October heat wave, arriving exhausted and irritable in Camden, New Jersey on the morning of 2 October, to be ushered into a studio in which two igloos with door-like openings had been constructed. In front of the igloos was a stand for the conductor; behind the conductor was the turntable for the master disc; according to one account, first-desk men played outside the igloos directly into horns of their own, but the rest of the orchestra was packed tightly inside – one igloo for the strings, the other for the wind – in order to maximise the sound available to the recording horns. Boaz Piller, a bassoon player in the orchestra, recalled that some instruments were not registering and were obliged to come out of the huts and sit right in front of the horn during solos. The oboe was most awkward during the 'transition section' of the finale of Tchaikovsky's Fourth and in the end they had him play directly into the horn.

Each side had to be repeated many times, first to obtain the right balance, which could only be judged by playing the wax just recorded (thereby destroying it), and then because of mistakes caused by the difficult playing conditions, tension and heat. The triumphant cymbal crashes were considered the last word in high-fidelity and put down a marker for future generations of orchestral recordings.[27] Pictures of other acoustic-recording sessions show that unusual seating arrangements were inevitable, though igloos of this sort were unusual.

The Tchaikovsky recording is impressive as presented on compact disc by Ward Marston.[28] One can hear more of the first desks than the whole string section: indeed, it is hard to believe that the orchestra was at full strength. The brass section registers well too, and one can detect at around 4:45, where the oboist had to penetrate the receiving horn, that the balance is unnatural. In spite of conditions, the performance is incisive and exciting. Marston even manages to uncover a deepish bass line, albeit from a tuba player, not the string basses. Signs of the old rubato style of playing are missing: there is little portamento and much of the playing is in tempo. In the rhythmic emphasis on rapidly progressing to the downbeat from the previous bar, rather than the modern manner of 'lengthening' the bar line, however, the performance is distinctly of its period.

Gennett jazz recordings

Some of the earliest jazz recordings, after the pioneering work of the Original Dixieland Jazz Band (1917), were made by a small company in Richmond Indiana called Gennett, an offshoot of Starr Piano, a manufacturer of pianos and phonographs. Compared with the East Coast's giants Victor and Columbia it was a modest operation, but historically it is crucial.[29] Debate will continue as to the impact recording had on the evolution of jazz, but it seems likely that it has been overstated. Certainly recording confined jazz numbers to three minutes for the ten-inch side and thereby misrepresented the style; it forced musicians to work out their performances in precise detail as time in recording sessions was limited, so improvisation was largely quashed. And the original instrumentation of jazz bands had to be modified to facilitate acoustic recording: string bass was replaced by tuba and a full percussion kit was reduced to wood blocks and/or cymbals. Such recordings were the means by which jazz spread throughout large parts of America and beyond. But, equally, much jazz was distributed in notated arrangements, and the notion of writing out what was to be played for a session was by no means uncongenial to the players, who were paid for arrangements. Moreover, the numbers recorded were often versions of existing songs with verse–chorus forms, which tended to coincide with the time requirements of recording.[30]

Nevertheless a glance at the early Gennett sessions reveals how much the musicians had to learn. The studio was a metre from a secondary railroad spur, which could interrupt sessions. The studio was 38 × 9 metres and adjoined a control room separated from the recording area by a double pane of glass. Drapery deadened the wooden walls so that the acoustic was quite dead. Players clustered around two horns, typically with the reduced percussion section close to one, next to the piano; woodwind and plucked strings were close but to one side, and brass players several metres away and off to the right. Local or passing bands were signed up and their first impression of the studio (as of all studios during the acoustic era, even if local weather conditions made this one worse than most) would be its heat – as high as 30 degrees Celsius, in order to keep the wax soft. Dozens of waxes might have to be cut and thrown away simply to get the balance correct. Even then many of the balances are bizarre. Once the recording began, a red light would flick on to indicate that 2 minutes 30 seconds had passed and the song should soon end. Each song would be recorded three times in order to produce one publishable copy, but many numbers were never issued. The artists had no say on what was issued and indeed made little money from the whole enterprise, but some received copies of the records which they could use to promote their careers.

The King Oliver band, signed in 1923, made twenty-seven takes. The poor Gennett sound quality sucks dynamic life out of the ensemble and lacks a bass line; trombone and clarinet dominate at the expense of the cornets; Louis Armstrong's counter melodies seem backward.

> Joe [Oliver] and Louis stood right next to each other as they always had, and you couldn't hear a note that Joe was playing … [so] they put Louis about fifteen feet over in the corner, looking all sad.[31]

Lillian Hardin Armstrong's famous story has been qualified since, but it indicates how balance was achieved. Rick Kennedy concludes from his discussion of these historic discs that the recordings were an 'ensemble effort': New Orleans jazz 'was not grounded in improvisation'.[32]

In 1925, still recording acoustically, Hoagy Carmichael and the Happy Harmonists recorded a number entitled 'Washboard Blues', which was rejected as it was twenty seconds short. Carmichael insisted and was told to come back in ten minutes and fill in the gap with a piano solo, which the terrified law student did magnificently.[33] Several transfers of this extra-ordinary recording have appeared, all different in the amount of surface noise removed, equalisation, and so on.[34]

Vaughan Williams, Symphony No. 4
Conscientious collectors of the time of the composer's 1937 recording had numerous means to optimise playback, including different grades of needle, various shapes of soundbox, weight adjusters and, for owners of acoustic record players, the Lifebelt, a tube for 'insertion between the tone-arm and sound-box … to give the reproducing stylus a certain quality of flexibility', promoted in *The Gramophone* by Compton Mackenzie (the novelist and founder of the magazine).[35]

(a)

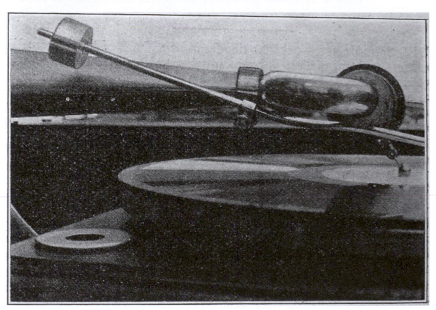

(b)

Figure 8.2 Lifebelt and Weight Adjuster, from an advertisement in *The Gramophone*, 1926

Anyone who has heard the exquisite sound obtainable from a well-adjusted EMG gramophone must surely admit that collectors in the early twentieth century had all they needed to bask in 'perfect' reproduction in their homes, enjoying a harmony with the media and means of reproduction comparable to hi-fi buffs in the LP era: reproduction was perfectible, just as it had been in 1907 and was to be again in 1967. Few people play their own 78s now, so somebody else has to do it. Transfer engineers usually work for themselves in studios conforming to no set format. Although many have audio-engineering backgrounds, they find their own way to obtaining a suitable product for modern consumption. In taking a set of 78s, such as the Vaughan Williams Fourth, and bringing it to CD, they interpret the discs according to an intricate set of criteria; no two transfers sound alike, as so many decisions are founded on personal taste and experience. The following list summarises the process:

- The record is cleaned and centred on the platter so the stylus does not swing from left to right.
- Pitch is checked for every side in case there are deviations; most engineers confronted with a record of this period would expect concert A to be at 440.
- A stylus that best fits the groove wall and therefore produces least surface noise in exchange for more audio information is chosen (it may not fit all sides).
- As the records were made with the lower frequencies attenuated, a suitable turnover curve has to be selected on a specialist amplifier; for an HMV recording of this period the turnover is likely to be around 200–250 Hz (around middle C), from whence there is a 6 dB attenuation every octave, though there are many variations; the treble should be played flat.
- High-frequency broadband noise above the musical signal has to be filtered.
- Most engineers do much more equalisation, often with a view to achieving as natural an orchestral sound as was heard in the hall in 1937 (most of the original recording venues used no longer exist so much guesswork and experience of other recordings is involved).
- Other processes are used to remove noise, including declicking and decrackling.
- New processes from CEDAR, for example, notably Retouch, can be used to remove almost any unwanted noise, including coughs, creaky chairs, and cutter rumble.[36]
- More touching up is possible, including the elimination of discrepancies of acoustic, microphone set-up, level, etc. between sides.
- The sides are joined up, sometimes wrongly, as in the last two sides of this symphony, where several transfers lop out a bar before the recapitulation.

The composer's recording of his Symphony No. 4 was made in Abbey Road Studio No. 1. It is a biting, incisive, disturbing recording, generally faster than any since. In the LP period one transfer was made (c. 1969–70), by Anthony Griffith, who used a razor blade, an analogue equaliser, a reel-to-reel tape recorder, and probably no form of analogue noise suppression other than some steep filtering. The *Gramophone* reviewer of 1970 was impressed; he wrote, 'The recording sounds extraordinarily good. Some things may seem "fiddled" (e.g. very forward woodwind at times) but it is full and still has plenty of quality.'[37]

Table 8.1

CD issue	Transfer engineer	Year
Koch 37018–2	Mark Obert-Thorn	1990
Dutton CDAX 8011	Michael Dutton	1995
Avid AMSC 599	David Wright, Dave Bennett	1998
Pearl GEMS 0062	Roger Beardsley	1999
Naxos 8.111048	Mark Obert-Thorn	2006

At least five CD transfers have been issued, as shown in Table 8.1.

The authors of the 1994 edition of the Penguin *Guide to Compact Discs* argue that Koch's 'transfer is less full-bodied than the LP version ... (the upper strings are lacking in timbre)'.[38] The *Gramophone* reviewer in April 1991 had been no happier:

> In 1970 World Records issued an Anthony Griffith LP transfer of the Fourth Symphony (6/70 – nla), which reproduced pretty well the blunt unvarnished but full-bodied sound of the original 78s. This transfer was used for a fairly recent LP reissue on EMI (2/88 – nla), but there the sound was rather smoothed out, so that body and impact were reduced. The new Koch International transfer, alas, is no better. Both ends of the sound spectrum have been compressed, and the performance again loses some of its weight and strength.[39]

The Koch release was presumably similar in technique to the LP: analogue tape and equalisation without CEDAR for declicking. Comparing it with Mark Obert-Thorn's latest transfer for Naxos, it is clear that heavier filtering was needed to dampen the shellac noise.

Dutton's transfer is markedly different. CEDAR processing has been liberally applied, to the extent that the scratch and much broadband noise have been magically washed away. Some artificial reverberation has been added to make up for what is lost in the processing. Also notable in this transfer is a heavy reduction in the frequencies between around 3 and 4 kHz, perhaps in response to a desire to ameliorate the old-sounding aspect of this recording and make it smoother, more modern in character. Left and right channels are slightly different, suggesting artificial-stereo processing.

Like Dutton, Avid attempts to belie the age of the recording. On the cover the interventions are trumpeted: 'Audiophile Quality Remastering' and 'In the Clarity of 3-Dimensional Sound'. The authors acknowledge in their notes that processing is not to everybody's taste but do not disapprove of it themselves: their 'aim is to produce as natural and pure a sound character that lacks harshness and possesses a smooth response that falls gratefully on the ear, being comfortable and clear'. As with Dutton the remaining background noise varies in intensity and the quieter passages, where the noise reduction has had to cut most deeply, have a quality that might be characterised as 'submerged'.

The Pearl issue reflects a less-interventionist philosophy than Dutton or Avid, but more than Koch and Naxos. It has the most generous bass of all the transfers and most vigorous attack in highly modulated passages. CEDAR or another process has removed the scratch almost completely but, as in the Naxos issue, no attempt is made to remove all the broadband noise; it is only attenuated by equalisation. It seems that some reverberation has been added to compensate for the rather lack-lustre acoustic of Abbey Road at the time.

The Naxos transfer illustrates a relatively purist approach to the process. I can detect no added reverberation; much of the broadband noise between around 8 and 10 kHz has been filtered out, but there is no evidence of digital hiss reduction. Compared with the Pearl transfer, sudden dynamic changes seem to have marginally less impact; this perhaps reflects the amplification system.

Differences between transfers affect the way the 78s are heard and their effect on listeners. For all the strong personality of the original 78s and the performance, each CD has its own distinct character.

The Beatles

The first two Beatles albums were recorded on two tracks (not stereo) in conditions similar to a live performance. The left channel was used for the rhythm section and the right for the voice. After that EMI switched to four-track recorders, which allowed for a more subtle mixdown to stereo, allowing the voice to be placed centrally in the mix and melody instruments to be in either the left or right channel. Although the early albums were recorded quickly with little manipulation, in contrast to the weeks of studio time expended on albums like *Revolver* (1966) and *Sergeant Pepper's Lonely Hearts Club Band* (1967), one might assume that the LPs issued by Parlophone offered definitive versions of the material. As exhaustive research, hundreds of bootlegs, and terabytes of internet discourse show, there is no standard version of some Beatles songs. The first four albums, *Please Please Me*, *With the Beatles* (1963), *A Hard Day's Night* and *Beatles for Sale* (1964) were simultaneously issued in mono and stereo. At the same time, Capitol issued the music in the United States; but, disliking the subtle, fairly dry acoustic of the originals which properly emphasises where reverberation has been used, such as on John Lennon's voice, Capitol drenched the songs in reverberation. The company remixed the stereo versions to eliminate the hole-in-the-middle effect on some of the EMI versions, thereby creating a wider but woollier soundstage. As twelve songs was the maximum ration allowed on their LP issues, two songs were lopped off, and the compilations were quite different (they included hit singles, including 'I Want to Hold Your Hand', which EMI had issued on EPs and therefore disdained to issue on LP as well). Dynamic contrast was reduced by compression and/or limiting. Recently Capitol reissued the US LP mixes on CD. Unlike EMI, who arbitrarily constrained the first four albums to mono and the remainder to stereo – much to the chagrin of the informed collector – Capitol included both stereo and mono mixes in the CD issues. In spite of this apparent concern for historical veracity, the CD issue has tended to reduce the already modest dynamic range present on the Capitol LPs between songs, and dynamic variety within individual songs has also been curtailed.

That there are not always single, definitive versions of some Beatles songs is evidenced by the manifold differences between the stereo and mono mixes, such as the forward presence of the vocal lead. Typical of the differences that may also arise between stereo mixes is 'Strawberry Fields Forever', one of the most studio-manipulated songs the group released. Mono remix 12 was issued by EMI in mono on EP on 17 February 1967 (Parlophone R 5570). Capitol issued a stereo mix, the first to appear, on 27 November 1967 on the *Magical Mystery Tour* LP (Capitol SMAL 2835). The same stereo mix was issued on LP in the UK by EMI in 1976 (Parlophone PCTC 255). In the interim German Apple issued a *Magical Mystery Tour* LP using a different stereo mix made in 1971 (SHZE 327), which now features worldwide on CD issues (all this emphasises the importance of mono throughout the 1960s for popular music and EMI's lack of prescience in issuing only stereo mixes on CD). Joseph Brennan writes in detail about the discrepancies between these two stereo versions:

> The most obvious difference in the 'German mix' is that it is much clearer, with a better percussion sound, and more stereo separation. Despite the improved reproduction, some nice touches of the earlier mix are lacking. If there is any doubt it is a different mix and not just a cleaner version of the same mix, listen for the first three instances of panning … On Stereo remix 3, when we first hear take 26, the cello and trumpet sound pans quickly from left to right, a little sleight-of-hand to distract the listener from the edit itself to the introduction of the new instruments to the song, while in the 'German mix' the cello and trumpet track is on the right to start with [etc.].[40]

Other versions of the song, which do not always have the official imprimatur of the group or EMI and Apple, but are intended to illuminate the complex recording history of the song, are available in volume 2 of *The Beatles Anthology* (Apple/EMI 8 34448 2) and numerous bootlegs.[41]

The sound of the CD issues of the Beatles closely reflects the LP mixes, many of which were made on four-track tape. To free up extra tracks, four tracks could be mixed down to two. Each time this happened a generation of sound quality was lost, and further degradation of the original song masters would be inflicted when the tapes were prepared for EP and LP release. The version of 'Penny Lane' in volume 2 of *The Beatles Anthology* sounds quite different from the version on the *Magical Mystery Tour* CD (EMI CDP 7 48062 2), not just because it is a composite version of several different takes, but because the original tracks were mixed down to digital tape, thereby preserving the very high quality of the first layer of recording.[42] Many hope EMI will eventually remaster the Beatles' recordings, but when they do the notion of a definitive version of each song will become even more strained.

Don Giovanni

Mackenzie poured scorn on the notion of stereophony in 1926, denouncing 'merely spatial illusion [as] worse than useless'.[43] Nevertheless, engineers on both sides of the Atlantic wanted it, especially for classical music. Tape made stereo recording straightforward, and it facilitated highly detailed editing, manipulation of the sound, such as the addition of reverberation, and multi-channel mastering for mixing down to mono or stereo. Early stereo records included trains, and pianos falling from high buildings, but tests conducted early in the history of stereo, and one's own experience, call into doubt the realism claimed for it. Test audiences were unable precisely to locate correctly the real position of instruments in an orchestra when a stereo signal was relayed live to another room, and when the microphones were moved the instruments moved and the image was changed. In a live concert it is usually hard to locate instruments with one's ears alone: the eyes have to assist. The reason for this may be that stereo audio systems and recordings tend to emphasise the frequencies holding much of the spatial information so the listener gets precise cues as to the location of instruments.[44] Stereo, in these circumstances, becomes an end in itself, a great improvement on mono, to be sure, because one hears so much more – violins placed either side of the conductor can be heard as such – but not necessarily a realistic reproduction of the live experience. Critics first encountering stereo nevertheless 'agreed that the stereophonic illusion was fascinating to hear', as they have ever since. John Crabbe's verdict on home listening is worthy of quotation in this context:

> There is a common assumption in the hi-fi community that our goal is the re-creation at the listener's ears of a sound pattern identical to that obtained at a good seat in the concert hall ... For good or ill we are in the hands of the recording producer, and the most we can hope of our domestic reproduction is to create the sort of balance ... determined by the producer during recording.[45]

For opera the attraction of stereo was that action on stage could be transmuted into movement between the left and right channels, accompanied by various distance effects. The producer and musicians would attempt to re-create the dramatic dialogue and an illusion of the real-time sequence of events, even though in recordings this is often an illusion. When, for example, Daniel Barenboim wished to record the *Don Giovanni* he was conducting at the 1973 Edinburgh Festival,[46] EMI set up a schedule, secure in the knowledge that all the singers were 'anchored to Edinburgh and available for all sessions'. The singer cast as the Don, Roger Soyer, sang *sotto voce* during the balancing session and it emerged that he was suffering from laryngitis. The first scene was put aside and the Masetto and Zerlina arias were taken in the first recording session. The remaining sessions in Edinburgh took all the music in which the Don was not directly involved, including the closing scene after he is dragged off to hell. Schedules were set up in London that would involve attempting to duplicate the complicated balance painfully achieved in Edinburgh (the Assembly Hall at the George Watson College was being redecorated during the recording). Just before the London sessions Helen Donath rang in sick. The producer, Suvi Raj Grubb, toyed with postponement or a new Zerlina, but finally made the agonising decision to record all the music minus Zerlina and superimpose her voice when she was fit. Soyer was horrified at the prospect of singing 'La ci darem' to an empty space, so a few recitatives and the duet were scheduled for a later time. Even so, Zerlina had to be superimposed elsewhere, as in the finale of the first act, for which session two tiny loudspeakers were placed behind Barenboim and Donath. Donath was reacting to the recording and came in late, so in the end she sang to silence, taking only Barenboim's beat for her cues.

The final master tapes comprised around half the opera on two-track tapes and three quarters of the rest on eight-track tapes made in Kingsway Hall; the rest had Zerlina's voice superimposed on two of these eight. Typical of the gruelling editing involved was joining up the recitative preceding Leporello's aria 'Madamina' – the join was to be made on the 's' of 'testimon':

> In the split second that [Geraint] Evans pronounced that 's' we had, simultaneously, to fade out the eight-track recording, fade in the two-track recording and make all the adjustments necessary for the two sounds to match.[47]

The first attempt at the edit had Leporello jumping like a 'startled rabbit' at the join;[48] it took over an hour to get it right.

This set may have been unusually awkward, but the process by which it came into being is representative of tape recording generally and of stereo.

The question of the extent to which so much artifice created an analogue of one of the Edinburgh performances is beyond the scope of this chapter. The recording is full of the dramatic detail and eventfulness that stereo brings, but it is possible that the 'phonograph effect' (a valuable concept used by Mark Katz in his dissertation and subsequent book),[49] perhaps part of which is described by Grubb in his marvellous account of the recording sessions, is present in the final product.

A view on recording

As these case studies attempt to demonstrate, a recording does not 'show' a performance to us, for the performance that generated the recorded artifact is hidden: the relationship is not mimetic; rather, we may regard a record as forming a diegesis with and within its domestic or other environment. The record and associated equipment are telling us about a performance, but it is not the performance itself; it is filtered through a large number of processes and contexts with which the original performer has nothing to do. The diegesis is dependent upon a long sequence that runs from the muscles of the pianist, through the coils of a microphone, down metres of wire, to a sapphire needle, past circuits amplifying some frequencies more than others, through murky black compounds, to the final phase, the installation of the listening event in the living room. The positioning of the record player, the condition of the record, the attention given to the playback equipment (such as the needle), the soundbox, and so on are part of the process. Much of this complex chain is hidden during the telling of the 'story' – playback – but unlike a live performance this story can be repeated, and each time it is different in some ways and alike in others, to the extent that a click in the record, a momentary drop in pitch, or a split horn note become part of one's knowledge of the music.

A curious slant on this comes from an unlikely source: Patti's niece Louise.

> I must say I was terribly disappointed with all the numbers except 'Voi che sapete'. How unsatisfactory it is that when you want a thing in a high key it alters the tempo so that things go at a terrific speed; and to lower it everything must drag. Still it is very wonderful, though not artistic.[50]

This performance of the records occurred after dinner with the diva herself present. It seems that the records were regarded as flexible in terms of their realisation: this exalted audience, the letter implies, experienced the music in a variety of keys.

Pursuing the issue of reproduction draws us into a labyrinth of knowledge that people no longer possess or have access to. The assumption that progress automatically invalidates the listening habits of a previous generation is bogus and does a disservice to the many dedicated listeners who believed they had found audio perfection: for them there was no urgent requirement that tomorrow would bring improvements, for they had found a delicate equilibrium with the resources then available. If we need a modern analogy we might take the user of the MPEG player: listening on trains and buses, the listener frequently plays the music in a degraded format (MP3, typically 10 per cent of the information on compact disc); and the earphones generally used are of poor quality and do not cancel out background noise. In spite of this, millions of people enjoy music in this way: social conventions, lifestyle, musical taste and many other elements affect the telling of the musical story, transmuting the materials by, for example, removing the original sequence of numbers by picking out favourite songs.[51]

The gramophone is in a sense the narrator; the playback and listening is the narration. Narrators lie, all the time. Extra information, new associations, may rupture the illusion. Records are complex documents. To treat them as if they are the same as performances we attend is inadvisable. They are products of an infinitely variable matching of medium and reproduction, allied to external knowledge culled from inserts, other knowledge, expectation, and so on. Nevertheless, at a key point in the chain that leads to the record, real historical performers exercised their larynxes and arms to make music: their exhalations and muscular gymnastics live on, engraved in the grooves, metamorphosed by a hundred different movements, electrical circuits, and razor blades.

Copyright and recordings

NICHOLAS COOK

Copyright in relation to recordings is something of a nightmare, though for different reasons in different places. A single recording may be covered by several separate copyrights. For a pop CD there will be copyright in the song (that is, the musical work), the lyrics, and the recording itself, as well as liner notes or illustrations. For a modern recording of Beethoven's Ninth Symphony there will not be copyright in Beethoven's music or Schiller's words (both are in the public domain), but there will be copyright in the recording. Even if a historic recording is out of copyright (as explained below), a CD reissue will have copyright in the transfer.

The practical significance of this depends on whether we are talking about the general dissemination of recordings, or their use for purposes of study and research. We'll take general dissemination first. In the EU, copyright in recordings lasts at the time of writing for fifty years, after which the recording goes into the public domain (though the musical work and lyrics may still be covered, since copyright on them lasts for seventy years after the author's death). At the time of writing, however, the record industry is trying to persuade the EU Commission to extend copyright on recordings to ninety-five years, citing the precedent of the USA, where most recordings (even those dating back to the 1890s) will remain in copyright until 2067, thereafter enjoying a term of 95 years. The result is that the bulk of the recorded heritage is not legally accessible in the US, since copyright owners have reissued only a very small proportion of it: the entire historical collection of Naxos Music Library, for instance, is barred to US subscribers. Should the EU follow the US, the outlook for the rapidly developing public interest in early recordings will be bleak.

In terms of access to recordings for purposes of study or research the picture is complicated but less bleak. In the USA, recordings fall under 'fair use' legislation, which sets out circumstances under which you are allowed to make copies of copyright items, and these circumstances include scholarship, research and criticism. So it is legal to copy an otherwise unobtainable recording for research purposes, and, if you are publishing a web article on it, you can include a clip from it, as long as you don't take too much (though it has no legal standing, 5 per cent is a generally accepted limit). The UK has 'fair dealing' legislation which is broadly comparable to American 'fair use', except that sound recordings fall only partly within it: you can copy recordings for purposes of 'criticism and review', so the web article example is covered, but not for research purposes. This is clearly anomalous, and in 2007 the Gowers Review of Intellectual Property recommended that copying of recordings for research purposes should be allowed; legislation is in train. This would of course be particularly important if the EU were to extend the copyright term.

Copyright is always complicated, especially as regards sound recordings, and the above is not a complete or authoritative statement of the law. For further information check the guidance available in your country.

One man's approach to remastering

TED KENDALL

It may be a shame that many significant performers did not arrange to live their lives in times when recording technology was fully developed, but that is no reason to dismiss their performances. The aim of remastering is to make these performances accessible to a modern audience, in terms of both physical availability and the most informative sonic presentation possible. This I call the music to muck ratio, as its determination is necessarily a subjective matter.

I shall outline the processes involved in remastering from 78 rpm originals, with particular reference to a specific example, George Formby Junior's recording of 'Rhythm in the Alphabet', issued in 1938 by Regal Zonophone (catalogue number MR 2890).

Having decided on the material required, a suitable source disc has to be found. Curiously enough, this is often easier with art music than more popular fare which, although it sold in greater numbers, was played far more often and looked after less well, being essentially *Gebrauchsmusik*. In the case of Formby, the situation is not helped by the ubiquitous banjolele solo, recorded close to the microphone and starting half way through the side, when the average steel needle would already be past its best. Aside from the question of wear, there is also the matter of pressing material to consider. The largest market for George Formby's recordings outside the UK was Australia, renowned for producing beautiful laminated pressings of superb appearance, although this was sometimes achieved by over-polishing the metal parts, causing some loss of high-frequency detail. Against this must be set the laminated pressing's tendency to rip on loud peaks when played with a typical pickup in less than perfect condition. English 'stock shellac' pressings, although generally noisier, tend to retain a sharper impression of the groove and to be somewhat more robust in terms of wear. In this particular case, the English pressing was the best available, and so this was used.

Small matter, then, of playing the record. There are aspects of the playing process which, if not sorted out at the time of transfer, are almost impossible to correct subsequently. The record must be centred as exactly as possible. The wow which emanates from an off-centre 78 pressing not only disturbs the time-base of the recording, but is at a frequency where the ear is at its most sensitive (about 1.2 Hz). Stock shellac pressings can usually be centred exactly; laminates nearly always have some random eccentricity, which is usually dealt with by minimising the run-out. If, however, there is one large disturbance, it will often be found that the best results are obtained by ignoring this and centring the rest of the rotation. This implies that the large disturbance is caused by distortion in the press, and is therefore geometrically self-cancelling.

Although the record may not have been cut at exactly 78 rpm, in practice most electrical recordings are fairly close to nominal speed. This, and the quality of modern digital varispeed algorithms, means that I usually transfer at the nominal 78 speed and adjust pitch later if required. In any case, the cutting speed itself may not have been constant, and several rehearsals may be necessary to get the compensation right. The repeatability and lack of further wear to the original given by digital correction are significant here. As it happens, 'Rhythm in the Alphabet' was squarely in key at 77.92 rpm, so it was left alone.

The correct stylus tip and pickup must be used. The optimum tip is that which is held by the walls of the groove without either being so high that surface scratches are picked up, or so low that the stylus rattles around in the bottom of the groove. A stereo pickup is generally used these days, primarily for reasons of availability, but also because it has advantages over a mono type. For one thing, adequate vertical compliance is assured, reducing the likelihood of pinch effect distortion. Also, the difference signal obtained by connecting the left and right outputs in antiphase gives a very sound idea of how the stylus fits in the groove. Any distress on peaks (generally caused by too large a tip) or excessive chatter (too small) is immediately apparent. It should be noted that groove profiles during the 78 era were far from standardised, but generally tended towards a U-section rather than the modern V-section. These grooves are usually best fitted by a truncated elliptical tip, such as those supplied by Expert Stylus Co. As so often happens with EMI recordings of this era, the Formby example played happily on a 2.8 thou truncated elliptical tip.

The choice of pickup cartridge is influenced by the need for robustness and the fact that shellac pressing materials are much harder than vinyl. These factors point to such designs as the Shure M44 series, which are at once sensitive enough not to inhibit information retrieval from the groove and tough enough to survive a hostile environment, where the forces involved can be up to six times as great as those encountered in LP replay. The choice of arm is similarly influenced – it must be of an effective mass which, in combination with the cartridge compliance, gives a reso-nant frequency that is clear of the 78 warp region, and also of sufficient mechanical integrity that the energy transmitted into the arm by the pickup does not excite other resonances or cause other problems. My own approach here is to use a modified Revox parallel-track arm, which is in fact a short unipivot mounted on a servo-controlled sliding carriage. This allows the pickup to work without hindrance, and the theoretical tendency to warp-wow given by the short arm has not been a problem in practice, partly because the unipivot is close to the disc surface, in the theoretically correct manner.

The signal from the pickup now needs to be amplified and the appropriate playback curve applied. All electrical recordings are recorded with a particular equalisation curve which defines the transition point between constant-amplitude and constant-velocity recording. The RIAA curve used for LPs is not appropriate, neither was there much in the way of a standard curve before the mid-1950s, by which time the 78 was practically dead anyway. My solution to this problem was to design a preamplifier with switchable bass, middle and treble time-constants to enable any published playback curve to be constructed. Evidently other people felt the need for one of these, for I soon had my arm twisted to make some for sale … and over a decade later The Front End still sells to archives, collectors and transfer engineers the world over. Our example required a single turnover at 350 Hz (450 uS).

Modern remastering inevitably involves analogue-to-digital conversion, which should be done at high quality. Stratospheric sampling rates and enormous bit-depths are of less importance than good clocking and low distortion. With these, 44.1 or 48 kHz sampling at 16–24 bits is entirely adequate. My initial recording is without processing. This provides both a known starting point and an archive copy for future use.

Once the audio is safely captured, the cleaning process can begin. I try to carry out most of this in one pass, as the settings for hiss reduction and EQ are interdependent and it is important not to apply more processing than is necessary to achieve the desired result. Impulsive noise is dealt with using CEDAR declick and decrackle, and hiss with CEDAR NR-5. The CEDAR software, while more expensive than most, is by far the best developed and most powerful for remastering. NR-5, in particular, allows subtle manipulation of the spectrum of the background noise, which is very useful for rendering it unobtrusive. The nearer the noise spectrum is to something found in nature, that is white or pink noise, the less noticeable it is. Most of the noise in a shellac pressing occurs in the low kHz region, below which it is relatively quiet. This is most convenient, because much of the ambience that gives clues as to the size of the room and the perspective in which the performers are placed is at the lower frequencies. By leaving these untouched, this subtle information is preserved. Note also that impulsive noise reduction is applied before anything else is done to the signal. The reason for this is that any phase shift in the signal makes it more difficult for the software to distinguish noise from wanted signal, and this can degrade sound quality through the software being driven too hard.

Equalisation is applied after the CEDAR processes. The selection of the correct playback curve ensures that only fairly small corrections are required, to tame odd resonances or reduce congestion. A good graphic equaliser, carefully driven, is a great aid to getting good results quickly. A roll-off in the extreme treble reduces out-of-band noise without straining the CEDAR too much. The final result is a balance between reduction of noise and diminution of 'life' and 'air', qualities that are difficult to define but easy to hear. In the case of *Rhythm in the Alphabet*[1] the particular challenge was to retain the bite on Formby's banjolele and preserve the distance cues which give a sense of perspective to the accompanying band. Thus the shouted 'Where's George?' is audibly more distant than Formby himself, and the drum break behind the banjolele solo has a sense of the drummer's position in the room. Formby, I think, intended the extended solo on this disc (which occupies the entire second half of the side) as an indication that he wasn't quite as gormless as his stage persona implied. Indeed, the whole side has the form of a typical heavy-metal number: start at a hell of a lick, two or three quick verses, then solo to the finish, and Devil take the hindmost!

The automatic CEDAR processes can only go so far. In any disc, there will be impulsive noises or thumps that defeat the software, and these have to be dealt with manually. In addition, bursts of noise or swishes can be removed with the aid of CEDAR Retouch, which allows a small section of sound to be manipulated with almost surgical precision. Once these complications are dealt with, the final step is to trim the start and end of the side such that the ear is guided swiftly but unobtrusively into and out of the surface noise. Again, the idea is to present the ear with something that does not obtrude and thereby distract attention from the performance.

And finally: I have always found it a prudent move to preserve my raw transfers. The art of remastering is still advancing, and the facility of revisiting a side without having to obtain it again for transfer is, on occasion, invaluable. Beecham's comment that it would be many hundreds of years before records reached perfection has some truth in it.

Technology, the studio, music

NICK MASON

It goes without saying that there have been huge changes in studio technology over the last forty years – but what's interesting is how at every stage in this evolution there has been a need to improvise with whatever the current technology provides. Pink Floyd's music has always made use of all kinds of what might be called 'environmental sounds', and EMI[1] had their own enormous library of sound effects on tape as well as the commercially available vinyl discs of sound effects. But often the quality simply wasn't good enough to take them off a vinyl record, and sometimes the specific sounds required weren't available, so we'd have to find our own ways to make or find the sounds. Examples would be the sound of footsteps for the 1973 album *Dark Side of the Moon*, recorded in the Abbey Road echo chamber; or the clock sounds, for which Alan Parsons, the engineer on that album, went out to a clock shop – in Islington I seem to remember – and recorded a lot of chiming and ticking and so on. Those were relatively straightforward, but when Roger Waters and I were doing the track 'Money', we ended up assembling a bunch of coins and drilling holes in them so that they could be dangled on strings in order to achieve the right sort of coin-jingling sound.

It's really quite surprising how difficult it is to get just the sound that you want: you think, 'Right, we need the sound of jingling coins', and you'd imagine that all you have to do is get hold of some coins and rattle them around in your hand. But it's really not that easy: the hand muffles the sound, and what you get doesn't sound anything like what you have in your mind's ear. I'm sure that sound effects departments over the years have been through the same exercise, discovering that what actually sounds right isn't necessarily the real thing at all. I know we used my fridge door for the spaceship-sounding door on *Wish You Were Here* …

We tended to use relatively simple techniques, even though people afterwards have assumed that we must have been at the cutting edge of technological development. In reality, things like the physical echo chamber at the Abbey Road studio were far superior to all the digital echo systems that were developed afterwards – or that's certainly what we thought. The echo chamber was just a soundproof room lined with tiles, and with ceramic pots laid out over the floor, as I remember it, in a gap between two studios. It had a microphone at one end, and a Tannoy monitor loudspeaker at the other, and you just fed the source sound from the control room to the loudspeaker, and then took a line back from the microphone. You adjusted the amount of echo you wanted by changing the balance between the source sound and the return from the microphone.

The thing with a digital approach is that you do get far better quality – you don't get that build up of hiss and noise and so on, which is the big plus – but I think one of the things that took a while to learn is that there are still some things that actually work far better done manually rather than digitally. The best example of that would be cross-fades: I've yet to find a computer that does cross-fades as well as simply sitting there with a pair of ears and a couple of faders. And another example would be wind sounds: there are an awful lot of wind noises on the 1971 album *Meddle*, and as far as I remember it was all done with the EMI wind machine, which was just a sheet of canvas over a drum which you rotated with a big handle. Very basic technology, but in the end far more effective than trying to record real wind; and perhaps that's because the wind sound that you want – that you imagine – on a rock album isn't what real wind actually sounds like, in the same way that the speed of a real heartbeat sounded too fast when we tried that on the intro to *Dark Side of the Moon*.

Which brings me to what a studio album really is, and the whole relationship between live performance and the studio. In the early days of the band, a lot of the songs were developed live, and then taken into studio. Certainly that was the case with our first album from 1967, *The Piper at the Gates of Dawn*. They were songs that were played live on the road, which made it a lot quicker to record them. Later on we ended up doing things very differently, for two reasons: first, to counteract bootlegging, we started to develop our songs in the studio so that we could finish and record them before we went public with them. But, second, we ended up using the studio as the place where we'd do the writing.

Dark Side of the Moon was the transition: most of the songs had been played live, although they then underwent considerable change in the studio before they ended up on the album. Over a number of years, we moved from a position of thinking that the studio album was something very different from playing live, and separation of instruments was critical – before coming full circle to thinking that it made better sense to try and get some spirit of playing together, rather than going for that completely sewn-together perfection that the modern studio seems to make possible. I think we almost got carried away with our reputation for beautifully controlled sound quality, and the idea that, to reach that holy grail, everything had to be recorded separately. It's very easy to lose the feel of the music when you do that – because that feel depends absolutely on the music being *played*. Our 1979 album *The Wall*, for instance, was a very technical studio album, and the engineer working on it was an absolute perfectionist, who wanted really clean, crisp sounds – which we were very happy to go along with. And since some of the music was more complicated than things that we'd played before, there was a drive to get really clean sounds, isolating everything, playing separately, trying to get it absolutely right. Whereas on the last album, *The Division Bell*, released in 1993, we really wanted to return to the business of playing in the studio together, and getting the feel that you get from that, rather than necessarily having to do everything separately. And that feeling of interacting with other people – who are with you there in the same room – I think it's called music, isn't it? It's not something I've ever really understood.

Reminder: A recording is not a performance

ROGER HEATON

Today's CD buyer/internet downloader demands, and mostly gets, a 'perfect' soundworld: sonic sumptuousness is as important as compositional content, and the performer's prowess goes without saying. If, in so-and-so's new Chopin recording, the piano is too distant, or too tinny, or in an acoustic so reverberant as to blur detail and condense the dynamic range, then it will simply collect dust on the shelf. Recordings with performer errors are similarly undesirable. I am, however, fond of Mary Garden's 1904 recording of Debussy's 'L'ombre des arbres' from *Ariettes oubliées*[1] with Debussy at the piano – an important document of course, but also memorable because after the opening piano introduction Garden enters on the wrong note. This is swiftly corrected by Debussy, who also (just in case) gives her the starting note for the second-verse entry. It always raises a smile. Wrong notes, untidy ensemble or imperfect intonation in live performance are, to some extent, the fragile nature of the business, and Garden's recording is a *performance* preserved for posterity. Yes, audiences are impressed by impeccably virtuosic playing (a spectator sport akin to gawping at a freak show), but we performers are also curiously and necessarily fallible: attempting, say, the extraordinarily slow speeds Messiaen asks for in the solo movements of *Quatuor pour la fin du temps*, or a real *tutta forza fffff* in works by Birtwistle or Maxwell Davies, is certainly technically challenging, and these kinds of dangerous moments in performance, even when they don't quite work, are exhilarating for performer and audience alike. But performers today can appear a little intimidated by the concert platform: the worry of technical perfection, living up to the recording with not a hair out of place, affords the listener a safer, one could say blander experience where spontaneity and risk-taking in the moment for musical ends seems somehow sacrificed to accuracy.

So is recording a good thing? Of course, it would be foolhardy to recommend otherwise, especially within these pages. My point is simply to remind performers that a recording and a performance are two entirely different endeavours, while listeners too should understand that in classical performance, unlike pop, the 'live' goal is not the faithful reproduction of the album, despite the recent trend for some string quartets and other small groups to amplify and add reverberation in concert.

The technological sophistication of the recording process with its easy correction of errors results in the 'perfect' construct. The recording takes place in an ideal acoustic, but one that is artificially enhanced. The skilfully placed microphones, not simply a stereo pair but close mixed with ambient ones farther away, create a depth and richness of balanced parts and voices, a clarity of foreground and background, left and right stereo spread, with the outcome most certainly not a document of a concert performance but something else – an idealised, irreproducible entity, the recording as art object in its own right. Recordings are 'engineered' and 'produced', the post-recording work an enormous jigsaw-like compilation of often hundreds of takes. This is a process that demands of the engineer an unforgiving attention to detail. A half-remembered story about a pianist (who may or may not have been Glenn Gould) listening to the final edit comes to mind. On expressing his satisfaction I'm sure the pianist was suitably chastised by the producer's quick-fire response: 'Don't you wish you could play it like that?'

At a recording session for Gavin Bryars's solo clarinet and ensemble piece *Allegrasco*,[2] a substantial single-movement work lasting twenty minutes, we recorded lengthy chunks, repairing as we went, regularly listening back to takes, the sound not only warmed by the large live studio acoustic but positively swimming in the producer Manfred Eicher's trademark ECM resonance. When all was completed Eicher asked for a final play-through of the piece, a 'performance'. The request seemed to me rather misguided, suggesting, quite erroneously, that what we had already recorded might in some way be imperfect or uninspired and that a final 'performance' would push us to greater heights. The result that appears on the CD *was* that performance: there are some slightly untidy moments in ensemble, and most irritating is a bubble (water/condensation in a hole caused by playing in overly chilly air-conditioned rooms) fizzing on a sustained climactic note which leaps out when I hear it. (Performer paranoia creeps in here: I'm sure other clarinettists are knowingly nudging and winking about it.) The decision to use this version on the CD was presumably in the belief that something other, something exceptional had been captured, but it represents a confusion between the archival or documentary nature of recording and the recording in its own right, a 'perfect' enhanced product rather like a painting: the result of work in the studio, repainting, retouching in sound, changing, a careful, slow process, not a photograph snapped in the moment. Performances, however well prepared, exist in a continuum: they are work-in-progress; they evolve; they will be different, even 'better' at some point. The recording is an object constructed in the studio, a perfected slice from somewhere along that continuum, frozen in time.

This idea of the recording studio as artist's studio is not unusual in popular music, with groups camping out in a studio (home or commercial) for weeks on end to create an album almost from scratch. The speed and flexibility of digital technology also allows the classical performer to make significant technical, artistic and interpretative choices during recording. My recording of the American minimalist Tom Johnson's *Rational Melodies* and *Bedtime Stories* was recorded in a church chosen for its excellent acoustics, with microphones carefully placed.[3] It is a lovely sound; I like to think that in concert my tone is that beautiful! It may be true, but despite the naturalness of the sound the CD is, as it should be, not a 'performance' but a false enterprise, an artifice. Johnson's pieces in performance often require circular breathing (many of the twenty-one *Rational Melodies* are continuous without rests) to give them their sense of momentum and rational inevitability, and the sniffing-while-blowing technique to keep the lungs' bellows full, almost inaudible in performance and actually rather adding to an audience's enjoyment of a different kind of virtuosity, is unacceptable on disc. Breaths have therefore been removed, giving a seamless flow. Many other noises-off have also disappeared: birdsong, aeroplanes, and the low frequency of London Underground's Northern Line trains rumbling in caverns beneath us, all erased later by clever software. But what was unusual in these sessions was the luxury to experiment. Johnson gives the performer the freedom to choose tempos, dynamics and articulation, and we were able to test out different approaches, record and hear them back, make adjustments, change our minds. It was a creative process.

Multitracking is *de rigueur* in pop music, a construction technique (I hesitate to call it composition because it involves adding things to existing songs: backing vocals, strings, sound effects and so on) which is mostly, if not completely, controlled by the producer rather than the artist. Critics might view this enhancement process as adding a superficial gloss, a kind of musical silk purse fashioned from a sow's ear. But it is in the truest sense creative work, often spontaneous and experimental during recording, and these added tracks will be used in live performance where possible to reproduce the studio version. Multitracking in classical music is rare. There is the odd gimmicky shot at it, as with the Emerson Quartet's doubling up for Mendelssohn's Octet;[4] Steve Reich's string quartets and other pieces require a recording for the live element to play along with, his *Different Trains* being the classic example. My own multitracked recording[5] also began with Reich – his *New York Counterpoint* for eleven clarinets, or more usually one live and the rest pre-recorded. This was a piece I'd played a few times with Richard Stoltzman's original backing tape; I have no quarrel with it but just wanted all the rest of the group to sound like me. The multitracking 'concept', if I dare use that word, then became the central theme of the disc. The recording, which also included a major new multi-clarinet work by Gavin Bryars, was exhausting, and there isn't space here to describe the many technical challenges for both player and producer encountered along the way. The disc's multitrackedness spilled over into other pieces such as new clarinet duets by Christopher Fox and Walter Zimmermann; also Morton Feldman's *Bass Clarinet and Percussion*, which requires two percussionists (here Simon Limbrick plays both parts). Glyn Perrin's *Like He Never Was*, composed for this project with two pairs of clarinets electronically treated in various ways, relishes the idea of perspective and distance, sound and silence, and only exists as this recording. As Perrin says, '[This piece] is scored for an unreal combination … It's very much a piece for the recording studio, which allows great control of timing and perspective.' This CD in many ways takes the pop album as its model and is perhaps a more extreme example of what a recording should be: an artifact that appears in your living room as a sound object, almost an installation. It is not a performance but a work of art, complete in itself.

9 Methods for analysing recordings

NICHOLAS COOK

If analysis means studying something in order to gain knowledge and understanding of it, then there are any number of ways of analysing recordings, and any number of reasons for doing so. Performers, recording engineers, historians of recording technology and historians of performance practice listen to recordings with quite different kinds of knowledge and understanding in mind: analysis means different things to them. The same applies to acoustic scientists, record collectors and archivists, or communication theorists, not to mention people in the A&R divisions of record companies whose job is to spot the next big hit. The list goes on.

This chapter basically assumes that your reason for analysing recordings is to gain a better understanding of them as culturally meaningful objects, and more specifically that you are primarily interested in the effect of music as experienced in performance, whether live or recorded. In that sense its orientation is musicological, although that too is a term that can be defined in different ways. Recordings are a largely untapped resource for the writing of music history, the focus of which has up to now been overwhelmingly on scores, and recent technological developments have opened up new ways of working with recordings – ways that make it much easier than before to manipulate them, in the sense that we are used to manipulating books and other written sources. I begin by introducing software that makes it possible to navigate a number of different recordings, and to create visualisations that help to heighten aural understanding of what is going on in the music. (Actually such software could be useful for practically all the people I mentioned in the first paragraph.) I move on to approaches that involve the comparison of large numbers of recordings in order to identify and characterise stylistic elements. Such approaches might be described as musicological in a relatively narrow sense. But then, in the final section, I consider some critiques of such approaches – critiques that have come from both within and outside musicology – and set them into the context of more broadly cultural approaches to recorded music.

Extending the ear

Important musicological work has been carried out using equipment no more specialised than a record or CD player, a pencil, and perhaps a stopwatch, coupled with the capacity for close listening that comes with experience. An example is the work of Robert Philip, whose two books between them represent a first draft of the history of classical music performance during the twentieth century. The quantitative dimension of his research hardly goes further than tables of performed tempi at various points in different recordings, while the quality of his listening is captured in passages such as that describing Ignaz Jan Paderewski's 1930 recording of Chopin's Mazurka Op. 63 No. 3:

> At the beginning he establishes a rhythm with a long first beat and a short second beat ... This is varied at points of particular emphasis. For example, the approach to the highest point of the melody at bars 4–5 is emphasized by shifting the tenuto to the second beat ... At bar 5 the lengthening of the second beat underlines the start of the phrase, and further emphasis is given by arpeggiating the accompaniment and delaying the melody note.[1]

Much the same might be said of the account of Jimi Hendrix's Woodstock performance of 'Star Spangled Banner' that Eric Clarke offers in his book *Ways of Listening*, which is not based on the empirical approaches through which Clarke made his reputation, but relies on straightforward verbal description. In the course of an argument that Hendrix's adaptation of the American national anthem derives much of its meaning from the clash between 'official' culture and (then) counter-culture, Clarke observes that the G♯ eight seconds into the performance (the highest note of the opening arpeggio) is 'approached by a small but clearly audible pitch bend or glide up to the note from the preceding E4 – a characteristic stylistic invariant for rock-guitar playing'.[2] He cites some more examples, and then concludes, 'At the same time as the anthem is specified by its intervallic and rhythmic invariants, rock as a genre is specified by invariants of performance. The cultural clash is directly specified in the material itself.' To be sure, my characterisation of this account as 'straightforward' may have been misleading, to the extent that Clarke's purpose is in part to set out an approach informed by the ecological psychology of J. J. Gibson. But however sophisticated the theoretical approach, it is grounded in the act of listening. For musicologists at least, that is where all analysis of recordings must start.

It is however possible to use new technology to create an environment that makes it easier to listen effectively, in the sense of moving around a recording to compare different parts of it, or moving between different recordings to hear one against another. In this chapter I demonstrate such possibilities through the use of Sonic Visualiser, a free program developed at Queen Mary, University of London, but some at least of its functionality is available in other programs, or is likely to be in the future: I don't provide detailed instructions on the use of Sonic Visualiser here, but they are available in web-based tutorials designed to complement this chapter.[3] In addition to the familiar wave-form representation and playback controls shown in Figure 9.1, Sonic Visualiser provides two features that are particularly powerful for working with recordings. One is the ability to annotate the sound file, for instance by marking where each bar occurs: you can tap to the music as you listen to it, and use the resulting barlines to navigate the recording. (You can see the barlines in Figure 9.1.) The other is the ability to align multiple recordings of the same piece: Sonic Visualiser will work out which point in one sound file corresponds to the same point in others, so that you can – for example – go straight to bar 9 of each. The importance of these apparently simple features should not be underestimated. They create the same kind of environment for recordings that is taken for granted when working with scores or other written documents, where you can flick back from one page to an earlier one, or place several scores side by side to compare them. The effect is to give a new dimension to close listening.

As its name implies, Sonic Visualiser also offers a range of features for visualising what you hear, but before I discuss these it's worth considering what is gained by visualising music. Actually visualisation is a fundamental analytical technique: established score-based analytical methods employ a wide range of notational or graphical representations that sometimes help to bring what you hear into focus, and in other cases complement what is readily audible (schematic representations of sonata form or the 12-bar blues, for instance, make it easier to perceive the pattern in what may sound like a mass of details). Of course, traditional printed images are less compelling than animations that move in time to the music, as anybody knows who uses Windows Media Player. And while Windows Media Player visualisations are not designed to focus attention on the music in an analytical sense, there are other ways of visualising music that do just that. Figure 9.2, for example, shows how the voices (shown by lips) and instruments are located within the stereo sound space during the opening verse (from 0′30″) and after the chorus (from 1′09″) of 'King Midas in Reverse' by the Hollies; in the original animation the image changes as the sound sources do. This visualisation represents something that is there to be heard in the music, but it adds something to the experience, refining and focusing your listening, and making you more aware of the sound space. It is in this sense analytical, and on the basis of a number of such analyses Ruth

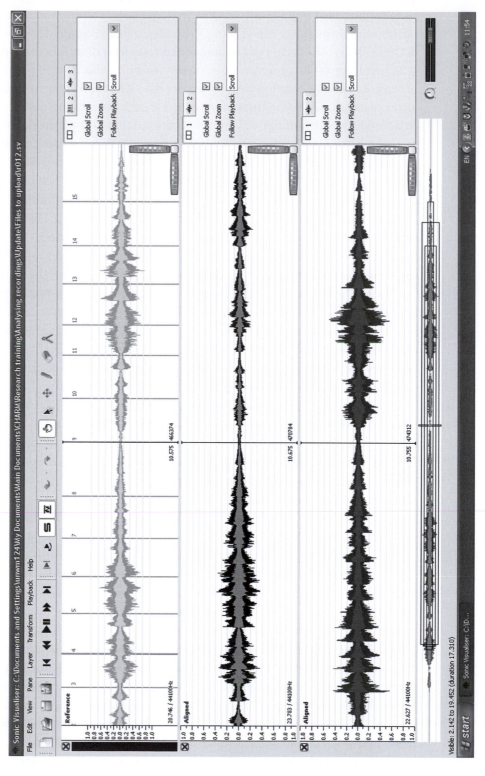

Figure 9.1 Working with multiple files in Sonic Visualiser

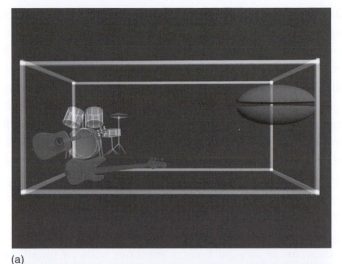

(a)

(b)

Figure 9.2 Soundbox images of the Hollies, 'King Midas in reverse'

Dockwray and Allan Moore, who developed this form of representation, have created a taxonomy of sound spaces and initiated historical interpretation of a previously undocumented aspect of recorded music practice.[4]

Figure 9.2 is computer-generated, but only in the sense that that is how the graphics have been created: it embodies the outcomes of close listening. Programmes like Sonic Visualiser, however, can generate a range of visualisations directly from the audio, and some of these are also effective in refining and focusing the listening experience. The most flexible of these visualisations are spectrograms, which represent sound in three dimensions: time (from left to right), frequency (from top to bottom), and intensity (by means of colour or, in black and white, shading).

Figure 9.3a is a very zoomed-in image of the passage from Hendrix's 'Star Spangled Banner' that Clarke discussed, showing just the fundamental frequency: the pitch bend, now seen in great detail, lasts from 8.0″ to 8.2″. More typical – less zoomed-in – spectrograms show pitches as several parallel lines because they include not just the fundamental (the frequency that corresponds to the pitch we usually hear) but also the individual harmonics at integer multiples of the fundamental: as an illustration, Figure 9.3b shows bars 42–6 from Sophie Braslau's 1928 recording of Schubert's song 'Die junge Nonne'. (The relative strength of the harmonics is important because it is one of the determinants of tone quality.) The sawtooth-like waves in Figure 9.3b represent Braslau's vibrato; you could easily measure its speed or depth if you wished. In the lower part of the image, and quite distinct, are the piano notes: because there is no vibrato they show up as straight lines, sometimes with an initial wedge shape resulting from their dynamic profile (sharp attack followed by decay). As Figure 9.3 demonstrates, spectrograms can be quite variable in appearance, because there are many different settings which enable you to focus on particular aspects of the sound at the expense of others, and there are also different colour schemes. But they all represent sounds using the same three dimensions, and are therefore read in the same basic manner.

Conventional score notation is extremely selective as a representation of musical sound: it provides a basic pitch and time framework with some annotations, but gives only broad indications regarding dynamics, articulation and timbre, and says virtually nothing about temporal or dynamic nuance. By being so selective, it can convey those aspects of music that it *does* convey very clearly. Spectrograms are just the other way round. Their attraction is that in principle all aspects of the sound are present in them; the downside is that in practice it may be hard to extract the information you want. They are most useful for homing in on the details of performance – the unnotated nuances that are responsible for so much of music's meaning – and it is in this role that they have been used by such musicologists as Robert Cogan or Peter Johnson in the field of classical music, and David Brackett or Serge Lacasse in popular music. When they are integrated into the working environment for studying recordings, as in Sonic Visualiser, they help to transform listening into analytical interpretation. Figure 9.3b comes from an article by Daniel Leech-Wilkinson which compares a number of recordings of 'Die junge Nonne' in order to show how different singers shape their performances so as to imbue the song with quite different expressive meanings. He writes of the passage shown in Figure 9.3 that the 'very fast (0.03 to 0.05 seconds) swoops up to notes, which until now have made Braslau sound dramatic (or matronly, if you prefer), suddenly become swoops down from above, sounds rarely

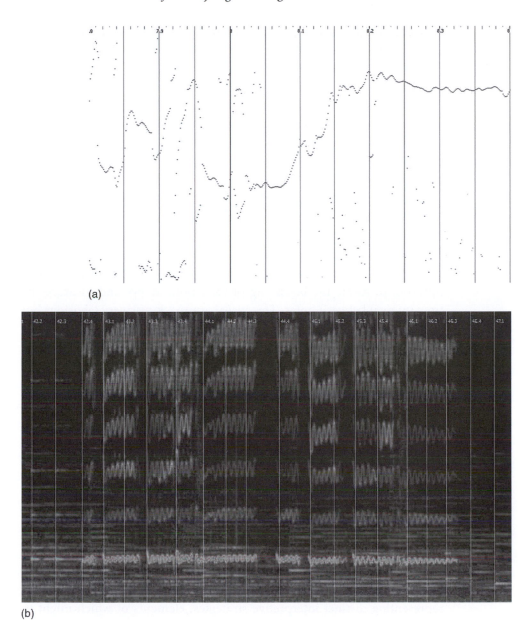

(a)

(b)

Figure 9.3 Spectrograms from (a) Jimi Hendrix's Woodstock recording of 'Star Spangled Banner' and (b) Sophie Braslau's recording of Schubert, 'Die junge Nonne'

used in song except in the Italian tenor sob: here also the start of each note is suggestive of crying'.[5] (The swoops from above are most easily seen in the lowest vocal line – the fundamental – for example on the first and third beats of bars 43 and 45: Leech-Wilkinson is arguing that inter-war recordings like Braslau's emphasise the dimensions of fear, horror and death, in contrast to later, less doom-laden interpretations.) Of course such effects might have been described without the use of a spectrogram, but it would have been harder to be sure exactly what aspects of the sound are responsible for them, or to communicate them to readers.

If a limitation of spectrograms is that it can be hard to extract the information that you want from them, then an alternative approach is to extract just those aspects of the sound you are interested in and create customised ways of representing or manipulating them for analytical purposes. Typically such aspects include timing and dynamic information. Though work of this kind has become increasingly common in musicology over the last two decades, the methods were principally developed in psychology and cognitive science. The extraction of timing information from recorded sound goes back to Carl Seashore's work in the 1930s, but the modern foundations of this approach lie in a series of articles published by Bruno Repp in the late 1980s and 1990s: Repp used a waveform editor (nowadays Sonic Visualiser could be used for this purpose) to locate the beginning of each note by eye and measure the time interval between notes. This visual approach was very laborious but yielded a representation of the temporal profile of each recording sufficiently accurate to support Repp's detailed analyses of the data.

A representative example is his 1992 study of twenty-eight recordings by well-known pianists of Schumann's 'Träumerei',[6] in which the analytical results might be summarised under three headings. First, virtually all the pianists marked the large structural divisions of the music by slowing down at the end of sections: there was little significant variation between pianists at this level. Next, Repp carried out a form of factor analysis on the timing profiles *within* these sections: this is a statistical technique that reduces the complexity of large data sets by extracting the principal components. If there was basically only one way of playing the piece, with a certain amount of semi-random variation, then the analysis would yield only one factor. In fact the analysis yielded three factors, one of which was shared by a large number of pianists and the other two of which were respectively associated with Horowitz and Cortot: Repp saw these as representing distinct interpretive strategies, elements of which might to some extent be mixed in specific performances. The final element of Repp's analysis consisted of extracting the timing data for the most striking melodic gestures in the music, and fitting them to mathematical functions: he found that parabolas generally yielded the best fit, which suggests that the practice of slowing down at the end of a melodic gesture may form some sort of correlate of the motion of objects in the physical world (if you throw a ball into the air, its arc will describe a parabola). Repp found that virtually all the performances exhibited these parabolic functions, but with significant differences of scale between different performers.

Repp's articles constitute a storehouse of analytical methods which musicologists have perhaps not sufficiently explored. At the same time, as a psychologist, Repp was more concerned with discovering general principles underlying the distribution of the data than trying to engage with the aesthetic properties of specific performances, and he was not concerned at all with issues of cultural meaning. This is a way of saying that not all analysis of recordings is musicological in intent, and the same applies to cognitive-scientific approaches, of which the outstanding example is perhaps the work of Gerhard Widmer and his co-workers at the Austrian Research Institute for Artificial Intelligence. Rather than using Repp's visual method to extract the basic data, this research was based on a semi-automatic system which extracted both the timing of the beats and their associated dynamic values (the system was semi-automatic because a fully automated system could not achieve the necessary accuracy, so that it was necessary to edit the data manually). The resulting tempo and dynamic data were then input to a visualisation system called the 'Performance Worm': this is a computer animation that moves as the music plays, with tempo on the horizontal axis and dynamics on the vertical axis. Figure 9.4 is the image generated by the first four bars of Daniel Barenboim's recording of the second movement of Mozart's

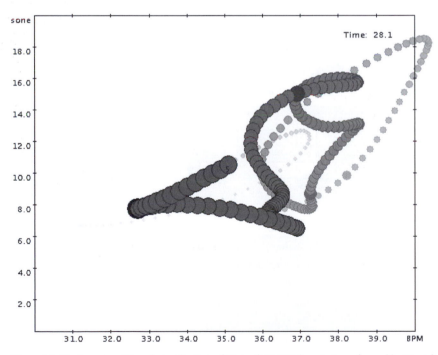

Figure 9.4 'Performance Worm' visualisation of Mozart's K. 332, bars 1–4, performed by Daniel Barenboim

Sonata K. 332,[7] with the darker sections representing the worm's most recent movements: the trails fade with time.

But while this is an intriguing way of visualising performance and bringing out certain of its gestural qualities, it was only the first step in a more elaborate analytical process of which I can give only a bare summary. The complete worm trails for four pianists' recordings of five Mozart sonatas were divided into short segments and subjected to cluster analysis, yielding an 'alphabet' of prototypical tempo–dynamic patterns as found in these performances. These prototypes were then organized into a matrix of 8 cells by 5, with a self-organising map algorithm being used to place similar cells adjacent to one another. The resulting images for each of the four pianists are shown in Figure 9.5, where the map-like shading shows how frequently the prototypical patterns were found in each pianist's performance. (Lighter shade means higher frequency.) It is obvious that the pattern for each pianist is quite distinct, with Pires perhaps being the most idiosyncratic.

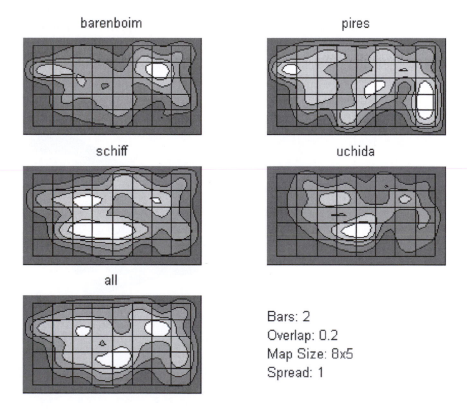

Figure 9.5 Images of four pianists' performances of five Mozart sonatas plus average values, based on tempo–dynamic associations

For the musicologist, work like this raises questions such as whether it is possible to make musical sense of the stylistic characterisations in Figure 9.5, or whether the analysis is at too abstract a level to be brought to bear on musicological issues such as aesthetic effect and cultural meaning. To raise such concerns is not to criticise Widmer's project, which is primarily a study in artificial intelligence rather than musicology: that is, it is a highly impressive attempt to model aspects of a particularly complex human behaviour – piano performance – through a range of objective methods. While musicologists have also used visualisations based on abstracting timing and sometimes dynamic information from the sound, they have done so with different purposes and, it has to be said, in general with much less technical sophistication. During the 1990s there was a considerable amount of work based on a tapping approach: you listened to the music, and tapped on a computer to mark certain points (usually bars or beats). The computer logged the times at which you tapped, and this information was imported into a spreadsheet, with the normal output being a tempo graph. Taken from my 1995 article on two recordings by Wilhelm Furtwängler of the first movement of Beethoven's Ninth Symphony,[8] Figure 9.6 was generated by tapping once a bar, with the plotted values being the average of three separate passes.

This method was relatively quick and easy, but limited in accuracy – partly because of problems in coordination between ear and hand, and partly because the resulting data were a mix of anticipation and reaction. (Really you were measuring not the music, but your own

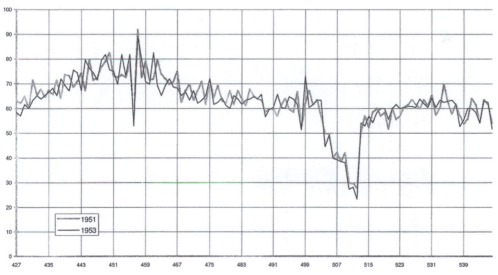

Figure 9.6 Tempo graph of Furtwängler's 1951 and 1953 recordings of Beethoven, Symphony No. 9, coda

physical response to it.) The data were probably good enough if you were tapping once a bar, but perhaps not if you were tapping once a beat. Nowadays, however, tapping can be carried out in an environment such as Sonic Visualiser, which offers crucial advantages: you can tap the beats and then listen to them as you play back the music, and you can then edit them, if necessary slowing down the playback, until you are confident they are where you want them. There are also plugins for Sonic Visualiser which make the onsets stand out visually in the waveform, while programs are being developed that take the tapped beats as their input and generate more accurate timing data, not only for beats but also for other onsets, along with associated dynamic data. While the data can then be analysed mathematically, as in Repp's and Widmer's work, tempo and dynamic graphs or other representations can be used together with spectrograms to create an integrated environment for working with recordings in which sound is combined with several complementary visualisations, each designed to bring out a particular aspect of the performance (see Figure 9.7). The result of all this is that the preparation of tempo or dynamic graphs no longer marks the end of the process, as all too often seemed to be the case in the past: nowadays it means you are ready to start on the real work of analysis.

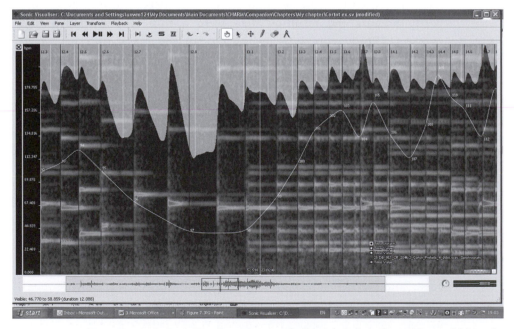

Figure 9.7 Using Sonic Visualiser to work with Chopin's *Prélude*, Op. 28 No. 4 in E Minor, bars 12–14, as recorded by Cortot in 1928 (Daniel Leech-Wilkinson). The display consists of a spectrogram, tempo graph, 'silhouette' representation of dynamics, and bar:beat numbers (measured in quavers). The main structural division of the piece falls at bar 13:1

An ear for style

The technical problems that constrained musicological analysis of tempo and dynamics are, then, being solved. Perhaps more intractable are the issues of interpretation involved in such work. The purpose of the 1995 study from which Figure 9.6 is taken was to investigate how far Furtwängler's performances could be understood in terms of Heinrich Schenker's analysis in his 1912 monograph on the Ninth Symphony. The underlying assumption was that what Schenker saw as discrete structural units would correspond to continuous tempo profiles – usually arch-shaped profiles – in Furtwängler's performance, with the breaks between sections being marked by rallentandi or caesurae. In this way the basic strategy was to begin with Schenker's analysis, and to see how far it could be mapped onto the performance. This, it seemed to me, was a valid approach because it is what Furtwängler himself must have done: he read Schenker's monograph shortly after it was published and was so impressed by it that he sought Schenker out, and the two men maintained a friendship until Schenker's death in 1935. More particularly, Furtwängler is known to have discussed the repertory he conducted with Schenker. The article, then, traced the musical consequences of a historical relationship.

But that was a special case. The problem occurs when the same approach is used in the absence of such a historical relationship, which can only make sense if one assumes that analytical approaches such as Schenker's embody fundamental musical principles that inform performances by artists who have never even heard of Schenker. That is a very large assumption to be making in the early stages of what is still a relatively new field of study. And the practice of working *from* a score-based analysis *to* a recording basically declares off limits all those aspects of performance that cannot be directly related to notational categories; it eliminates most of what there is to study before you even start, including all the rhetorical, persuasive, or expressive effects that contribute so much to the meaning of music as performance yet have little or nothing to do with structure as the music theorist sees it. (I note with embarrassment a cheap jibe against Mengelberg in my 1995 article, whom I described as 'a rubato conductor, a virtuoso', in other words, not a structural performer.[9]) Finally, to work from page to stage, as they say in theatre studies, is to treat a performance as first and foremost a reproduction of the musical work as embodied in the score; nobody would wish to say that that is *all* a performance is, but once you have started down this road, it is very hard to do justice to the creative dimension that makes it worth studying performance in the first place. And of course page to stage approaches simply do not apply to most music outside the Western classical tradition.

There is one further criticism I would direct at traditional musicological analysis of performance, recorded or otherwise. I mentioned the underlying principles regarding the relationship between score-based analysis and performance on which my 1995 article was based, but they are neither well developed nor explicitly set out. This failing is quite general among musicologists,[10] and the lack of well-articulated principles for the mapping between analytical and performance data results in a rather loose discourse in which tempo or dynamic graphs may not really provide the empirical support that is ascribed to them. There is also a tendency to see tempo profiles as objects of analysis in their own right, whereas according to Henkjan Honing and Peter Desain the tempo curve (as they term it) 'lulls its users into the false impression that it has a musical and psychological reality. There is no abstract tempo curve in the music nor is there a mental tempo curve in the head of a performer or listener.'[11] It is hard to be sure what to make of this argument: tempo is obviously linked to the ebb and flow of what we experience when we listen to music. But even so, Honing and Desain would claim that the tempo profile results from an indefinite number of different factors which really need to be understood individually. They propose that relevant factors might include the 'composers' pulse' patterns associated with the work of Manfred Clynes, the hierarchical phrase arching associated with Neil Todd, and the rule-based model of expressive performance developed by Johan Sundberg and his co-workers: to make sense of a tempo profile, then, it is necessary to break it down or 'decompose' it into its various components.[12] Whether these particular factors are necessarily the right ones is a matter for debate (especially since there is considerable overlap between Clynes's, Todd's and Sundberg's models), but the principle is persuasive.

Taken together, these criticisms suggest some profitable directions for musicological analysis of recordings. In the first place, both the availability of more robust data, and the possibilities afforded by programs like Sonic Visualiser of integrating them into the study environment, should encourage work that is grounded in close observation of recordings and builds towards appropriate analytical models, rather than importing its models wholesale from score-based analysis. Second, whereas both the CD-and-pencil and early tapping approaches encouraged work based on perhaps just one or two recordings analysed in relation to the score – as in the case of my Furtwängler study – new technology makes it much easier to draw comparisons between large numbers of different recordings, whether by means of Sonic Visualiser's alignment facility or the data extraction approach pioneered by Repp: this is tantamount to a shift of emphasis from the work (understood in relation to the score) to performance style, understood through comparisons between recordings. The final element would be a move towards the identification of significant features that underlie tempo or dynamic profiles, and when I say 'significant' I mean to imply a need to consider the role that such features play in the communication of structural, expressive, or connotational information through performance.

There is a good deal of work that illustrates the first two of these directions. José Bowen and Eric Grunin,[13] among others, have made use of scattergrams that map simple performance features such as average tempo or duration (not necessarily the same thing, owing to repeats) against date of recording or performer's date of birth; their use of large numbers of recordings bolsters confidence that the resulting distributions are statistically significant.[14] Figure 9.8 is a rather more sophisticated example, showing how performances of the exposition from Beethoven's Third Symphony have in general become less flexible over some ninety years of recordings. Those by Furtwängler have been picked out, and are rather consistent in their degree of flexibility. (To measure flexibility, the exposition was divided into twelve sections and the relationship between their average tempi calculated.) Again, Richard Turner has used clustering software to group recordings of Brahms's First Symphony according to the similarity of their tempo profiles.[15] But although such analyses are based on direct comparisons between different recordings, rather than referencing them to the work they are performances of, they actually tell us little

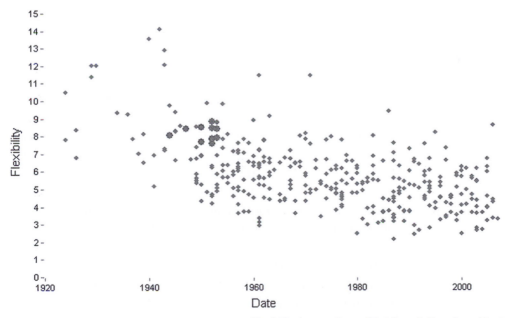

Figure 9.8 A comparative measure of flexibility in recordings of Beethoven's Symphony No. 3 plotted against date of recording, with Furtwängler's recordings highlighted

about performance style. The reason is obvious: not only are they exclusively based on tempo data – just one aspect of the performance, though an important one – but they also reduce the temporal evolution of the music to a single value, and in this way conflate quite different things. (A performance that swings wildly between frenetic tempi and funereal pauses may end up with exactly the same average tempo as one in the post-war sewing-machine style.) They are also heuristically unproductive. By this I mean that they are hard to relate to the music as experienced, and hence not effective in directing attention to specific points in the music that might reward further study. The danger is that they may close down rather than open up further investigation.

Other recent approaches retain the temporal dimension and so overcome some of these problems. Craig Sapp's multicorrelational plot of Artur Rubinstein's 1966 recording of Chopin's Mazurka Op. 30 No. 2 is shown in Figure 9.9a.[16] It is based on tempo data (like the Grunin and Turner analyses), and shows which other recording of the same piece is most similar at any given point; the various shades of grey are keyed to the other thirty-two recordings in this sample. What the plot is saying is that – despite Rubinstein's reputation as a performer who successively reinvented himself – much the closest match is with his own 1952 recording, with his 1939 recording also being closer than anyone else's (though not as close as the 1952 one). Here, however, it is possible to locate the particular points at which other recordings are most similar, and in this way gain some insight into what underlies the overall correlations. The similarity with Chiu's 1999 recording, for example, is confined to one particular point about three quarters of the way through (it is represented by the diamond-like shape), so you could listen to this passage in the two recordings and assess how far the connection makes musical sense. In this way a visualisation based on objective measurement can act as a prompt to further critical study, sending you back to the recordings with specific questions in mind.

Sapp's visualisations focus on style, in the sense that they are based wholly on comparison, and are resolutely bottom-up. But they are vulnerable to the Honing–Desain critique, in that the analysis is based on the overall tempo profile without any attempt to distinguish the different features contributing to it. The problem is one that Repp encountered in his 'Träumerei' analysis: he initially carried out factor analysis on the complete timing data, but only one component emerged, as the data were swamped by the slowing down at the end of major sections that was a feature of virtually all the performances – which is why he then carried out his factor analysis *within* these sections.[17] Sapp has addressed this problem through alternative visualisations based on smoothed and residual data: you smooth the original data mathematically, which brings out larger features such as phrasing, and then you subtract the smoothed

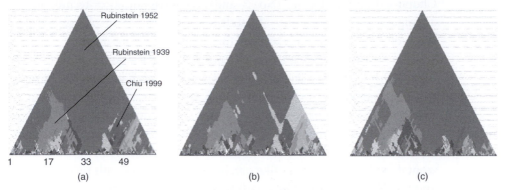

Figure 9.9 Multicorrelational tempo plots of Rubinstein's 1966 recording of Chopin's Mazurka, Op. 30 No. 2, using (a) full, (b) smoothed and (c) residual tempo data (Craig Sapp). Numbers represent bars. The base of the triangle represents the moment-to-moment succession of the music; the vertical dimension shows similarities at successively higher levels

data from the original data, so eliminating the large-scale features that swamped Repp's results and in this way focusing on smaller-scale features such as accentuation. Figures 9.9b and 9.9c show the smoothed and residual equivalents of 9.9a, and as can be seen the correlations change quite noticeably: the similarity to Chiu virtually disappears in the residual data, so must relate to larger-scale features. Sapp also uses similar full, smoothed, and residual plots based on global dynamics, and on the combination of tempo and dynamics.

In a sense, both Repp's distinction between what happens at the level of the whole piece, within sections, and in terms of melodic gestures, and Sapp's use of smoothed and residual data represent attempts to decompose the overall tempo into distinct features, in the way that Honing and Desain called for. But such approaches are perhaps most musicologically interesting when they correspond to features of the performance that make immediate musical sense, such as the hierarchical phrase arching that Honing and Desain put forward as a candidate for decomposition. As I mentioned, such phrase arching is associated with the work of Neil Todd, who developed a model of expressive performance based on the idea that performers give temporal and dynamic shaping to musical phrases through the use of parabolic functions (there is a link with Repp's work on melodic gestures), and that this applies at multiple levels such as 2, 4, 8 and 16-bar units.[18] Todd's work was based on laboratory performances, and his articles convey the impression that he is talking about a general psychological principle of expressive performance. Musicologists, however, tend to view such general principles with suspicion: perhaps the most striking lesson to be drawn from the recorded legacy of the last hundred years is the extent to which performance practices have changed. Accordingly, in a project based on recordings of

Chopin's Mazurka Op. 63 No. 3 and Sapp's visualisation techniques, I attempted to develop a way of modelling the practice of phrase arching that would make it possible to trace this historical development.

This work is based on two customised visualisations, as shown in Figures 9.10 and 9.11. The first is what I call an 'arch combiscape' and is related to Sapp's multicorrelational plots: here, however, the correlation is between the tempo or dynamic data and the shape of a rising or falling arch. The plots in Figure 9.10 consist of two triangles, the upper one representing tempo and the lower one dynamics, with time on the horizontal axis: the light flame-like patches show matches with rising arches, and the dark patches matches with falling arches. A complete arch profile is accordingly marked by the conjunction of a light and a dark patch, with the height of the patches giving an indication of the length of the arch (4 bars, 8 bars, etc.).[19] Figure 9.10a, then, is saying that Neuhaus's recording from 1955 is a perfect example of phrase arching as defined by Todd: the bilateral symmetry reveals the extent to which tempo and dynamics are coordinated with one another, as well as with the composed phrasing. By contrast Friedman's recording of 1923 (Figure 9.10b) shows very little evidence of phrase arching at all; there is a major caesura around bar 25, but a caesura is not the same thing as a regular pattern of phrase arching. In a nutshell, the story that emerges is that the elements of phrase arching exist in recordings from before the 1939–45 war, but that fully coordinated phrase arching – with tempo, dynamics, and the composed phrasing all locked together – emerges only after the war. Of course, this story is just based on an incomplete (though substantial) collection of the recordings of Op. 63 No. 3, and without doing the work one can't know how far it might apply to other mazurkas, let alone other repertories. The pivotal role of the war, however, has been remarked by scholars working on other repertories: why this might be the case is not clear, but one should probably understand the practice of phrase arching in relation not only to other aspects of performance practice at that time, but also to contemporary developments in other cultural spheres, such as architecture and design.[20]

In Figure 9.10 phrase arching at the 8-bar level is so strong that it is hard to see it operating at other levels. Figure 9.11 shows an alternative visualisation, based on the same arch-matching principle but now implemented as an Excel spreadsheet. Here the extent of tempo and dynamic phrasing at each level (2, 4, 8 and 16 bars) is shown separately. Whereas in the Neuhaus recording both tempo and dynamic arching are much stronger at the 8-bar than at other levels, Friedman's tempo arching is generally weaker and more dispersed between levels. But the values in the bar chart account for only part of the effect of expressive phrase arching. The effect of

(a)

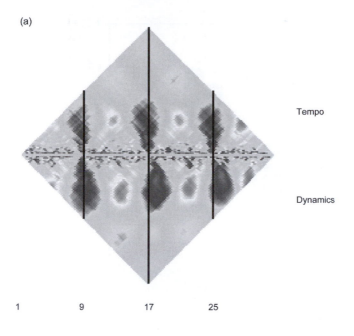

Tempo

Dynamics

1   9   17   25

(b)

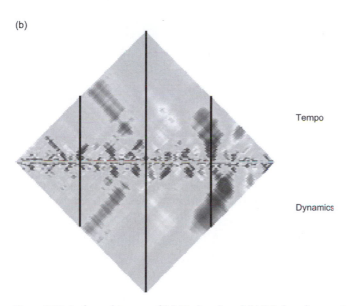

Tempo

Dynamics

Figure 9.10 Arch combiscapes of (a) Neuhaus's and (b) Friedman's recordings of Chopin, Mazurka Op. 63 No. 3, bars 1–32: light patches correspond to rising, and dark patches to falling, arches

8-bar phrasing is so strong in Neuhaus's performance because it is re-inforced by the high degree of correlation between tempo and dynamic arching, as shown in the line graph: the scale relates to this graph, with 0 signifying no correlation, and 1 signifying identity. And by combining these two distinct factors into a single formula,[21] it is possible to devise

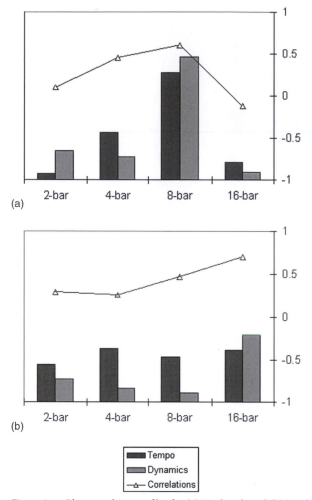

Figure 9.11 Phrase arching profiles for (a) Neuhaus's and (b) Friedman's recordings of Chopin, Mazurka Op. 63 No. 3, bars 1–32, with strength of arching and the degree of correlation between tempo and dynamic arching shown separately at each level (2, 4, 8, and 16 bars)

a rough overall measure of phrase arching. Figure 9.12 is a scattergram based on this measure, with the strength of phrase arching (highest at the top of the chart) plotted against the date of recording. One interesting finding is that the three performers of whom we have multiple recordings – Friedman, Rubinstein and Uninsky – all come out with rather consistent overall values, even though the individual profiles of their recordings vary. (In other words they achieve similar levels of phrase arching in their different recordings – rather as Grunin found similar levels of flexibility in Furtwängler's recordings of the 'Eroica' – but they do so in different ways.) Another finding is the extent to which phrase arching is associated with Russian or Russian-trained pianists (represented by the squares in

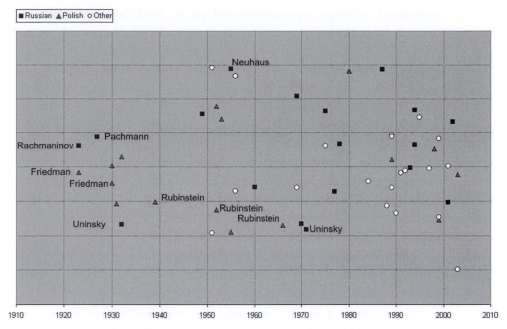

Figure 9.12 A comparative measure of the overall strength of phrase arching in recordings of Chopin's Mazurka Op. 63 No. 3, bars 1–32, plotted against date of recording

Figure 9.12): 68 per cent of them fall into the top half of the chart. Finally, the scattergram shows that, while highly coordinated phrase arching emerged after the war, performances that did not feature it continued. There is little evidence here of the narrowing range of stylistic options which many commentators have put down to the baleful influence of recordings.

The hope, then, is that analysis focused on specific features of performance will give rise to more meaningful interpretations of changes in performance style than analysis based on such undifferentiated data as total duration or overall tempo profile. It is possible to imagine a set of style-analytical tools, of which phrase arching might be one, that could be used together to characterise the style of individual performers, so facilitating the same kind of aesthetic and interpretive study of performers that traditional musicology has lavished on composers. The result would be a musicology that does better justice to music as a performing art.

The ear in culture

But can empirical, computationally based approaches such as I have been discussing really help us understand music as a cultural practice? Powerful voices have been raised both within and beyond musicology against formalised analytical approaches in general. Richard Taruskin writes that 'turning ideas into objects, and putting objects in place of people, is the essential modernist fallacy – the fallacy of reification, as it is called. It fosters the further fallacy of forgetting that performances, even canned performances, are not things but acts.'[22] And Carolyn Abbate goes further. She claims that the experience of live performance is the only authentic musical reality and hence the only valid subject for musicology: scores and recordings – what she calls 'the tactile monuments in music's necropolis'[23] – are no more than cyphers of that experience, employed by musicologists to distance and domesticate an experience that is uncanny, unruly and ultimately irreconcilable with scholarly discourse. From such a point of view, the empirical and computational analyses discussed in this chapter must look like the ultimate sell-out.

Taruskin's reference to 'canned performances' echoes a tradition of disparaging mechanically reproduced music (which is to say music as most people today experience it) that goes back almost as far as the technology itself. But the criticisms deserve a more considered response. Analyses, whether we are talking about Schenkerian voice-leading or combiscapes, may be things, but they are meaningful only in so far as they prompt acts of informed listening: Taruskin's critique of analysis itself puts objects in place of people, the people in this case being analysts. As for Abbate, the idea of a musicology without representation is a dead end, for musical cultures are, as much as anything, cultures of representation. The way to avoid the dead hand of rationalisation – to keep music live, as the Musicians' Union slogan has it – is to understand scores and recordings semiotically, that is to say, as possessing meaning not because they are things but because they reference acts. On the one hand, recordings can be understood as the traces of performative events, whether located in a concert hall, a studio or control room (the performers in question include producers and engineers), or a teenager's bedroom. On the other hand, they are prompts to performative acts by listeners, whether in the social circumstances of a pre-war gramophone club, the domestic space of a 1950s home, a 1980s cityscape musicalised by the Walkman, or twenty-first-century clubbing culture. As we shall see, however, the distinction between trace and prompt is usually more blurred than this suggests.

The most obvious, not to say naive, way to think of a recording is as an aural snapshot.[24] On 3 April 1902, Fred Gaisberg – the Gramophone Company's first sound engineer and talent scout – visited the Vatican and made a recording of Alessandro Moreschi, who sang in the Sistine Chapel Choir and was possibly the last of the professional castrato singers. The session began with the 'Crucifixus' from Rossini's *Petite messe solennelle*, and, though the resulting recording sounds very uncontrolled to modern ears (perhaps as a result of nerves and the unfamiliar circumstances), it was issued in the same year on the Red G & T's label.[25] This is as close as a recording can be to the trace of a performative event, although how far that event can be retrieved at this distance of time is doubtful: as the liner notes of the Pearl Opal reissue say, 'The pitching of Moreschi's records presented us with some problems since no-one had the slightest idea what his voice ought to sound like'. (Early disc recordings varied a great deal from the nominal 78 rpm.) The nearest contemporary equivalent might be the CD which the audience members of John Eliot Gardiner's Cadogan Hall (London) concert walked away with on 9 February 2006: consisting of Mozart's Symphonies Nos. 39 and 41, the CD was recorded during the first half of the concert, with 1,000 copies being made during the interval and second half.[26] Here the recording functions as a souvenir, the trace of a personal experience.

But this model obviously does not apply to recordings produced by studio multitracking, such as Mike Oldfield's *Tubular Bells* (1973), or Queen's 'Bohemian Rhapsody' (1975), the album version of which was built up layer by layer, giving it a tightness that Queen could never achieve in live performance. Nor does it apply to the Wagner recordings produced during the 1950s and 1960s by John Culshaw, who manipulated the virtual space of the stereo recording in order to compensate for the loss of the visual dimension of live opera, or Glenn Gould's 1976–7 recordings of piano pieces by Sibelius: Gould employed separate banks of microphones placed in and around the piano, alternating between and mixing the separate inputs in a manner coordinated with the musical structure.[27] Such production techniques cannot be compared to a snapshot, and indeed Gould likened his approach to film editing. Nobody who sees a film thinks it was made by leaving the camera running for two hours: films consist of the traces of a large number of performative events taking place over a period of weeks or months, edited, crosscut, and nowadays digitally manipulated, and the same is to a greater or lesser degree true of virtually all sound recordings made since tape editing became widespread. But the film still references an event or series of events of which it presents itself as a trace: it is just that the diegesis, as film theorists call it, is fictive, and understood as such by audiences. The concept of diegesis applies just as well to sound recordings, and demonstrates the sense in which the relationship between the recording (the thing, as Taruskin would have it) and the experience is a semiotic one. In other words, it is through the act of listening which the recording prompts that we understand it as the trace of an event.

And that takes me back to where I started, to the different methods of analysing recordings and purposes for doing so. In this chapter I have frequently used the words 'performance' and 'recording' as if they were more or less interchangeable, and that is because most of the time musicologists are interested in recordings as documents of performance. But even here there is a distinction to be made. It is possible to focus quite specifically on the actual performance events of which the recording is a trace: you might do this if your aim was to reconstruct live performance practice (a difficult project, apart perhaps from the period between the introduction of electrical recording and the adoption of tape editing[28]), or in order to reconstruct the studio production processes that were involved in making the recording. But musicologists are more often interested in recordings for the listening experience they afford, and the conceptions of how music might go that they embody. From this point of view, it is not only probably undecidable but also not to the point whether a given effect was created by the performers, the producer, or the postproduction engineer: as inherently collaborative products, recordings 'are what they are', in Peter Johnson's words,[29] and it is as what they are that they circulate and are consumed as integral elements of contemporary musical culture.

One way to express this is that recordings do not so much reproduce musical performances as redefine what performance is. And if we see recordings as an integral part of a more generously conceived practice of performance, then it makes sense to apply the approaches developed by interdisciplinary performance theorists directly to recordings. Philip Auslander has written that 'to think of music as performance is to fore-ground performers and their concrete relationships to audiences, *rather than* the question of the relationship between musical works and perfor-mances' (this is one of the critiques of analysis from outside musicology to which I referred).[30] In saying this, Auslander primarily has in mind the extent to which performers construct – perform – identity, not generally their own identity as an individual but rather a fictive identity as an artist, what Auslander calls a persona. His point is obvious when applied to Bob Dylan or Madonna, but hardly less applicable to Karajan or Gould. And recordings play as crucial a role as live performance in such identity construction: if, in Baz Kershaw's words, it is 'a fundamental tenet of performance theory… that no item in the environment of performance can be discounted as irrelevant to its impact',[31] then this, too, applies to recordings. One obvious example concerns what Serge Lacasse calls 'pho-nographic staging', the creation of particular sound images through pro-duction effects such as reverberation, compression and phase shifting, as well as the stereo positioning with which Dockwray and Moore are concerned. Lacasse proposes a taxonomy of such effects, and explains that, 'rather than describing the ways in which different sound effects are *produced* in the studio, the model aims to account for these effects mostly from the point of view of the listener: how do these effects alter the ways in which we *perceive* recorded sound sources?'.[32] And if such effects contribute crucially to phonographic performances of personae, and more generally to what recordings mean, then so do such non-auditory dimensions of recordings as cover images and liner texts, not to mention the physical and social circumstances within which recordings are experienced. No analysis of the cultural meaning of recordings can be regarded as really complete without consideration of all these matters.

Predictably, where I disagree with Auslander is over his use of the words 'rather than'. I would have preferred 'as well as'. To be sure, as I said before, an approach based exclusively on the fully fledged 'work of music', as constructed by aestheticians of musical autonomy, will be very limited in its application; actually, it will be deficient even as applied to the performance of the Beethoven symphonies, the touchstone of what might be termed 'opus composition'. But there is no either/or here. Any performance, live or recorded, can be the performance of a musical work (arguably must be for, as Bruno Nettl says, it is something close to a musical universal that 'one does not simply "sing", but one sings something'),[33] and at the same time a performance of individual or communal identity, an embodiment of the acts of actual people in concrete situations and in real time. It follows from this that there is no one way of analysing recordings, and that we should be prepared to work with as many different analytical methods as there are dimensions within which recordings signify (and one can always think of one more dimension that might be significant). But I would add that we should expect the most fruitful results when we link different, even apparently opposed, methods. The kind of computer-assisted close listening I described in the first part of this chapter can refine an analysis of identity construction in terms of phonographic staging as well as of the expressive effects through which performers create meaning; conversely, consideration of the performative effects and social consumption of recordings provides a context within which to make sense of observations resulting from close listening or computational evaluation. In short, cultural analysis can be supported by empirical analysis, and empirical analysis given purpose by cultural analysis. It's a win–win relationship.

10 Recordings and histories of performance style

DANIEL LEECH-WILKINSON

Introduction

Recordings show us that music we think we know intimately sounded quite different in the past. When music sounds different it *is* different, because music's meaning depends to a very important extent on its sound. Even if you sit at home and read an orchestral score (let's assume you have exceptional powers of musical imagination), the sounds you imagine are those made by a modern orchestra playing as orchestras play today. So however you hear it, there's no experiencing music except through the way it's performed: when the performance changes, the music changes. I think we have to assume, therefore, that pieces we believe we know rather well actually felt different a hundred years ago. We can get some sense of this by reading what people thought about pieces then. Scott Messing's studies of Schubert reception give some idea of how views of him and his music have changed.[1] I've argued in another study that we can hear these changes also in recorded performance, indeed, that in some cases it was recordings of powerful performances (those of Dietrich Fischer-Dieskau especially) that shaped the things people thought and wrote about the composer, bringing to him a new seriousness and psychological depth that was not there in earlier commentary or – it would seem – for earlier listeners.

Similarly, Jim Samson has argued that by the end of the nineteenth century (when recording begins) there were at least four distinct views of Chopin, split along nationalist lines: a French view, which saw Chopin as essentially French, a master of expression, nuance and refinement; a Russian view, according to which Chopin was a Slavic composer, fascinated with the rhythms of national dance; a German view, which incorporated Chopin into the pantheon of Germanic masters thanks to his sophisticated control of harmony and form; and an English view, which simplified his complex textures to make them more suitable for the drawing room.[2] One can hear these approaches in early recordings if one takes, for instance, Alfred Cortot as representative of the French view, Ignaz Friedman the Slavic, and Artur Schnabel the German. (Fortunately, perhaps, simplified English Chopin is not readily available now in recordings.) Today we don't find so many self-consciously different approaches; ease of travel, and perhaps also recording itself, has spread styles far and wide, encouraging homogenisation.[3] There may be less variety – although in fact that remains to be shown through detailed study – but if there is that hasn't inhibited change. On the contrary, styles are changing as fast now as they were a century ago; and, as ever, performance and conceptions of music today remain closely interlinked.

Writers have from time to time used recordings as historical evidence. Louis Lochner quotes a study of the violinist Fritz Kreisler's vibrato from as early as 1916, based on a recording.[4] But most discussion of performance style until quite recently was to be found in the work of collectors and enthusiasts, whose minute and deep knowledge of recorded performances remains as yet unmatched. It was producers and music journalists who created such monuments to the history of performance as *The Record of Singing* and *The Violin on Record* and innumerable collected editions of performers' recorded works,[5] as well as the main journals (*Gramophone, Record Collector, Classic Record Collector* and others). In this context musicologists are *arrivistes*. Since Robert Philip's ground-breaking book of 1992, *Early Recordings and Musical Style*, and Timothy Day's *A Century of Recorded Music* (2000), performance style has begun to receive close academic scrutiny.[6] Martin Elste and Dorottya Fabian have published important work on Bach recordings, and Michael Musgrave and Bernard Sherman edited a fine volume on Brahms.[7] There has been a major genre study by David Milsom;[8] and an increasing number of PhD theses points towards a vigorous future. There is a great deal to learn and to do, but it may not be too soon for this chapter to offer a view of the nature of performance style and the mechanisms underlying its change.

It is not a trivial subject. The evidence of changes in performance style provided by recordings has profound implications for studies of historical performance. If we want to know about the performance practice of eras before recording began – the baroque and classical periods, for example – we have only writings as evidence. But from around 1900 treatises and teaching books on how to play and sing can be compared with recordings – often recordings of their authors (examples include Lilli Lehmann, Lotte Lehmann, Leopold Auer, Carl Flesch, Harry Plunket Greene and Alfred Cortot, among others) – and what we find is devastating to the whole notion of historically informed performance. It would be impossible to come anywhere near the sounds people actually make by following only what they write. Documentary evidence now seems hopelessly insufficient without sound. Moreover, if performance style changed as fast before 1900 as it has since, anything we did think about one small time period could be irrelevant to the previous or succeeding generation. Changes in recorded style force us to rethink the whole subject of performance practice before 1900, and perhaps even to abandon it as having any practical application.

And the same evidence has profound implications, too, for studies of scores, since their meanings appear to change far more quickly and radically than we could have supposed. Clearly, what music means to us today must be just as temporary and contingent.

Performance style

What do we mean by performance style? Conceptually, performance style is very like composition style. Composers as they grow up develop artistic habits in their melodic, harmonic, textural and formal composition that are characteristic both of them and of their generation. Some of these habits are inherited from their immediate predecessors, some are borrowed from contemporaries, some (chiefly perhaps the interaction between all these) are new and influence others in turn. Similarly, performers who have sufficient technical control and musical imagination develop ways of making sounds on their instruments and relationships between adjacent sounds in their performances that identify them, place them in relation to their predecessors and contemporaries, and are striking enough for others to be influenced by them. Over time general style changes. It's arguable that composition style changes more obviously and suddenly than performance style (more in the manner described in Thomas Kuhn's *The Structure of Scientific Revolutions* than Charles Darwin's *The Origin of Species*). It's easier for a composer to be a revolutionary and yet gain an audience (indeed it's almost a qualification) than for a performer, who is expected always to please. And therefore performance style changes not so much by intention, by the determined self-confident act of an individual, as by accident, by gradual changes, made almost without anyone noticing, that accumulate rapidly. And to that extent performance style needs different models if we're to understand its mechanisms.

Like composition style, performance style can easily be seen to work on a number of different levels. All performers have a slightly different collection of habits, which we can call their 'personal style'. Yet each of these collections is inevitably going to be highly characteristic of its time. It would be impossible for performers to please audiences, promoters and critics, or even as students to have pleased examiners and teachers, if their way of making music were as different from the current norm as we hear on earlier recordings. Consequently, current taste selects performers who conform, and in so doing it creates a 'period style' which may be defined by habits that many of them have in common. Equally, gifted young performers are selected because within all this conformity they show some distinguishing features that seem compatible with general style and yet mark them out as new. So selection involves a preference for novelty, but novelty that works well with current general habits. Strong exceptions are so rare that one can cite only Glenn Gould; the way in which he managed to find work despite his difference offers important lessons.[9]

Other kinds of group style are also possible. National style is the most obvious, and as we've seen that needs particular social environments if it's to evolve. (At the moment in Western art music it barely exists.) Styles might also develop according to religious or other ideological allegiances. It is very likely that period style itself operates on different levels. We may not have had recordings for long enough to be able to see this yet. But it seems probable that, while some ways of being musical change as quickly as we hear on recordings, others last rather a long time, perhaps for centuries, yet not indefinitely. For example, it seems possible that polyphony before around 1600 could have involved ways of connecting notes quite unlike those that have been used since. Perhaps if atonality continues to be developed over many centuries it will gradually come to be handled by performers in ways fundamentally unlike those of the twentieth century or of any continuing tonality. Only many centuries of recording will allow us to hear. In these ways there may be extended period styles.

It seems reasonable to suppose that instruments and human bodies impose limits on the extent of style change. Voices may be capable of a greater variety of sounds and manners of expression than violins, for example, and certainly more than most wind instruments. So it's probable that singing changes more than playing. Recordings seem to bear that out. We can assume, then, that instruments provide some long-term constraints and consistencies; and perhaps we can think of ways of using instruments as constituents in extended period style. Performance style must owe many of its characteristics to an interaction between what instruments can do and what bodies can do with them. But the relationship is two-way. What bodies can do depends partly on practice, and what is practised depends on the sounds one is aiming to achieve.[10] Inevitably, the causes and effects of performance style are complex. One fixed element – in this case the instrument – is not enough to allow us to reconstruct the others.

One might also suppose there to be a causative relationship with composition, but which is the cause and which the effect is far from clear. The performance of atonal classics offers an instance.[11] As Miriam Quick has proposed, Webern expected his music to be played in what Richard Taruskin calls the 'vitalist' manner of the 1930s, with great flexibility of tempo and dynamics.[12] When it was revived and promoted in the 1950s it was played as inflexibly as possible: by its new generation of performers this was taken to be its very essence, though an older generation (including vociferously Theodor Adorno) fruitlessly argued that this was a radical misunderstanding. Since the 1980s these scores have been performed ever more flexibly, not for historical reasons (historically informed performance has not yet reached Webern) but simply in the normal course of reactive events, in which a new generation insists on the necessity of finding music different. Note that, although Webern's music was new, its original performance style was not. On the contrary, the composer expected and desired a conventional performance. In many contexts this is probably normal. Once atonality had been assimilated, however, performance and composition came closer into line. In the 1950s, Pierre Boulez, who was leading the Webern revival in polemics and as a conductor, was composing with notes whose individually, fully specified characteristics mattered more than their continuity. Likewise his early recorded performances sound *pointilliste* in treating each note as an individual event. In the 1980s and 1990s, still conducting Webern but now emphasising its linearity and harmonic richness, he was composing with sonorities and structurally melodic continuities.[13] Performance style, then, is thoroughly bound up with other kinds of style, not necessarily just musical style, and is as representative of its time as they.

How styles changed

A brief chapter is no place for a detailed history of changing performance styles over the past century. But a sketch may be useful before we go on to think about underlying mechanisms.

   When recordings began, a handful of very old but very famous performers were enticed into the studio (sometimes, the studio was taken to them). We hear in their playing and singing a style (perhaps styles) that had already almost gone and was certainly not typical of younger recording artists. There are too few of them for us to know how representative they are. But one thing that emerges strongly from a study of later musicians is that, far more often than not (this is my impression, but one that seems increasingly borne out by recorded evidence), musicians played in consistent ways throughout their professional careers. (We'll see why in the next section.) There were notable exceptions, so this can never be taken for granted, but on the whole most recorded musicians for whom we have a lifetime's output seem to have developed a personal style early in their career and to have stuck with it fairly closely for the rest of their lives. In that case, we have some basis for supposing that these oldest recorded musicians may have been playing in a manner current in their twenties.[14] So the spreading of chords by Carl Reinecke (born 1824) in a Mozart piano concerto may be a feature of some playing in the late 1840s (the time of Schumann and Chopin: certainly there are Chopinesque moments in his melodic elaborations).[15] Or he may be an exception, or a maverick. But it would be unwise to dismiss his evidence too soon. Joseph Joachim (born 1831) may be showing us something of the range of violin performance styles practised in the 1850s (early Brahms). He plays with a somewhat different style for each repertory of music: there is virtually no vibrato in his Bach (this would remain unthinkable again for over a century), whereas more vibrato and a much stronger sound characterise his Brahms as well as his own music. Adelina Patti (born 1843) may be singing with something of the manner of the mid-1860s (middle-period Verdi), and if so we would need to rethink much nineteenth-century music, because Joachim and Patti share (with the other oldest recorded performers) a much plainer and smaller sound than we might expect, extremely flexible within the metre, with shallow vibrato but a lot of portamento, yet far from the sentimentality that portamento came to signal much later (in the 1920s). Their attention is focused on line and on lyrical continuity uninterrupted by sudden change in any dimension of the sound; their expression is heartfelt but without histrionics. In them we may well be hearing musical performance style as it was before the changes required by the huge scorings and expressive extravagance of Wagnerian and *verismo* opera.

From slightly younger singers and players we hear a different kind of musicianship. Lilli Lehmann (born 1848), an admired Wagnerian soprano, already sings with much greater contrasts within a phrase and with fast but deep scoops up to notes she wishes to stress; Eugène Ysaÿe (born 1858), coming from a Franco-Belgian tradition, plays the violin with slower and more frequent portamento than Joachim and with much more vibrato; Vladimir de Pachmann (born 1848) plays the piano with extravagant (sometimes mischievous) elaborations, and with rubato at both beat and bar levels deployed according to the character and role Pachmann perceives each moment to have within the phrase. Clearly we are now hearing a different stylistic world in which moments in scores with expressive potential are felt to need the listener's attention drawn to them.

This is a tendency that increases further and for longer than we might today imagine possible. Pianists with a Polish background born from the 1850s to the 1880s (Michałowski (1851), Paderewski (1860), Hofmann (1876), Friedman (1882)) play Chopin with ever more widely varying beat-lengths, in patterns that differ according to the form far more than they have since. Mazurkas, nocturnes, polonaises and waltzes are not only different from one another but considerably different between pianists, so that it seems to be not so much the form as the need to differentiate that drives expressivity. Pachmann's Mazurka Op. 50 No. 2 is shaped at phrase level and relatively light compared to Friedman's, which is much more involved in beat-to-beat changes of emotional temperature, with shifts in the musical surface tending to generate major changes of mood. Similarly, among violinists we find Huberman (born 1882) using very wide vibrato and ubiquitous portamento where Flesch (born 1873) used less though still more than Auer (born 1845) or Rosé (born 1863).

The implication that there was expressive inflation through these generations, making itself heard in recordings through the 1900s to the 1920s, is amply confirmed by looking at singers. Among those born between the 1850s and the 1880s (and always recognising that individuals are very different) there appears to be a gradual shift away from shaping the phrase through broad changes in tempo towards a smaller-scale rubato responsive to melodic and harmonic twists which themselves respond to the text: emotional detail becomes the focus of attention as moods swing from moment to moment. By the time we reach Lotte Lehmann (born 1888), each word and each note is mined for all its expressive potential: it seems as though the singer feels everything felt by the characters in the text and aims to get the audience to feel it too. Lehmann has her counterpart among pianists in Alfred Cortot (born 1877), for whom extreme tempo flexibility is supplemented by octave reinforcements and other adjustments to the composer's text in the interest of intensified feeling. Both Lehmann and Cortot devoted minute attention to explaining to their students what each moment in the score seemed to them to represent. It was an emotional-pictorial approach to understanding and communicating musical meaning.

For reasons that remain to be properly investigated (but can all too easily be guessed at), the Second World War cut off this view of musical performance and made it seem obsolete.[16] For a new generation a new approach seemed necessary, and suddenly those performers who had been playing all along in a more restrained fashion seemed newly relevant. Among pianists we can see Schnabel (born 1882) becoming iconic, followed by Kempff (1895), Solomon (1902) and Horowitz (1903), while (exceptionally) Rubinstein (born 1887) changed his performance style after the war, cutting back on rubato to bring it into line with the new approach. Meanwhile Tureck (born 1914) led Bach playing in a new, almost mechanical direction towards something perceived to be more faithful to the score (which is to say, less sensitive to potential meanings beyond the structural relationships between the notes).

Among violinists and singers, however, the reaction against subjectivity took a rather different turn, away from portamento and rubato, but at the same time towards much heavier vibrato. A permanent wider and slower vibrato applies now to everything, regardless of the changing musical surface, as if its width and speed could signal feeling in the abstract while its regularity could guard against feeling in the moment. In Germany the generation of Schwarzkopf (born 1915) and Fischer-Dieskau (born 1925) initiated this tradition; in Italian opera it was that of Callas (born 1923), leading to a soundworld in which vibrato is so prominent as to make ensemble singing harmonically incomprehensible – a measure of how much expressive weight it was being asked to bear. Among violinists we can hear the counterpart in players such as Stern (born 1920) and Haendel (born 1928), and still in the playing of Perlman (born 1945), Kremer (born 1947) and even Mutter (born 1963).

This post-war style settled into something like a norm for several decades, surviving to a considerable extent even into modern times (reflected in the example of Mutter). Pianists Brendel (born 1931), Ashkenazy (1937), Argerich (1941), Perahia (1947); violinists Chung (1948), Kennedy (1956), Shaham (1971); and singers Baker (1933), Janowitz (1937), Domingo (1941), Battle (1948), Bonney (1956) and Bartoli (1966), as well as many younger singers, work broadly within this stylistic world in which vibrato and dynamics bear most of the expressive load, with rubato constrained by a steady beat, the tone rich and relatively unvaried. If performance style was ever 'romantic' it was here and not before, wholly separate from romantic movements either in literature or in musical composition.[17]

It is this comfortable stylistic consensus against which what we now call the Historically Informed Performance (HIP) movement reacted so strongly from the late 1960s through the 1980s, led by performers born from around 1930 onwards and thus growing up through the years of post-war reconstruction (for example, Harnoncourt (1929); Brüggen, Bylsma, Norrington (all born 1934); Hogwood (1941); and Sigiswald Kuijken (1944)). This was the late modernist reaction against materialist and technological complacency, a turning back to a more primitive original state which the modern world had comfortably covered over. Fortepianos, gut strings, natural brass and raucous woodwind all seemed to represent truthfully the plainness of Urtext editions and (though they dare not say it) the primitiveness of the pre-industrial societies imagined as the proper home of early music. Above all, ruthlessly fast and articulated rhythms removed the expressive hallmarks of traditional post-romantic performance.

Two things seem outstandingly interesting about this development at the moment. One, by far the more important, is that, probably for the first time since at least *c.* 1600, perhaps for the first time ever, an entirely new performance style was forged deliberately from nothing more than the will to change, and – most remarkable of all – it was made to work. Where styles change normally by chance mutations and others' (largely unconscious) responses to them, here a new style was made by reading, thinking and playing, proceeding by trial and error until something worked. Within a decade a new style had carved a niche, while within two it had taken over a large share of the market, so that conventional orchestras now began to leave baroque (and, more and more, classical) music alone, certain that anything they did there would be slammed by the critics.

The other fascinating development was that HIP performers very quickly became much more expressive, using wide dynamic and rhythmic fluctuation to do deep expressive work. At the same time the next genera-tion of mainstream players and singers began to adopt HIP characteris-tics – cleaner sound, smaller-scale articulations – until at present it is often hard to tell what one is listening to. Postmodernists of this sort include among violinists Mullova (born 1959), Vengerov (born 1974), Hahn (1979); among singers von Otter and Fink (both born 1955), Koženà (born 1973), Royal (born 1979); and among conductors Jurowski (born 1972), Rattle (born 1955) and also Mackerras (born 1939), whose once lone compromise position has now become mainstream. Most character-istic of the early twenty-first century, it seems to me, is the coupling of this amalgam with a returning and continuing inflation in expressive performance. How far it will go remains to be seen.

The preceding paragraphs have mapped out some of the most obvious developments of the past century, but they are also grossly oversimpli-fied. Any performer takes in a complex mix of elements which might (if only there were a way to do it) be traced to innumerable sources from the more or less recent past. Each element in the mix works differently in its particular context from the way it would work in another. A rhythmic articulation, for example, produces a different effect when combined with altered habits of dynamic shaping. A vibrato of 0.6 seconds per cycle sounds quite different in 2000 than it did in 1900 because so many other elements have changed. It's possible, therefore, to point in any performer's work to details that may seem to contradict a general-ised story of style change, but that may be to overlook the changed significance of those details in their respective contexts. Or perhaps not. To make progress we really need now to undertake many detailed studies of local and especially of personal styles, and only then, using that detail as a secure base, will we be able to build up new and better pictures of general period or national style. I suggest that it's on these much more detailed studies that attention could best be focused in the immediate future.

How style changes

At the same time, we may begin to think about the mechanisms by which style changes. How do we get from Joachim to Vengerov (or even to Ysaÿe)? To understand that, we need a more detailed grasp of the elements of which a style is made up. What are the units of style? I've said that performance style is a collection of habits. What do these habits consist of? Quite simply, they consist of ways of not performing scores literally. A literal sounding (one can hardly call it a performance) of the pitches and durations of a score is perceived as mechanical and 'unmusical'. To say that a performance is 'musical' in effect means that aspects of what is notated are performed non-literally, with some variation from the notated value which brings a sense of beauty or a feeling of communicated meaning to a performance of the score. Listeners tend to feel that their emotions have been touched in some way. (There are excellent reasons, revealed by a great deal of experimental psychology, to think that that is broadly correct.[18]) These changes to the literally notated score are made in as many of the three principal dimensions of sound (pitch, timing, loudness) as can be adjusted by the instrument being used. A voice or a bowed string instrument and (to more limited extents in pitch) most wind instruments can adjust all three; a piano can modify timing and loudness; a harpsichord only timing. Musicians develop ways of managing these possibilities and of applying them to scores. The way they manage them is a matter of technique, the way they apply them a matter of style. Of the two, style changes much more quickly because there is a much wider range of possible combinations of compositional context (a note or chord with particular structural functions), pitch, loudness and timing. Timbre, although it is in fact simply a function of pitch and loudness, may also be considered in effect as a further dimension, which only increases the almost infinite range of possible ways of 'shaping' each note in a score.

Patterns of shaping applied to notes constitute habits of performance style. We can define performers' habits in terms of the precise ways in which they modify pitch, timing and loudness in particular situations. At the level of the individual note and below – for example, the way a note is started or the way sound in each dimension is altered during it – performance style can be defined quite precisely in units that are comparable to genes in the evolution of life, or memes in the evolution of culture,[19] or which might best (since the meme has only a notional existence and since cultural transmission typically involves imprecise copying)[20] be thought of as 'cultural variants'.[21] We can think of culture as high-speed adaptation,[22] with social learning as its mechanism.[23] It is a system of inheriting acquired variation.[24] Invoking theories of cultural evolution is therefore a rather good way of understanding how these collections of performance habits change over time.

In their formative years, the ways in which performers are musical will be shaped by a number of factors. They will be learning from teachers, who will instil technique, but technique applied in real situations which therefore involve performance style. Teachers will by definition encourage a style that is (or was when they were young) accepted in the wider musical world, and young players at a certain level will often choose a teacher because they already like his or her style. So teaching tends to aim to transmit traditional style quite exactly. At the same time, however, and much more since the widespread availability of recording, aspiring performers are also listening to others, both to older musicians with their own personal styles and also to their peers who are trying out different habits for themselves. (Indeed, research has found – unsurprisingly – that the influence of peers tends to be stronger than that of teachers.[25]) Further experimentation comes through practising, and through the interaction there of what is learned, heard, tried out, imagined and discovered by accident. More is learned through performing to an audience, and then through responding to audiences', examiners' and, later, critics' responses: one's performance style gets adjusted accordingly. Eventually, as successful young performers begin to acquire work and to manage their careers, a style is arrived at that seems to fit into current general norms, yet to have something distinctive and fresh about it, and that achieves an optimal balance between the effort required to maintain it and the reward that accrues. The young performer succeeds in making a career if he or she is highly competent and also has something noticeably but not upsettingly new to offer.

This process is a classic example of cultural evolution as theorised by Peter Richerson and Robert Boyd, and (building on their work) by Stephen Shennan. The key process is that of listening to and learning from others, adopting features of their style that seem useful and abandoning those that do not. Because there are so many aspiring performers at any one moment, a very widespread interaction between individuals causes substantial change over time at the population level.[26] Individuals are highly responsive (because so much hangs for them on their success), and therefore change at the population level can be very rapid. Yet for each individual the amount of innovation can be quite small, using the easiest modifications to hand, with the least change for the greatest effect. And for individuals innovation need not continue. In fact there are pressures that discourage it. Once a career has become established there is little incentive to upset the balance of effort and reward by innovating further. As they in turn become teachers and models for younger aspirants to the profession, their achievement seems to be confirmed by their increasing status, and there is a strong incentive to attempt to pass on their own style (in which their most gifted pupils will always frustrate them).

Now we can see why it is common for performers on record to have their personal styles established quite early in their careers and not to change them radically thereafter. (Exceptions are interesting and worth special attention.) And we can see too why performance style changes inaudibly from year to year, just noticeably over twenty years or so, observably with ease over fifty years, and astonishingly over the history of recording. The changes introduced by individual performers are so small that they may even be unrecognised by them, in effect unconscious. Large changes, which are much riskier and correspondingly rare, take longer to be assimilated by others (if not simply rejected). So Historically Informed Performance, a rare instance of a very radical change within a tiny population, took some time to become established and even now, after forty years and conspicuous success, is still being integrated into mainstream playing.

We can better understand the general direction of style change by invoking the theory of runaway sexual selection. Variants that bring advantages (in animals, mates; in musicians, work) will be copied in an exaggerated form, as rivals attempt to outbid others for the available resources. Over time, attractive traits will become inflated until eventually the cost of maintaining them outweighs the benefits. (Peacock tails are the usual example, attracting mates to the point where males with the largest tails can no longer escape predators, in which case the genes for the largest tails die out.) In music we can see a very clear example of this process in the gradual inflation of expressivity from the oldest recorded performers up to the generation of Cortot and Lotte Lehmann, at which point the costs (in terms of inaccuracy and theatricality) seemed to many to outweigh the benefits in emotional engagement. Younger performers attracted attention and approval by playing with more accuracy and greater restraint, causing a gradual deflation in expressivity as faithfulness to the score became seen as a virtue. At much the same time (the 1920s and 1930s) neo-classicism proved to be a successful change of a more radical kind, although, probably due in part to the transference of cultural consumption away from the elite towards the middle classes, sentimental performance continued alongside, dominating record company output, until the end of the Second World War, after which it seemed inappropriate to too many people.[27] Both World Wars offer obvious instances of a social-historical factor with a powerful bearing on change in performance style. (And seen as part of a decline in divisive nationalism that fed two wars and others since, the decline of national styles is not necessarily to be regretted.)

A further factor was certainly change in technology. Often musical technology seems to bring an increased ability to generate expressivity. The development of the piano through the eighteenth and nineteenth centuries offers one example, the expansion of the orchestra another. The latter forced a new vocal method, and increases in portamento, vibrato and rubato into the twentieth century may in part have been consequences. But by the time we reach the apogee of hyperexpressivity, with Cortot and Lehmann, a new technology is playing a major role. The microphone and the valve amplifier allow intimacy as a new or reinvented dimension of musical expressivity. This also applies to popular music in a big way, allowing new kinds of intimate sentimentality, and later to the electric guitar, linking minimum effort with maximum sound, truly a revolution in the cost/benefit equation. Arguably, HIP may have offered a kind of new intimacy: smaller bands, smaller gestures, requiring smaller spaces on apparently unsentimental (historical) grounds, but actually allowing closer engagement than the deliberately cool nature of the expressivity at first implied. Yet in time runaway selection has led HIP expressivity to become inflated, its present state. This example emphasises how many are the factors that bear on changes in performance style, and how complex their interaction. Much more research is needed before we can delineate any example with confidence.

Another aspect of runaway selection theory that is relevant is the tendency for sexual display, like musical style, to swing between ritualisation and innovation. After reaching an extreme point, style tends to return towards a mean, a point at which successful attractive behaviours are maintained for some time. We could think of mainstream performance between the 1950s and the 1980s in these terms, a time when ideas about vibrato and rubato, for example, were fairly stable. The longer this lasts, the stronger the likelihood that an inventive individual or group will seek to attract by departing substantially from the norm. Again, this well explains the appearance of HIP. HIP also nicely illustrates the potential in cultural behaviours for some entirely external factor to intervene, in this case a moral imperative to be more faithful to the composer's historical environment. Runaway selection is particularly characteristic of changes in Western music because Western music is *relatively* unrestrained by cultural pressure to conform. (And judging by the consistently rapid change of styles in art since at least the thirteenth century this seems to have been so for a long time.) And needless to say, all these processes are sped up by commercial pressures, most evidently in the context of popular music production where fashion is driven by irresistible economic forces.

In general, performers will follow what theorists of evolution call optimal foraging principles, adopting either the nearest modifications to hand that will give the least change to existing expressive techniques (the least surprise) for maximum effect, or (more rarely, and HIP is again an example) a more radical change that will continue to attract attention for a long time to come.[28] The principle of gaining the best return for a given amount of effort is most clearly exemplified in the nineteenth-century rise of the virtuoso. For social-economic reasons (new audiences, public concerts) putting in much more practice and a longer apprenticeship became worthwhile because the returns for astonishing performance were much greater than before. Moreover, 'the individual with the greater ability pays a lower marginal cost for a given increase in the intensity of the competition'.[29] For the rest, a high price has to be paid in attempting to keep up (in evolutionary terms, costly signalling). The benefits were economic, social and sexual (as Liszt discovered). In modern times, a very large audience, through recordings, encourages a very large investment in performing prowess, to the point where now there are so many highly skilled performers emerging from the conservatories that there have to be other distinguishing factors determining success. One that has emerged in the current younger generation of top-rank performers is a selective advantage in being very easy to work with: as a result the prima donna has declined, but young performers have to pay a very high price in disguising their effort and anxiety.

Looking ahead

It's easy to see how recordings contribute to patterns of change in performance style. Recordings function as one-to-many disseminators that can spread stylistic variants very fast. On the one hand this can encourage homogenisation, but on the other it engineers rapid change, and however strong the homogenising tendency a new recording can always spread new variants. So it's highly likely that performance style has changed more rapidly since recordings became commonly listened to by musicians than before. It was perhaps not until the 1920s (this needs more formal research) that the gramophone was sufficiently universal, accepted and well supplied with records for it to play a normal role in transmitting performance styles to performers. (Bear in mind that it was still considered unwise for young musicians to listen to recordings until very recently.) Equally, notable commercial success would have a powerful effect on the direction of future change. Yet again HIP provides a very clear example. Once it became normal to record baroque and then classical scores with period-instrument orchestras, and to broadcast these performances in preference to traditional ones (as was the case by the 1990s), it became inevitable that traditional orchestras would begin to engage period-instrument conductors (Harnoncourt, Norrington) and to adopt HIP techniques (smaller bands, faster speeds, less vibrato), just as it was inevitable that young traditionally trained performers (Rattle, Mullova) would take on HIP characteristics, all of which is now common. At the same time, expressive inflation in HIP performance practice, as performers competed to attract attention, has led HIP unrecognisably far from its deliberately inexpressive starting point in the pre-original-instrument baroque performances of the 1950s, resulting in a merger on record and in the concert hall of HIP and mainstream in a kind of highly articulated romanticism which is itself a response to public acclaim made evident above all through the sales of recordings.

These mechanisms, which we're just beginning to understand, are now on the verge of being torn apart, I suggest, by the arrival of machine-made expressive performances. What happens when computers can generate performances that sound indistinguishable from human recordings – which, given the already manufactured nature of 'human' recordings and the increasing sophistication of algorithms for expressive performance, will not be long now – will depend on the ways in which, if at all, the algorithms allow for the possibility of evolving performance style. If they are to succeed, they will need to do that rather well. Human performers, competing with machines to attract our attention, will then need to be inventive in extremely unpredictable yet pleasing ways to have an economically viable role.

Birth dates

A selective listing of recorded musicians facilitating style comparison

Pianists, harpsichordists		*String players*		*Singers*	
Reinecke (roll)	1824				
Leschetizky (roll)	1830				
		Joachim	1831	Santley	1834
Grieg	1843	Sarasate	1844	Patti	1843
Diémer	1843	Heermann	1844	Lloyd, E.	1845
Pachmann	1848	Auer	1845	Albani	1847
				Maurel	1848
				Lilli Lehmann	1848
Michałowski	1851			Henschel	1850
Pugno	1852			Tamagno	1850
Grünfeld	1852			Battistini	1856
Janotha	1856	Viardot	1857	Nordica	1857
		Ysaÿe	1858	Sembrich	1858
		Hubay	1858	Calvé	1858

Paderewski	1860			Melba	1861
Davies	1861			Schumann-Heink	1861
Debussy (roll)	1862	A Rosé	1863	Eames	1865
		Soldat	1864	Plunket Greene	1865
Lamond	1868	Powell	1867	Urlus	1867
Godowsky	1870	Squire	1871	Tetrazzini	1871
De Lara	1872	Capet	1873	Slezak	1873
Eibenschütz	1873	Flesch	1873	Caruso	1873
Rachmaninoff	1873	Suk	1874	Chaliapin	1873
		Kreisler	1875		
Hofmann	1876	Casals	1876	Mysz-Gmeiner	1876
Cortot	1877			Erb	1877
Hambourg	1879			Destinn	1878
Landowska	1879	Kubelik	1880		
Friedman	1882	Thibaud	1880	Farrar	1882
Schnabel	1882	Huberman	1882	Galli-Curci	1882
Backhaus	1884	Hall	1884	Gerhardt	1883
Fischer	1886	Sammons	1886	Hempel	1885
Rubinstein	1887	Fachiri	1886	Schumann, E.	1888
Scharrer	1888	Spalding	1888	Lehmann, Lotte	1888
Murdoch	1888			Schlusnus	1888
Raucheisen	1889	Zimbalist	1890	Gigli	1890
Hess	1890			Melchior	1890
Moiseiwitsch	1890	Elman	1891	Kipnis	1891
		Szigeti	1892	Schöne	1891
		Telmanyi	1892	Dal Monte	1892
Cohen	1895	Harrison	1892	Braslau	1892
Haskil	1895	Menges	1893	Austral	1894
Kempff	1895	Fiedler	1894	Flagstad	1895
Gieseking	1895	Kolisch	1896	Ponselle	1897
Long, K.	1896			Anderson	1897
Moore	1899	Kulenkampff	1898	Patzak	1898
Solomon	1902	Heifetz	1901	Hüsch	1901
Horowitz	1903	Krasner	1903	Klose	1902
Serkin	1903	Milstein	1904	Giannini	1902
Arrau	1903	Primrose	1904	Schiøtz	1906
Curzon	1907	Oistrakh, D	1908	Hotter	1909
Kirkpatrick	1911	Navarra	1911	Björling	1911
Tureck	1914			Ferrier	1912
Richter	1915	Schneiderhan	1915	Schwarzkopf	1915
Gilels	1916	Shumsky	1917		
Lipatti	1917	Neveu	1919	Nilsson	1918
Michelangeli	1920	Stern	1920	Jurinac	1921
Anda	1921	Grumiaux	1921	Los Angeles	1923
Cziffra	1921			Callas	1923
Loriod	1924	Kogan	1924	Fischer-Dieskau	1925
Rosen	1927	Rostropovich	1927	Crespin	1927
Leonhardt	1928	Suk	1929	Ludwig	1928
Brendel	1931	Oistrakh, I.	1931	Ameling	1933
Gould	1932			Baker	1933
Cliburn	1934	Bylsma	1934	Caballé	1933
				Rogers	1935
		Pauk	1936	Schreier	1935
Ashkenazy	1937			Janowitz	1937
Gage	1939	Kuijken, W.	1938	Auger	1939
Kovacevich	1940			Fassbaender	1939

Argerich	1941	Standage	1941	Domingo	1941
Barenboim	1942			Walker	1943
Pollini	1942	Luca	1943	Allen	1944
Koopman	1944	Kuijken, S.	1944	Palmer	1944
Lupu	1945	Perlman	1945	Norman	1945
Perahia	1947	Kremer	1947	Carreras	1946
Uchida	1948	Chung, K.-W.	1948	Battle	1948
Schiff	1953	Huggett	1953	Holzmair	1952
Staier	1955	Ma	1955	Fink	1955
Zimerman	1956	Kennedy	1956	Bonney	1956
Aimard	1957			Prégardien	1956
Pogorelich	1958	Isserlis	1958	Bär	1957
MacGregor	1959	Mullova	1959	Fleming	1959
Hamelin	1961	Mutter	1963	Oelze	1963
Rousset	1961	Manze	1965	Bostridge	1964
		Bell	1967	Bartoli	1966
Anderszewski	1969			Coote	1968
Andsnes	1970	Repim	1971	Maltman	1970
Kissin	1971	Shaham	1971	Netrebko	1971
Lewis	1972	Vengerov	1974	Genz	1973
				Kožená	1973
		Hahn	1979	Royal	1979
		Chang	1980		
		Fischer	1983		
de la Salle	1988				

Recreating history: A clarinettist's retrospective

COLIN LAWSON

My first practical engagement with historical performance occurred in the early 1980s. This was an intoxicating time for period recordings, thanks largely to the new medium of the compact disc. Christopher Hogwood's pioneering Mozart Symphonies for L'Oiseau Lyre was proving an important driver in propelling the entire movement towards classical repertory. In 1976 Neal Zaslaw had heralded Hogwood's project by taking as inspiration the celebrated orchestra at Mannheim, as it was recalled by Burney and Schubart.[1] The rallying cry of 'an army of generals equally fit to plan a battle as to fight it' was a true promise of historical riches. Little of this heady ambition was reflected in Eric van Tassel's review of the complete set some eight years later, which observed tartly that 'the ... minimalist approach, which even in the last symphonies consists simply in getting all the details right, need not prevent our penetrating the surface of the music if we are willing to make some imaginative effort ... a performance not merely under-interpreted but un-interpreted offers potentially an experience of unequalled authenticity'.[2] The role of character and personality in 'historical' music-making was beginning to attract wider discussion that went far beyond the argument that *any* decision on tempo or dynamics must constitute interpretation. For example, Laurence Dreyfus pointed out that the 'authentic' musician acted willingly in the service of the composer, denying any form of glorifying self-expression, but attained this by following the text-book rules for 'scientific method', with a strictly empirical programme to verify historical practices. He was suspicious that these rules, when all was said and done, were magically transformed into the composer's 'intentions'.[3] Richard Taruskin was already viewing the need to satisfy a composer's intentions as a failure of nerve, if not infantile dependency.[4]

By the time I joined The Hanover Band in 1987 as principal clarinet, Beethoven was very much on the agenda. In 1980, Howard Mayer Brown had remarked in his article 'Performing practice' in *The New Grove* that it would be revealing to hear Beethoven symphonies on period instruments, 'but the practical difficulties of assembling and equipping such an orchestra would be almost insuperable'. Nevertheless, from 1982 The Hanover Band was recording Beethoven's orchestral music for Nimbus 'in a form he would recognize', attracting positive reviews that included the notorious strap-line, 'the most original Beethoven yet recorded'.[5] The 'Pastoral' Symphony felt like a serious challenge, but the recording sessions were knife-edge and exciting. After responding enthusiastically to Roy Goodman's high-voltage conducting, I was somewhat surprised to read in the booklet notes that the Band was directed either from the violin or from the keyboard, 'as is in keeping with the period and according to the repertoire'. Furthermore, Clive Brown was certainly justified in querying the historical parameters of the Beethoven 'period' cycles that by then were proliferating. In 1991 he declared roundly that the pedigree of many of the instruments was of doubtful authenticity, observing that there was infinitely more to historically sensitive performance than merely employing the right equipment, and that the public was in danger of being offered 'attractively packaged but unripe fruit'.[6] 'Original instruments' certainly included many copies that had been tweaked in the direction of twentieth-century sensibilities. There is of course a long and under-researched tradition of such practices. For example, as early as 1932 Robert Donington was praising the improvements made to the harpsichord by his teacher Arnold Dolmetsch.[7] More recently, Robert Barclay has drawn attention to the anachronistic features that characterise certain modern natural trumpets.[8]

The Nimbus label had a declared policy of encouraging artists who were willing and able to approach recording without recourse to the edit, which the company regarded as 'destructive, indefensible and fraudulent'. Like many Nimbus artists, the Band queried the policy, only to be told that 'the quality of communication is absolute' and that modest corrections already made produced a quality that was actually 'beyond the competence of the Band to reproduce in a live concert'.[9] From the first clarinet chair this issue seemed far more complex, encouraging caution in recording sessions for fear that technical slips would ruin a long take. After recording the Mozart Clarinet Concerto for Nimbus in 1989, I asked the producer about an untidy solo entry, only to be met with sympathy for my inadequacies rather than any sense of responsibility for what had happened during the session. The Nimbus sound was itself controversial, given the use of a single 'soundfield' microphone. The so-called 'Ambisonic sound system' was reckoned to achieve a natural balance that took greater account of room acoustics, though it often seemed to mask the detailed phrasing the Band was attempting to produce. I became even more suspicious of this set-up when recording *Peter and the Wolf* for Nimbus in a modern-instrument orchestra under Yehudi Menuhin, since all the 'animals' sounded on the playback as if they had been banished to a distant corner of the paddock.

Later experiences with DG Archiv and EMI revealed the producers' lack of involvement with explicitly historical issues, even when leading figures were on the podium. Recording with Trevor Pinnock revealed his inspirational prioritisation of sound and intonation, whereas Roger Norrington used sound as a means to illuminate the language of gesture, shape and form. These conductors' musical personalities were well served by producers and engineers of fine artistic judgement. But, overall, no one ever queried even the basic national playing styles that might make the sound of Beethoven, Cherubini and Rossini individual and distinctive. During my time as principal clarinet of the London Classical Players, Norrington wrote in one of his CD booklet notes that the earliest gramophone recordings were of limited help in seeking a historical viewpoint. It was somehow reassuring that a mere dozen years later he could write in relation to his crusade against pervasive orchestral vibrato that most of today's musicians had no notion of what could be so simply revealed in a good gramophone collection. Significantly, only one conductor – Roy Goodman – has ever asked about the pedigree of my clarinets. Pinnock, for example, showed absolutely no interest in such matters, apparently dreading only that unacceptable sounds would be emitted, especially from the winds. Yet in celebration of twenty years of The English Concert in 1993, he wrote: 'Some of the publicists' myths about "authenticity" have been exploded, but for us the simple fact remains the same: we like to use the tools designed for the job in hand. Instruments good enough for Bach should surely be good enough for us.'[10]

Some of my most inspirational sessions were recordings of Mozart's Piano Concertos K. 482 and K. 488 with a stylish Hogwood and brilliant fortepianist Robert Levin. But does this repertory actually need a conductor, I began to wonder? In any event, Levin's improvisations throughout each take were an integral part of his contribution. He later indicated that the producer Chris Sayers was left to select from a variety of interpretations and improvisations, pending developments in technology that would enable every version to be programmable. As Levin has said, there is something about recording that is antithetical to the freedom of improvisation. Indeed, this is just one aspect of the sometimes uneasy partnership of modern technology and early instruments.

Most clarinettists, whether on modern or period instruments, aspire to engage in some artistic projects over which they have a reasonable degree of control. Recording the Weber concertos on a ten-keyed clarinet together with Roy Goodman and The Hanover Band was a special opportunity. The packaging of that particular CD reflects current debate as to whether music needs merely to be absorbed or whether it should be understood at a deeper level. The disc was prepared with reference to primary sources and in discussion with appropriate scholars, including editor Jonathan Del Mar. Yet, as a Classic FM release, it came with a mood guide, gaining two rosettes in the 'soothing' category and five under 'exhilarating'. The disc is part of a 'full works' series, in which Classic FM made a feature of presenting complete pieces, rather than compilations of bleeding chunks or sound-bites.

My chamber music recordings, whether on classical clarinets and basset horns, early nineteenth-century instruments or simple-system clarinets, have woven a variety of paths between historical accuracy and practical expediency. Overall, I have always been eager to assimilate historical evidence into articulation and phrasing, but also to prioritise sound quality, even where the means were not strictly historical. I argued to myself that C. P. E. Bach's remarks about the importance of moving an audience were of special value. After the premiere of Mozart's Serenade K. 361 in 1784, one critic described Anton Stadler's clarinet as having so soft and lovely a tone that no one with a heart could resist it. In the recording studio as in the concert hall, such primary evidence – relating as much to the art of music-making as its craft – can be particularly influential and inspirational.

11 Going critical: Writing about recordings

SIMON FRITH

Introduction: Criticism and commerce

> The talking machine, as is well-known, found its first sponsor in the cycle
> trade – the music trade would have none of it.
>
> *Phono Trader and Recorder*, 1911[1]

For about twenty years, between 1972 and 1992, I practised as a rock critic.
While this did mean reviewing concerts and sometimes talking to performers, to be a rock critic was to be a record critic. My first published work
was a record review in *Rolling Stone*, and rock, as a new kind of musical
institution, was centred on the record.[2] The founding fathers of rock
criticism, Greil Marcus and Jon Landau, both edited *Rolling Stone*'s record
review pages, while Robert Christgau, the self-titled Dean of Rock
Criticism, started his Consumer Guide, capsule reviews of every rock
record released, in 1969.[3]

Towards the end of my time as a critic I began to notice articles about
the decline of rock criticism. 'Where have all the rock critics gone?' asked
Ed Ward, editor of the *Rolling Stone* history of rock 'n' roll, in August
1988, following up his question later that year with the more assertive
'Rock Critics RIP!'[4] This was to become a recurring feature-story line. In
1998 Gina Arnold, a leading voice in the next generation of American rock
critics, reflected in her turn 'On the death of rock criticism' ('Once it was
about passion. Now it's all puff') in the online *Flagpole Magazine*, while
veteran Italian rock critic, Gino Castaldo, deplored the 'strong decrease in
the *demand* for critics'.[5] What is being described in such laments is a
perceived change in the conditions of rock criticism: on the one hand,
record companies were signing the wrong sort of acts, releasing the wrong
sort of records, overwhelming the critic with the scale and effectiveness of
their marketing; on the other hand, newspapers and magazines no longer
gave music writers the space or freedom to be critical.

Such arguments have become the commonplace of rock critics' conversations with each other – their worst fears realised by Robert Christgau's forced
departure from the *Village Voice* in 2006[6] – and they are supported by
academic study. Ulf Lindberg *et al.*'s magisterial *Rock Criticism from the*

Beginning reads like an obituary, and sociological studies of the British music press chart the increasing limits on space, the rising influence of brand managers, the reduction of critic to PR accessory, the ubiquitous star rating, the fragmentation of the rock market into taste publics, and so forth.[7] There's more than a whiff of nostalgia here. There may once have been a golden age for rock writers but as record critics they have always played a role in music marketing. Turn to classical music critics' reflections on their present situation and we therefore find similar arguments but with a different inflection: the decline of classical music criticism in the quality press is related to the dire effects of record selling generally. Max Bridle, editor of the online classical music magazine, *Seen and Heard*, thus suggested in 2001 that classical critics 'lost their influence as movers and shakers' in the early 1990s thanks to 'philistinism amongst arts editors and decreased critical coverage in newspapers'. Bridle linked the decline of classical music criticism to the rise of popular music and 'the nefarious (and probably incorrect) belief that this is what readers want'.[8]

Academic work on classical music coverage in the press does indeed confirm that over the last fifty years there has been an increasing tendency to treat classical music as entertainment and that this reflects the marketing practices of the record industry.[9] Such changes are obvious in *The Times*. In 1955 classical record reviews took their place among the concert reviews and notices of recitals; the paper didn't carry any reviews of pop records. Fifty years later, classical CD reviews appeared among a rather larger number of rock, pop, jazz, folk and world music reviews, and the paper is more likely to run features on popular than classical recording artists.

To treat the 'commercialisation' of record reviewing as something recent, though, is misleading. As Ronald Wellburn has suggested, the first record review probably appeared in a British magazine, *Talking Machine News* (the trade paper for the phonograph retail industry – 'the dealers' paper' as it was later to call itself), in March 1913.[10] The record review was born as a consumer guide and marketing device; it involved comparing different recorded versions of the same number and rating them, and such an approach immediately became the norm for popular record criticism. The first issue of Compton Mackenzie's *The Gramophone* in April 1923 was devoted to classical records but included brief notes on popular and dance records by James Caskett (Christopher Stone), who commented:

> One of the most widespread uses of the gramophone is for providing dance music. Every month new and more exciting dance tunes are produced which, as they weary us, are discarded for newer and still more exciting ones. For it is notorious that jazz tunes, admirable as they are, do soon become a

burden … The gramophone is most convenient; no need to be too careful of the life of the records, you can wear them out and get the latest.[11]

By issue four, *The Gramophone*'s dance record notes were by 'F. Sharp', who assured readers that 'the following have all been danced to, and a dancing expert has given her valuable opinion on their merits'; and by 1924 dance records were just listed, with asterisks against especially good ones.

Such instant consumer guidance wasn't altogether spurned by classical music record reviewers either. W. A. Chislett notes that:

> 1927 was the Beethoven centenary year and brought a veritable spate of records from all the companies, with Columbia in the lead with an enormous batch. These inspired Sir Compton to suggest an order of preference among them for the guidance of the proverbial man in the street.[12]

And in 1928 the *Gramophone Critic and Society News* was launched as 'the voice of the average plain man (or woman) who takes a real interest in gramophone music, and who is neither a hopeless low-brow nor a supercilious head-in-the-air highbrow'. (*Gramophone Critic* was obviously conceived as competition for *The Gramophone*.) This new magazine was to be 'a guide and counsellor for record buyers', and to that end each issue featured a 'critics' choice' of releases (primarily classical) from each record label. Meanwhile, across the Atlantic, the *Music Lovers' Guide* (which had begun life in 1926 as the *Phonograph Monthly Review*, and was to become in 1935 the *American Music Lover*) applied stars to the records reviewed in its popular music section, 'In The Popular Vein', a practice eventually (in 1936) followed by *The Gramophone* too in its review of jazz and swing releases.[13] Guiding consumers is what record reviewing has always been about. This is what record criticism is for, and why it has been valuable for record companies and newspapers/magazines alike.

What has to be remembered is that while, as Richard Osborne documents, 'the recording of music was mentioned in association with the phonograph from its first conception' (Edison claimed as early as 1878 that 'The phonograph will undoubtedly be liberally devoted to music'), the established music business remained wary of the new technology: 'Phonographs and gramophones were occasionally sold alongside musical instruments or scores, but the mechanical music industry had to find its own retail outlets.'[14]

One consequence was record companies' heavy use of advertising, 'a sensible policy,' in Osborne's words, 'as magazines and newspapers gave little editorial space to the talking machine trade'.[15] Another was the significance of classical music for this sales strategy:

> Eldridge R. Johnson realized that for this object [the gramophone] to gain cultural acceptance the associative qualities that needed to be generated were

musical, not technical. He later stated that 'only great musical talent could transform the phonograph record from a toy into the greatest medium of home entertainment this country [the USA] had known'. To this end Victor and the Gramophone Company pioneered the practice of signing the most renowned musical artists to exclusive, long-term contracts (at first they targeted the operatic stars of Europe; later, as the recording of orchestras improved, they also employed conductors). These celebrity artists – and their art-forms – were vigorously promoted in the companies' advertising. With their names on the companies' record labels it was believed that the surrounding grooves would be 'mellowed ... with the patina of high art'.[16]

Gramophone and gramophone record companies' continuing investment in an upmarket (rather than popular) music sales strategy is reflected in both EMI's interest in *The Gramophone* in the 1920s and Warners's investment in *Rolling Stone* in the 1970s. The most influential outlets for record criticism, one could say, were materially beholden to the companies that issued the records they criticised. Both record producers and record magazines, to put it less cynically, were interested in the long-term development of record consumption.

This was not simply a matter of record companies using record magazines to advertise their wares, although there are examples of such magazines. *Record Mail* was launched in January 1958 as a 'monthly review of "popular" records issued by EMI Records Ltd', to be joined in February by *Record Times*, 'featuring the latest CLASSICAL recordings of EMI'. Decca followed in June the same year with *Records*, 'Britain's first colour illustrated monthly guide to new LPs and EPs featuring all that is best in the world of records'. In 1959 this became *Records Magazine*, 'the monthly guide to good record buying', with a classical pull-out supplement. But such straightforward promotional outlets (which didn't survive long in the rock era) lacked what defined (if in different ways) the purpose of record reviews in *The Gramophone* and *Rolling Stone*: to educate as well as influence the listener.

From the perspective of the record companies this was, in part, an aspect of the continuing belief that recording culture needed to be 'given the patina of high art'. In the 1920s *Talking Machine News*, the UK record dealers' paper, always led its review section with classical releases, and an editorial in November 1921 even wondered, 'Popular Music on Records. Is there too much of it?' The magazine's concern followed a report in the Canadian *Phonograph Journal* that the 'best music' was being submerged by 'the popular hits, the latest fox-trots and jazzy blues', which now accounted for 83 per cent of the Canadian market. *Talking Machine News* thought that the British market was not so distorted.

> Record companies are not philanthropists and it is more than probable that it is the light and popular music of the moment that pays them best, and that it is through the profits on such records that others of a higher and more classical description are made possible. In which case real music lovers have cause for thankfulness.[17]

But such a distinction between 'light' and 'real' music also reflected an assumption about customers' use of records and the implications of this for the business's long-term profitability. The problem of pop records, as the *Talking Machine News* editor put it, was that they are 'easily tired of, for none of them live, and the records being scrapped newer ones are soon demanded, whereas a classical record is often kept carefully for years'. (The same distinction would be drawn between pop singles and rock albums fifty years later.) The latter mode of consumption was judged to be more in the record sellers' interest than the former, and so by July 1922 the editor was wondering 'how dealers can improve public taste' and reporting new evidence of customers turning against 'unsavoury fare' (jazz and ragtime) 'and developing a taste for something more refined and beautiful'. To help this trend, he suggested, the music dealer 'should be a man not only of musical taste, but of musical culture', and to this end he recommended the free tuition offered by the Gramophone Company in 'the foundations of a knowledge of musical works' which would guide their tastes 'in the right direction'. Hence too the importance for the industry of *The Gramophone*.

Objects of criticism

> These records, containing pure tones of varying intensity and pitch, between 14,000 and 10 cycles per second, are of particular interest to technically-minded gramophone users who wish to test the response of their instruments.[18]

The history of record criticism can be understood according to three different narratives: the history of music criticism, the history of the record business, and the history of newspapers and magazines. The record itself is a musical object, a commercial object and an acoustic object. To write about records is necessarily to write about all these things, but the record has been shaped above all by technology. The object record reviewers wrote about in 1923 was different from the object they wrote about in 1943, in 1963, in 1983 and in 2003 (though the music the various kinds of 'record' carried might remain the same). And just as the history of recording technology was shaped by cultural forces, by arguments about value and what listening to music should involve, so recording technology shaped the listening experience and musical judgements: the early 1950s manufacture of the long-playing record and the single, for example, marked the difference between serious and popular music in a quite different material way than the price differentiation between various kinds of 78, which is why the album was crucial to the way in which rock distinguished itself from pop. When EMI launched the 45 rpm record in Britain all but one of its first batch of forty-eight releases carried a classical recording, but, as Richard Osborne writes, 'within a year customers were commenting that "those of us whose equipment can play these discs, and who prefer the so-called 'classical' music, are sorry to find that almost all the new releases of 45 rpm records are of 'popular' music"'. When Decca Records followed EMI's lead, in 1954, their 45 catalogue featured no classical music at all.[19] A cultural distinction had been given technological form.

To write about records, then, is to write about a number of things at once, and in looking at the record review over the last century we can find four overlapping kinds of critical discourse.

The record as record

First of all, the record is treated literally as a record – a record of a performance or event, a technical (and initially remarkable) device for giving listeners access to something not directly available to them. This was the initial way of thinking about records and it has continuing significance in all musical genres. It is, in particular, how the recording business itself has tended to account for the appeal of its products. An advertisement for the Bestone Stereophone in *The Gramophone* in December 1923 is typical in its declaration that 'The elimination of surface noises, the life-like rendering of the human voice, the personality of the violinist and the pianist, the extraordinary detail revealed in orchestral records are qualities which are unique in these wonderful instruments.'[20] Colin Symes has documented the history of the classical record industry's concern for 'fidelity', its ongoing attempts to give record buyers the concert-hall experience in their living rooms.[21]

From a reviewer's perspective, though, the poor sound quality of early sound recording limited its documentary value.[22] In *The Gramophone*'s early reviews recordings are described primarily by reference to the score, as in this review of Tchaikovsky's Fifth Symphony:

> The motto theme now in the major key is invested with the full majesty of the strings; brass have some ponderous chords and then above string triplets and brass the motto theme on woodwind becomes a triumphal march. The music changes from major to minor in a new tune and quickens (*allegro vivace*), but the note of rejoicing persists.[23]

Reviewers were concerned with the quality of the recording as a performance, but as measured by the relationship of recorded sound to the score
(it is often assumed that readers would be listening to their records with
scores in hand), rather than with any sense that the pleasure of the record
had anything to do with being somehow at the original studio event.

> This is *Eine kleine Nachtmusik* with the double bass omitted. Being without a
> score and pressed for time, I must confine myself to saying that the
> recording (new style) seems all that one could wish. The balance is good, and
> each instrument is distinctly audible without being too obtrusive. The
> *timbre* too is as near that of a string quartet as the gramophone has so far
> been able to reach, at least on the new HMV machine. Readers, however,
> should bear in mind that a scoreless reviewer cannot tell if any of the detail
> has been suppressed.[24]

Reference is made to what a performance ideally sounds like in the concert
hall, rather than to what this particular performance might have sounded
like originally.

> I am inclined to think this is the best piece of piano recording I have heard.
> In the *Fantaisie-Impromptu* I do not detect a single harsh note or other
> blemish, and the Impromptu in A flat is almost equally good. Never before
> have I heard that 'pearly' quality which a good pianist can impart to runs in
> the upper part of the piano so faithfully reproduced on a gramophone
> record. I notice that Irene Scharrer plays softly most of the time, even when
> Chopin marks a distinct *forte* in the score, and in this she is wise; she has a
> sufficient variety of touch to make changes of quality where they are wanted
> without resorting to those strenuous methods which, however satisfactory in
> the concert hall, seldom record well.[25]

The record as collectable
Second, the record is treated as something to collect, to put in a domestic
library, as an object of study and appreciation. This was, of course, the
initial thinking behind *The Gramophone* (in his first editorial Compton
Mackenzie explained the magazine's purpose as being 'to encourage
record companies to build up for generations to come a great library of
good music'), and it continues to be the organising principle of review
sections in classical music magazines, book guides to classical records and
such radio programmes as BBC Radio 3's *CD Review*. It is an approach
also to be found now in all popular music genres and is rooted in
comparison – why you should own this recording of Handel's *Messiah*
rather than that one; in a notion of the canon – what are the essential
works; and in an underlying suggestion that good music is good for you,
even – especially – if one has to work at one's appreciation, to listen to the
record repeatedly (and to study the review).

> To some people it may seem that we are giving undue space to two slight,
> however charming, works, these latest National Gramophonic Society
> recordings. But, in the first place, they are works which should be valued by
> every reader of *The Gramophone*; in the second place, they are clear and
> typical examples of chamber music; in the third place, while a mere outline
> of a work may help one to find one's way about it, to get at the heart of it, to
> discover all that it signifies, we have to look at it far more closely – to see why
> this movement is what it is, what is the effect of that phrase, what is its
> relation to another, in a word, all that the composer has put into it.[26]

There is a thin line, though, between encouraging readers to build up a
library of great music on record and encouraging the love of record
collecting for its own sake, where what matters is completion, the acquisition of rare items, the records rather than the music on them. This was
apparent very early in *The Gramophone*'s history.

> I took an early opportunity of visiting the HMV shop in the Hohestrasse,
> and at once proceeded to turn the place upside down. One of my first
> purchases was a record of the quintet from the *Meistersinger*, and, on the
> other side, *Pogner's Anrede*, from the same opera splendidly sung by Paul
> Bender – who, by the way, has sung in various bass parts this year at the
> Metropolitan Opera House, New York, with great success. His record of
> *Wahn, Wahn*, from the same opera was not nearly so well recorded, but I
> subsequently bought the song on an Odeon record by Michel Bohnen …
> After four days at Wiesbaden we returned to Cologne, and I again raided
> the gramophone places, and added to my stock two beautiful records by
> Hermann Yadlowker of Schubert's *An die Musik* and his *Gute Nacht* from
> the Winter Journey Cycle. Paul Knüpfer was probably the finest bass
> produced by Germany for half a century, and he has fortunately made
> numerous records, of which I acquired Schumann's *Wohlauf noch
> gertrunken den funkelnden Wein;* Schubert's *Song of Old Ag*e, and a fine
> 'Rhinegold' record of the Entry of the Giants.[27]

This is the familiar voice of the record collector that one can still hear (in
the person of Rob Cowan) on Radio 3 and which has its rock equivalent in
the magazine *Record Collector*.

The record as acoustic device
Third, the record is treated as a material object, a technological product
with particular qualities of sound and durability. For reviewers this meant,
on the one hand, paying attention to a recording's acoustic characteristics.

> The inability of the gramophone to reproduce heavily hit piano notes,
> particularly when those notes occur in the first few grooves of a twelve-inch
> record, is particularly apparent in two or three of these records, and the
> complaint is aggregated by the harshness of the piano tone. No wonder the
> beginning of Schumann's *Aufschwung* was said to be 'frantic banging': it is.

But curiously enough, the very passage that causes the terrible noise at the beginning of the record acquires a splendid sonority when it reappears later on in the record. This complaint of inability to reproduce low notes well at the beginning of a twelve-inch record has been successfully overcome in the latest records issued by the Gramophone Company, but whether the methods they applied to Cortot and Thibaud will prove successful as applied to Paderewski and his harsh toned pianoforte, the future bulletins must be allowed to prove.[28]

On the other hand, it meant a concern for good sound equipment, an interest in technical experiment – *The Gramophone* reviewed record-playing devices as well as records. W. A. Chislett's reminiscence of the magazine's first fifty years documents the various ways record reviewers tried to get the best sounds that they could from their records.

By this time [1928] microphonic (or electrical as it was then called) recording had got into its stride but electrical reproduction was still feeling its way and the Expert Committee were inclined to advocate acoustical reproduction but with two or more sound-boxes tuned to suit not only the forms of recording but also differentiating between, say, orchestral, vocal and piano records. I myself had four soundboxes, and had to note on the record labels which one gave the best results. What enthusiasm there was then, although most of us experimented on a trial and error rather than scientific basis.[29]

By the end of the 1920s *The Gramophone* had established a template for the classical record review that is still familiar. The review described the music in analytic terms drawn from academic musicology (and with a strong sense of what was proper according to the score); the record's acoustic qualities were assessed. The critics' authority rested on their knowledge of both the history of music and record company catalogues. The best – most elegant and effective – versions of such reviews are to be found, though, not in *The Gramophone* itself but in Edward Sackville-West and Desmond Shawe-Taylor's *The Record Guide*, published in 1951 as the UK's 'first guide to recorded classical music', the book 'that takes the expensive guesswork out of record-buying and ensures that you get the *best* records for your money'.[30] Here, in commentaries on music by Mozart and Stravinsky, we find the requisite combination of musicological and acoustic authority:

The performance is a very fine one, and the Berlin cast about as good as could have been secured, though the Sarastro is a little rough; Sir Thomas Beecham's handling of the score is exemplary, and he has been well served by the recording engineers; the incisive tones of the tenor, Helge Roswaenge, sound a little fierce in the early sides, but this is a fault which disappears as the work proceeds. There are some interesting examples of 'manipulation' to secure particular results: for example, the *pianissimo* of Monostatos's aria sounds as though it were assisted by the turn of a knob, and, contrariwise, the upper register of the Queen of the Night is made to sound more powerful and brilliant by the addition of 'studio' resonance. In principle, such tamperings with 'the truth' are undesirable, but in these instances it must be allowed that the controls have been judiciously handled. (These comments, it should be added, are based solely on aural evidence.)[31]

This astonishing work made musical history. Listening to it now, we may find difficulty in realising the uproar of anger and dismay that shook the Champs-Elysées Theatre in Paris … The discords, the violent cross-rhythms, the blunt, uncompromising themes – all these seem mild, compared with much that we have heard in the intervening period. We can take *Sacre* for granted now, because its lessons have been assimilated; yet a really fine performance – and the two most recent recordings are variously splendid – can give us back some of the original excitement caused by the work. The Monteux set has a special interest, since it was he who conducted the first performance of the ballet. As we should expect, his interpretation is extremely dramatic and the tempi are more strongly contrasted than Van Beinum's. The set is not over-recorded, and contains some sensational passages of sheer sound; but it has little or no recession and the tutti are mere din. The Decca version, on the other hand, is beautifully stereophonic, the bass clearer, the woodwind better played and blended.[32]

The Record Guide is written with such self-assurance that it is hard to resist going through the 'suggestions for beginners' and listing must-have 78s, and harder still to realise how much of such criticism is actually vacuous. What does it mean to call something 'over-recorded'? What is 'sheer sound'? What is a 'blunt' theme? Would we understand any of these terms if we weren't already familiar with Stravinsky's work? But there are two other points I want to make about this sort of discourse.

First, there's no doubt that classical record reviewers lived in a man's world. Writers in *The Gramophone* made routine (if light-hearted) reference to wives not understanding their obsessions with records and record technology. While listening to classical music was ostensibly about spiritual uplift, listening to classical music records often seemed to have more to do with the arcane rituals of a masculine hobby. W. A. Chislett describes visiting his fellow *Gramophone* contributor, Percy Wilson, at his home in Putney in 1927: 'I found that he was using the wall of his sitting room as a baffle for a moving-coil speaker. He had knocked out some bricks dividing the room from the hall and installed the speaker there. His wife took rather a poor view of the appearance but the results were an eye-opener, or perhaps I should say ear-opener, for those days.'[33]

Second, the terms of standard classical record review were set in the age of the 78, before the emergence of microgroove recording, the long-player, tape, stereophonic sound, etc.[34] For a modern reader it is easy to forget that these are reviews of 78s, with a playing time of no more than three and a half minutes per side and with a sound quality that we would not nowadays accept. Reviews described an ideal experience that for many listeners would have been unrealisable (no wonder *The Gramophone*'s reviewers were so obsessed with their equipment). In Frank Swinnerton's words in the magazine in 1923, 'the confirmed gramophone-user does not hear the needle, although he may shiver at the crackle; but the novice at first hears nothing else'.[35]

The record as work of art

It is not surprising, then, that the fourth critical discourse, in which the record is treated as a work of art in its own right (the recording studio a site of creativity like the artist's studio), was developed not by classical music critics but by rock critics. This was a discourse that followed the emergence of the album in the 1960s not as a collection of works that existed independently, as scores, but as something that was created by the act – the art – of recording itself.

Jazz and rock criticism

As I've already noted, the classical record review, whether in magazines like *The Gramophone* or on the arts pages of newspapers, developed alongside (and in deliberate contrast to) a different way of writing about popular records.

> Among the vocal records are some of interest, notably a set of five by Frances Langford. A sentimental nostalgia runs through this set, which I found almost attractive – a reminder that some of us are approaching an age when we shall find ourselves growing old with only jazz memories. I used to wonder what would happen to band leaders when they became grandfathers. Now I know. They just play the old tunes and make us all feel as sentimental as fools … I should like to give a special hand to Eddie Carroll for a Piano Medley on HMV. This simple playing with no frills of any kind has style. It is difficult to say why; it may be a negative virtue, but this is different from the general run of such things.[36]

But even in 1940 we can contrast such light reviewing of light music with Edgar Jackson's approach to 'Swing Music' – here jazz records get the same sort of respect as on the classical pages.

> Basie at his best, playing with unusual touch and technique tasteful, tuneful music which sounds disarmingly simple even though in fact it is in the intangibly complicated Basian idiom.
> *Reproduction*: POOR. One day perhaps the American Decca Company will realise how distressing this raspy surface of nearly all their records is, and do

something about it. Meanwhile, if you go in for high fidelity reproduction I should take home every Decca disc and try it out before you buy it.[37]

Jackson, *The Gramophone*'s jazz and swing critic, also edited *Melody Maker* (launched in 1926), and *Melody Maker* along with *Rhythm* (launched in 1927) was undoubtedly more significant than *The Gramophone* for British jazz record collectors. In Catherine Parsonage's words,

> The magazines helped listeners to choose which records to purchase as their record review pages featured extensive critical and comparative study of the latest releases and offered insights into the musical material and performance style. As such they were extremely influential on the perception and understanding of jazz in Britain at the time.[38]

Through Edgar Jackson, though, the jazz record review took similar shape in *The Gramophone*. Jazz records came to be written about as something apart from commercial popular music. They were taken as seriously as classical records, and the jazz record review was organised in a similar way. Records were described analytically (if drawing on genre-specific rather than classical musicological terms); performances were placed historically; individual performers – soloists – were assessed if not for their truth to a score then for their truth to a musical form (what was or was not 'authentic' jazz was a critical issue in jazz record reviewing almost from the beginning); and reviewers were expected to provide as much information as possible about the recording session.

> First choruses are often used for just straightforward statements of later-developed themes, and one has only to listen to some of [Benny] Goodman's first choruses to realise that the task of stating the theme often leaves even him cold and uninspired.
>
> But listen to his first chorus in *Shine*, and you will find a very different story.
>
> On the face of it Benny does little more in this first chorus than he does in most of his others. He just states the theme with the minimum of embellishment.
>
> But I don't think anyone will need to be a connoisseur to appreciate the artistry with which he does it. The outline of his phrases is as perfect as is the style with which he plays them. His embellishments are as few as they are economically constructed, but their placing and architecture make them the dewdrops which add beauty to the rose.[39]

Like the classical record review, then, the jazz record review was educational (and became even more so in the 1950s with vinyl reissues of classic tracks) and helped construct a community of collectors. But jazz criticism was different from classical criticism in two respects. On the one hand, jazz was constantly changing and critics had to make sense of a series of new jazz forms as well as its 'commercialisation' as swing. On the other hand,

British jazz critics were in crucial respects outside the musical world they were assessing. Jazz was American music and, as the reviewers began to grasp in the 1930s, significantly black American music.[40] The basis of jazz record critics' authority – their writing voice – was different from that of their classical colleagues. Read *The Gramophone*'s and *Melody Maker*'s 1940s and 1950s jazz record reviews now and what is striking is the emphasis on good taste (jazz was, in this respect, distinguished from the vulgarity and gimmickry of R&B and rock 'n' roll).

> With delicacy and restraint, his trumpet tightly muted most of the time, Miles Davis creates solos possessing a remarkable inner tension.[41]

> There is a particular quality in his playing, a melodic grace, a use of certain individual cadences, that is very much his own. And when he turns to the piano – as he does on half of these tracks – the crispness, the percussiveness, of his vibes-playing gets reflected in the litheness of his technique on that instrument.[42]

> Two Ray Charles releases (gospel songs in manner if not content) are just as poor, although for different reasons. *I'm Moving on/I believe to my soul* (London 45) have train effects and choral backing which merely add to the horror of Charles's singing. 'What'd I say' (London 12-inch LP) is a mixture ranging from fairly average 1940s jump blues singing on *Roll With My Baby*, through a rocked-up *My Bonnie*, to such unpleasantly distorted sounds as those on *Tell The World About You. Rockhouse*, an instrumental number is credited to Ray Charles, but I seem to have heard the riff theme on many other occasions. The recording balance varies a great deal. The Raylettes provide an incongruous vocal backing on six of the ten tracks. *Tell Me How Do You Feel* has Hammond organ instead of piano, and *What Kind Of A Man Are You* has no Ray Charles vocal at all: it is, instead, a feature for Mary Ann Fisher, a slightly suave female counterpart of the leader. Charles's piano playing is as crisp as ever; if only he did not insist on singing![43]

Given this dismissal of one of the most influential records for British beat groups, it is perhaps not surprising that *The Gramophone* never got to grips with rock music. In Britain as in the USA, rather than being absorbed into jazz discourse, a distinct form of rock criticism emerged. In the USA, this meant the failure of *Downbeat*'s critics to make sense of the new music and the success, instead, of *Rolling Stone*.[44] In the UK the rise of rock was marked not by the emergence of a new kind of record magazine, but by the transformation of *Melody Maker*. In 1968 its standard record review was still formulated in pop terms:

> THE BOX TOPS 'Cry Like A Baby' (Bell). Yes, indeed, they can sing. Fine, cohesive group sound brilliantly led by Alex Chilton, a soulful and exciting singer. A very commercial album which should sell in vast quantities.[45]

By 1978 the rock record review had incorporated elements of the jazz review but with a much clearer sense of the record itself as the artwork.

> It has a sense of purpose, and the three men produce a remarkably powerful sound. Much of the credit for this can be given to Tony Banks, whose keyboard work gives an almost symphonic texture. Mike Rutherford steps forward as well, his guitar playing filling the gap left by Steve [Hackett].
> While one misses Hackett's original style, such are the miracles of electronics and recording techniques that it is often difficult to place who is playing what, anyway, when guitars sound like keyboards and vice versa. Apart from unifying into an extremely tight three-piece, the band have also loosened up and started to improvise in an un-Genesis fashion.
> This is particularly noticeable on the beautifully relaxed and grooving 'The Lady Lies', where Banks plays acoustic piano over a kind of beat Keith Jarrett might employ. There is a combination of fine instrumental work, interesting lyrics and that feeling for singles-oriented material exemplified by 'Follow You Follow Me'.[46]

And by 1988 the rock record review had fully evolved: descriptive terms were now entirely metaphorical; the critic's knowledge was displayed by virtuoso comparison between bands; and musicians' intentions were less significant than the overall effect of the record on the listener.

> 'Traitor' starts the album with a pointlessly brilliant soliloquy starring Einar as the ultimate revolutionary – the sarcastic anarchist who mocks the revolution – while a stratospheric choir of Björks whip up a horsetail trail of Banshee vapour over something like The Birthday Party only transfused. Nimble, 'Motorcrash' is spooky Madness jostling with delectable detail, Björk relating the tragic story of the child drawn to disaster and Einar employing his best disembodied Big Brother voice of authority …
> 'Birthday' is the waterbaby subaqua stun-jazz that first seduced these ears and still spreads a smile at its alien aural fauvism. Only the Cocteaus's 'Head Over Heels' ever roamed plains so free, so fertive [sic], so frisky. 'Delicious Demon' could scarcely differ more – a mumbo-jumbo rodeo of lassoing whoops splitting its sides over the heavy metal chorus and getting pretty pissed and partied-up at the end.[47]

Conclusion: Record criticism and the consumer

> **A good critic** is authoritative; passionate; surprising; open minded; entertaining; interesting; well-informed; committed; original; free thinking; independent.
> **A bad critic** is uncaring; uncommitted; predictable; ignorant; negative; a show off; too fashion conscious; unoriginal; clichéd; too susceptible to hype.[48]

In the twentieth century, writing about records became a specific occupation. The record critic came to occupy a significant role for both record
companies (the critic's importance to the recording industry indicated by
its provision of records, associated concert tickets and access to privileged
information) and newspapers and magazines (which paid for the reviews).
There are two aspects of this worth noting.

First, a critic's value as a critic lies in his or her *independence* of both
music and print institutions. A record reviewer must not be a record
company propagandist. In practice even well-respected rock critics have
moved across the boundary. For example Britain's finest rock critic,
Richard Williams,[49] moved from *Melody Maker* to Island Records and
then to The *Times* and the *Guardian*; Paul Nelson worked for Mercury
Records during his distinguished career at *Rolling Stone* and other US
journals. In the classical and jazz worlds critics have often worked directly
for record companies, not least as writers of sleeve notes – another form of
record review. Their critical autonomy is preserved, it seems, because
classical and jazz recordings are thought to be somehow not commercial.
And from this perspective the critic's direct engagement with record
production confirms their sense of difference within the journalistic
field. Gemma Harries and Karin Wahl-Jorgensen's interviews with arts
journalists in Britain show how critics deploy their place within their art
and its world to separate themselves from 'ordinary' news reporters and
feature writers and to resist 'hack work'.[50]

Second, the record critic is self-appointed: there are no formal qualifications for the job. W. A. Chislett describes *The Gramophone* as a
magazine launched by amateurs for amateurs. His own route into record
criticism was typical:

> It was also in 1924 that I wrote a letter (found to be too strongly worded for
> publication) about some comments on band records. I was as astonished as I
> was delighted to receive in reply from Christopher Stone, the London Editor,
> a letter inviting me to review the band records of 1924 for publication early
> in 1925. The records were duly sent to me and the review appeared in the
> February issue. Thus began a very happy association which has continued
> ever since ...[51]

The only tool necessary for a record-reviewing career, it seems, is enthusiasm. Chislett is certainly not the only record critic whose first publication was a letter complaining about a magazine's reviews, and many 1970s
and 1980s rock critics first emerged as writer/publishers of their own
fanzines.[52]

In her history of dance criticism in the USA, Lynne Conner usefully
distinguishes between evaluative, descriptive and prescriptive ways of

writing. Prescriptive writing – suggesting how a performance could be improved – is rare in record criticism, not only because such criticism is always after the event, as it were (nothing the critic writes is going to lead to the record being remade), but also because the presumed readers are not musicians or producers but record buyers. Most record criticism in newspapers and magazines just describes and evaluates.

A record critic has to describe a recording that the reader hasn't yet heard but he or she must also suggest how this music should be heard/made sense of. So a record critic must be able to describe music both in its immediacy and in its implications, and to do both these things while instantly engaging the reader's attention – and, at least in newspapers, with very limited time and space.

It is hardly surprising that most published record criticism is not very good. Critics (of all sorts of record) are inclined to the use of clichés, imprecise metaphors and (in rock criticism at any rate) inept musical comparisons. Such writing (like most newspaper writing) is of the moment and does not stand up well to retrospective reading. And yet even such rough-and-ready writing is essential to recording culture. To be interested in music is to be interested in records, which is to be interested in what people write about those records. The record critic is a necessary part of the conversations people have about music. A declining interest in what critics say about records marks a declining interest in records. Record critics let us know what's out there *and* they provide the terms in which to debate what is worth having and what is not. They are a necessary part of record-based musical communities.[53] Back in the late 1970s, when I wrote for *Melody Maker*, market research for a putative redesign/relaunch (which never happened) revealed that by far the most read section of the paper was the record reviews. Readers particularly liked reading reviews of records they already had, and were particularly engaged (and enraged) by reviews with which they disagreed. Buying a record and reading its reviews were – and are – part of the same cultural process.[54]

Something in the air

CHRIS WATSON

I first heard it late one night in a bed and breakfast on the outskirts of Glasgow. It was October 1993 and I was on my way to the Scottish Highlands and breaking my journey overnight in a large Victorian ter-raced house with old, loose-fitting, sash windows. A strong northeasterly wind battered the gable end. My room was on the second floor and around 2am the blast percolated through the window frame, at first a low tone then rising in pitch and intensity as the wind strength varied. I was drawn out of sleep and lay there in the dark inside an unfamiliar room. The window rattled gently, but the sounds from it twisted and turned all around in the darkness. Warm, secure and drowsy, the details of these wildly varying sounds stirred something in my imagination as I slowly drifted back off into sleep.

As a location sound-recordist with a particular interest in wildlife sounds and their associated habitats I had, prior to this event, always tried to avoid wind 'noise' on my recordings. I used large efficient wind-shields to screen my sensitive directional microphones from the effects of the elements and later, in post-production, filtered my tracks using a variety of equalisers to reduce the broad band frequencies associated with wind noise. All that has changed. I have now radically altered my recording techniques to try to incorporate almost all the sounds I hear in any chosen location, including those made by the elements, and now regard the sounds made by the wind as just that – sound, rather than noise.

A week or so into my journey to the Highlands, standing in Glen Cannich in the grip of a fierce westerly gale, I realised that the only sounds present were those produced by the wind. Coniferous forests have their own signature sound, and in light to moderate winds the needles hiss and sigh up in the canopy producing an almost continuous, and quite choral, drifting series of voices. Now, however, the rusty red bark of the ancient Caledonian pines howled, and the outermost branches waved and raged as strong gusts blew through the needles and cones. There was also some-thing else. Along the forest edge was a line of power poles strung with three cables hanging vertically coincident, and they sang. As the gale winds varied, the sounds from the forest and the wires blew a thin two-part harmony that filled the air, and, although impossible to localise, its force and sheer physicality focused my attention. So instead of using directional microphones to highlight individual elements in this wall of sound I chose a spaced pair of omnidirectional mikes, and found my recording position by walking round the site listening for a preferred natural balance of all the parts, similar perhaps to the conductor's position in front of an orchestra. Omnidirectional microphones respond well to low frequencies, and they are also very naturalistic so that listening for extended periods is not hard or tiring on the ears. Recordings made in this way sound, to my ears at least, the closest to hearing the actual event.

These experiences taught me to listen in another way and to focus through foreground or featured sounds and hear them in relation to the background ambience, or acoustic properties, of the habitat. The balance between the two is something I now create by microphone placement and careful listening, and has opened my ears to the creative potential of what I once regarded as unwanted sound – i.e., noise. Recently I have been recording on the Scottish island of Islay where the prevailing westerlies drive straight off the Atlantic ocean and across the island. On the west coast these blustery conditions create a dominant low roar from the sea, but delving at close perspective into the low vegetation with miniature microphones reveals a remarkable and colourful array of sounds. At the back of Saligo beach the deep, soft, harmonic swish of marram grass has a lush and continuous feel, yet in the nearby wet flushes the broad blades of yellow flag iris beds have a distinctive and striking clatter as they are blown together in the gusts. I collect many such sounds to create a palette from which to work in my compositions, and describe them under three categories: Atmospheres, Habitats and Featured sounds. Atmospheres generally have a wide, ambient, perspective and help to create a real sense of place. As these recordings are often combined in a mix, I require them to have two particular characteristics: they must be continuous, at least two minutes in length; and they must have a small dynamic range. 'Small dynamic range' does not mean quiet, just a relatively narrow band between the loudest and quietest sounds. For example, I have recorded an atmosphere at midnight in the Sinai desert, at Wadi Saghara, which was continuously quiet; and more recently I recorded an atmosphere in Grand Central Terminal, New York, which was constantly loud. Both recordings, however, exhibit a small dynamic range.

The second category I use are Habitats. These I define as recordings that effectively speak for themselves, in that they exhibit narrative characteristics and present a variety of sounds or species heard within that place. They have a 'voice' and consequently may carry a wide dynamic range. The Farne Islands off the Northumberland coast have spectacular seabird colonies, and during April through until June these sites ring with some of the wildest and most inspiring of nature's music – a sea-cliff habitat. Onomatopoeic kittiwakes cry and shriek as they launch themselves from high ledges, fulmars cackle and growl a gurgling bass line, while the deep rush of sea wash below provides a slow accompanying pulse. Despite the apparent contrast, even the most industrial habitats can also conjure up fascinating rhythms and habitat sounds. While recording in a railway goods yard in Chihuahua, Mexico, I captured a series of spontaneous and hugely dynamic shunting sounds punctuated by train horns, air brakes and feral diesel purrs – together with the familiar metal rhythm of the tracks: a *chemin de fer* habitat for the twenty-first century.

Featured sounds are always forward in the mix. These are effectively the solo or focal point at any given moment during a track. Perhaps a phrase of bird song, the whoop of a spotted hyena, a lightning strike or the deep crunch of shifting glacial ice. I select them for their beauty, timbre or sheer power, and treat them as reference points in the timeline of a piece – since I often work with varying temporal scales or 'time compressions'. For example, to create the recorded piece *Oloololo* the sonic events and drama experienced during a fourteen-hour day from 5am to 7pm in Kenya's Masai Mara were edited, mixed and segued down to just eighteen minutes without transforming any of the original sounds. And in a different, more recent, example I placed a pair of miniature microphones down low into the rough pastures of a field edge in Kentucky, USA, and recorded several takes from this fixed position from 7pm until after midnight. From this selection of tracks across five hours I edited and mixed down a piece that runs for just two minutes. The result charts the wonderful changing rhythms and harmonic textures of a massively polyphonic insect chorus and reveals the real music down among the bluegrass.

Afterword
Recording: From reproduction to representation to remediation

GEORGINA BORN

The literary form of the Afterword is an attractive one: it gives one licence to reflect on this *Companion to Recorded Music* as a whole, compendious and diverse as it is, while bringing out and expanding upon some of its core themes. In this sense the Afterword itself recapitulates one of the key properties of media: the capacity to rework existing ideas or cultural material. In relation to literary media, the seminal work of Jack Goody and Ian Watt identified how the transition from oral to written transmission of knowledge and information enabled the development of a series of externalised aids to thought:[1] the production, in written or graphic form, of lists and summaries, groupings and categories, classification and comparison, and hence the potential for a reflexive and critical engagement with past ideas, and for objectified histories. Visual media such as painting, photography and film proffer their own particular versions of these techniques, among them, variously, framing and focusing, close up and long shot, montage and jump cut. Electronic sound and auditory media proffer yet other analogous properties: splicing and editing, sequencing and looping, sampling and remixing. Writers on 'new' or digital media, in turn, have identified in them a series of capacities, many of them prefigured by the properties of 'old' (or earlier) media, but all of them reinflected by the physical and symbolic architectures of computer software and hardware: automation, modular and fractal organisation, replicability and variability, and transcoding – the repeated translation of a concept, process, object, image or sound from one format into another.[2] Jay Bolter and Richard Grusin coin the encompassing term *remediation* for these collective properties,[3] pointing to the way that digital media like the computer and the internet foster a convergence of previously distinctive media forms – literary, visual and sonic – such that their content is both parasitic and aggregative, amounting to the *re*-presentation in novel combinations and contexts of pre-existing media content. I'll suggest later that remediation is particularly suggestive when thinking about music.

The foregoing sketch of some of the material properties of distinctive media, and of their complex differences and interrelations, is stimulated by the resurgent interest across the social sciences and humanities in the

[286]

materiality of culture and communication.[4] This is an approach that in media research is often traced back through the work of such Canadian media theorists as Harold Innis as well as Marshall McLuhan, with his famous dictum that 'the medium is the message'.[5] Today, rather than succumb to the seductions of technological determinism – of understanding cultural historical evolution as driven by changes in technology, changes that are themselves assumed to be prime movers – there is a concern both to uncover the industrial, scientific, political, social and cultural conditions that have fostered innovation in technology and media, and to analyse how each new medium, as it stabilises and comes into common usage, proffers or affords new kinds of cultural, aesthetic, intellectual, social and embodied experience. Technologies, in this last sense, can be understood to have *affordances* that can be weak or strong.[6] Not only do the contents of media re-work prior media and cultural content, but analysts of technological change point to the way that 'new technology … typically emerges not from flashes of disembodied inspiration but from existing technology by a process of gradual change to, and new combinations of, that existing technology'.[7] Technological change is, then, path-dependent, contingent and catalysed by broader forces – the interests of the state, existing and emerging markets, social relations and cultural trends – all of which synergistically condition the kinds of technologies that result from the cauldron of transnational industrial and scientific competition.[8] Exemplary studies of music technologies in this regard are Jonathan Sterne's account of the evolution of sound recording across the nineteenth and twentieth centuries, and James Lastra's history of the development of sound technology in American cinema.[9]

It is ironic that this *Companion* appears towards the end of a decade in which the death is being heralded both of the music recording as a physical object (the CD, and before that the cassette tape, LP or wax cylinder) and of the music industry as we have known it.[10] Digitisation and the internet have fostered a range of accelerating transformations that radically alter the environment for both the creation and consumption of music. Downloading and peer-to-peer file sharing, social networking sites like MySpace and Facebook, and Creative-Commons-based sound-sharing websites such as freesound.org have led to an explosion of decentralised music distribution. In turn this has caused a crisis in the business model – essentially, the sale of music in the form of a physical object – that has served the music industry and its precursors well for over two hundred years.

The *Companion* appears, then, at a critical period of transition in music's relations with cultural and economic life; but it also inaugurates an interesting moment in the reconfiguration of the interrelations between the several disciplines that study music. Retrospectively, it is extraordinary to consider how belated is the development in musicology of a concern with recording, or what Benjamin, writing of art, photography and film, called 'mechanical reproduction'.[11] It was in the 1930s and 1940s that Adorno and Benjamin, cultural theorists associated with the Frankfurt School, wrote treatises that foresaw the profound transformations of cultural and musical experience being wrought by capitalism and its industrial technologies. In relation to music, these included sound recording and the other already highly developed music media that ensued – film music, radio music, and music's use by advertising – but also performance spectaculars. According to Adorno,[12] under the sway of the 'culture industry', music and art have been turned into mere commodities, their former autonomy sacrificed to the profit imperative, as so many standardised or 'pseudo-individualised' cultural goods are produced and reproduced through the hyper-rationalized processes of mass manufacture. The reception of culture and music is also transformed, subordinated to the realisation of exchange value, while use value ebbs away; audiences increasingly value what they paid for the product more than the musical experience that it affords. For Adorno, as for Marx, commodity fetishism determines that the human relations that underpin cultural production take on the reified appearance of a thing, in the guise of the commodity. Leisure time amounts to a false refuge, a prolongation of work, as individual freedom is caught up in the fetishism of cultural goods that enslave through amusement. Audiences for the musical output of the culture industry become forcibly regressed as they compulsively consume generic music commodities in the attempt to enrich and humanise the depleted social and cultural fabric of their lives. These transformations hold true, according to Adorno, for 'high' as well as 'light' music and art. Only genuine 'popular culture which remains recalcitrant to centralized production and distribution' and 'that advanced autonomous art which "has renounced consumption"' escape capture by the culture industry.[13]

Benjamin's account of the industrialisation of culture in his essay 'The work of art in the age of mechanical reproduction' is almost the antithesis of Adorno's. For Benjamin, the prime consequence of the mechanical reproduction of the artwork is the decay of its aura, that is, its embeddedness in tradition and its 'parasitical dependence' on cult or ritual, qualities that derive from its unique existence in time and space. It is the auratic presence of the original artwork that secures its authenticity; but 'to an ever greater degree the work of art reproduced becomes the work of art designed for reproducibility … The instant the criterion of authenticity ceases to be applicable to artistic production, the total function of art is reversed. Instead of being based on ritual, it begins to be based on another

practice – politics.'[14] Benjamin contends that the unprecedented availability of commodified art changes its functions. Rather than fetishism,
mass reproduction engenders a new kind of distracted reception accompanied by the growth of expertise among audiences, such that in cinema
there is a 'direct, intimate fusion of visual and emotional enjoyment
with the orientation of the expert … The critical and receptive attitudes
of the public coincide.'[15] Culture is, then, democratised and demystified
by mechanical reproduction, released from its role in shoring up social
hierarchies and class relations. Moreover, the techniques of film and
photography – the close-up, slow motion, montage – act in their essential
artificiality as perceptual prostheses, augmenting human perception.
'With the close-up, space expands; with slow motion, movement is
extended. The enlargement of a snapshot … reveals entirely new structural
formations of the subject … The camera intervenes with the resources of
its lowerings and liftings, its interruptions and isolations … The camera
introduces us to unconscious optics as does psychoanalysis to unconscious
impulses.'[16] Here Benjamin identifies the modernist potential of mass-
media technologies, echoing the early twentieth-century avant-gardes.
Not only is consumption democratised, but, with the expansion of cultural
production and reproduction, so is creativity. The distinction between
author and public is eroded and the activity of artistic creation becomes
'common property': 'at any moment the reader is ready to turn into a
writer'.[17]

The opposed analyses of Adorno and Benjamin continue to undergird
much contemporary thinking on the mass reproduction of culture in
philosophy and sociology, cultural and media theory. Yet until recently
musicology evaded the challenges posed by their work, including the need
to theorise the existence and the impact of recording and music media.
This is evident in writings that employ a classic rhetorical device, men-
tioning the significance of music technologies, as though they had never
been the subject of research, only to neglect to pursue their implications
for the argument at hand. Two examples are symptomatic in this regard.
Lydia Goehr, in her seminal analysis of the 'imaginary museum of musical
works', productively contrasts idealist conceptions of the musical work
with music's plural material forms. She states, 'There is nothing about
the concept of a work, the relations between works and performances,
or works and scores, or works and experiences of them, that is going
to tell us where the locus of musical meaning "really" resides.'[18] In this
way she highlights music's mediation, acknowledging that there is no
single privileged location of musical meaning or experience. Late in the
book Goehr considers twentieth-century challenges to the musical-work
concept, among them (echoing Benjamin) 'mechanical reproduction'.[19]

Despite this gesture, and its potential significance for her materialist deconstruction of idealist philosophies of music, Goehr provides no systematic discussion of the effects of technologies of music production and reproduction on contemporary musical life. More recently Carolyn Abbate, in her essay 'Music – drastic or gnostic?', calls for a musicology centred on 'actual performances', 'music's materiality rather than disembodied texts', and the 'delivery systems that bring music into ephemeral phenomenal being' – by which she refers to recording technologies and studio practices.[20] But having signalled their importance, Abbate makes no reference to the copious existing scholarship on performance and technological 'delivery systems' in popular music studies and ethnomusicology; equally puzzling, and perhaps a consequence, is her equation of the recognition of music as 'a material form' and a 'social event' with its 'ineffability'.[21]

Rather than in musicology, the origins of academic research on recording and music media lie in the inception in the 1980s of the interdisciplinary field of popular music studies as it developed at the intersection of ethnomusicology, sociology, and media and cultural studies. With its greater concern with the common, lived realities of musical experience in all areas of social life in terms of both creation and consumption, and its sometime commitment to empirical social and cultural research, this intersecting field could not ignore the centrality of recording and music media over the twentieth century. Between the end of the 1970s and the turn of the 1990s a trickle of disparate early articles and books appeared, including works by Edward Kealy, Antoine Hennion, Chris Cutler, Alan Durant, Shuhei Hosokawa, David Toop, Dave Laing, Simon Frith, Georgina Born, Dick Hebdige, John Mowitt, Andrew Goodwin, Paul Thébèrge, Richard Middleton and Steve Jones.[22] It took until the mid-1990s and early 2000s for this trend to produce a series of formative books on recording and electronic music media, notably those of Peter Manuel, Tricia Rose, Michael Chanan and Thébèrge and, on computer music, Born; and it took until the late 1990s and early 2000s for consolidated research to appear on the history and cultures of recording and music media, as in Timothy Taylor and Sterne, as well as, from musicology and classical music studies, Nicholas Cook and Timothy Day.[23] What began as a trickle is now a fragmentary sub-discipline, or, rather, a sub-interdiscipline, and one that has rarely been acknowledged by musicology. It is to be welcomed that the *Companion* and the institution responsible for its appearance and some of its contents – Britain's AHRC Research Centre for the History and Analysis of Recorded Music – mark a sea-change in this intellectual history, a history the object of which (recorded music) is being noticed just as the gradient of its historical significance, after a century of steep incline, is tipping over into free-fall.

If, as I have suggested, music has long been subject to remediation, it is difficult to assess what is new in the history of its encounter with technologies and media. Music encoded as MP3 files, music circulating on the internet, on digital platforms and hand-held devices: these modes of musical experience extrapolate from earlier, analogue electronic music media, at the heart of which was recording – the mechanical capture, storage, circulation and capacity repeatedly to hear at will prior musical events. The question is: what does analogue recording do to music, and how does this change with the transition from analogue to digital technologies? In the remainder of the chapter I want to offer several perspectives on this haunting question.

A good starting point is to problematise that anxious sense of loss of musical authenticity and presence associated with sound recording in the eyes of those for whom recording is secondary in comparison with the primacy of face-to-face musical communication in live performance. As Sterne shows, historically this perspective has often formed part of a larger metaphysics – an 'audiovisual litany' – in which hearing is idealised as a more organic, affective sense than sight, and as 'manifesting a kind of pure interiority'.[24] In this metaphysics of musical presence, 'sound reproduction is doomed to denigration as inauthentic, disorientating', a fragmentation of musical experience.[25] It is striking that a similar lament for loss of authenticity and presence is recapitulated in some writers' concern with the shift from analogue to digital recording. Thus, for Eric Rothenbuhler and John Peters, analogue recording (like photography) is what the semiotician Charles Peirce called indexical:[26] it entails direct physical traces of, and therefore a fragile connection to, a prior musical event; in this sense it partakes in the original moment of performance, in 'nature' and history, such that 'there is the possibility of a communion that reaches all the way back to the music's source of inspiration'. In contrast, according to these writers, digital recording lacks these qualities and amounts to a symbolic (numerical) encoding of the music's waveforms; it is 'fundamentally arbitrary' and effects an ontological rupture both with the original musical event and with analogue recording.[27]

In place of such ontologised and totalising approaches, Sterne argues that it is imperative to historicise the changing nature of musical experience wrought by different sound technologies as they coalesce into full-blown media, appraising each in its own terms. Indeed, his study develops the thesis that 'insofar as sound technologies are ever organised into sound media, the medium ... precedes even the technology itself'.[28] That is, broader cultural, social and economic conditions must be in place in order for a particular technology to become established as a mass medium. The social and cultural precedes the technology; just as, we might add, the aesthetic can precede the technology, prefiguring what is to come, as shown by Ives's experiments in the orchestral juxtaposition of materials – the musical montages that he composed as orthodox scores in such works as *Central Park in the Dark* (1906) and *Decoration Day* (1911–31) – which preceded by decades the recording technologies that would make tape-based sound and musical montages very easy.

With reference to the material in this book and a few earlier studies, I want to pursue Sterne's insistence on not beginning from an *a priori* loss, and instead sketch some lines of analysis that attend to the distinctive properties of music recording and related media – and thus accord them a material, cultural and social *positivity*. It bears pointing out that to historicise in this way does not prevent judgements being made about the qualities of musical experience entailed by particular music media; the point is that they can now be made on the basis of a rich comparative understanding of their distinctive affordances. To grasp the complexity of these changes, it is useful to follow media theory in distinguishing between three phases in the communication process – production or creation, text or object, and consumption or reception – and in assuming no necessary symmetry between production and reception in their engagements with the musical object.[29]

To begin at the end of the circuit: how has the consumption of music been affected by recording and ensuing music media? In this book, Arild Bergh and Tia DeNora broadly follow Benjamin: in their account recording and distribution technologies 'have potentially democratised the field of aesthetic music experiences', and erase 'the line between listener/fan and record producer/patron'.[30] Music listening is empowering, aiding the accomplishment of 'identity work' both individually and collectively.[31] These are certainly clear tendencies, and they are now decades old. But, while acknowledging them, I would also follow Adorno in analysing the evolving strategies of the music recording and media industries as, through the commercial release of a stream of musical consumer goods and services, they condition contemporary listening. In this light, the hegemony of recorded music expands via the industry's repeated coining of new listening devices and new ways to engender consumption. At the same time it is surely necessary to depart from Adorno by probing the novel aesthetic modalities that these devices afford. In recent years corporate strategies have attempted to incorporate both non-commoditised musical experience and non-musicalised temporal, spatial and embodied experience, proffering entirely new kinds of aesthetic experience: both an aesthetic of music's fluidity and openness to recombination in internet-based music applications, and an aesthetic of the simultaneous or multiple in the Walkman and iPod – music *and* movement *and* place. This additive aesthetic logic is captured well by Michael Bull's work on the Walkman and iPod, and by Hosokawa, who writes of the Walkman experience as 'walk 'n' eat 'n' drink 'n' play 'n' listen' (boy on roller skates eating McDonalds, drinking Coke, listening to Michael Jackson …) – a kind of 'secret theatre' in which 'the user controls the art of their coordination'.[32] The industry's drive to proliferate music's mediatised consumption therefore multiplies both the spaces and activities colonised by consumption (the car, pub, mall, underground, queue …; walking, jogging, driving, eating, waiting …) and the forms of aesthetic experience proffered by these media.

Bergh and DeNora identify an apparent paradox: new media platforms make it possible to listen to music in an expanding number of spatial locations and existential situations, while this unprecedented availability of music is accompanied by a lessening of focused listening. This, say Bergh and DeNora, amounts to 'ubiquitous listening', the aural equivalent of ubiquitous computing, such that 'it is possible to speak of music "choosing" listeners as well as the opposite'.[33] The paradox points in the direction of earlier, empirically grounded sociological studies of music consumption by DeNora and Bull, which give access to the otherwise invisible subjectivities and elaborate everyday rituals and practices of heightened and regulated emotion, and of the choreography of memory and identity, that appear to be the stuff of ordinary, mediated musical experience.[34] Bull, in particular, offers acute analyses of the Walkman's and iPod's affordances in terms of how they affect the subjective perception of urban time, space and movement. He recounts their users' aestheticising practices and 'ambiguous imperatives of constructed … "individualism"', their 'minimalisation of the social through [an] "imaginary" social inhabited within personal stereo space', and their 'narcissistically orientated' disposition towards the urban 'other' manifest in 'culturally solipsistic travelling'.[35] In this way Bull highlights the 'atomistic subjective expressiveness and instrumentalism' of many users.[36] From these studies of contemporary music consumption, two dominant effects are palpable: an intensified semanticisation in the reception of mediated music, along with an intensified sovereign and narcissistic individualism. We might sum up these twin effects with the epithet 'late-liberal listening'; both resonate uncannily with Adorno's predictions. It is difficult, then, to reconcile the contradictory tendencies evident in these studies, which recall the thought of both Benjamin and Adorno. To an unprecedented extent music is individually chosen and engaged with, forming a 'democratised' part of everyday existence. At the same time music is folded into the psyche as an extension of self that occludes any distance between subject and object, and thus any resistance that the musical object may contribute to subsumption by the consuming subject.[37]

If we turn to the second of the three phases in the communication process, recorded music as musical object or text, the material in this book suggests the necessity of moving from a conception of recording as a reproduction or copy of an original, live musical event, and thus as secondary or derivative, to an understanding of recording as *representation* – as both verb and noun. Such a conceptual shift breaks with the anxieties over loss immanent in notions of reproduction, yielding an utterly distinctive musical object – a second primary object, if you will, and one that, in its difference, augments rather than either echoing or replacing music's live performance. In Ian Hacking's terms, representation must be grasped as at once both translation and intervention.[38] This conceptual shift can be registered at several levels, and it has revolutionary implications for our understanding of music today. It points, first, to the profoundly *illusionistic* nature of the recorded text, especially since – unlike in analogue film editing, where the cuts between shots are generally visible – sound recording and editing techniques are often made imperceptible in the finished tape, as though the seamless sonic and musical events represented were simply 'found' in 'nature'. This points in turn to the predominance of a *realist* sonic discourse in both classical and many popular music recordings, one in which the goal has been a finished recording that appears simply to capture, and to be faithful to, a prior musical event.[39] Thus music recording, with the aesthetic and rhetorical traditions and practices that it has engendered historically, has at its core an antimony in which illusionism and realism are emphatically not in contradiction.

This is nowhere better illustrated than in Steve Savage's personal take in this book, where he describes attempts to produce an edit of recorded blues voices with the digital audio workstation, given the subtle variations in real-time performance in the studio and a resultant 'flawed' recording, through intensive manipulation. As he puts it, the ultimate aim in his recording practice is to achieve what he calls an 'it could have happened' aesthetic – something that did not happen but appears as though it has. For Savage this amounts to nothing less than a 'new paradigm of construction'.[40] Recording as construction or representation is manifest equally in Nigel Simeone's account of the musical thinking that underlay the first ever recording of Bernstein's *West Side Story* – the attempts to rearrange the stage musical for recording, which involved considerable aesthetic changes from the theatrical form including altered speed, orchestration and even harmony. The result, according to Simeone, was a text that is more musically cogent precisely because it is appropriate for the recording medium: a new representation of *West Side Story*. What we have, then, is the recording studio not as a means of capturing a pale imitation of an original musical event, nor of rendering a lesser kind of aesthetic object, but as an instrument for realising novel, previously unachievable, aesthetic potentials on the basis of recorded music's distinctive phenomenal forms. Indeed, a powerful argument for the phenomenological impossibility of conceiving of recording as the reproduction of live performance is voiced by Peggy Phelan when she states: 'Performance's only life is in the present. Performance cannot be saved, recorded, documented, or otherwise participate in the circulation of representation: once it does so, it becomes something other than performance.'[41]

But recording has the paradoxical capacity both for a deeper illusionism and for highlighting its own construction as a musical practice. The first propensity is evident when recording makes possible a compositional practice that takes recorded ambient sounds as its raw material, sounds and timbres that could not be achieved with an acoustic instrumentarium. The resulting tape composition could therefore never be recreated by instrumentalists in live performance; yet it appears to partake, again, in 'nature' through the realism and indexical qualities of its sound materials. Chris Watson, in this book, gives a poetic evocation of the 'creative potential of what I once regarded as unwanted sound – i.e., noise' in his site-specific, part-realist, yet heavily time compressed sound pieces.[42] The second propensity, highlighting recording's construction, comes to the fore through excavating the aesthetic lineage behind Watson's experiments in recorded sound montage: *musique concrète*. In *musique concrète*, initiated by Pierre Schaeffer, Pierre Henry and others in the 1940s, tape music was composed of recordings of 'found' or ambient sounds ('sound objects') that were stripped of their real-life associations, treated, rearranged and edited together. Schaeffer had been a radio engineer and announcer for the French radio network Radiodiffusion Française, and one of his key contributions was to establish a studio at RF that supported experiments in music and radio-theatre.[43] An early piece by Schaeffer, *Etude aux chemins de fer* (1948), was the first composition constructed entirely from recorded sounds. As Joel Chadabe describes, it 'contains juxtaposed sections of locomotive steam and wheel sounds, their periodic rhythms punctuated with whistles'; Schaeffer originally spoke of it as a 'concert of locomotives'.[44] In the same period the German radio studio in Cologne was supporting a different approach, 'pure' *elektronische Musik* created not by transforming natural sounds but by the generation and manipulation of electronic tones via sine wave generators.[45] From the early 1950s Stockhausen worked at Cologne, and in *Gesang der Jünglinge* (1955–6) he innovated and combined traditions by integrating recordings of natural sounds with electronically generated material. Both historical lineages of electronic art music amount to the antithesis of the prevailing illusionism. The studio is used as a creative apparatus, but in the service of a modernist, anti-realist aesthetic of sound montage (the equivalent of modernist abstraction in the visual arts). The result is to highlight the artificiality and constructedness of electronic and recorded sound, with the potential to distance the listener from any assumed familiarity with the sound materials and to resist ready semantic assimilation.

For Watson's sound-based pieces, as for the mid-twentieth-century pioneers of *musique concrète* and *elektronische Musik*, there is no 'real', live musical event predating the recording. It follows that in musics of this kind, and for all those musicians, composers and bands for whom the recording studio becomes *the* crucible for musical creativity and experimentation, the recorded musical text *is* the primary text. This is not restricted to electronic art musics; indeed it is more characteristic of popular musics, given the central role that recording, studio practices and their aesthetic potentials play in them. In most genres of twentieth-century popular music, musical interest resides not so much in harmonic, melodic or formal complexity or development, as it does in Western art music, but in timbral and rhythmic nuance and subtlety within fairly fixed and repetitive structures – aesthetic qualities that Charles Keil and Steven Feld condense in the term *groove* – and in the rapid re-inflection, branching and hybridisation of genre.[46] While these qualities evade and exceed orthodox musical notation, they are easily captured by the direct sonic representations given by recording. Moreover, the various electronic and digital techniques available in the recording studio can enhance these aesthetic qualities, extending the timbral palette and heightening the impact of rhythmic gestures, as similar techniques do in more limited, real-time ways in live popular music performance. The attempt in the recording studio aesthetically to enhance or exceed what is possible in live musical performance, then, has been a defining feature of most twentieth-century popular musics. In his personal take, Richard Witts recounts an anecdote from the early 1980s in which an audience member objects when she finds the performance of a song by his new wave band a mere shadow of the recording: 'To her mind the song was what she heard on the disc, not what we, who made it, played before her ears and eyes. So much for authenticity.'[47] In this ontological inversion it is performance, not recording, that is experienced as secondary and as involving a loss: performance cannot achieve the same aesthetic powers as the recorded musical text.

But recording's aesthetic valencies are not uniform. They vary historically, geographically and culturally, associated with specific technologies and practices, such that it is possible to identify distinctive eras, sites and personas of recording aesthetics as they imbue particular musical genres. Historically, Witts suggests, changes of aesthetic paradigm in recording may parallel wider socio-economic changes. He charts a transition from the smooth, elaborate soundworld of progressive rock in the late 1960s to mid-1970s, produced at smart 24-track studios financed by the 'credit swimming round the international rock music scene between 1967 and 1973', to the raw, 'unfinished', 'ecstatic' sounds on disc of pub rock, punk, post-punk and free improvisation in the late 1970s and early 1980s. Witts argues that this stylistic shift responded to the severe economic downturn and social crises unleashed in the mid-1970s by the oil crisis and 'the first stirrings of mass unemployment as new technology impacted on the labour market'.[48]

In terms of geography, Witts describes vividly the 'different technological tendencies' that characterised the Liverpool and Manchester sounds of post-punk, noting that the Liverpool scene had recourse to synthesisers, drum machines and other 'toys' to fabricate ' "acousmatic" sonorities that they could replicate on stage', while the Manchester sound made greater use of treatments at the mixing desk. For example, the Mancunian Martin Hannett, producer of Joy Division, 'emulated the "heavy dub" sound pioneered in the early 1970s by Jamaican producers like Lee "Scratch" Perry – radical, druggy studio mutations of reggae instrumentals by means of reverb, echo and sound effects'. Here is evidence, then, of a veritable genealogy of transnational, inter-generic aesthetic influences at work in the popular music recording practices of the time. Witts notes also the different aesthetics afforded by particular studios, contrasting Manchester's 'recording business' Arrow (used by Granada Television to record voice-overs and trails), with Liverpool's Open Eye (publicly subsidised), with cheap domestic studios where musicians would 'record in the lounge, mix-down in the attic, and [play back] … in the kitchen'.[49] Mention of Hannett's influence raises, in turn, the distinctive recording aesthetics embodied in particular individuals and musical cultures, an issue central to Louise Meintjes's chapter, where she expands on the notion of producers and engineers having their 'own sound'. She begins with a story that revisits one of the most controversial episodes in late twentieth-century popular music, a trauma at the birth of the world music genre: Paul Simon's appropriation of the aesthetic labour of South African producers and musicians in the recording of his 1986 *Graceland* album.[50] Meintjes evokes the issues concretely: Simon 'needed to borrow [South African producer Koloi] Lebona's ears … [Lebona] sat there for days, listening and advising, while South African musicians played and the tape rolled and rolled … He gave Simon the sound of his own mix'.[51]

If recording, its techniques, practices and aesthetic potentials have been central to the development of twentieth-century popular musics, for other musics recording's effects are perceived with ambivalence and its musical value is more contested. In her personal take, Susan Tomes exemplifies such ambivalence and explores recording's negative valencies when reflecting on her experience as a performer of classical chamber music. She observes cogently that, compared to live music-making, recording tends to elicit 'hyper-critical' performances, that it brings 'unprecedented challenges' and a 'bell jar of self-consciousness'.[52] The resulting recording has an unreal 'surface perfection' which is invariably manufactured from a 'mosaic of the best attempts'.[53] For Tomes, these recording realities dehumanise chamber music – the epitome of a music created through communion in live performance: 'this is closing down instead of opening up, and … against the essential spirit of chamber music, as well as the spirit of communication'.[54] Clearly, different musics entail radically unlike experiences and valuations of, and accord a different prominence to, recording and its aesthetic potentials. This suggests that we should conceive of recording as but one, variable element in the make-up of particular music ontologies.

Coming now to the first of the three phases, the production or creation of recorded music, we can now grasp recording as a novel historical form of musical practice. As is well evidenced in the chapters by Albin Zak, Andrew Blake and Meintjes, recording involves a complex musical division of labour, and introduces new roles – producer, sound engineer and sound technicians.[55] Indeed, recording studios are the locus of intimate and creative human relations with technologies, a hybrid musical-technical labour that adds yet more strata of technical mediation to, without replacing, the musical-technical labours of instrumentalists. The actor-network theory of Bruno Latour may be productive here in enabling us to conceptualise studio practices in terms of a network of interrelations and interdependencies between human and non-human 'actors', both of which contribute agency while also setting limits to the creative outcome. In this sense recording technologies effect translations of the sound materials that they treat or represent; in Latour's lexicon they are mediators, where the term refers to all those actors – human and non-human – that 'transform, translate, distort, and modify the meaning or the elements they are supposed to carry'.[56] The aesthetically generative nature of the corporeal-mechanical practice at the core of this mediation process is conveyed by Witts in his description of post-punk recording: 'By the early 1980s … we still edited by slicing magnetic tape with razor blades, and standard analogue techniques included echo plates, reverberation units, double-tracking using varispeed, flanging, direct-injecting …, equalisation (EQ) effects, chorusing, bouncing-down, and tape loops. Through constructs of spatial location and motion these FX produced a sense of distance, depth, of flows, "other-worldness" or alienation.'[57]

It is, however, the social dynamics of the recording studio that have preoccupied many writers. Musical relations in the studio are at the same time social relations and interactions; they are often absorbing and intense, as signalled by the common experience during recording of a loss of awareness of chronological or 'outer' time.[58] As with human relations in general, the social relations of recording are invariably hierarchical: between producer, engineer and musicians, as well as within bands, ensembles and orchestras (stars versus session musicians, soloists versus orchestral players, and so on). Issues of power and control, collaboration and interdependence arise particularly sharply in the social microcosm of the studio, which has in some ways a less extensive and rigid arrangement of roles than other musical practices (such as the concert hall, orchestra or string quartet), while at the same time introducing new and often gendered technical hierarchies. It has therefore elicited reflection on and contestation of these very dynamics.

Yet, as with consumption, there appear to be contradictory forces at work in production. Thébèrge adds acuity to Tomes's personal observations by analysing the effects of standard practices in the recording studio that arose with analogue multitracking.[59] These include the layered, sequential recording of tracks through separate takes by individual musicians or sections; and to facilitate this, musicians' isolation in soundproof booths so as to enable control over the separate tracks, as well as repeated takes and drop-ins, without the sounds spilling over. The consequence has been a routine negation of live ensemble playing in studio performance, such that the ensemble's capacity for real-time musical mutuality and co-responsiveness is lost. Thébèrge therefore identifies the studio as a locus of rationalised and alienated musical labour, arguing that whatever the deceptive organicism and simulated 'co-presence' of the resulting recordings – in which the separate takes and edits are rendered imperceptible – this is a music made out of bits and pieces of players and performances figured as the idealised image of 'community' and technical perfection in music. In stark contrast to this critical portrayal, the studio has also been identified as affording a newly collaborative and democratised creative practice – as Cutler has it, echoing Walter Ong, a new orality which encourages improvisation and realises the studio's potential for an empirical and re-socialised music-making, one that is exemplified in popular music's notion of the 'group'.[60] Collaborative musical creativity in the studio therefore transcends the romantic individualism of the author function vested in the composer, and foresees what might be called distributed or social creativity.[61]

Not only does the recording studio as a social microcosm produce its own social dynamics, but it refracts social relations beyond the studio.

It is this 'double' understanding of the social in music that underlies Meintjes's analysis of creative practices in the recording studio as they are conditioned by the cultural dislocations, social relations and politics of late-apartheid and post-apartheid South Africa.[62] Meintjes emphasises the necessity of examining South African studio practices against this historical background, suggesting that the politics of recording occur on two intersecting planes: first, in the micro-politics of the studio – evident in who has musical power and control, whose fantasies prevail about how things should sound; and, second, in how these micro-politics are crossed by wider political dynamics, raising the question, 'How do social practices and values about race, ethnicity, class and gender ... impinge upon the recording process and affect the creative outcome?'[63] It is in this light that Meintjes traces the transition from 'apartheid studio practices' to the present.[64] In the apartheid era, recording was the site of struggles over the control of musical inflections and sound qualities – struggles in which, through covert interventions, black musicians would secretly attempt to wrest back control from the white engineer at the mixing desk. Meintjes contrasts this period with the post-apartheid present, which has seen the development of a generation of black engineers and so altered dynamics in the studio; she observes of the fledgling, as yet imperfect, attempts by a young black engineer to learn the engineer's aesthetic trade that 'he has yet to develop an engineer's hearing acuity and the skills to translate the musicians' poetic lexicon into the language of acoustic and electronic science'.[65] In sum, the recording studio engenders a distinctive form of creative practice, one that draws attention to its social dynamics and to musicians' intimate relations with technologies, while for some writers it signifies a transition in the very paradigm of musical creativity.

I have suggested that this *Companion* marks a critical shift from the widespread notion of recording as reproduction or copy to a conception of recording as representation. I follow Benjamin in arguing that recording as representation should be grasped as fully, positively artificial, and as having the potential to extend the ambit of human musical perception and aesthetic response. If, given the predominance of realist illusionism, recording's existence as both representation and remediation was veiled in the analogue era – with the exception of musical styles such as *musique concrète* and a number of black electronic popular musics, notably dub, toasting, scratching, rap and their issue, which prefigured later developments by making aesthetic virtue out of musical cut-up and montage[66] – with digitisation these propensities are enormously magnified. Indeed, in the digital age it is remediation that comes to the fore in musical experience, while not effacing music as representation.

This state of affairs originated in the early 1980s when digital sampling and sequencing technologies announced that music made out of the fabric of remixed other musics and sounds would become the normal aesthetic mode; in parallel, the DJ as musical (re-)mediator became established as another new, formative, creative role. Available in many forms including, from 1983, the Yamaha DX7, digital synthesisers, samplers and sequencers soon became ubiquitous. From the mid-1980s they ushered in a sound exemplified by techno, the next genre in the aesthetic lineage of black electronic popular musics. Techno is a DJ-based digital dance music that expands on the aesthetics of dub and rap. It is composed of juxtaposed layers or plateaux of compulsive, repetitive rhythmic beats and figures based on sequenced loops of musical materials; these materials are treated by various types of signal processing (such as filtering) and play out until their arbitrary end. Structurally, in its avoidance of musical development, its insistent rhythmic plateaux and non-teleological form, techno exhibits striking parallels with minimalism in art music. More ambitious forms of techno involve the use of algorithmic compositional tools to generate material and of digital synthesis to experiment with timbre, and the design of temporal frameworks to control how a track unfolds in time. Techno might therefore be described as semi-automatic, if also semi-improvised, composition.

Sequencing and sampling point to the two core material properties of digitised music; both indicate music's movement beyond representation to remediation. The first concerns remediation as a property of the digital musical object. Digital music consists of numerical code aggregated into sound files that can be manipulated by computers; they are produced through the translation, by analogue–digital converters, of analogue electronic audio signals into numerical code, a process that can follow any of a series of alternative coding standards, such as the MP3 or .wav formats. Digitised music amounts, then, to a kind of *immaterial materiality*: with music's physical and commodity forms rendered liquid as code, digital musical objects are immanently mutable and malleable, open to re-working not only structurally, through their recombination as discrete objects, but even in their internal processes – particularly in their timbral qualities. It follows that experimentation with new timbres unavailable in the acoustical soundworld, and with creating transitions between timbral 'objects', has been a major goal of computer music.[67] Even more than its electronic precursors, digitised music – in both its art and popular music incarnations – encourages an open sequence whereby the closing down of a musical object or process and its circulation are followed by its repeated re-opening and re-creation. This is manifest in the popularity of websites such as ccMixter, a music-sharing site licensed under Creative Commons in which users 'can listen to, sample, mash-up or interact with music in whatever way you want … [and then] upload your version for others to … re-sample'.[68] It is equally manifest in the compositional procedures of today's digital art music in which, according to Simon Waters, 'the status of [musical] material becomes extraordinarily fluid – what might have been a relatively complete musical "statement" can reappear as a sample source for improvisatory inclusion in another work; distinctions between "source material", "transformations" and "completed sections" are contingent … [and] a degree of continuity is established between works'.[69] In both cases, the musical object or work becomes relatively unfixed, its completeness or openness a question both of pragmatics and of serial musical reflection. The very nature of the musical work is transformed, such that it makes sense to speak of the provisional work.[70]

Mutability of the musical object is also evident in the reception of digitised music, as consumers exercise the power, through 'ripping', to personalise their musical experiences by accumulating multiple versions of the same track, versions about which they are discriminating and often knowledgeable, and by disassembling and re-assembling albums.[71] Here, then, as well as in the role of the DJ – at once consummate consumer and gatekeeper of musical taste, and creative (re-)mediator – we approach again the question of the blurring of the boundary between production and consumption signalled by Benjamin, Bergh and DeNora. What is clear is that digitisation – far more than analogue recording technologies – has enabled consumers to become active participants in the circulation and remediation of tracks and sounds. In addition, social networking sites encourage these circulation practices to be linked tightly to self-conscious identity projects, such that musical consumption is experienced as a concrete form of 'self-creation'. However, whether these circulation and identity activities really represent a significant convergence between consumption and production, as DJ practices unquestionably do, seems to me to be doubtful.

The second core property of digitised music follows: it is a different modality of remediation, one that focuses on circulation and its aesthetic affordances – a circulation that is at once spatial, geographical and cultural.[72] Encoded as digital sound files, transcending physical form, digitised music is instantly replicable and hyper-mobile, amenable to being embedded in and transcoded for any digital environment. This is shown by the three main forms of music's contemporary circulation: not only through the internet via peer-to-peer file sharing, and legal or illegal downloading sites, as well as through individualised and portable listening devices, but also in the guise of 'ubiquitous' music embedded in and interactively triggered by movement through particular locations, buildings and spaces. All three forms amount to music's intensified circulation. But it is the internet that has the most profound implications. As digitised music 'travels' instantaneously from point to point and through ramifying networks, it is re-grounded in new geographical locations where it encounters new musical cultures, favouring further musical hybridities – that is, aesthetic remediation.

These processes can be illustrated by the circulation of a genre of digitised, hybrid Asian dance music which, as Dhiraj Murthy shows, has played a formative part in the creation of an international diaspora of affluent South Asian youth based in major urban centres in Britain, the USA, Australia, Singapore and India. Music distributed by the diasporic Asian cultural industries and relayed by the internet, music which is then 'realised' and remixed in each city by DJs in club performances, forms these young people into a disparate global subculture. Tracks that were popular in London or Bradford reach New York months later; they hit Melbourne a couple of months after that, and move on to Singapore and New Delhi. This movement results, then, in a prolix hybridity of Asian and other musics encountered in each locale: 'South Asian DJs in the subculture appropriate, through sampling, everything from Brick Lane to Harlem to Bollywood to construct a music they label "Asian".'[73] The mercurial speed at which the music is relayed by the internet, and its translation in each place from virtual form into the grounded materiality of performance, dance, bodies and place – and therefore new musical contacts – give the music the property of mediating the extended social relations that constitute both its history and its continual remaking.

Digitised music therefore exhibits a double mutability: first, in the guise of its immanent mutability as a musical object, and thus the potential for relayed creativity through cumulative aesthetic hybridities, yielding a provisional musical work that both retains and blurs the traces of individual and collective authorship; and, second, in the oscillation between a globally virtual internet form and a localised corporeal form, as live performance and embedded consumption. In digitised music, even more than in analogue recording, the conceptual dualism of authenticity or artificiality is effaced; there is no original and no copy, only rapidly proliferating, variant representations (or versions). Distributed across space, time and persons, digitised music eschews any finished state; it becomes an object of relayed creativity – that is, of recurrent de-composition, composition and re-composition by a series of creative agents.[74]

It is a final paradox of the digital age that, just as music reaches this condition of extreme flux, there appears to be a return to the materiality, sociality and corporeality of live performance – but on altered terms. This renewal of performance is suggested not just by its significance in the

South Asian diasporic musical subculture, but by the extraordinary international public response to the socio-musical experiments represented by two contemporary ensembles: the Simon Bolivar Youth Orchestra of Venezuela,[75] and the West-Eastern Divan Orchestra which unites young Israeli and Arab musicians under the direction of Daniel Barenboim. Both form the apex of larger educational and peace-building movements aimed at healing social divisions and religious and ethnic conflicts. What is striking in both cases is the new meaning attributed to live music-making – a new sense of the alchemy afforded by the vital interactions of musical performance as they foreground the social relations that compose the ensemble, an alchemy in which musical integration is intended to act as a metonym, performatively, for social integration.[76] The renewal points also to the unending complexity of the entanglement and the recursive, mutual mediation between live performance, on the one hand, and recording, representation and remediation, on the other. Indeed, at the same time that the digital music economy makes available on the internet the complete world-historical archive of recorded musics, aided by the niche musical interest markets conjured up and made contactable via the internet, the same economy stimulates the repeated discovery and release of long-lost recordings of live performance: a continually expanding simulation of the 'live'. In the process these releases tend to re-sacralise the 'live' and stoke the auratic qualities of recordings of live performance as against mere studio recordings.[77]

So to return to the question of what is new in the present state of music: everything and nothing. Nothing is totally novel; and yet, certainly, music's remediation is more intensive, extensive and rapid in the several senses outlined than in any previous era – profound transformations that arguably amount to an entirely new condition of music. It hardly needs adding that, while these transformations may afford musical invention, they do not guarantee it. Returning to the larger project of the *Companion*: perhaps as significant as these immediate findings is how, by addressing the problem of recording and thus of the myriad forms of music's mediation and remediation, the prospect is opened up of a systematic and integrated comparative analysis that encompasses both art and popular musics, Western and non-Western, present and past. To remediate, and reconfigure, the very boundaries of the disciplines of music study – musicology, ethnomusicology, sociology and psychology of music, popular music studies – would be a fitting legacy indeed for this stimulating volume.

Notes

Introduction

1 CHARM (www.charm.rhul.ac.uk) was established in 2004 with a five-year grant from the Arts and Humanities Research Council (then Board); a further five-year term has been awarded, but the Centre is changing its name to the AHRC Research Centre for Musical Performance as Creative Practice (www.cmpcp.ac.uk), signalling an evolution in its research agenda.

2 In particular, while strictly speaking a 'phonograph' uses cylinders and a 'gramophone' uses discs, American writers tend to use the first to refer to playback devices more generally.

1 Performing for (and against) the microphone

1 I would like to acknowledge the help of Tessa Bonner and Sally Dunkley from the classical field, and Mary Carewe and Janet Mooney from the pop field. I am also most grateful to Steve Smith of Gimell Records, with whom I have discussed various technical issues, and for the comments of Daniel Leech-Wilkinson, Mark Katz and John Rink.

2 In the field of early music I have recorded and performed extensively with, among many others, The Tallis Scholars, the Orlando Consort and Gothic Voices; on the 'lighter' side I have worked with groups such as the Stephen Hill Singers and Metro Voices, and with various unnamed groups of session singers.

3 The 'session' here simply refers to a recording session, usually of three hours' duration. For reasons of stamina and concentration, and because the musician's working day is split into morning, afternoon and evening, the three-hour session is by far the most common, dating from at least the 1940s. It is firmly established in current British Actors' Equity and Musicians' Union guidelines.

4 Classical and pop music are by no means as cleanly separated as they used to be, though the distinction remains valid to some extent. In classical music there is an observable trend towards 'crossover' artists, and the increased issue of CDs of classical music in pop terms ('Chill Out Classics', etc.) suggests a blurring of the boundaries. A defunct distinction from the early days of BBC Radio between Radio 3 as the classical music station and Radio 2 as the Light Programme is particularly useful.

5 Gould quit the concert stage in 1964. Two years later the Beatles, for different reasons and in a quite distinct field, also abandoned live performance and concentrated exclusively upon recording.

6 A fixer is the person approached by the production company who is then sub-contracted to book the singers.

7 See M. Katz, '(In)visibility', in *Capturing Sound: How Technology Has Changed Music*, Berkeley, University of California Press, 2004, pp. 18–24.

8 See R. Jakobson, 'Closing statement: Linguistics and poetics', in T. A. Sebeok (ed.), *Style in Language*, New York, Technology Press of MIT, 1960, pp. 350–77.

9 This has been addressed most fully within a semiotics of theatre. For a helpful precis see K. Elam, *The Semiotics of Theatre and Drama*, London, Methuen, 1980. On phatic language see M. de Marinis, *The Semiotics of Performance*, A. O'Healy (trans.), Bloomington, Indiana University Press, 1993, pp. 139–42. On rhythmic indicators see E. Clarke and J. Davidson, 'The body in performance', in W. Thomas (ed.), *Composition–Performance–Reception: Studies in the Creative Process in Music*, Aldershot, Ashgate, 1998, pp. 74–92. Clarke and Davidson refer to swaying with or against the beat as 'a "surface" level of movement – a kind of rhetoric – which the performer adds to the performance' (p. 79).

10 It is worth pointing out here that the lack of the visual dimension does not necessarily mean the listener is not engaged in a relationship with the body of the performer. That, at least, is how Roland Barthes responds to listening to *recordings* of Charles Panzera and Dietrich Fischer-Dieskau (see R. Barthes, 'The grain of the voice', in *Image–Music–Text*, S. Heath (ed. and trans.), London, Fontana, 1977, pp. 179–89).

11 See P. Schaeffer, *Traité des objets musicaux*, Paris, Editions du Seuil, 1966, pp. 91–9.

12 Performers frequently express disdain for recording's demands for perfection and the word most commonly used in that context is 'sterile'. André Previn's comments offer a case in point:

'I tend to let small flaws go for the sake of the performance, because I think that if you really start patching every possible note that has gone slightly awry, you wind up with a performance that is perfect and, at the same time, completely sterile.' Quoted from J. Harvith and S. E. Harvith (eds.), *Edison, Musicians, and the Phonograph: A Century in Retrospect*, New York, Greenwood Press, 1987, p. 211.

13 A recurring theme of the collection of interviews with classical performers in Harvith and Harvith, *Edison*. This contrasts strongly with the 'hands-on' approach of pop performers hunched over the mixing desk in TV's Classic Albums series.

14 For an account of amplification in musical theatre and the 'classical' voice, see S. Banfield, 'Stage and screen entertainers in the twentieth century', in J. Potter (ed.), *The Cambridge Companion to Singing*, Cambridge, Cambridge University Press, 2000, pp. 63–82 (pp. 74–8).

15 Foldback refers to the mix that is played back simultaneously to the singer either through speakers (on stage) or by headphones (in the recording situation).

16 Recording sessions of film music are the most common occasions.

17 I am indebted to Mary Carewe for this point. She commented that there is a slight delay, almost only a feeling, when listening to voices through headphones as they are relayed back to the singer.

18 Katz, *Capturing Sound*, p. 40. Certainly Crosby's voice had a certain quality which simply suited the microphone, but much of his success must also be attributed to a mastery of microphone technique.

19 Access to the production booth is hierarchised and alters according to the numbers involved. The members of a choir of twenty would not expect to hear the balance decided upon by the production team. However, a small group of four or five will generally listen to first takes and make small changes to their position and vocal production on the basis of what they have heard, and also heed the suggestions of the producer and colleagues.

20 See, for example, an interview with Jindrich Rohan, quoted in Harvith and Harvith, *Edison*: 'A recording can never be done without performing in small sections. It's really kind of a fraud, because by doing small sections, rehearsing them, doing some of them many times again, and taping them until perfection is achieved, you're doing something that you never could do in an actual performance with your public present. So it really is a kind of cheating – cheating the public' (p. 181). See also note 12 above.

21 The obvious example here is Glenn Gould's account of recording the *Well-Tempered Clavier* in his 'manifesto', 'The prospects of recording', in T. Page (ed.), *The Glenn Gould Reader*, New York, Vintage, 1990, pp. 331–52.

22 See Gould's experiment on lay listeners and their assumptions about editing as reported in his 'The grass is always greener in the outtakes: An experiment in listening', in Page, *Glenn Gould Reader*, pp. 357–67.

23 'That which withers in the age of mechanical reproduction is the aura of the work of art' (W. Benjamin, 'The work of art in the age of mechanical reproduction', in H. Arendt (ed.), H. Zhon (trans.), *Illuminations*, London, Fontana, 1973, pp. 211–44 (p. 221) (original published in 1936)). By 'aura' Benjamin means the uniqueness of a work of art – its singular existence in a specific time and place which is inevitably lost when the work is replicated.

24 According to Timothy Day (*A Century of Recorded Music: Listening to Musical History*, New Haven, Yale University Press, 2000, p. 25), 'in the 1980s and 90s a general trend toward simplification in the recording techniques was discernible, a tendency to ensure that the balance was right in the studio and to remove the necessity even to consider complex post-recording manipulation'. Interestingly, this shift towards a more organic, simple recording set-up, undoubtedly aided by the miniaturisation of recording technology and necessitated by recording outside the studio, coincides with the rise of recordings of early music. Steve Smith has pointed out to me that the simpler recording set-ups were also the result of the improvement in quality of the equipment chain – from microphones through to the compact disc. The simple matched pair in a directional mono microphones set-up proved to be of particular success on compact disc, which enjoys a much wider dynamic range than its vinyl predecessor.

25 This is particularly true for medieval music. See D. Leech-Wilkinson, *The Modern Invention of Medieval Music*, Cambridge, Cambridge University Press, 2002.

26 The bibliography is too extensive to cite here, but the work of organisations such as CHARM should be acknowledged.

27 This is a surprisingly common refrain from performers cited throughout Harvith and Harvith, *Edison*, when asked what, for them, is the main function of recording.

28 Peter Phillips, in his liner notes to his recording with The Tallis Scholars of *Obrecht: Missa Maria zart*, Gimell CDGIM032 (1996),

suggests that the piece is un-performable in concert – yet obviously recordable.

29 I think it is correct here to talk of ethics. In an article on the subject ('The ethics of musical performance', in Thomas, *Composition–Performance–Reception*, pp. 157–64), J. O. Urmson sets up a comparison that demonstrates increasing levels of ethical responsibility, from playing music for oneself through to playing music for a paying audience. In the case of recording one is playing for paying audiences.

30 The following example was given only one public performance, at a Promenade Concert on 19 July 1986, but was later recorded and made into a film for Swiss television: Andrew Parrott, Taverner Players Orchestra, Taverner Choir and Taverner Consort Choir, *Una Stravaganza dei Medici – Florentine Intermedi (ed. Keyte)*, EMI Reflexe 47998, reissued Virgin Classics 77877 and HMV 5 73863 2 (1986).

31 Day (*A Century of Recorded Music*, p. 12) cites a 1924 recording of the Choir of St George's Chapel, Windsor, where the usual forces of the choir could not be used due to the inefficiency of recording hardware at the time.

32 See L. Goehr, 'The perfect performance of music and the perfect musical performance', *New Formations*, 27 (1995–6), 1–22.

33 On the invisibility of the early music performer, see D. Greig, 'Sight readings: Notes on *a cappella* performance practice', *Early Music*, 23 (1995), 125–48.

34 Goehr, 'The perfect performance', 14.

35 The Borodin Quartet made two recordings of the Shostakovich quartet cycle, initially for Melodiya between 1967 and 1971, at which time the thirteenth and fourteenth quartets had not been written. Subsequently the reincarnated group recorded the complete cycle for EMI in the 1980s. The first set has most recently been reissued on the Chandos Historical series CHAN 10064 (2004). Also: the Hilliard Ensemble, *Gesualdo: Tenebrae*, ECM New Series 1422/23 843 867–2 2CDs (1991); Parrott and Taverner Players Orchestra, Taverner Choir and Taverner Consort Choir, *Una Stravaganza dei Medici – Florentine Intermedi (ed. Keyte)*; Phillips and The Tallis Scholars, *Obrecht: Missa Maria zart*; Georg Solti and the Vienna State Opera, with various soloists, *Der Ring des Nibelungen (Ring Cycle)*, Decca 414 100–2 (1958–65); Herbert von Karajan and Berliner Philharmoniker, with various soloists, *Beethoven: 9 Symphonien*, Deutsche Grammophon DGG 4290362 (1963).

2 Recording practices and the role of the producer

1 B. Kernfeld (ed.), *The New Grove Dictionary of Jazz*, London, Macmillan, 1988. Norman Granz, apparently an exception to this rather depressing rule, is given a named entry (pp. 446–7) but is described only as an entrepreneur and label owner, not as a record producer.

2 A. Bennett, B. Shank and J. Toynbee (eds.), *The Popular Music Studies Reader*, London, Routledge, 2006. The index entry is on p. 405. Compare J. Toynbee's own *Making Popular Music*, London, Arnold, 2000, another wide-ranging text which deals only with 'producers' of drum'n'bass (see pp. 156–7) in relation to DJs who actually play their music at clubs. Producers in this sense are performer-assembler-composers, based in bedroom studios.

3 One welcome example of this re-evaluation was the BBC Radio 2 series in August 2007 on well-known record producers from the 1960s, compèred by a record producer, Steve Levine; similarly, the obituaries of Tony Wilson, who died in August 2007, identified him as a record producer as well as a television presenter and music-business entrepreneur. The academic *Journal on the Art of Record Production*, founded in 2006, can be found at www. artofrecordproduction.com.

4 www.aimhigher.ac.uk/dontstop/ doing_what_you_love/music/ record_producer.cfm (accessed August 2007).

5 According to Symes, this is the 'keystone discourse' of all classical music recording. See C. Symes, *Setting the Record Straight: A Material History of Classical Recording*, Middletown, CT, Wesleyan University Press, 2004, pp. 60–87.

6 S. A. Pandit, *From Making to Music: The History of Thorn EMI*, London, Hodder and Stoughton, 1996, pp. 64–5.

7 J. Culshaw, *Putting the Record Straight*, London, Secker and Warburg, 1981, pp. 320–1.

8 Ibid., pp. 228–9. But cf. the more recent comments of Decca producer Andrew Cornall: 'I don't think anyone ever decides to do classical music production as a career move. I know I didn't,' quoted in R. J. Burgess, *The Art of Music Production*, second edition, London, Omnibus Press, 2001, p. 188.

9 On BBC radio and modernism in the 1920s to 1930s see J. Doctor, *The BBC and Ultra-modern Music 1922–36: Shaping a Nation's Tastes*, Cambridge, Cambridge University Press, 1999; and, in the 1960s to 1970s, W. Glock, *Notes in Advance: An*

Autobiography in Music, Oxford, Oxford University Press, 1991.

10 Culshaw, *Putting the Record Straight*, p. 176.

11 Ibid., p. 340.

12 This isn't the place to deal with the issues of race, ethnicity and empire that are raised by Grubb's career, but, in brief, such an approach might take us to Grubb's learning the repertoire from records sold by Indian HMV. Thinking about HMV in India might in turn take us back to the conservative repertoire, and we might also compare the arguments made in the early 1990s about the formation of English Literature within India, as argued by Sara Suleri in *The Rhetoric of English India*, second edition, Chicago, Chicago University Press, 1992. We should remember that the foundation of the Philharmonia Orchestra was supported in large part by money given by the Maharajah of Mysore (see E. Schwarzkopf, *On and Off the Record: A Memoir of Walter Legge*, London, Faber and Faber, 1982, pp. 95–6).

13 There are two: in D Minor, K. 466, and C Minor, K. 491. Schubert's Octet is for clarinet, bassoon, horn, string quartet and double bass.

14 S. R. Grubb, *Music Makers on Record*, London, Hamish Hamilton, 1986, p. 68.

15 It's worth noting that his contemporary John Culshaw, while busily 'simulating' the opera stage in stereo for the Decca recording of Wagner's *Ring* – and indeed the *Peter Grimes* that frightened Decca – was even happy to manipulate the basic sound and add sound effects when it suited score or voices. Grubb, *Music Makers on Record*, p. 64.

16 Ibid., pp. 16–17.

17 Ibid., pp. 128–9. For further discussion of Grubb's use of these techniques, see Simon Trezise's chapter in this volume, pp. 206–7.

18 M. Chanan, *Repeated Takes: A Short History of Recording and Its Effects on Music*, London, Verso, 1995.

19 By way of comparison, a bass voice starts from *c.* 65 cycles per second, and a soprano can easily reach *c.* 1,046 cycles per second. Grubb, *Music Makers on Record*, p. 113.

20 The absences can be found in Schwarzkopf, *On and Off the Record*, and in A. Sanders (ed.), *Walter Legge: Words and Music*, London, Duckworth, 1998.

21 Count Basie, *April in Paris*, Verve MG-V 8012 (1955).

22 J. Szwed, *So What: The Life of Miles Davis*, London, William Heinemann, 2002, p. 280.

23 Ibid., p. 297.

24 A good succinct account of Spector's work is in V. Moorefield, *The Producer as Composer: Shaping the Sounds of Popular Music*, Cambridge, MA, MIT Press, 2005, pp. 9–15.

25 See J. Boyd, *White Bicycles: Making Music in the 1960s*, London, Serpent's Tail, 2006, pp. 135–41.

26 Nile Rodgers, interviewed in H. Massey, *Behind the Glass: Top Record Producers Tell How They Craft the Hits*, San Francisco, Backbeat Books, 2000, p. 178.

27 Less epoch-making, but still in the realm of global commercial success, is Queen's 1980 single 'Another One Bites the Dust', which clearly uses Bernard Edwards's bass guitar riff from 'Good Times'.

28 Prince did and does self-produce all of his commercially released material, though the original demo tapes that got him his record deal with Warner were produced by Chris Moon.

29 Eno's work is discussed in E. Tamm, *Brian Eno: His Music and the Vertical Color of Sound*, London, Faber and Faber, 1990. Eno's thoughts about production – among many other things – can be found in B. Eno, *A Year with Swollen Appendices*, London, Faber and Faber, 1996.

30 J. Baudrillard, *Simulacra and Simulation*, S. F. Glaser (trans.), Ann Arbor, University of Michigan Press, 1994.

31 T. Taylor, *Strange Sounds: Music, Technology and Culture*, London, Routledge, 2001, pp. 232–3.

32 This is a late-1980s 'factory sample' that was provided by Akai for use with their samplers such as the S1000 model. This particular sample of the shakuhachi has a characteristic swooping glitch towards the end of the note (despite which it is not credited to a named performer).

33 S. Lake and P. Griffiths (eds.), *Horizons Touched: The Music of ECM*, London, Granta, 2007, p. 2.

34 The phrase is taken from Roland Barthes's essay 'The grain of the voice', to be found in his *Image–Music–Text*, S. Heath (ed. and trans.), London, Fontana, 1977, pp. 179–89.

35 Lake and Griffiths, *Horizons Touched*, p. 309.

Still small voices

1 G. Steiner, *Real Presences*, London, Faber and Faber, 1989, p. 8.

2 Ernest Ansermet and the Decca String Orchestra (leader, William Primrose), *Ernest Ansermet Conducts Handel*. Koch Historic 3-7708-2H1 (1996, originally recorded in 1929).

3 G. Gould, *The Hereafter*, a film by B. Monsaingeon, Ideale Audience International DVD9DM20 (2006).

3 Getting sounds: The art of sound engineering

1 H.-J. Braun, 'Introduction: Technology and the production and reproduction of music in the 20th century', in *Music and Technology in the Twentieth Century*, H.-J. Braun (ed.), Baltimore, Johns Hopkins University Press, 2002, p. 9.

2 Quoted in O. Read and W. L. Welch, *From Tin Foil to Stereo: The Evolution of the Phonograph*, Indianapolis, Howard W. Sams, 1959, p. 384.

3 M. B. Sleeper, 'By way of introduction', *High Fidelity*, 1/1 (Summer 1951), 6.

4 D. Randolph, 'Records in review', *High Fidelity*, 3/1 (March/April 1954), 49.

5 C. L. Granata, *Sessions with Sinatra: Frank Sinatra and the Art of Recording*, Chicago, A Cappella, 1999, p. 47.

6 T. G. Porcello, 'Sonic artistry: Music, discourse, and technology in the sound recording studio', PhD thesis, University of Texas at Austin (1996), 188.

7 O. Daniel, *Stokowski: A Counterpoint of View*, New York, Dodd, Mead and Co., 1982, p. 306.

8 Granata, *Sessions with Sinatra*, p. 73.

9 J. S. Wilson, 'Creative jazz', *New York Times*, 5 April 1953, X9.

10 M. Lewisohn, *The Beatles Recording Sessions: The Official Abbey Road Studio Session Notes 1962–1970*, New York, Harmony Books, 1988, p. 77.

11 J. Gallagher, 'Cosimo: A conversation with the Dean of New Orleans recording', *Mix* (March 1996), 99.

12 K. Mathieson, *Giant Steps: Bebop and the Creators of Modern Jazz*, Edinburgh, Canongate, 1999, p. 90.

13 T. Fox, *In the Groove: The People Behind the Music*, New York, St Martin's Press, 1986, p. 110.

14 B. Sidran, *Talking Jazz: An Oral History*, New York, Da Capo, 1995, p. 140.

15 D. Daley, 'Kevin Killen: The engineer becomes producer', *Mix* (October 1989), 64.

16 C. A. Robertson, 'Jazz and all that', *Audio* (October 1957), 49.

17 E. Kealy, 'The real rock revolution: Sound mixers, social inequality, and the aesthetics of popular music production', PhD thesis, Northwestern University (1974), 44.

18 S. Schmidt Horning, 'Chasing sound: The culture and technology of recording studios in America, 1877–1977', PhD thesis, Case Western Reserve University (2002), 206. Emphasis added by Horning.

19 B. Owsinski, 'You don't know jack', *EQ* (May 1996), 55.

20 R. Clark, 'Mixing forum: Four top professionals talk gear and techniques', *Mix* (May 1997), 50.

21 For an example of pre-digital practices, see D. Simons, *Studio Stories*, San Francisco, Backbeat, 2004, pp. 29–31. Engineer Frank Laico describes his techniques, working with such performers as Tony Bennett and Johnny Mathis, for crafting a specific ambient image unique to a particular voice.

22 P. Verna, 'Marching to his own drum sound, Hugh Padgham beats a path to the top of the industry', *Billboard* (27 July 1996), 54.

23 See C. Anderton, *The Digital Delay Handbook*, New York, Amsco, 1985.

24 See, for example, P. Doyle, *Echo and Reverb: Fabricating Space in Popular Music Recording 1900–1960*, Middletown, CT, Wesleyan University Press, 2005; A. Zak, *The Poetics of Rock: Cutting Tracks, Making Records*, Berkeley, University of California Press, 2001.

25 B. Jackson, 'Los Lobos paint their masterpiece', *Mix* (October 1992), 202. The project Blake refers to is Los Lobos's *Kiko*. Massenburg's recordings range from the tight funk textures of Earth, Wind and Fire's *That's the Way of the World* (1975) to the crystalline detail of Lyle Lovett's *Joshua Judges Ruth* (1992). Massenburg's concern for sonic precision is further evinced in the design and manufacture of his own line of signal processors.

26 D. Marsh, *Glory Days: Bruce Springsteen in the 1980s*, New York, Pantheon, 1987, p. 121.

27 Quoted in G. Ballou (ed.), *Handbook for Sound Engineers: The New Audio Cyclopedia*, second edition, Carmel, MN, SAMS, 1991, p. 1158.

28 T. G. Porcello, 'Music mediated as live in Austin: sound, technology, and recording practice', in P. D. Greene and T. G. Porcello (eds.), *Wired for Sound: Engineering and Technologies in Sonic Cultures*, Middletown, CT, Wesleyan University Press, 2005, p. 107.

29 See C. Keil, 'Participatory discrepancies and the power of music', *Cultural Anthropology*, 2 (1987), 275–83. Reprinted in C. Keil and S. Feld, *Music Grooves: Essays and Dialogues*, Chicago, University of Chicago Press, 1994, pp. 96–108.

30 Owsinski, 'You don't know jack', 52.

31 Daley, 'Kevin Killen', 64.

32 M. Molenda, 'Production values: Listen to the music', *Electronic Musician* (April 1996), 69.

33 Fox, *In the Groove*, pp. 110–11.

34 A. Kazdin, *Glenn Gould at Work: Creative Lying*, New York, E. P. Dutton, 1989, pp. 39–40.

35 C. Morris, 'We're an American band', *Pulse* (April 1996), 45.

36 P. D. Greene, 'Introduction: wired sounds and sonic cultures', in Greene and Porcello, *Wired for Sound*, pp. 1–22 (p. 1).

Limitations and creativity in recording and performance
1 A central, but at one time rather run-down, area of the city.
2 Little Mesters were self-employed cutlery makers, who formed the backbone of Sheffield's international cutlery industry.
3 The British Electric Foundation is my production company, set up after I left the Human League in 1980.
4 A virtual synthesiser is a piece of software running on a computer that exactly replicates the sound-generating possibilities of what used to be a particular piece of hardware. It is possible, for example, to get a software version of a ring modulator (a generic synthesis device), or a software version of a specific proprietary synthesiser (e.g. a specific Roland or Korg model).

Records and recording in post-punk England, 1978–80
1 Acknowledgements – the author wishes to thank the following for their help: Mark Crabtree, Tony Friel, Mike 'Noddy' Knowler, Joe McKechnie and James Nice.
2 The first was *Short Circuit – Live at the Electric Circus*, a Virgin label 10ins EP recorded at the Manchester club and featuring the Fall, Joy Division, John Cooper Clark ('the punk poet') and reggae band Steel Pulse (June 1978). Factory Records's first release was *A Factory Sampler* (1978), while the Manchester Musicians' Collective released *A Manchester Collection* (1979) and *Unzipping the Abstract* (1980). In Liverpool Open Eye put out *Street To Street* (Aug 1979) with liner notes by John Peel; a second volume followed a year later.
3 The Buzzcocks's record label, New Hormones (formed January 1977) was the first of hundreds of British 'indie' labels, some of which published only one or two releases. By 1978 there were at least 120, and by 1980 there were 800 such labels, according to the Zigzag Catalogue of Small Labels for those years (I'm grateful to Mike Knowler for hunting down these catalogues in his garage).
4 See P. Devine, 'The 1970s and after: The political economy of inflation and the crisis of social democracy', *Soundings*, 32 (Spring 2006), www.lwbooks.co.uk/journals/articles/devine05.html.
5 By January 1972 British unemployment had risen above 1 million (4 per cent of the economically active population aged over

sixteen) for the first time since the 1930s. By 1978 it had risen to 1.5m (5 per cent) and would peak under the Thatcher government in 1985 at 3.25m (12 per cent). Source: Labour Force Survey, Office for National Statistics. Post-punk's emergence and demise crossed this period.
6 Although the Sex Pistols's *Never Mind the Bollocks* album used traditional and high-standard recording methods at London's Wessex Studio, employing Pink Floyd's producer, Chris Thomas.
7 The Japanese companies Tascam and Fostex were together responsible around 1981 for introducing cassette-based Portastudio and semi-professional multitrack recording machines, heralding the do-it-yourself 'bedroom studio' movement.
8 Leeds's Gang of Four retained this plain, dry sound on their recordings.
9 See T. Wishart, *On Sonic Art*, revised edition, London, Harwood Academic Publishers, 1996, pp. 80, 142, 195. See also P. Doyle, *Echo and Reverb: Fabricating Space in Popular Music Recording 1900–1960*, Middletown, CT, Wesleyan University Press, 2005, pp. 4–19.
10 'Echo' was the name of the band's drum machine.

4 The politics of the recording studio: A case study from South Africa
1 Simon heard recordings of Tau ea Matsekha produced by Koloi Lebona. The *Graceland* album draws on the Sotho musical style of Tau ea Matsekha, reproduces the sound of the accordion on the recordings, and pairs Bakithi Khumalo's bass playing with the Sotho accordion – an innovation in Lebona's Tau ea Matsekha productions.
2 Koloi Lebona, interview with the author, Johannesburg, 9 August 2001.
3 Koloi Lebona, interview with the author, Johannesburg, 17 May 1991.
4 See R. Allingham, CD sleeve notes to *1992 Gallo Gold Awards: 65 Years*, promotional CD, Johannesburg, Gallo (Africa) (1992); R. Allingham, 'South Africa: The nation of voice', in S. Broughton, M. Ellingham and R. Trillo (eds.), *World Music The Rough Guide: An A–Z of the Music, Musicians and Discs*, London, The Rough Guides, 1999, pp. 638–57; and L. Meintjes, *Sound of Africa! Making Music Zulu in a South African Studio*, Durham, NC, Duke University Press, 2003.
5 Peter Ceronio, interview with the author, Randpark Ridge, 9 January 1992.
6 D. Coplan, *In Township Tonight! South Africa's Black City Music and Theatre*, second

edition, Chicago, University of Chicago Press, 2008, pp. 311–22.

7 This and subsequent stories of moments in the studio in 1991 and 1992 appear in Meintjes, *Sound of Africa!* with expanded discussions. All studio sessions occurred at Gallo (Africa)'s Downtown Studios, except where otherwise noted.

8 *Uyezwa ukuthi bayicula kamnandi njani? Imnandi!* (Transcribed from field tape recording, 30 March 1992.)

9 *Eyi! Lento ungaze uyibone incane, iphethe yonke inhlobo yento ezakurekhodwa manje sikulekwaya* (ibid.).

10 R. Plant Armstrong, *The Affecting Presence: An Essay in Humanistic Anthropology*, Urbana, University of Illinois Press, 1971.

11 *Asisayiboni ipanya-panya – bavele bayipanya-panya bona.* (Transcribed from field tape recording, 30 March 1992.)

12 Isigqi sesi Manjemanje, *Lomculo Unzima*, produced by W. Nkosi, LP RPM Records, AFRLP 029 (1992).

13 *Ayifakile nje ikwaai-kwaai Peter!* (Transcribed from field tape recording, 18 November 1992.)

14 Zulu verb: *ukushaya* (infinitive).

15 *Modumo wa Afrika! Afrika!* (Transcribed from field tape recording, 18 November 1992.)

16 From the point of view of women artists, studio possibilities are also constrained on the basis of gender: electronic technology is considered to be the domain of men. It is unusual to find women with experience of electronic technology in South African studios.

17 T. Taylor, *Global Pop: Global Music, Global Markets*, London, Routledge, 1997.

18 This story appears in L. Meintjes, 'Reaching overseas: South African sound engineers, technology and tradition', in P. D. Greene and T. G. Porcello (eds.), *Wired for Sound*, Middletown, CT, Wesleyan University Press, 2005, pp. 23–46 (pp. 32–3).

19 Recording digitally began at Downtown Studios in the early 1990s. At this time, tracks were recorded either onto two-inch analog tape or onto DAT tape. Recording directly onto a hard disc was not yet a common local practice.

20 West hitches a grammatically appropriate Zulu prefix onto the Afrikaans word *klok* just as he had onto the English 'bell'.

21 *Yathi ingquza emayaka-yaka yathintha enye intambo lapho eyihlabeni isiyogcina. Asiphinde futhi.* (Transcribed from field tape recording, 12 February 1991.)

22 *Ayikho inkinga, mfowethu sekusho ukuthi mina ngigade wena mangizwe uthinta la angafuni khona ngiyoyimisa phela lento* (ibid.).

23 Peter Pearlson, interview with the author, Johannesburg, 15 April 1991.

24 Darryl Heilbrunn, interview with the author, Johannesburg, 19 November 1992.

25 *Nê*: Afrikaans question form implying a positive response is anticipated.

26 See T. G. Porcello, 'Speaking of sound: Language and the professionalization of sound-recording engineers', *Social Studies of Science*, 34/5 (2004), 733–58.

27 In his campaigning in the run-up to the 1994 elections, Thabo Mbeki spoke of an 'African renaissance' as a component of the African National Congress's political programme under his presidency.

28 See G. Maré, *Ethnicity and Politics in South Africa*, London, Zed Books, 1993; E. Wilmsen, S. Dubow and J. Sharp (eds.), 'Ethnicity and identity in Southern Africa', *Journal of Southern African Studies*, special issue, 20/3 (1994), 347–53; and S. Nombuso Dlamini, 'The construction, meaning and negotiation of ethnic identities in KwaZulu-Natal', in A. Zegeye (ed.), *Social Identities in New South Africa: After Apartheid*, Cape Town, Kwela Books, 2001, pp. 195–222 for discussions of the development of the Zulu nationalism that eventually materialised into the Inkatha Freedom Party, one of the parties at the negotiating table during the transition period.

29 Pakie Mohale, interview with the author, Johannesburg, 29 July 2002.

30 South Africa's studios were slower to make the transition to fully digital technology than were the major studios in the North. In the early-1990s sessions discussed in this chapter, the sound engineer and producer could watch dials or a diminutive screen set into the console, but this was not a site attended to by musicians nor was it a point of reference in discussions about the sound.

31 Siyazi Zulu's group, Umzansi Zulu Dance, have subsequently released another CD: Umzansi Zulu Dancers, *Zindala Zombili*, Izimpande IZI003 (2007).

From Lanza to Lassus

1 Arturo Toscanini and the New York Philharmonic-Symphony Orchestra, *Beethoven: Symphony No. 7 in Major*, HMV DB 2986/90 (1936); Leopold Stokowski and the Philadelphia Orchestra, *Stravinsky: Petrushka*, HMV DB 3511-4 (1937); Benno Moiseiwitsch and the Hallé Orchestra conducted by Leslie Heward, *Grieg: Piano Concerto in A Minor*, HMV C 3264/7 (1941); Henri Busser and the Paris Opéra Chorus and Orchestra, *Gounod: Faust*, HMV C 2122/41 (1932); Fritz Busch and the Glyndebourne Festival Chorus and Orchestra, *Mozart: Don Giovanni*, HMV DB 2961/83 (1936); Ugo Tansini and the EIAR

Chorus and Orchestra, *Donizetti: Lucia di Lammermoor*, Parlophone R 20454/66 (1939); Carlo Sabajno and the Chorus and Orchestra of La Scala, *Verdi: Rigoletto*, HMV C 1483/97 (1927/8); Vincenzo Bellezza and the Rome Opera Chorus and Orchestra, *Verdi: La traviata*, Columbia DX 1324/38 (1949).

2 Enrico Caruso, *Puccini: Tosca* ('*Recondita armonia*' *and '*E lucevan le stelle*'), HMV DA 112, Victor Matrices 8347 & 8346 (1909).

3 Amelita Galli-Curci with Louise Homer, Beniamino Gigli, Angelo Bada, Giuseppe De Luca and Ezio Pinza, *Donizetti: Lucia di Lammermoor* ('*Chi mi frena*') and *Verdi: Rigoletto* ('*Bella figlia dell'amore*'), HMV DQ 102, Victor Matrices CVE-41232-3 and 41233-3 (1927).

4 Vittorio Gui and the Glyndebourne Festival Chorus and Orchestra, *Mozart: Le nozze di Figaro*, HMV ALPS 1312 & ALP 1313/5 (1955); Herbert von Karajan and the Philharmonia Orchestra and Chorus, *Mozart: Così fan tutte*, Columbia 33CX 1262-4 (1954).

5 Victor de Sabata and the Chorus and Orchestra of La Scala, *Puccini: Tosca*, Columbia 33CX 1094/5 (1953).

6 Ferenc Fricsay and the Berlin Philharmonic Orchestra, *Tchaikovsky: Symphony No. 6 in B Minor*, Deutsche Grammophon Gesellschaft DGM 18104 (1954).

7 Isobel Baillie with the Hallé Orchestra conducted by Leslie Heward, *Handel: Messiah* ('*I know that my redeemer liveth*'), Columbia DX 1036 (1941).

8 Yehudi Menuhin with Rudolf Barshai and the Bath Festival Orchestra. *Mozart: Sinfonia concertante in E-flat Major, K. 364*, HMV ASD 567 (1963).

9 Rudolf Serkin with Adolf and Hermann Busch, *Schubert: Piano Trio in E-flat Major, D929*, HMV COLH 43, from HMV DB 2676/80, Matrices 2EA 2466/75 (1935); Otto Klemperer and the Philharmonia Orchestra. *Beethoven: Symphony No. 5 in C Minor*, Columbia 33C 1051 (1955); Emil Gilels, *Haydn: Piano Sonata in C Minor, Hob. XVI:20*, Le Chant du Monde LDA 8310-1 (1960); Aksel Schiøtz with Gerald Moore. *Schubert: Die schöne Müllerin* and *Schumann: Dichterliebe*, Odeon MOAK 1 and MOAK 3, from HMV DB6252/9 (1945) and HMV DB6270/2 (1946); Felix Prohaska and the Vienna Chamber Choir and State Opera Orchestra, *Bach: Cantatas BWV78 and BWV106*. Vanguard/Bach Guild BG 537 (1954).

10 Sviatoslav Richter. *Schumann: Humoreske in B-flat Major, Op. 20*, Monitor MC 2022 (1956); Emil Gilels with Leonid Kogan and Mstislav Rostropovich, *Beethoven: Piano Trio in B-flat Major, Op. 97*, Monitor MC 2010 (1956).

11 Milton Katims and the Budapest Quartet, *Mozart: Quintet in C Major, K. 515*, Columbia ML 4034 (1945); Smetana Quartet, *Beethoven: Quartets in C Minor, Op. 18 No. 4 and C Major, Op. 59 No. 3*, Westminster WST 14119 (1959).

12 Smetana Quartet, *Janáček: Quartet Nos. 1 and 2*, Electrola SME 91442 (1965); Smetana Quartet, *Shostakovich: Quartet No. 3*, Supraphon SV 8223 (1961).

13 Busch Quartet, *Beethoven: Quartets in C-sharp Minor, Op. 131, and A Minor, Op. 132*, Electrola E 80968 and 80969 from HMV DB 2810/4, Matrices 2EA 3120/9, (1936), and DB 3375/9, Matrices 2EA 5464/8 & 5471/6 (1937).

14 Sir Adrian Boult and the Scottish National Orchestra, *Elgar: Symphony No. 2 in E-flat Major*, Waverley SLLP 1022 (1963).

15 Christopher Finzi with Wilfred Brown and the English Chamber Orchestra, *Finzi: Dies Natalis*, World Record Club/Recorded Music Circle CM 50 (1963).

16 Bruno Turner with Pro Cantione Antiqua and the Hamburger Bläserkreis für alte Musik, *Ockeghem: Missa pro defunctis*, Archiv Produktion 2533 145 (1973).

17 Sir David Willcocks with the Jacobean Consort of Viols and the Choir of King's College, Cambridge, *Gibbons: 'Glorious and powerful God'*, Argo ZRG 5151 (1958).

5 From wind-up to iPod: Techno-cultures of listening

1 See, for example, www.youtube.com/watch?v=8ZhuLFcw1qY (accessed 26 June 2008).

2 V. Chew, *Talking Machines*, London, Her Majesty's Stationery Office (1981).

3 S. Broughton (ed.), *The Rough Guide to World Music. Vol. 2: Latin and North America, Caribbean, India, Asia and the Pacific*, London, Rough Guides, 2000.

4 J. H. Johnson, *Listening in Paris: A Cultural History*, Berkeley, University of California Press, 1995; J. Parakilas (ed.), *Piano Roles: Three Hundred Years of Life with the Piano*, New Haven, Yale University Press, 2002.

5 T. DeNora, *Beethoven and the Construction of Genius: Musical Politics in Vienna 1792–1803*, Berkeley, University of California Press, 1997; W. Weber, 'Did people listen in the 18th century?', *Early Music*, 4 (1997), 678–91.

6 T. Day, *A Century of Recorded Music: Listening to Musical History*, New Haven, Yale University Press, 2000.

7 M. Perlman, 'Golden ears and meter readers: The contest for epistemic authority in audiophilia', *Social Studies of Science*, 5 (2004), 783–807.

8 W. Weber, 'From miscellany to homogeneity in concert programming', *Poetics*, 2 (2001), 125–34.

9 R. Leppert, *The Sight of Sound: Music Representation and the History of the Body*, Berkeley, University of California Press, 1995.

10 A. Kertz-Welzel, 'The "magic" of music: Archaic dreams in romantic aesthetics and an education in aesthetics', *Philosophy of Music Education Review*, 1 (2005), 77–94; J. Attali, *Noise: The Political Economy of Music*, Minneapolis, University of Minnesota Press, 1985.

11 T. Adorno, *Introduction to the Sociology of Music*, E. B. Ashton (trans.), New York, Continuum, 1989.

12 R. Eyerman and L. McCormick (eds.), *Myth, Meaning and Performance: Toward a New Cultural Sociology of the Arts*, Boulder, Paradigm Publishers, 2006.

13 K. Hetherington, *Expressions of Identity*, London, Sage, 1998.

14 T. DeNora, 'Music as agency in Beethoven's Vienna', in Eyerman and McCormick, *Myth, Meaning and Performance*, pp. 103–20; S. Pederson, 'Beethoven and masculinity', in S. Burnham and M. P. Steinberg (eds.), *Beethoven and His World*, Oxford, Princeton University Press, 2000, pp. 313–31; G. Smith, *Lost in Music*, London, Picador, 2000.

15 A. Bergh, 'Everlasting love: The sustainability of top-down versus bottom-up approaches to music and conflict transformation', in S. Kagan and V. Kirchberg (eds.), *Sustainability: A New Frontier for the Arts and Cultures*, Frankfurt-am-Main, VAS-Verlag, 2008, pp. 351–82.

16 S. M. Lash and J. Urry, *Economies of Signs and Space*, London, Sage Publications, 1994.

17 C. Small, *Musicking: The Meanings of Performing and Listening*, Hanover, NH, Wesleyan University Press, 1998.

18 For Gaisberg's globe-trotting see David Patmore's chapter in this volume, p. 122.

19 For a sample of these debates, see P. Kivy, *The Possessor and the Possessed: Handel, Mozart, Beethoven and the Idea of Musical Genius*, New Haven, Yale University Press, 2001 or A. Bloom, *The Closing of the American Mind*, New York, Simon and Schuster, 1988 (both of which articulate or seek to reinstate canonic values): these sources arguably misconstrue the reasons for the alternative position of aesthetic relativism, which rarely theorises the processes through which a form or work comes to assume canonic status within a social group or for an individual.

20 T. DeNora, 'Aesthetic agency and musical practice: New directions in the sociology of music and emotion', in P. N. Juslin and J. A. Sloboda (eds.), *Music and Emotion: Theory and Research*, Oxford, Oxford University Press, 2001, pp. 161–80; A. Hennion, 'Music lovers: Taste as performance', *Theory, Culture and Society*, 5 (2001), 1–22.

21 J. Cage, *Silence: Lectures and Writings*, Middletown, CT, Wesleyan University Press, 1961.

22 Juslin and Sloboda, *Music and Emotion*; T. DeNora, *Music in Everyday Life*, Cambridge, Cambridge University Press, 2000.

23 S. Acord, 'Beyond the code: New aesthetic methodologies for the sociology of the arts', *Sociologie de l'art: OPUS* (Questions du méthod), 9 (2006), 69–86.

24 DeNora, *Music in Everyday Life*.

25 E. Gomart and A. Hennion, 'A sociology of attachment: Music amateurs, drug users', in J. Law and J. Hassard (eds.), *Actor Network Theory and After*, Oxford, Blackwell, 1999, pp. 220–47.

26 A. Hennion, *La passion musicale: Une sociologie de la mediation*, Paris, Diffusion Seuil, 1993; G. Born, 'On musical mediation: Ontology, technology and creativity', *twentieth-century music,* 2 (2005), 7–36.

27 R. W. Witkin, *Adorno on Popular Culture*, London, Routledge, 2002.

28 J. C. Lena, 'Meaning and membership: Samples in rap music, 1979 to 1995', *Poetics*, 32/3-4 (2004), 297–310; Hennion, *La passion musicale.*

29 www.news.com/Apple-strikes-cell-phone-music-deal/2100-1027_3-5284580.html (accessed 26 June 2008); www.time.com/time/business/article/0,8599,1658484,00.html (accessed 26 June 2008).

30 Attali, *Noise.*

31 S. Maisonneuve, 'Between history and commodity: The production of a musical patrimony through the record in the 1920–1930s', *Poetics*, 2 (2001), 89–108.

32 E. Eisenberg, *The Recording Angel: The Experience of Music From Aristotle to Zappa*, New York, Penguin Books, 1987.

33 A. Hennion, 'Baroque and rock: Music, mediators and musical taste', *Poetics*, 6 (1997), 415–35; J. W. Davidson and A. Coulam, 'Exploring jazz and classical solo singing performance behaviours: A preliminary step towards understanding performer creativity', in G. Wiggins (ed.), *Musical Creativity: Current Research in Theory and Practice*, Oxford, Oxford University Press, 2006, pp. 181–99.

34 S. Melchior-Bonnet, *The Mirror: A History*, New York, Routledge, 2002.

35 DeNora, *Music in Everyday Life*.

36 Maisonneuve, 'Between history and commodity', p. 104.

37 A. Kershaw, 'Bob Dylan: How I found the man who shouted "Judas"', *Independent* (23 September 2005), www.independent.co.uk/arts-entertainment/music/features/bob-dylan-how-i-found-the-man-who-shouted-judas-507883.html.

38 T. Adorno, 'On the fetish character in music and the regression of listening', in A. Arato and E. Gebhardt (eds.), *The Essential Frankfurt School Reader*, New York, Continuum, 1982, pp. 270–99.

39 R. Wallis and K. Malm, *Big Sounds from Small Peoples: The Music Industry in Small Countries*, London, Constable, 1984.

40 S. Frith, *Performing Rites: On the Value of Popular Music*, Cambridge, MA, Harvard University Press, 1996.

41 C. Mugan, 'With the rise of downloads are albums now dead?', *Independent* (29 June 2007), www.independent.co.uk/arts-entertainment/music/features/with-the-rise-of-downloads-are-albums-now-dead-455056.html.

42 www2.le.ac.uk/ebulletin/news/press-releases/2000-2009/2006/01/nparticle-wxc-b9c-7hd (accessed 26 June 2008).

43 C. Williams, 'Does it really matter? Young people and popular music', *Popular Music*, 2 (2001), 223–42.

44 A. Gabrielsson, 'The influence of musical structure on emotional expression', in Juslin and Sloboda, *Music and Emotion*, pp. 223–48; Eisenberg, *The Recording Angel*; J. Sloboda, A. Lamont and A. Greasley, 'Choosing to hear music', in S. Hallam, I. Cross and M. Thaut (eds.), *Oxford Handbook of Music Psychology*, Oxford, Oxford University Press, 2009, pp. 431–40; Kertz-Welzel, 'The "magic" of music'.

45 T. Lesiuk, 'The effect of music listening on work performance', *Psychology of Music*, 2 (2005), 173–91.

46 T. DeNora, 'The role of music in intimate culture: A case study', *Feminism and Psychology*, 2 (2002), 176–81; A. C. North, J. David and J. McKendrick, 'The influence of in-store music on wine selections', *Journal of Applied Psychology*, 2 (1999), 271–6; S. Pettan (ed.), *Music, Politics, and War: Views From Croatia*, Zagreb, Institute of Ethnology and Folklore Research, 1998. H. Jones, 'US military lawyer slams Guantanamo procedures', Paper Chase, 2006 (http://jurist.law.pitt.edu/paperchase/2006/03/us-military-lawyer-slams-guantanamo.php) (accessed 26 June 2008).

47 Eisenberg, *The Recording Angel*.

48 A. Hennion, 'Those things that hold us together: Taste and sociology', *Cultural Sociology*, 1 (2007), 97–114.

49 B. Anderson, 'A principle of hope: Recorded music listening practices and the immanence of Utopia', *Geografiska Annaler B*, 3 & 4 (2002), 211–227; S. D. Crafts, D. Cavicchi and C. Keil, *My Music*, Hanover, NH, University Press of New England, 1993; DeNora, *Music in Everyday Life*.

50 O. Stockfelt, 'Adequate modes of listening', in D. Schwarz, A. Kassabian and L. Siegel (eds.), *Keeping Score: Music, Disciplinarity and Culture*, Charlottesville, University Press of Virginia, 1997, 129–46.

51 Hennion, 'Music lovers: Taste as performance'; C. Martin, ' "We feed off each other": Embodiment, phenomenology and listener receptivity of Nirvana's *In Utero*', MA dissertation, Bowling Green State University (2006).

52 See R. A. R. MacDonald, D. J. Hargreaves and D. Miell (eds.), *Musical Identities*, Oxford, Oxford University Press, 2002 for detailed discussion of this from a number of perspectives.

53 A. Swidler, 'What anchors cultural practices', in K. D. Knorr-Cetina, T. R. Schatzki and E. Savigny (eds.), *The Practice Turn in Contemporary Theory*, London, Routledge, 2001, pp. 74–92.

54 R. Eyerman and A. Jamison, *Music and Social Movements: Mobilizing Traditions in the Twentieth Century*, Cambridge, Cambridge University Press, 1998.

55 R. Jenkins, *Social Identity*, London, Routledge, 2004.

56 A. Bergh, 'Med-music on the move: Music of immigrants in Europe', radio programmes for BBC World Service (1995, see http://musicalista.net/background/archive/med-music-on-the-move-music-of-immigrants-in-europe.html).

57 T. DeNora, 'Health and music in everyday life – a theory of practice', *Psyke & Logos*, 1 (2007), 271–87; K. Batt-Rawden, 'Music: A strategy to promote health in rehabilitation? An evaluation of participation in a "music and health promotion project" ', *International Journal of Rehabilitation Research*, 2 (2006), 171–3; S. Trythall, 'Live music in hospitals: A new "alternative" therapy', *Journal of the Royal Society for the Promotion of Health*, 3 (2006), 113–14; A. Bergh, 'I'd like to teach the world to sing: Music and conflict transformation', *Musicae Scientiae*, special issue (2007), 141–57; V. Jordanger, A. Popov, S. Aas Rustad and A. Vitvitsky, *The North Caucuses Dialogue*

Project: Report on the IPC Two-Years Project 2004–2006, Trondheim, Building Peaces, http://buildingpeaces.org/filer/TheIPCtwoyearproject2004-2006.pdf.
58 DeNora, *Music in Everyday Life*; Lash and Urry, *Economies of Signs and Space*; R. Garofalo, *Rockin' the Boat: Mass Music and Mass Movements*, Boston, MA, South End Press, 1992; C. A. Lockard, *Dance of Life: Popular Music and Politics in Southeast Asia*, Honolulu, University of Hawaii Press, 1998.
59 Batt-Rawden, 'Music'.
60 Bergh, 'Everlasting love'.
61 A. Bennett, 'Heritage rock: Music fandom and preservation', Conference of the European Sociological Association (ESA), Research Network for the Sociology of the Arts, Glasgow (3–6 September 2007).
62 A. Bergh, 'Tape Europe express' 86', *Puls*, 8 (1986), 52–3.
63 P. Manuel, *Cassette Culture: Popular Music and Technology in North India*, Chicago, University of Chicago Press, 1993.
64 Bennett, 'Heritage rock'.
65 J. Lanza, *Elevator Music: A Surreal History of Muzak, Easy-Listening and Other Moodsong*, Ann Arbor, University of Michigan Press, 2004.
66 M. Prendergast, *The Ambient Century: From Mahler to Trance – the Evolution of Sound in the Electronic Age*, London, Bloomsbury, 2000.
67 M. Bull, *Sounding Out the City: Personal Stereos and the Management of Everyday Life*, Oxford, Berg, 2000.
68 K. O'Hara and B. Brown (eds.), *Consuming Music Together: Social and Collaborative Aspects of Music Consumption Technologies*, New York, Springer, 2006.
69 Bull, *Sounding Out the City*; Schwarz, Kassabian and Siegel, *Keeping Score*.
70 A. Reyes Schramm, 'Music and tradition: From native to adopted land through the refugee experience', *Yearbook for Traditional Music*, 21 (1989), 25–35; Bergh, 'Everlasting love'.

A matter of circumstance: On experiencing recordings
1 Harry Belafonte, *Banana Boat [Song] (Day-O)*, His Master's Voice 45 POP 308 (*c.* 1957). Most likely I bought a German issue equivalent to this release. My copy does not exist any more.
2 See M. Elste, 'Hindemiths Versuche "grammophonplatten-eigener Stücke" im Kontext einer Ideengeschichte der Mechanischen Musik im 20. Jahrhundert', *Hindemith-Jahrbuch. Annales Hindemith*, 25 (1996), 195–221.

3 See M. Elste, 'Die Musik, der Lautsprecher, der Bildschirm und ich. Ein Essay über Musik im Fernsehen', *Musica*, 40/1 (1986), 18–21.
4 Rudolf Serkin, Adolf Busch and Hermann Busch, *Schubert: Piano Trio No. 2, Op. 100*, Electrola E 80 792 (1963/4).
5 Friedrich Gulda, Hans Swarowsky and the Orchester der Wiener Staatsoper, *Mozart: Piano Concertos No. 21, K. 467 and No. 27, K. 595*, Concert Hall M 2319 (recorded in *c.* 1963).
6 Nikolaus Harnoncourt, Hans Gillesberger and the Concentus Musicus Wien, Wiener Sängerknaben, Chorus Viennensis, *J. S. Bach: Mass in B Minor BWV232*. Telefunken Das Alte Werk SKH 20 (1968); see M. Elste, *Meilensteine der Bach-Interpretation 1750–2000: Eine Werkgeschichte im Wandel*, Stuttgart and Weimar, Metzler; Kassel, Bärenreiter, 2000, pp. 180–95.
7 Lukas Foss and the Zimbler Sinfonietta, *Bartók: Divertimento for Strings*, Turnabout Vox TV 34 154 S (reissued in *c.* 1967).
8 W. Rosenberg, review of Lukas Foss and the Zimbler Sinfonietta, *Bartók: Divertimento for Strings*, *Hi F.-Stereophonie*, 7/9 (1968), 670.
9 K. Myers, *Index to Record Reviews*, volume IV, Boston, MA, G. K. Hall and Co. (1978), p. 445.

6 Selling sounds: Recordings and the record business
1 C. Ehrlich, 'Mechanisation takes command: A century of cultural upheaval', Keynote address, 'Record time' conference, Jerusalem Music Centre (10–14 May 1998).
2 For a more detailed discussion of early recording technologies see the chapter in this book by George Brock-Nannestad.
3 P. Gronow and I. Saunio, *An International History of the Recording Industry*, London, Cassell, 1998, p. 9. This publication is highly recommended to those seeking further knowledge of the history of the recording industry.
4 Ibid., p. 12.
5 P. Martland, 'A business history of the Gramophone Company Ltd (1887–1918)', PhD thesis, University of Cambridge (1992).
6 Gronow and Saunio, *International History*, p. 31.
7 Ibid., p. 12.
8 Ibid., p. 28.
9 Ibid., p. 38.
10 R. Miller and R. Boar, *The Incredible Music Machine*, London, Quartet/Visual Arts, 1982, p. 139.
11 Gronow and Saunio, *International History*, p. 57.
12 Ibid., p. 39.

13 Ibid., p. 57.

14 Ibid., p. 86.

15 Ibid., p. 89.

16 Ibid., p. 96.

17 D. Patmore, 'The business of musical culture', paper delivered to the Association of Business Historians conference, Wolverhampton (30 June 2007).

18 Gronow and Saunio, *International History*, p. 38.

19 J. Horowitz, *Understanding Toscanini*, London, Faber and Faber, 1987.

20 F. W. Gaisberg, *Music on Record*, London, Robert Hale, 1946.

21 A. Sanders (ed.), *Walter Legge: Words and Music*, London, Duckworth, 1998.

22 C. O'Connell, *The Other Side of the Record*, New York, Alfred A. Knopf, 1947.

23 J. Hammond, *John Hammond on Record: An Autobiography*, New York, Ridge Press/ Summit Books, 1981.

24 Gronow and Saunio, *International History*, p. 98.

25 Ibid., p. 96.

26 Ibid., p. 118.

27 Ibid., p. 99.

28 Ibid., p. 102.

29 D. Patmore and E. Clarke, 'Making and hearing virtual worlds: John Culshaw and the art of record production', *Musicae Scientiae*, 11/2 (2007), 269–93. For more on Martin's production of the Beatles albums, see Andrew Blake's chapter in this volume, pp. 45–6.

30 Gronow and Saunio, *International History*, p. 135.

31 Ibid., p. 188.

32 Ibid., p. 183.

33 Ibid., p. 137.

34 Ibid., pp. 191–2.

35 Ibid., p. 193.

36 Recording Industry Association of America, quoted in 'The CD is dead, long live the CD!' MSN Slate, 27.03.07, 4.01pm EST. www.slate.com/id/2162771/?GT1=9231 (accessed 26 June 2008).

37 For instance, see D. Kusek and G. Leonhard, *The Future of Music: Manifesto for the Digital Music Revolution*, Boston, MA, Berklee Press, 2005.

Revisiting concert life in the mid-century: The survival of acetate discs

1 A. Watts, *Cecil E. Watts: Pioneer of Direct Disc Recording*, London, Agnes Watts, 1972.

2 M. J. L. Pulling (ed.), 'The magnetophon sound recording and reproducing system', British Intelligence Objectives Subcommittee, B.I.O.S. Final Report No. 951 (1946).

3 P. Fitzgerald, *Human Voices*, London, Collins, 1980, p. 7.

4 R. Dougall, *In and Out of the Box: An Autobiography*, London, Collins and Harvill Press, 1973, p. 63.

5 Where details of performers are not given on labels they have been deduced from known details in *Radio Times* and the BBC Written Archive Centre files at Caversham.

6 L. Foreman, 'Thirties off the air', *International Classical Record Collector*, 6/21 (Summer 2000), 7–8.

7 See P. Wilson, 'Home recording', *The Gramophone* (March 1931), 513–14; and D. Aldous, 'Specialist contributions – I', in Watts, *Cecil E. Watts*, p. 103.

8 See L. Foreman, 'Saved from oblivion', *Classic Record Collector*, 49 (Summer 2007), 21–3.

9 Although *Radio Times* bills the conductor as Barbirolli, the label reveals that the Bush Concerto was conducted by George Weldon.

7 The development of recording technologies

1 G. Brock-Nannestad, '150 years of time-base in acoustic measurement and 100 years of audio's best publicity stunt – 2007 as a commemorative year', Audio Engineering Society (AES), 122nd Convention, Vienna (5–8 May 2007), Paper No. 7007.

2 Letter from Calvin Child (Victor Talking Machine Company) to T. Birnbaum (Gramophone Company), now in EMI Music Archives (10 December 1906).

3 R. Beardsley, 'Waxes, shells and stampers', available from the CHARM website at www. charm.kcl.ac.uk/history/p20_4_7.html (accessed 19 June 2008).

4 G. Brock-Nannestad, 'How is discography related to the physical object?', presented at the seminar 'Dokumentation av 78-varvsepoken i Skandinavien', SLBA, Stockholm (12–13 February 2005), Svenska Ljud- och Bildarkivet, Stockholm, Catalogue No. bib05-0257.

5 G. Brock-Nannestad, 'The objective basis for the production of high quality transfers from pre-1925 sound recordings', Audio Engineering Society (AES), 103rd Convention, New York (26–29 September 1997), Preprint No. 4610.

6 This grandfather of all magnetic pickups is described in full detail in Edward Kellogg's US patent 1,783,044 (published 25 November 1930).

7 The TriErgon process for editing invented by Vogt, Engl and Massolle in Germany was used commercially (*c.* 1927–30). Sound was recorded on film, which was edited and

subsequently transferred at fractional speed to disc records.

8 For more on this topic, see Lewis Foreman's contribution to this volume.

9 M. Camras (ed.), *Magnetic Tape Recording*, New York, van Nostrand Reinhold, 1985.

10 Typical of the reports is M. J. L. Pulling (ed.), 'The magnetophon sound recording and reproducing system', British Intelligence Objectives Subcommittee, B.I.O.S. Final Report No. 951 (1946).

11 H. E. Roys, 'Reminiscing – the stereophonic record', *Journal of the Acoustical Society of America*, 77/4 (1985), 1332.

12 GB patent 394,325, p. 16, line 110 – p. 17, line 10.

13 For instance, in the BBC already in the 1930s, the recording and reproducing system was just another black box (like filters, attenuators, or switches) to be plugged into any chain in any order as required. What actually went on inside was of no interest to the users of the system. See G. Brock-Nannestad, 'Comment on "Peter Copeland, *Equalisation of BBC Disc Recordings*" ', *IASA Journal*, 10 (November 1997), 77–81.

14 T. Fine, 'The dawn of commercial digital recording', *ARSC Journal*, 39/1 (Spring 2008), 1–17.

15 J. Watkinson, *RDAT*, Oxford, Focal Press, 1991.

16 P. B. Fellgett, 'Some comparisons of digital and analogue audio recording', *The Radio and Electronic Engineer*, 53 (February 1983), 55–62.

17 J. Watkinson, *The Art of Digital Audio*, third edition, Oxford, Focal Press, 2001.

18 Optical detection of the signal on mechanical records has always created great interest, because there is no wear of the carrier, see G. Brock-Nannestad, 'The attraction of optical replay of mechanical recordings', in Z. Vajda and H. Pichler (eds.), *Proceedings of AES 20th International Conference 'Archiving, Restoration, and New Methods of Recording'*, Budapest (5–7 October 2001), pp. 157–61. The latest approaches are for instance based on interferometric measurement of the height differences with respect to the surface of the record, or use a colour-coded light source in which the reflection from the undulating groove provides information on its instant direction by the reflected colour. In a related approach a 1:1 photograph of the record surface is scanned for digitisation.

19 G. Brock-Nannestad, 'Pre- and de-emphasis – a forgotten necessity', AES Convention Paper No. 5360, 110th Convention, Amsterdam (12–15 May 2001).

20 H. H. Scott, 'The design of dynamic noise suppressors', *Proceedings of the National Electronics Conference*, volume III, Chicago (3–5 November 1947), p. 25.

21 J. Beament, *How We Hear Music*, Woodbridge, Suffolk, Boydell Press, 2001.

22 Individuals like the jazz historian and sound restorer John R. T. Davies (1927–2004) employed very successful but slow manual methods of selective removal of the magnetic layer on tape to remove clicks and distortion.

23 F. J. W. Rayner, S. V. Vaseghi and L. Stickells, 'Digital signal processing methods for the removal of scratches and surface noise from gramophone recordings', in *Archiving the Audio-Visual Heritage – A Joint Technical Symposium*, Berlin, Stiftung Deutsche Kinemathek, 1988, pp. 109–11.

24 G. Brock-Nannestad, 'What are the sources of the noises we remove?', in Vajda and Pichler, *Proceedings of AES 20th International Conference*, pp. 175–82.

The original cast recording of *West Side Story*

1 The LP was first issued in mono as OL 5230 and was certainly in stores during the week beginning 7 October. The stereo version, with the number OS 2001, was issued in 1958. The principals included Carol Lawrence (Maria), Chita Rivera (Anita), Marilyn Cooper (Rosalia), Larry Kert (Tony) and Mickey Calin (Riff). As well as singing Consuelo, Reri Grist was also the solo singer in 'Somewhere'. The conductor was Max Goberman. The production team for the sessions included Goddard Lieberson (producer), Howard Scott (associate producer), and Fred Plaut and Edward T. Graham (engineers).

2 G. Lieberson, 'The non-visual theatre', in *Essays* (privately printed, 1957), unpaginated.

3 Gary Marmorstein, *The Label: The Story of Columbia Records*, New York, Thunder's Mouth Press, 2007, p. 271.

4 Library of Congress, Music Division, Leonard Bernstein Collection.

5 O. L. Guernsey Jr (ed.), *Broadway Song and Story: Playwrights, Lyricists, Composers Discuss Their Hits*, New York, Dodd, Mead, 1985, p. 46.

6 Library of Congress, Music Division, Leonard Bernstein Collection, Correspondence Files, Box 36.

7 Interview with the present author on 20 September 2006.

8 Library of Congress, Music Division, Leonard Bernstein Collection, Correspondence Files, Box 52. I am grateful to Mark Eden Horowitz at the Library of Congress for drawing my attention to this

letter, and especially to Stephen Sondheim for kindly allowing the relevant parts of it to be reproduced here.

9 *West Side Story* was among the earliest Columbia cast recordings to be made in stereo. The open-reel tape mentioned by Sondheim was issued as a pair of two-track tapes with the number TOB 13, put on sale in late 1957 or early 1958.

10 References are to the full orchestral score of *West Side Story*, New York and London, Jalni Publications and Boosey & Hawkes, 1994. The cut music appears on pp. 165–6 of the full score.

11 In an interview with the present author on 20 September 2006, Sondheim described this decision – which was Lieberson's – in more positive terms: not as a 'drawback' to the recording, but as an example of Lieberson following his record producer's instincts to good effect.

12 Larry Kert, the original Tony.

13 Green played Mouth Piece in the original production.

14 Orchestral forces for show recordings were almost always augmented from those of the actual pit band.

15 Jerome Robbins.

16 Irwin Kostal and Sid Ramin were co-orchestrators with Bernstein of *West Side Story*.

8 The recorded document: Interpretation and discography

1 For a wide-ranging view of issues surrounding discography before the internet see M. Gray, 'Discography: Its prospects and problems', *Notes* 35/3 (March 1979), 578–92.

2 www.geocities.com/Tokyo/1471/ ormandy_disk_e.html.

3 http://lso.co.uk/downloadables/lumps/ upload/472-35.pdf.

4 Why, for example, does the Library of Congress place a question mark after the date 1929 for Rachmaninov, Piano Concerto No. 2 on Victor? The year is correct.

5 An extensive list of web sources may be found via the CHARM website, www.charm.kcl.ac.uk/ discography/weblinks/disco_links.html.

6 F. Clough and G. Cuming, *The World's Encyclopaedia of Recorded Music* (including First Supplement 1950–1), London, Sidgwick and Jackson, 1952; Second Supplement 1951–2 (1953); Third Supplement 1953–5 (1957); online at www.charm.kcl.ac.uk/discography/ disco_resources.html.

7 R. D. Darrell, *The Gramophone Shop Encyclopaedia of Recorded Music*, New York, The Gramophone Shop, 1932.

8 B. Rust, *Jazz Records, 1897–1942*, fourth edition, New Rochelle, Arlington House, 1978; J. G. Jepsen, *Jazz Records, 1942–1969*, Copenhagen, Nordisk Tidsskrift Forlag, 1963; W. Bruyninckx, *60 Years of Recorded Jazz, 1917–1977*, Mechelen, Belgium, Bruyninckx, 1980.

9 See for example B. Rust, *The American Dance Band Discography*, New Rochelle, Arlington House, 1975; K. Ritosalmi-Kisner and D. D. Rooney, 'Minneapolis Symphony Orchestra/Minnesota Orchestra: A discography of recordings, 1924–2003', *ARSC Journal*, 34/2 (2003), 160–93.

10 Both Gray volumes are available online via the CHARM website (see note 6 above).

11 P. Fülöp, *Mahler Discography*, New York, Kaplan Foundation, 1995.

12 See the controversial 'Guidelines of discographies in the *ARSC Journal*', *ARSC Journal*, 37/1 (Spring 2006), 17, www.arsc-audio.org/pdf/DiscographicalGuidelines.pdf.

13 John Hunt, *Giants of the Keyboard: Kempf, Gieseking, Fischer, Haskil, Backhaus, Schnabel*, London, John Hunt, 1994.

14 Review in *ARSC Journal*, 26/1 (Spring 1995), 83.

15 A. Kelly, *His Master's Voice: The German Catalogue: A Complete Numerical Catalogue of German Gramophone Recordings Made from 1898 to 1929 in Germany, Austria, and Elsewhere by the Gramophone Company Ltd = Die Stimme seines Herrn*, Westport, CT, Greenwood, 1994.

16 For more information on the complex and often contentious field of surface markings, see H. S. Friedman, 'Surface markings on Gramophone Company and Victor Records', *ARSC Journal*, 34/2 (2003), 135–59.

17 Available at the time of writing from Alan Kelly as a MS Word file on CD Mat 201. The data is also included in the CHARM online discography.

18 The recording is available on IMG 5 75486 2, which gives the recording details: Kingsway Hall, 5–6 November 1929.

19 On www.charm.kcl.ac.uk/discography/ search/search_simple.html, search on 'Mendelssohn', 'midsummer' and 'Beinum'.

20 Michael Gray, private email.

21 All information concerning the recording is taken from liner notes by Mark Obert-Thorn, also the transfer engineer, accompanying Biddulph LHW 036, which gives the alternative version of the recording. The original may be heard on a number of CD issues, including those of Naxos and BMG/ Sony.

22 Friedman, 'Surface markings', 136.

23 Now incorporated in the CHARM discography.

24 Gray, private email.

25 www.prex.com, www.academy-records. com, www.jerrysrecords.com, www. glaspolerecords.com, www.mikrokosmos.com, www.norpete.com, www.78rpm.com (Nauck), www.holdridgerecords.com. These are just examples used by colleagues at the time of writing. There are many more to be found online.

26 J. F. Cone, *Adelina Patti: Queen of Hearts*, Aldershot, Scolar Press, 1993, p. 246.

27 See M. Bookspan, 'The BSO and the talking machine', *High Fidelity Magazine* (January 1958), 50–1, 124–6; B. Bell, liner notes, *The First Recordings of the Boston Symphony Orchestra*, BSO Classics 171002 (1995).

28 Karl Muck and the Boston Symphony Orchestra, *Tchaikovsky: Symphony No. 4*. BSO Classics 171002 (1995).

29 Information about Gennett Studios and the recording sessions is taken from R. Kennedy, *Jelly Roll, Bix, and Hoagy: Gennett Studios and the Birth of Recorded Jazz*, Bloomington, Indiana University Press, 1994, pp. 27–34.

30 A valuable discussion of the dissemination of jazz through recording may be found in A. Shipton, *A New History of Jazz*, New York, Continuum, 2007, pp. 402–6.

31 Ibid., pp. 63–4.

32 Ibid., p. 65.

33 Ibid., p. 125.

34 Hoagy Carmichael and the Happy Harmonists. *Washboard Blues*. Gennett 3066A (recorded 19 May 1925). Contrasting compact-disc transfers may be found on *Those Fabulous Gennetts Vol. 2*. Timeless CBC 1-080 (2002; transfer by Hans Eekhoff) and *Hoagy Carmichael: The First of the Singer Songwriters. Key Cuts 1924–1946*. JSP Records JSP918 (2004; transfer by Doug Pomeroy).

35 Leaflet included with the device, quoted by Mackenzie in his editorial for the February 1926 edition of *The Gramophone*, 416.

36 www.cedaraudio.com/products/ cambridge/camretouch.html.

37 Review in *The Gramophone* (June 1970), 89.

38 E. Greenfield, I. March and R. Layton, *Guide to Compact Discs*, London, Penguin, 1994, p. 1221.

39 Review taken from Gramofile at www. gramophone.co.uk/cdreviews.asp (author's name not given).

40 www.columbia.edu/~brennan/beatles/ strawberry-fields.html. See also A. Wiener, *The Beatles, the Ultimate Recording Guide*, New York, Facts on File, 1992, p. 201; M. Lewisohn, *The Beatles Recording Sessions: The Official Abbey Road Studio Session Notes 1962–1970*, New York, Harmony Books, 1988.

41 Among several sites listing and critiquing the bootlegs, this one is typical: http://fabfour. de/beatles_bootlegs.html.

42 See the booklet accompanying the set.

43 C. Mackenzie, *The Gramophone* (January 1926), 349.

44 D. Morton, *Sound Recording: The Life Story of a Technology*, Westport, CT, Greenwood Press, 2005, p. 147.

45 J. Crabbe, *Hi Fi in the Home*, London, Blandford, 1973, p. 264.

46 This account is taken from S. R. Grubb, *Music Makers on Record*, London, Hamish Hamilton, 1986, pp. 145–54 (discussed by Andrew Blake in this volume, pp. 40–3).

47 Ibid., p. 153.

48 Ibid.

49 M. Katz, 'The phonograph effect', PhD thesis, University of Michigan (1999).

50 Cone, *Adelina Patti*, p. 245.

51 For a discussion of cyberspace and the impact of MPEG players see M. Katz, *Capturing Sound: How Technology Has Changed Music*, Berkeley, University of California Press, 2004, pp. 158–87.

One man's approach to remastering

1 *Rhythm in the Alphabet* remastered by Ted Kendall is issued in the box set *George Formby: England's Famed Clown Prince of Song*, JSP Records, JSPCD 1901 (2004); download available from www.emusic.com.

Technology, the studio, music

1 All of Pink Floyd's albums were made for the recording company EMI.

Reminder: A recording is not a performance

1 Claude Debussy, *Claude Debussy: The Composer as Pianist*, Pierian Recording Society, Pierian 0001 (2000).

2 Gavin Bryars Ensemble, *Gavin Bryars: After the Requiem*, ECM Records ECM1424 (1991).

3 Roger Heaton, *Tom Johnson: Rational Melodies, Bedtime Stories*, Ants AG12 (2006). *Rational Melodies* is scored for solo clarinet, while *Bedtime Stories* is for narrator and clarinet.

4 Emerson String Quartet, *Mendelssohn: The Complete String Quartets*, Deutsche Grammophon B0006TN9G2 (2005).

5 Roger Heaton, *New Music for Multi-tracked Clarinets*, Clarinet Classics CC0009 (1994).

9 Methods for analysing recordings

1 R. Philip, *Early Recordings and Musical Style: Changing Tastes in Instrumental Performance, 1900–1950*, Cambridge, Cambridge University

Press, 1992, p. 51; also R. Philip, *Performing Music in the Age of Recording*, New Haven, Yale University Press, 2004.

2 E. Clarke, *Ways of Listening: An Ecological Approach to the Perception of Musical Meaning*, New York, Oxford University Press, 2005, p. 54; timing based on *Jimi Hendrix: Live at Woodstock*, MCD 11987/111 987-2 (1999) (disc 2, track 4). Clarke sourced the recording from the collection *Jimi Hendrix: The Ultimate Experience*, where the G♯ comes at 0'14".

3 N. Cook and D. Leech-Wilkinson, 'Techniques for analysing recordings: an introduction', accessible at www.charm.kcl.ac.uk/analysing/p9_0_1.html.

4 R. Dockwray and A. Moore, 'The establishment of the virtual performance space in rock', *twentieth-century music* (forthcoming). My thanks to the authors for providing me with this image in advance of publication.

5 D. Leech-Wilkinson, 'Sound and meaning in recordings of Schubert's "Die junge Nonne"', *Musicae Scientiae*, 11/2 (2007), 209–33 (220). Figure 9.3b is the Sonic Visualiser session file specified on p. 219, with the addition of bar numbers.

6 B. Repp, 'Diversity and commonality in music performance: An analysis of timing microstructure in Schumann's "Träumerei"', *Journal of the Acoustical Society of America*, 92/5 (1992), 2546–68.

7 For an outline of the project see G. Widmer, 'In search of the Horowitz factor: Interim report on a musical discovery project', *Proceedings of the 5th International Conference on Discovery Science*, London, Springer Verlag (2002), 13–21; my thanks to Gerhard Widmer for supplying Figures 9.4 and 9.5. Sample Performance Worm animations may be downloaded at www.ofai.at/~werner.goebl/animations/.

8 N. Cook, 'The conductor and the theorist: Furtwängler, Schenker, and the first movement of Beethoven's Ninth Symphony', in J. Rink (ed.), *The Practice of Performance: Studies in Musical Interpretation*, Cambridge, Cambridge University Press, 1995, pp. 105–25 (Figure 5.4).

9 Ibid., p. 120.

10 But not among more psychologically oriented researchers, such as Clarke and Caroline Palmer.

11 H. Honing and P. Desain, 'Tempo curves considered harmful', in J. Kramer (ed.), 'Time in contemporary musical thought', *Contemporary Music Review*, 7/2 (1993), 123–38 (136).

12 See, e.g., M. Clynes, 'Expressive microstructure in music, linked to living qualities', in J. Sundberg (ed.), *Studies of Musical Performance*, Stockholm, Royal Swedish Academy of Music, 1983, pp. 76–181; N. Todd, 'A model of expressive timing in tonal music', *Music Perception*, 3 (1985), 33–58; J. Sundberg, A. Friberg and L. Frydén, 'Rules for automated performance of ensemble music', *Contemporary Music Review*, 3/1 (1989), 89–109. The Sundberg *et al.* rules are implemented in the program Director Musices (www.speech.kth.se/music/performance/download/).

13 J. Bowen, 'Tempo, duration and flexibility: Techniques in the analysis of musical performance', *Journal of Musicological Research*, 16 (1996), 111–56; E. Grunin, 'An Eroica project', www.grunin.com/eroica/ (accessed 1 March 2008), from which Figure 9.8 is taken.

14 Eric Grunin (personal communication) notes of his Eroica project, which at the time of writing encompasses 387 recordings of the complete symphony, that the data stopped evolving at about 200 recordings. Few if any other studies are so extensive.

15 R. Turner, 'Conductors compared: Individual interpretation and historic trends in Brahms' First Symphony', paper given at 'Musicology and Recordings', CHARM/RMA conference, Egham, UK (13–15 September 2007).

16 From www.mazurka.org.uk/ana/pcor-perf/rubinstein/index-noavg.html (accessed 1 March 2008); the black-and-white reproductions in Figure 9.9 do not retain all the information in the colour originals.

17 Repp, 'Diversity and commonality', 2555.

18 Todd, 'A model of expressive timing'.

19 Figure 9.10 was created using the online 'Scape plot generator' at www.mazurka.org.uk/software/online/scape/ (set to 'arch'), with data drawn from www.mazurka.org.uk/info/excel/beat/ and www.mazurka.org.uk/info/excel/dyn/gbdyn/. Again the black-and-white reproduction in Figure 9.10 is less informative than the colour original.

20 See Leech-Wilkinson's chapter in this volume on the effect of the Second World War (p. 252), and on the continuous, heavy vibrato in violin performance which became general after the war and might be considered a parallel practice to post-war phrase arching (pp. 252–3). Further details concerning phrase arching in Op. 63 No. 3, and the methods used here to quantify it, may be found in N. Cook, 'Squaring the circle: Phrase arching in recordings of Chopin's mazurkas', *Musica Humana*, 1 (forthcoming).

21 The strength of phrase arching at the 8-bar level relative to other levels is multiplied by the degree of correlation between tempo and dynamics at the 8-bar level, with the former being weighted twice as highly as the latter.

22 R. Taruskin, *Text and Act: Essays on Musical Performance*, New York, Oxford University Press, 1995, p. 24.

23 C. Abbate, 'Music – drastic or gnostic?', *Critical Inquiry*, 30 (2004), 505–36 (510).

24 This corresponds to the first of the four types of critical discourse discussed by Simon Frith in this volume, chapter 11, pp. 272–3.

25 Catalogue No. 54764, transfer issued in 1987 on *Alessandro Moreschi, the Last Castrato: Complete Vatican Recordings*. Pavilion Pearl Opal CD 9823.

26 C. Higgins, 'Look sharp: Chance to buy live CD straight after the concert', *Guardian*, 7 February 2006 (www.guardian.co.uk/uk/2006/feb/07/arts.artsnews1, accessed 1 March 2008).

27 D. Patmore and E. Clarke, 'Making and hearing virtual worlds: John Culshaw and the art of record production', *Musicae Scientiae*, 11/2 (2007), 269–93; K. Bazzana, *Glenn Gould: The Performer in the Work*, Oxford, Clarendon Press, 1997, pp. 249–52.

28 As described by Simon Trezise in chapter 8 of this volume, see pp. 193–6.

29 P. Johnson, 'The legacy of recordings', in J. Rink (ed.), *Musical Performance: A Guide to Understanding*, Cambridge, Cambridge University Press, 2002, pp. 197–212 (p. 198).

30 P. Auslander, 'Musical personae', *Drama Review*, 50 (2006), 100–19 (117); my emphasis.

31 B. Kershaw, *The Politics of Performance: Radical Theatre as Cultural Intervention*, London, Routledge, 1992, p. 22.

32 S. Lacasse, 'Persona, emotions and technology: The phonographic staging of the popular music voice', paper presented at 'The Art of Record Production' conference, London (17–18 September 2005) (www.charm.kcl.ac.uk/redist/pdf/s2Lacasse.pdf). For an application of the idea of phonographic staging to analysis of vocal recordings see Lacasse's 'The phonographic voice: Paralinguistic features and phonographic staging', in A. Bayley (ed.), *Recorded Music: Performance, Culture, and Technology*, Cambridge, Cambridge University Press (forthcoming).

33 B. Nettl, *The Study of Ethnomusicology: Twenty-nine Issues and Concepts*, Urbana, University of Illinois Press, 1983, p. 40.

10 Recordings and histories of performance style

1 S. Messing, *Schubert in the European Imagination*, volumes I and II, Rochester, NY, University of Rochester Press, 2006–7.

2 J. Samson, 'Chopin, Fryderyk Franciszek', section 11: Reception, *Grove Music Online*, L. Macy (ed.), www.grovemusic.com (accessed 27 November 2007).

3 Robert Philip argues that there has been homogenisation in *Performing Music in the Age of Recording*, New Haven, Yale University Press, 2004. Mark Katz argues that recording itself has been responsible: *Capturing Sound: How Technology Has Changed Music*, Berkeley, University of California Press, 2004.

4 L. P. Lochner, *Fritz Kreisler*, New York, Macmillan, 1950, pp. 272–3. Another early study was S. N. Reger, 'The string instrument vibrato', in C. E. Seashore (ed.), *The Vibrato*, Studies in the Psychology of Music 1, Iowa City, University of Iowa, 1932, pp. 305–43. See also Józef Kański's investigation of Chopin playing on record from 1960: 'Über die Aufführungsstile der Werke Chopins: Einige allgemeine Probleme der Aufführung auf Grund von Schallplattenaufnahmen', in Z. Lissa (ed.), *The Book of the First International Musicological Congress devoted to the Works of Chopin: Warszawa 16th–22nd February 1960*, Warsaw, PWN Polish Scientific Publishers, 1963, pp. 444–54.

5 *The Record of Singing*: Vol. 1, 12 LPs, EMI RLS 724 (1977, reissued with a supplementary record in 1982); Vol. 2, 13 LPs, RLS 743 (1979); Vol. 3, 13 LPs, EMI EX 2901693 (1984); Vol. 4, 8 LPs, EMI EX 7697411 (1989). Vols. 1 and 2 were selected by collector Vivian Liff, Vols. 3 and 4 by producer Keith Hardwick. At the time of writing (27 November 2007) there is an excellent article in Wikipedia including an outline of the contents: http://en.wikipedia.org/wiki/The_Record_of_Singing. *The Violin on Record* (Pearl BVA I and II, 1990), from the collection of Raymond Glaspole with notes by Tully Potter. Other examples include *Great Pianists of the 20th Century*, 100 CDs, Philips 462 845-2 (1999), collected by Tom Deacon; *A–Z of Pianists* (Naxos 8558107-10, 2007), collected by Jonathan Summers; and (the first by an enthusiast welcomed into musicology) *A–Z of Conductors* (Naxos, 8558087-90, 2007) by David Patmore.

6 R. Philip, *Early Recordings and Musical Style: Changing Tastes in Instrumental Performance, 1900–1950*, Cambridge, Cambridge University Press, 1992; T. Day, *A Century of Recorded Music: Listening to Musical History*, New Haven, Yale University Press, 2000.

7 M. Elste, *Meilensteine der Bach-Interpretation 1750–2000: Eine Werkgeschichte im Wandel*, Stuttgart and Weimar, Metzler; Kassel, Bärenreiter, 2000; D. Fabian, *Bach*

Performance Practice, 1945–1975, Aldershot, Ashgate, 2003; M. Musgrave and B. D. Sherman, *Performing Brahms: Early Evidence of Performance Style*, Cambridge, Cambridge University Press, 2003.

8 D. Milsom, *Theory and Practice in Late Nineteenth-Century Violin Performance*, Aldershot, Ashgate, 2003.

9 See especially K. Bazzana, *Wondrous Strange: The Life and Art of Glenn Gould*, New Haven, Yale University Press, 2004.

10 A diagram showing these interrelationships is included in D. Leech-Wilkinson, *The Changing Sound of Music: Approaches to Studying Recorded Musical Performances* (www.charm.kcl.ac.uk/studies/chapters/chap7.html).

11 Day, *Century of Recorded Music*, pp. 178–85; D. Leech-Wilkinson, 'Musicology and performance', in Z. Blazekovic (ed.), *Music's Intellectual History: Founders, Followers and Fads*, New York, RILM (forthcoming).

12 M. Quick, 'Making sense of structure: Recordings of Webern's Variations for Piano, Op. 27', paper delivered to the Sixth European Music Analysis Conference/VII, Jahreskongress der Gesellschaft für Musiktheorie, Freiburg (11 October 2007).

13 Boulez has argued that the performers in his early concerts simply didn't know how to make sense of the music (*Boulez on Conducting: Conversations with Cécile Gilly*, R. Stokes (trans.), London, Faber and Faber, 2003, pp. 64–6). He may well have a point. But it is also true that his developing performance and compositional styles are uncannily alike, and that a changing view of his own musical past, in line with changes in personal and period style, is exactly what one would expect.

14 That being so, it is more important to know a performer's birth year than the date of the recording. A table of birth dates for selected recorded performers is included at the end of this chapter in the hope that it may facilitate further comparative work and encourage the idea that common features may be traced between performers and their period contexts.

15 Welte piano roll No. 237 (recorded 1905).

16 There is some discussion of this change in D. Leech-Wilkinson, 'Portamento and musical meaning', *Journal of Musicological Research*, 25 (2006), 233–61.

17 On romanticism in performance see R. Philip, 'The romantic and the old-fashioned', in E. Kjellberg, E. Lundkvist and J. Roström (eds.), *The Interpretation of Romantic and Late-Romantic Music: Papers Read at the Organ Symposium in Stockholm,*

3–12 September 1998, Uppsala, Uppsala Universitet, 2002, pp. 11–31.

18 An excellent starting point for reading on music and emotion is P. N. Juslin and J. A. Sloboda (eds.), *Music and Emotion: Theory and Research*, Oxford, Oxford University Press, 2001.

19 R. Dawkins, *The Selfish Gene*, Oxford, Oxford University Press, 1979 (revised edition 1989); S. Blackmore, *The Meme Machine*, Oxford, Oxford University Press, 1999. Memes are perhaps best defined as 'patterned neurological connections' (S. Shennan, *Genes, Memes and Human History*, London, Thames and Hudson, 2002, p. 46). A bold application of memetic theory to musical scores is S. Jan, *The Memetics of Music: A Neo-Darwinian View of Musical Structure and Culture*, Aldershot, Ashgate, 2007.

20 D. Sperber, *Explaining Culture: A Naturalist Approach*, Oxford, Blackwell, 1996, pp. 100–18 (discussed by Shennan, *Genes, Memes*, p. 47); P. J. Richerson and R. Boyd, *Not by Genes Alone: How Culture Transformed Human Evolution*, Chicago, University of Chicago Press, 2005, pp. 63, 85.

21 Richerson and Boyd, *Not by Genes*, pp. 60f.

22 Ibid., p. 7.

23 Shennan, *Genes, Memes*, p. 38.

24 Richerson and Boyd, *Not by Genes*, p. 74.

25 Shennan, *Genes, Memes*, p. 49.

26 Richerson and Boyd, *Not by Genes*, p. 13.

27 Leech-Wilkinson, *The Changing Sound*, chapter 5.

28 Shennan, *Genes, Memes*, p. 199.

29 Ibid., p. 225.

Recreating history: A clarinettist's retrospective

1 N. Zaslaw, 'Toward the revival of the classical orchestra', *Proceedings of the Royal Musical Association*, 103/1 (1976), 158.

2 E. Van Tassel, 'Recordings', *Early Music*, 12 (1984), 125.

3 L. Dreyfus, 'Early music defended against its devotees: A theory of historical performance in the twentieth century', *Musical Quarterly*, 49 (1983), 300.

4 R. Taruskin, 'The pastness of the present and the presence of the past', in N. Kenyon (ed.), *Authenticity and Early Music*, Oxford, Oxford University Press, 1988, p. 146.

5 *Early Music News*, July 1982, cited in J. Griffiths, *Nimbus: Technology Serving the Arts*, London, Andre Deutsch, 1995, p. 178.

6 C. Brown, 'Historical performance, metronome marks and tempo in Beethoven symphonies', *Early Music*, 19 (1991), 248.

7 Cited from Dreyfus, 'Early music', 305–6.

8 R. Barclay, 'A new species of instrument: The vented trumpet in context', *Historic Brass Society Journal*, 10 (1998), 1–13.
9 Griffiths, *Nimbus*, pp. 179–81.
10 T. Pinnock, '20 years of The English Concert', *Early Music News*, 174 (May 1993), 1.

11 Going critical: Writing about recordings
1 R. Osborne, 'An historical anatomy of the vinyl record', PhD thesis, London Consortium/ Birkbeck College (2008), 48–9.
2 For Osborne this is what differentiates rock from both classical music (primarily shaped by live performance) and pop (primarily shaped by broadcasting). The significance of recording for the development of jazz is apparent, but jazz didn't originate in recording as rock did and even now a record for most jazz musicians is just that, a record of musical ideas and relationships developed through performance and of no further interest. This is a very different attitude from that of most rock musicians, for whom the studio is the site in which to develop new material which is performed live after the record is released. Jazz musicians' approach to recording is a problem for labels seeking to market their recorded output; see S. Frith, *Review of Caber Music*, Edinburgh, Caber and the Scottish Arts Council, 2005.
3 The key rock critical texts are focused primarily on records. See G. Marcus, *Mystery Train*, New York, Dutton, 1975; J. Landau, *It's Too Late To Stop Now*, San Francisco, Straight Arrow, 1972; R. Christgau, *Any Old Way You Choose It*, Baltimore, Penguin, 1973; and D. Marsh, *The Heart of Rock and Soul: The 1001 Greatest Singles Ever Made*, New York, NAL, 1989. See also *The Rolling Stone Record Review*, New York, Pocket Books, 1971.
4 The first article was in the *Austin Chronicle* (August 1988), 14; the second in *American Way*, the American Airlines magazine (Autumn 1988), 72–6.
5 Arnold's article appeared in *Flagpole* on 5 February 2001; Castaldi's remark is taken from private correspondence on the issue the same year.
6 He's now senior critic at *Blender*.
7 U. Lindberg, G. Guomundsson, M. Michelsen and H. Weisethaunet, *Rock Criticism from the Beginning: Amusers, Bruisers and Cool-Headed Cruisers*, New York, Peter Lang, 2005. And see P. Gorman, *In Their Own Write: Adventures in the Music Press*, London, Sanctuary, 2001; E. Forde, 'Music journalists, music press officers and the consumer music press in the UK', PhD thesis, University of Westminster (2001);

J. Williamson, 'The British music press', PhD thesis, Queen Margaret University (in progress).
8 M. Bridle, 'The art of critics and criticism?', *Seen and Heard* editorial (November 2001), www.musicweb-international.com/Sand H.2001/Nov01/editorial.htm.
9 See K. Bruhn Jensen and P. Larsen, 'The sounds of change: Representations of music in European newspapers 1960–2000', in J. Gripsrud and L. Weibull (eds.), *Stable Change: European Media and Public Spheres 1960–2000*, Bristol, Intellect (in press); G. Harries and K. Wahl-Jorgensen, 'The culture of arts journalists: Elitists, saviors or manic depressives?', *Journalism*, 8 (2007), 619–39.
10 R. G. Wellburn, 'The early record review: Jazz criticism's first-born child', *Annual Review of Jazz Studies 3*, New Brunswick, Transaction Books, 1985.
11 J. Caskett, 'Dance records', *The Gramophone* (April 1923), 21.
12 W. A. Chislett, 'The Gramophone: 1923–1973. A personal reminiscence', *The Gramophone* (June 1973), 31.
13 The reviewer, Edgar Jackson, explained that 5 stars meant Admirable, 4 Bountiful, 3 Commendable, 2 Doubtful and 1 Execrable.
14 Osborne, 'Historical anatomy', 48–9.
15 Ibid., 61.
16 Ibid., 68. The final phrase is from R. Gelatt, *The Fabulous Phonograph 1877–1977*, second revised edition, London, Cassell, 1977, p. 129.
17 'Popular music on records. Is there too much of it?', *Talking Machine News*, 3 (November 1921).
18 E. Sackville-West and D. Shawe-Taylor, *The Record Guide*, London, Collins, 1951.
19 Osborne, 'Historical anatomy', 188.
20 *The Gramophone* (December 1923), 124.
21 C. Symes, *Setting the Record Straight: A Material History of Classical Recording*, Middletown, CT, Wesleyan University Press, 2004.
22 'The ability to document live performances was a late development in sound recording history, and was only really made possible with the shift from acoustic to electric recording in the mid 1920s' (Osborne, 'Historical anatomy', 112). Even after electric recording, classical reviewers tended to treat records as documents only in relation to opera.
23 *The Gramophone* (June 1924), 20. From this perspective there is not a great deal of difference between the reviews of the latest sheet music on a music publisher's list that appeared in the *Musical Times* ('We have lately received a large number of interesting new songs – so many that we can find space for little more than the barest mention … The music

throughout is appropriately simple, but full of interesting harmonic touches, including some dallying with the modes. Altogether a fascinating set of delicately-finished trifles,' *Musical Times* (1 March 1919), 117) and the reviews of the latest batch of releases from a record company that appeared in *The Gramophone*.

24 Review of Mozart's Serenade for strings in G, K. 525 ('Eine kleine Nachtmusik'), *The Gramophone* (June 1926), 33.

25 Review of Chopin's Fantaisie-Impromptu and Impromptu in A flat, *The Gramophone* (June 1926), 34.

26 Review of Mozart's Clarinet Trio, K. 498, *The Gramophone* (June 1931), 10.

27 F. Foster Williams, 'Records and music in Germany', *The Gramophone* (December 1923), 126–7.

28 B. D. W., 'Paderewski's records. A note', *The Gramophone* (June 1925), 25.

29 Chislett: 'The Gramophone: 1923–1973', 31.

30 Sackville-West and Shawe-Taylor were described on the book cover as 'two most experienced record reviewers – critics for the BBC, the *Observer*, the *New Statesman* and *The Gramophone*'.

31 On *The Magic Flute*; in Sackville-West and Shawe-Taylor, *The Record Guide*, p. 409.

32 On *Le Sacre du Printemps*; in Sackville-West and Shawe-Taylor, *The Record Guide*, p. 584.

33 Chislett, 'The Gramophone: 1923–1973', 32.

34 *The Record Guide* included an Appendix on Long Playing Records. These are welcomed by the authors for their ability to play long pieces of music without interruption, and for their lightness and ease of storage. But the welcome is not unreserved: 'An essential merit of the gramophone has always been the power it gives us to select and discriminate; it will be a sad day when performance of miscellaneous short pieces or songs have to be bought in bulk' (p. 719). The authors thus welcome the LP on the condition that it does not 'push 78s off the market' (p.720). By the time of the book's first supplement, published by Collins in 1952 as *The Record Year*, the aim was no longer simply to cover records released in 1951–2 but to provide a systematic guide to *all* classical LPs on the market. The nature of the reviews, though, was unchanged.

35 Quoted in Osborne, 'Historical anatomy', 38.

36 From Roger Wimbush's roundup of miscellaneous and dance music releases, *The Gramophone* (June 1940), 16.

37 *The Gramophone* (June 1940), 17.

38 C. Parsonage, *The Evolution of Jazz in Britain, 1880–1935*, Aldershot, Ashgate, 2005, p. 69.

39 Edgar Jackson on Benny Goodman's 78, *Shine* coupled with *The World Is Waiting for the Sunrise*, *The Gramophone* (June 1946), 7. The review included a list of recording personnel, composing details, dates of recording sessions, and the catalogue numbers of the tracks' original US releases.

40 I have discussed this elsewhere. See S. Frith, *Performing Rites: On the Value of Popular Music*, Cambridge, MA, Harvard University Press, 1996, pp. 43–4.

41 Charles Fox on Miles Davis, *The Gramophone* (June 1957), 32.

42 Charles Fox on Victor Feldman, *The Gramophone* (June 1959), 34.

43 From the round-up of new releases of 'Negro gospel music' by Alexis Korner, *The Gramophone* (June 1960), 46.

44 See M. Brennan, 'Down beats and rolling stones: An historical comparison of American jazz and rock journalism', PhD thesis, University of Stirling (2007).

45 *Melody Maker* (22 June 1968), 14.

46 From Chris Welch's half-page review of Genesis's *... And Then There Were Three*, *Melody Maker* (1 April 1978), 20.

47 From Steve Sutherland's full-page review of the Sugarcubes's *Life's Too Good*, *Melody Maker* (23 April 1988), 38.

48 Adjectives taken from an unpublished survey of record buyers' use of record reviews that I carried out in 2006.

49 For Williams's work see R. Williams, *Long Distance Call*, London, Aurum Press, 2000.

50 Harries and Wahl-Jorgensen, 'The culture of arts journalists'. For a useful historical account of the emergence of the newspaper arts critic's complex 'autonomy' see L. Conner, *Spreading the Gospel of Modern Dance: Newspaper Dance Criticism in the United States, 1850–1935*, Pittsburgh, University of Pittsburgh Press, 1997.

51 Chislett, 'The Gramophone: 1923–1973', 31. I became a rock critic after I met Greil Marcus, a friend of a friend, at graduate school in the University of California, Berkeley, and talked to him about records. It was 1968; he was already involved with *Rolling Stone*.

52 The letters pages of Greg Shaw's pioneering fanzine, *Who Put the Bomp*, include a number of correspondents who went on to have rock-writing careers.

53 For an example of the significance of record critics for the contemporary British jazz scene, for example, see M. Brennan, 'The rough guide

to critics: Musicians discuss the role of the music press', *Popular Music*, 25/2 (2006), 221–34.

54 For help with the research for this chapter many thanks to Ana de Oliveira Silva.

Afterword

1 J. Goody and I. Watt, 'The consequences of literacy', *Comparative Studies in Society and History*, 5/3 (1963), 304–45.

2 L. Manovich, *The Language of New Media*, Cambridge, MA, MIT Press, 2001, chapter 1.

3 J. D. Bolter and R. Grusin, *Remediation: Understanding New Media*, Cambridge, MA, MIT Press, 1999.

4 H. U. Gumbrecht and K. L. Pfeiffer, *Materialities of Communication*, Stanford, Stanford University Press, 1994; D. Miller, *Materiality*, Durham, NC, Duke University Press, 2005.

5 H. Innis, *The Bias of Communication*, Toronto, University of Toronto Press, 1991 (1951); M. McLuhan, *Understanding Media: The Extensions of Man*, London, Routledge, 2001 (1964).

6 On the concept of affordance, see J. J. Gibson, 'The theory of affordances', in R. E. Shaw and J. Bransford (eds.), *Perceiving, Acting, and Knowing*, Hillsdale, NJ, Erlbaum, 1977, pp. 67–82; E. Clarke, 'Music and psychology', in M. Clayton *et al.* (eds.), *The Cultural Study of Music*, London, Routledge, 2003, pp. 113–23; and I. Hutchby, 'Technologies, texts and affordances', *Sociology*, 35/2 (2001), 441–56.

7 D. MacKenzie and J. Wachjman, *The Social Shaping of Technology*, second edition, Buckingham, Open University Press, 1999, p. 9.

8 The classic critique of technological determinism is MacKenzie and Wachjman, *Social Shaping*, especially the 'Introductory essay'.

9 J. Lastra, *Sound Technology and the American Cinema: Perception, Representation, Modernity*, New York, Columbia University Press, 2000; J. Sterne, *The Audible Past: Cultural Origins of Sound Recording*, Durham, NC, Duke University Press, 2003.

10 One version of this argument, focused on the classical music industry, is N. Lebrecht, *The Life and Death of Classical Music*, New York, Anchor, 2007.

11 W. Benjamin, 'The work of art in the age of mechanical reproduction', in H. Arendt (ed.), H. Zhon (trans.), *Illuminations*, London, Fontana, 1973, pp. 211–44 (original published in 1936). For some commentators this phrase, '*technischen Reproduzierbarkeit*' in the original, is rendered 'technical reproducibility'.

12 T. Adorno and M. Horkheimer, 'The culture industry: Enlightenment as mass deception', in *Dialectic of Enlightenment*, J. Cumming (trans.), London, Verso/NLB, 1997 (1944), pp. 120–67; T. Adorno, 'On the fetish character of music and the regression of listening', in A. Arato and E. Gebhardt (eds.), *The Essential Frankfurt School Reader*, New York, Continuum, 1982, pp. 270–99.

13 S. Jarvis, *Adorno: A Critical Introduction*, Cambridge, Polity, 1998, p. 73.

14 All Benjamin, 'The work of art', p. 226.

15 Ibid., p. 236.

16 Ibid., pp. 238–9.

17 Ibid., p. 234.

18 L. Goehr, *The Imaginary Museum of Musical Works: An Essay in the Philosophy of Music*, Oxford, Clarendon Press, 1992, p. 278.

19 Ibid., p. 266.

20 C. Abbate, 'Music – drastic or gnostic?', *Critical Inquiry*, 30 (2004), 505–36 (505, 506, 513 n. 23).

21 Ibid., pp. 534, 532.

22 E. Kealy, 'From craft to art: The case of sound mixers and popular music', *Work and Occupations*, 6/1 (1979), 3–29; A. Hennion, *Les professionnels du disque: Une sociologie des variétés*, Paris, Métailié, 1981; A. Hennion, 'An intermediary between production and consumption: The producer of popular music', *Science, Technology and Human Values*, 14/4 (1989), 400–24; C. Cutler, 'Technology, politics, and contemporary music', *Popular Music*, 4 (1984), 279–300; A. Durant, *Conditions of Music*, New York, State University of New York Press, 1984; D. Toop, *The Rap Attack: African Jive to New York Hip-Hop*, London, Pluto, 1984; D. Laing, *One Chord Wonders: Power and Meaning in Punk Rock*, Milton Keynes, Open University Press, 1985; S. Frith, 'Art versus technology: The strange case of popular music', *Media, Culture and Society*, 8/3 (1986), 263–79; G. Born, 'On modern music culture: Shock, pop and synthesis', *New Formations*, 2 (1987), 51–78; D. Hebdige, *Cut 'n' Mix: Culture, Identity and Caribbean Music*, London, Routledge, 1987; J. Mowitt, 'The sound of music in the era of its electronic reproducibility', in R. Leppert and S. McClary (eds.), *Music and Society*, Cambridge, Cambridge University Press, 1987, pp. 172–97; A. Goodwin, '"Sample and hold": Pop music in the digital age of reproduction', in S. Frith and A. Goodwin (eds.), *On Record*, London, Routledge, 1990, pp. 258–73; P. Théberge, 'The "sound" of music: Technological rationalisation and the

production of popular music', *New Formations*, 8 (1989), 99–111; R. Middleton, *Studying Popular Music*, Philadelphia, Open University Press, 1990, chapter 3; S. Jones, *Rock Formation: Music, Technology and Mass Consumption*, London, Sage, 1992.

23 P. Manuel, *Cassette Culture: Popular Music and Technology in North India*, Chicago, University of Chicago Press, 1993; T. Rose, *Black Noise: Rap Music and Black Culture in Contemporary America*, Hanover, NH, Wesleyan University Press, 1994; M. Chanan, *Repeated Takes: A Short History of Recording and Its Effects on Music*, London, Verso, 1995; P. Thébèrge, *Any Sound You Can Imagine: Making Music/Consuming Technology*, Hanover, NH, University Press of New England, 1997; G. Born, *Rationalizing Culture: IRCAM, Boulez, and the Institutionalization of the Musical Avant-Garde*, Berkeley, University of California Press, 1995; T. Taylor, *Strange Sounds: Music, Technology and Culture*, London, Routledge, 2001; Sterne, *The Audible Past*; N. Cook, *Analysing Musical Multimedia*, Oxford, Oxford University Press, 1998; T. Day, *A Century of Recorded Music: Listening to Musical History*, New Haven, Yale University Press, 2000.

24 Sterne, *The Audible Past*, p. 15.

25 Ibid., p. 21.

26 C. S. Peirce, *Collected Writings*, C. Hartshorne, P. Weiss and A. Burks (eds.), eight volumes, Cambridge, MA, Harvard University Press, 1931–58.

27 E. Rothenbuhler and J. D. Peters, 'Defining phonography: An experiment in theory', *Musical Quarterly*, 81/2 (1997), 242–64 (253, 250).

28 Sterne, *The Audible Past*, p. 214.

29 S. Hall, 'Encoding/decoding', in Centre for Contemporary Cultural Studies (ed.), *Culture, Media, Language*, London, Hutchinson, 1980, pp. 128–38; J. Thompson, *Ideology and Modern Culture*, Cambridge, Polity, 1990.

30 See Bergh and DeNora's chapter in this volume, p. 113.

31 Ibid., p. 112.

32 M. Bull, *Sounding Out the City: Personal Stereos and the Management of Everyday Life*, Oxford, Berg, 2000; M. Bull, *Sound Moves: iPod Culture and Urban Experience*, London, Routledge, 2007; S. Hosokawa, 'The walkman effect', *Popular Music*, 4 (1984), 176.

33 Bergh and DeNora, this volume, p. 115.

34 T. DeNora, *Music in Everyday Life*, Cambridge, Cambridge University Press, 2000; M. Bull, *Sounding Out the City: Personal Stereos and the Management of Everyday Life*, Oxford, Berg, 2000; Bull, *Sound Moves*. It

should be noted that the empirical focus of the studies by Bull and DeNora is British music consumers.

35 All Bull, *Sounding Out the City*, pp. 180–1.

36 Ibid., p. 194.

37 While this analysis may recall aspects of Adorno's critical typology of listening, such as the 'emotional' listener (*Introduction to the Sociology of Music*, E. B. Ashton (trans.), New York, Continuum, 1989, pp. 8–9), there is a significant difference between my argument and his. M. Paddison (*Adorno's Aesthetics of Music*, Cambridge, Cambridge University Press, 1993, p. 216) notes that Adorno's analysis of music consumption 'gives priority to the Object [the musical work] and to the sphere of production'; he continues that it 'recognizes the socially and historically mediated character both of the Object and of the experiencing Subject'. Yet, *pace* Paddison, while Adorno certainly develops an analysis of the social and historical mediation of the musical object, he does not do this for listening in the guise of ordinary subjects. His account of consumption centres on a normative account of 'structural listening' and, in its absence, a hypothesised set of ideal types of regressive listening. In contrast, my approach starts from the assumption that it is not in the power of the musical object alone to effect resistance to subsumption. Any capacity for resistance must instead be theorised in terms of the relations between musical object and listening subject, where the latter demands an analysis of the social and historical conditions of listening, such as those sketched here, as well as the changing forms of subjectivity that are brought to listening.

38 I. Hacking, *Representing and Intervening: Introductory Topics in the Philosophy of Natural Science*, Cambridge, Cambridge University Press, 1983.

39 For an account of how a rhetoric of fidelity attached to recording from its earliest forms, see E. Thompson, 'Machines, music, and the quest for fidelity: Marketing the Edison phonograph in America, 1877–1925', *Musical Quarterly*, 79 (1995), 131–71; and, for an elaboration on this discussion, Rothenbuhler and Peters, 'Defining phonography'.

40 See Savage's personal take in this volume, p. 34.

41 P. Phelan, *Unmarked: The Politics of Performance*, New York, Routledge, 1993, p. 146. I am indebted to Karl Coulthard for this quotation (K. Coulthard, 'Constructing liveness in Duke Ellington's *Ellington at Newport 1956 (Complete)*', paper presented at the 'Text, Media, and Improvisation'

conference, McGill University, Montreal, 21–2 June 2008.

42 See Watson's personal take in this volume, p. 284.

43 D. Kahn, *Noise, Water, Meat: A History of Sound in Art*, Cambridge, MA, MIT Press, 1999, chapter 5, especially pp. 137–9.

44 J. Chadabe, *Electronic Sound: The Past and Promise of Electronic Music*, New Jersey, Prentice-Hall, 1997, p. 26; see also P. Schaeffer, *Traité des objets musicaux*, Paris, Editions du Seuil, 1966.

45 P. Griffiths, *Modern Music: A Concise History from Debussy to Boulez*, London, Thames and Hudson, 1978.

46 C. Keil, 'Motion and feeling through music', *Journal of Aesthetics and Art Criticism*, 24 (1966), 337–49; C. Keil, 'Participatory discrepancies and the power of music', *Cultural Anthropology*, 2 (1987), 275–83; C. Keil, 'The theory of participatory discrepancies: A progress report', *Ethnomusicology*, 39/1 (1995), 1–19; C. Keil and S. Feld, *Music Grooves: Essays and Dialogues*, Chicago, University of Chicago Press, 1994.

47 See Witts's personal take in this volume, p. 80.

48 Ibid., p. 81.

49 Ibid.

50 Meintjes, 'Paul Simon's *Graceland*, South Africa, and the mediation of musical meaning', *Ethnomusicology*, 34/1 (1990), 37–74.

51 See Meintjes's chapter in this volume, p. 84.

52 See Tomes's personal take in this volume, pp. 10–11.

53 Ibid., p. 11.

54 Ibid.

55 See also the early studies of the recording studio by Kealy ('From craft to art') and Hennion (*Les professionnels du disque* and 'An intermediary between production and consumption').

56 B. Latour, *Reassembling the Social: An Introduction to Actor-Network Theory*, Oxford, Oxford University Press, 2005, p. 39.

57 Witts, this volume, p. 82.

58 I refer to Schutz's analysis, after Bergson, of music's capacity to draw performers and listeners into its own temporal unfolding, which he terms music's 'inner time' and opposes to outer, chronological time. The recording experience seems to compound music's inner time. See A. Schutz, 'Making music together', in *Collected Papers*, volume II, The Hague, Nijhoff, 1971, pp. 159–78.

59 Thébèrge, 'The "sound" of music'.

60 Cutler, 'Technology, politics, and contemporary music'; W. Ong, *Orality and Literacy*, London, Methuen, 1982.

61 For the author function see M. Foucault, 'What is an author?', in D. F. Bouchard (ed.), D. F. Bouchard and S. Simon (trans.), *Language, Counter-Memory, Practice*, Oxford, Blackwell, 1977, pp. 124–7; for distributed creativity see G. Born, 'On musical mediation: Ontology, technology and creativity', *twentieth-century music*, 2/1 (2005), 7–36.

62 On the existence of several orders of the social in music, see Born, 'On musical mediation' and 'On the publicisation and privatisation of music', paper presented at conference Music, Sound, and the Reconfiguration of Public and Private Space, University of Cambridge (18–19 April 2008).

63 Meintjes, this volume, p. 86.

64 Ibid., p. 85.

65 Ibid., p. 97.

66 Hebdige, *Cut 'n' Mix*; Toop, *The Rap Attack*; Rose, *Black Noise*.

67 Born, *Rationalizing Culture*, chapters 7 and 8.

68 See www.ccmixter.org.

69 See S. Waters, 'The musical process in the age of digital intervention', online paper, Music Department, University of East Anglia: Advanced Research in Aesthetics in the Digital Arts, 2000, www.ariada.uea.ac.uk/ariadatexts/ariada1/content/Musical_Process.pdf, reflecting on his own compositional practice as conditioned by digital technologies.

70 Born, 'On musical mediation', 34.

71 N. Robertson, 'Music, agency and reproduction in the Internet Age', University of Cambridge (2005). Dissertation submitted for Part 2 of the Social and Political Sciences degree.

72 For recent analyses of circulation in cultural theory, see D. P. Gaonkar and E. Povinelli, 'Technologies of public forms: Circulation, transfiguration, recognition', *Public Culture*, 15/3 (2003) 385–97; J. Heiser, 'Good circulation', *Frieze*, 90 (April 2005), 79–83.

73 D. Murthy, 'Globalization and South Asian musical subcultures: An investigation into music's role in ethnic identity formation amongst second generation diasporic South Asians', PhD summary, University of Cambridge, 2003.

74 Born, 'On musical mediation'.

75 The SBYO is the culmination of a larger movement in which intensive instrumental training is offered to children from low-income neighbourhoods and slums, resulting in a national network of hundreds of youth orchestras and choirs (see M. Shank and L. Schirch, 'Strategic arts-based peacebuilding', *Peace and Change: A Journal of Peace Research*, 33/2 (2008), 217–42).

76 For a critical commentary on the West-Eastern Divan Orchestra, however, see B. Etherington, 'Instrumentalising musical ethics: Edward Said and the West-Eastern Divan Orchestra', *Australasian Music Research*, 9 (2007), 121–9.

77 See Coulthard ('Constructing liveness') for an exemplary case study of the complex mutual mediation between recording and the 'live', and how this has been renewed by digital techniques that make it possible repeatedly to reconstruct and release 'new, improved' representations of mythical past (in this case improvised jazz) performances.

Bibliography

Abbate, C. 'Music – drastic or gnostic?', *Critical Inquiry*, 30 (2004), 505–36

Acord, S. 'Beyond the code: New aesthetic methodologies for the sociology of the arts', *Sociologie de l'art: OPUS* (Questions du méthod), 9 (2006), 69–86

Adorno, T. *Introduction to the Sociology of Music*, E. B. Ashton (trans.), New York, Continuum, 1989

'On the fetish character in music and the regression of listening', in A. Arato and E. Gebhardt (eds.), *The Essential Frankfurt School Reader*, New York, Continuum, 1982, pp. 270–99

Adorno, T. and Horkheimer, M. 'The culture industry: Enlightenment as mass deception', in *Dialectic of Enlightenment*, J. Cumming (trans.), London, Verso/NLB, 1997 (1944), pp. 120–67

Aldous, D. 'Specialist contributions – I', in A. Watts, *Cecil E. Watts: Pioneer of Direct Disc Recording*, London, Agnes Watts, 1972, p. 103

Allingham, R. 'South Africa: The nation of voice', in S. Broughton, M. Ellingham and R. Trillo (eds.), *World Music The Rough Guide: An A–Z of the Music, Musicians and Discs*, London, The Rough Guides, 1999, pp. 638–57

Anderson, B. 'A principle of hope: Recorded music listening practices and the immanence of Utopia', *Geografiska Annaler B*, 3 & 4 (2002), 211–27

Anderton, C. *The Digital Delay Handbook*, New York, Amsco, 1985

Attali, J. *Noise: The Political Economy of Music*, Minneapolis, University of Minnesota Press, 1985

Auslander, P. 'Musical personae', *Drama Review*, 50 (2006), 100–19

B. D. W. 'Paderewski's records. A note', *The Gramophone* (June 1925), 25

Ballou, G. (ed.). *Handbook for Sound Engineers: The New Audio Cyclopedia*, second edition, Carmel, MN, SAMS, 1991

Banfield, S. 'Stage and screen entertainers in the twentieth century', in J. Potter (ed.), *The Cambridge Companion to Singing*, Cambridge, Cambridge University Press, 2000, pp. 63–82

Barclay, R. 'A new species of instrument: The vented trumpet in context', *Historic Brass Society Journal*, 10 (1998), 1–13

Barthes, R. 'The grain of the voice', in *Image–Music–Text*, S. Heath (ed. and trans.), London, Fontana, 1977, pp. 179–89

Batt-Rawden, K. 'Music: A strategy to promote health in rehabilitation? An evaluation of participation in a "music and health promotion project"', *International Journal of Rehabilitation Research*, 2 (2006), 171–3

Baudrillard, J. *Simulacra and Simulation*, S. F. Glaser (trans.), Ann Arbor, University of Michigan Press, 1994

Bazzana, K. *Glenn Gould: The Performer in the Work*, Oxford, Clarendon Press, 1997
  Wondrous Strange: The Life and Art of Glenn Gould, New Haven, Yale University
  Press, 2004
Beament, J. *How We Hear Music*, Woodbridge, Suffolk, Boydell Press, 2001
Benjamin, W. 'The work of art in the age of mechanical reproduction', in H. Arendt
  (ed.), H. Zhon (trans.), *Illuminations*, London, Fontana, 1973, pp. 211–44
Bennett, A., Shank, B., and Toynbee, J. (eds.). *The Popular Music Studies Reader*,
  London, Routledge, 2006
Bergh, A. 'Everlasting love: The sustainability of top-down versus bottom-up
  approaches to music and conflict transformation', in S. Kagan and V. Kirchberg
  (eds.), *Sustainability: A New Frontier for the Arts and Cultures*, Frankfurt-am-
  Main, VAS-Verlag, 2008, pp. 351–82
  'I'd like to teach the world to sing: Music and conflict transformation', *Musicae
  Scientiae*, special issue (2007), 141–57
  'Tape Europe express '86', *Puls*, 8 (1986), 52–3
Blackmore, S. *The Meme Machine*, Oxford, Oxford University Press, 1999
Bloom, A. *The Closing of the American Mind*, New York, Simon and Schuster,
  1988
Bolter, J. D. and Grusin, R. *Remediation: Understanding New Media*, Cambridge, MA,
  MIT Press, 1999
Bookspan, M. 'The BSO and the talking machine', *High Fidelity Magazine* (January
  1958), 50–1, 124–6
Born, G. 'On modern music culture: Shock, pop and synthesis', *New Formations*, 2
  (1987), 51–78
  'On musical mediation: Ontology, technology and creativity', *twentieth-century
  music*, 2/1 (2005), 7–36
  *Rationalizing Culture: IRCAM, Boulez, and the Institutionalization of the Musical
  Avant-Garde*, Berkeley, University of California Press, 1995
Boulez, P. *Boulez on Conducting: Conversations with Cécile Gilly*, R. Stokes (trans.),
  London, Faber and Faber, 2003
Bowen, J. 'Tempo, duration and flexibility: Techniques in the analysis of musical
  performance', *Journal of Musicological Research*, 16 (1996), 111–56
Boyd, J. *White Bicycles: Making Music in the 1960s*, London, Serpent's Tail, 2006
Braun, H.-J. 'Introduction: Technology and the production and reproduction of
  music in the 20th century', in *Music and Technology in the Twentieth Century*,
  H.-J. Braun (ed.), Baltimore, Johns Hopkins University Press, 2002, pp. 9–32
Brennan, M. 'Down beats and rolling stones: An historical comparison of American
  jazz and rock journalism', PhD thesis, University of Stirling (2007)
  'The rough guide to critics: Musicians discuss the role of the music press', *Popular
  Music*, 25/2 (2006), 221–34
Bridle, M. 'The art of critics and criticism?', *Seen and Heard* editorial (November
  2001), www.musicweb-international.com/SandH/2001/Nov01/editorial.htm
Brock-Nannestad, G. 'The attraction of optical replay of mechanical recordings', in
  Z. Vajda and H. Pichler (eds.), *Proceedings of AES 20th International Conference
  'Archiving, Restoration, and New Methods of Recording'*, Budapest (5–7 October
  2001), pp. 157–61

'Comment on "Peter Copeland, *Equalisation of BBC Disc Recordings*" ', *IASA Journal*, 10 (November 1997), 77–81

'What are the sources of the noises we remove?', in Z. Vajda and H. Pichler (eds.), *Proceedings of AES 20th International Conference 'Archiving, Restoration, and New Methods of Recording'*, Budapest (5–7 October 2001), pp. 175–82

Broughton, S. (ed.). *The Rough Guide to World Music. Vol. 2: Latin and North America, Caribbean, India, Asia and the Pacific*, London, Rough Guides, 2000

Brown, C. 'Historical performance, metronome marks and tempo in Beethoven symphonies', *Early Music*, 19 (1991), 247–60

Bruhn Jensen, K., and Larsen, P. 'The sounds of change: Representations of music in European newspapers 1960–2000', in J. Gripsrud and L. Weibull (eds.), *Stable Change: European Media and Public Spheres 1960–2000*, Bristol, Intellect (in press)

Bruyninckx, W. *60 Years of Recorded Jazz, 1917–1977*, Mechelen, Belgium, Bruyninckx, 1980

Bull, M. *Sounding Out the City: Personal Stereos and the Management of Everyday Life*, Oxford, Berg, 2000

Sound Moves: iPod Culture and Urban Experience, London, Routledge, 2007

Burgess, R. J. *The Art of Music Production*, second edition, London, Omnibus Press, 2001

Cage, J. *Silence: Lectures and Writings*, Middletown, CT, Wesleyan University Press, 1961

Camras, M. (ed.). *Magnetic Tape Recording*, New York, van Nostrand Reinhold, 1985

Caskett, J. 'Dance records', *The Gramophone* (April 1923), 21

Chadabe, J. *Electronic Sound: The Past and Promise of Electronic Music*, New Jersey, Prentice-Hall, 1997

Chanan, M. *Repeated Takes: A Short History of Recording and Its Effects on Music*, London, Verso, 1995

Chew, V. *Talking Machines*, London, Her Majesty's Stationery Office (1981)

Chislett, W. A. 'The Gramophone: 1923–1973. A personal reminiscence', *The Gramophone* (June 1973), 31

Christgau, R. *Any Old Way You Choose It*, Baltimore, Penguin, 1973

Clark, R. 'Mixing forum: Four top professionals talk gear and techniques', *Mix* (May 1997), 50

Clarke, E. 'Music and psychology', in M. Clayton *et al.* (eds.), *The Cultural Study of Music*, London, Routledge, 2003, pp. 113–23

Ways of Listening: An Ecological Approach to the Perception of Musical Meaning, Oxford, Oxford University Press, 2005

Clarke, E., and Davidson, J. 'The body in performance', in W. Thomas (ed.), *Composition–Performance–Reception: Studies in the Creative Process in Music*, Aldershot, Ashgate, 1998, pp. 74–92

Clough, F., and Cuming, G. *The World's Encyclopaedia of Recorded Music* (including First Supplement 1950–1), London, Sidgwick and Jackson, 1952; Second Supplement 1951–2 (1953); Third Supplement 1953–5 (1957); online at www.charm.kcl.ac.uk/discography/disco_resources.html

Clynes, M. 'Expressive microstructure in music, linked to living qualities', in J. Sundberg (ed.), *Studies of Musical Performance*, Stockholm, Royal Swedish Academy of Music, 1983, pp. 76–181

Cone, J. F. *Adelina Patti: Queen of Hearts*, Aldershot, Scolar Press, 1993

Conner, L. *Spreading the Gospel of Modern Dance: Newspaper Dance Criticism in the United States, 1850–1935*, Pittsburgh, University of Pittsburgh Press, 1997

Cook, N. *Analysing Musical Multimedia*, Oxford, Oxford University Press, 1998

  'The conductor and the theorist: Furtwängler, Schenker, and the first movement of Beethoven's Ninth Symphony', in J. Rink (ed.), *The Practice of Performance: Studies in Musical Interpretation*, Cambridge, Cambridge University Press, 1995, pp. 105–25

  'Squaring the circle: Phrase arching in recordings of Chopin's mazurkas', *Musica Humana*, 1 (forthcoming)

Coplan, D. *In Township Tonight! South Africa's Black City Music and Theatre*, second edition, Chicago, University of Chicago Press, 2008

Crabbe, J. *Hi Fi in the Home*, London, Blandford, 1973

Crafts, S. D., Cavicchi, D., and Keil, C. *My Music*, Hanover, NH, University Press of New England, 1993

Culshaw, J. *Putting the Record Straight*, London, Secker and Warburg, 1981

Cutler, C. 'Technology, politics, and contemporary music', *Popular Music*, 4 (1984), 279–300

Daley, D. 'Kevin Killen: The engineer becomes producer', *Mix* (October 1989), 64

Daniel, O. *Stokowski: A Counterpoint of View*, New York, Dodd, Mead and Co. 1982

Darrell, R. D. *The Gramophone Shop Encyclopedia of Recorded Music*, New York, The Gramophone Shop, 1932

Davidson, J. W., and Coulam, A. 'Exploring jazz and classical solo singing performance behaviours: A preliminary step towards understanding performer creativity', in G. Wiggins (ed.), *Musical Creativity: Current Research in Theory and Practice*, Oxford, Oxford University Press, 2006, pp. 181–99

Dawkins, R. *The Selfish Gene*, Oxford, Oxford University Press, 1979 (revised edition 1989)

Day, T. *A Century of Recorded Music: Listening to Musical History*, New Haven, Yale University Press, 2000

de Marinis, M. *The Semiotics of Performance*, A. O'Healy (trans.), Bloomington, Indiana University Press, 1993

DeNora, T. 'Aesthetic agency and musical practice: New directions in the sociology of music and emotion', in P. N. Juslin and J. A. Sloboda (eds.), *Music and Emotion: Theory and Research*, Oxford, Oxford University Press, 2001, pp. 161–80

  Beethoven and the Construction of Genius: Musical Politics in Vienna 1792–1803, Berkeley, University of California Press, 1997

  'Health and music in everyday life – a theory of practice', *Psyke & Logos*, 1 (2007), 271–87

  'Music as agency in Beethoven's Vienna', in R. Eyerman and L. McCormick (eds.), *Myth, Meaning and Performance*, Boulder, Paradigm Publishers, 2006, pp. 103–20

  Music in Everyday Life, Cambridge, Cambridge University Press, 2000

  'The role of music in intimate culture: A case study', *Feminism and Psychology*, 2 (2002), 176–81

Devine, P. 'The 1970s and after: The political economy of inflation and the crisis of social democracy', *Soundings*, 32 (Spring 2006), 146–61

Dockwray, R., and Moore, A. 'The establishment of the virtual performance space in rock', *twentieth-century music* (forthcoming)

Doctor, J. *The BBC and Ultra-Modern Music 1922–36: Shaping a Nation's Tastes*, Cambridge, Cambridge University Press, 1999

Dougall, R. *In and Out of the Box: An Autobiography*, London, Collins and Harvill Press, 1973

Doyle, P. *Echo and Reverb: Fabricating Space in Popular Music Recording 1900–1960*, Middletown, CT, Wesleyan University Press, 2005

Dreyfus, L. 'Early music defended against its devotees: A theory of historical performance in the twentieth century', *Musical Quarterly*, 49 (1983), 297–322

Durant, A. *Conditions of Music*, New York, State University of New York Press, 1984

Eisenberg, E. *The Recording Angel: The Experience of Music From Aristotle to Zappa*, New York, Penguin Books, 1987

Elam, K. *The Semiotics of Theatre and Drama*, London, Methuen, 1980

Elste, M. 'Hindemiths Versuche "grammophonplatten-eigener Stücke" im Kontext einer Ideengeschichte der Mechanischen Musik im 20. Jahrhundert', *Hindemith-Jahrbuch. Annales Hindemith*, 25 (1996), 195–221

    Meilensteine der Bach-Interpretation 1750–2000: Eine Werkgeschichte im Wandel, Stuttgart and Weimar, Metzler; Kassel, Bärenreiter, 2000

    'Die Musik, der Lautsprecher, der Bildschirm und ich. Ein Essay über Musik im Fernsehen', *Musica*, 40/1 (1986), 18–21

Eno, B. *A Year with Swollen Appendices*, London, Faber and Faber, 1996

Etherington, B. 'Instrumentalising musical ethics: Edward Said and the West-Eastern Divan Orchestra', *Australasian Music Research*, 9 (2007), 121–9

Eyerman, R., and Jamison, A. *Music and Social Movements: Mobilizing Traditions in the Twentieth Century*, Cambridge, Cambridge University Press, 1998

Eyerman, R., and McCormick, L. (eds.). *Myth, Meaning and Performance: Toward a New Cultural Sociology of the Arts*, Boulder, Paradigm Publishers, 2006

Fabian, D. *Bach Performance Practice, 1945–1975*, Aldershot, Ashgate, 2003

Fellgett, P. B. 'Some comparisons of digital and analogue audio recording', *The Radio and Electronic Engineer*, 53 (February 1983), 55–62

Fine, T. 'The dawn of commercial digital recording', *ARSC Journal*, 39/1 (Spring 2008), 1–17

Fitzgerald, P. *Human Voices*, London, Collins, 1980

Forde, E. 'Music journalists, music press officers and the consumer music press in the UK', PhD thesis, University of Westminster (2001)

Foreman, L. 'Saved from oblivion', *Classic Record Collector*, 49 (Summer 2007), 21–3

    'Thirties off the air', *International Classical Record Collector*, 6/21 (Summer 2000), 7–8

Foucault, M. 'What is an author?', in D. F. Bouchard (ed.), D. F. Bouchard and S. Simon (trans.), *Language, Counter-Memory, Practice*, Oxford, Blackwell, 1977, pp. 124–7

Fox, C. (comment on Miles Davis), *The Gramophone* (June 1957), 32

    (comment on Victor Feldman), *The Gramophone* (June 1959), 34

Fox, T. *In the Groove: The People Behind the Music*, New York, St Martin's Press, 1986

Friedman, H. S. 'Surface markings on Gramophone Company and Victor Records', *ARSC Journal*, 34/2 (2003), 135–59

Frith, S. 'Art versus technology: The strange case of popular music', *Media, Culture and Society*, 8/3 (1986), 263–79

　Performing Rites: On the Value of Popular Music, Cambridge, MA, Harvard University Press, 1996

　Review of Caber Music, Edinburgh, Caber and the Scottish Arts Council, 2005

Fülöp, P. *Mahler Discography*, New York, Kaplan Foundation, 1995

Gabrielsson, A. 'The influence of musical structure on emotional expression', in P. N. Juslin and J. A. Sloboda (eds.), *Music and Emotion; Theory and Research*, Oxford, Oxford University Press, 2001, pp. 223–48

Gaisberg, F. W. *Music on Record*, London, Robert Hale, 1946

Gallagher, J. 'Cosimo: A conversation with the Dean of New Orleans recording', *Mix* (March 1996), 99

Gaonkar, D. P. and Povinelli, E. 'Technologies of public forms: Circulation, transfiguration, recognition', *Public Culture*, 15/3 (2003), 385–97

Garofalo, R. *Rockin' the Boat: Mass Music and Mass Movements*, Boston, MA, South End Press, 1992

Gelatt, R. *The Fabulous Phonograph 1877–1977*, second revised edition, London, Cassell, 1977

Gibson, J. J. 'The theory of affordances', in R. E. Shaw and J. Bransford (eds.), *Perceiving, Acting, and Knowing*, Hillsdale, NJ, Erlbaum, 1977, pp. 67–82

Glock, W. *Notes in Advance: An Autobiography in Music*, Oxford, Oxford University Press, 1991

Goehr, L. *The Imaginary Museum of Musical Works: An Essay in the Philosophy of Music*, Oxford, Clarendon Press, 1992

　'The perfect performance of music and the perfect musical performance', *New Formations*, 27 (1995–6), 1–22

Gomart, E., and Hennion, A. 'A sociology of attachment: Music amateurs, drug users', in J. Law and J. Hassard (eds.), *Actor Network Theory and After*, Oxford, Blackwell, 1999, pp. 220–47

Goodwin, A. ' "Sample and hold": Pop music in the digital age of reproduction', in S. Frith and A. Goodwin (eds.), *On Record*, London, Routledge, 1990, pp. 258–73

Goody, J. and Watt, I. 'The consequences of literacy', *Comparative Studies in Society and History*, 5/3 (1963), 304–45

Gorman, P. *In Their Own Write: Adventures in the Music Press*, London, Sanctuary, 2001

Granata, C. L. *Sessions with Sinatra: Frank Sinatra and the Art of Recording*, Chicago, A Cappella, 1999

Gray, M. 'Discography: Its prospects and problems', *Notes* 35/3 (March 1979), 578–92

Greene, P. D. 'Introduction: Wired sounds and sonic cultures', in P. D. Greene and T. G. Porcello (eds.), *Wired for Sound: Engineering and Technologies in Sonic Cultures*, Middletown, CT, Wesleyan University Press, 2005, pp. 1–22

Greenfield, E., March, I., and Layton, R. *Guide to Compact Discs*, London, Penguin, 1994

Greig, D. 'Sight readings: Notes on *a cappella* performance practice', *Early Music*, 23 (1995), 125–48

Griffiths, J. *Nimbus: Technology Serving the Arts*, London, Andre Deutsch, 1995

Griffiths, P. *Modern Music: A Concise History from Debussy to Boulez*, London, Thames and Hudson, 1978

Gronow, P., and Saunio, I. *An International History of the Recording Industry*, London, Cassell, 1998

Grubb, S. R. *Music Makers on Record*, London, Hamish Hamilton, 1986

Guernsey Jr, O. L. (ed.). *Broadway Song and Story: Playwrights, Lyricists, Composers Discuss Their Hits*, New York, Dodd, Mead, 1985

Gumbrecht, H. U. and Pfeiffer, K. L. *Materialities of Communication*, Stanford, Stanford University Press, 1994

Hacking, I. *Representing and Intervening: Introductory Topics in the Philosophy of Natural Science*, Cambridge, Cambridge University Press, 1983

Hall, S. 'Encoding/decoding', in Centre for Contemporary Cultural Studies (ed.), *Culture, Media, Language*, London, Hutchinson, 1980, pp. 128–38

Hammond, J. *John Hammond on Record: An Autobiography*, New York, Ridge Press/Summit Books, 1981

Harries, G., and Wahl-Jorgensen, K. 'The culture of arts journalists: Elitists, saviors or manic depressives?', *Journalism*, 8 (2007), 619–39

Harvith, J., and Harvith, S. E. (eds.). *Edison, Musicians, and the Phonograph: A Century in Retrospect*, New York, Greenwood Press, 1987

Hebdige, D. *Cut 'n' Mix: Culture, Identity and Caribbean Music*, London, Routledge, 1987

Heiser, J. 'Good circulation', *Frieze*, 90 (April 2005), 79–83

Hennion, A. 'Baroque and rock: Music, mediators and musical taste', *Poetics*, 6 (1997), 415–35

 'An intermediary between production and consumption: The producer of popular music', *Science, Technology and Human Values*, 14/4 (1989), 400–24

 'Music lovers, taste as performance', *Theory, Culture and Society*, 5 (2001), 1–22

 La passion musicale: Une sociologie de la médiation, Paris, Diffusion Seuil, 1993

 Les professionnels du disque: Une sociologie des variétés, Paris, Métailié, 1981

 'Those things that hold us together: Taste and sociology', *Cultural Sociology*, 1 (2007), 97–114

Hetherington, K. *Expressions of Identity*, London, Sage, 1998

Higgins, C. 'Look sharp: Chance to buy live CD straight after the concert', *Guardian*, 7 February 2006, www.guardian.co.uk/uk/2006/feb/07/arts.artsnews1

Honing, H., and Desain, P. 'Tempo curves considered harmful', in J. Kramer (ed.), 'Time in contemporary musical thought', *Contemporary Music Review*, 7/2 (1993), 123–38

Horowitz, J. *Understanding Toscanini*, London, Faber and Faber, 1987

Hosokawa, S. 'The walkman effect', *Popular Music*, 4 (1984), 165–80

Hutchby, I. 'Technologies, texts and affordances', *Sociology*, 35/2 (2001), 441–56

Innis, H. *The Bias of Communication*, Toronto, University of Toronto Press, 1991 (1951)

Jackson, B. 'Los Lobos paint their masterpiece', *Mix* (October 1992), 202

Jackson, E. Review of Benny Goodman recordings, *The Gramophone* (June 1946), 7

Jakobson, R. 'Closing statement: Linguistics and poetics', in T. A. Sebeok (ed.), *Style in Language*, New York, Technology Press of MIT, 1960, pp. 350–77

Jan, S. *The Memetics of Music: A Neo-Darwinian View of Musical Structure and Culture*, Aldershot, Ashgate, 2007

Jarvis, S. *Adorno: A Critical Introduction*, Cambridge, Polity, 1998

Jenkins, R. *Social Identity*, London, Routledge, 2004

Jepsen, J. G. *Jazz Records, 1942–1969*, Copenhagen, Nordisk Tidsskrift Forlag, 1963

Johnson, J. H. *Listening in Paris: A Cultural History*, Berkeley, University of California Press, 1995

Johnson, P. 'The legacy of recordings', in J. Rink (ed.), *Musical Performance: A Guide to Understanding*, Cambridge, Cambridge University Press, 2002, pp. 197–212

Jones, H. 'US military lawyer slams Guantanamo procedures'. Paper Chase, 2006, http://jurist.law.pitt.edu/paperchase/2006/03/us-military-lawyer-slams-guantanamo.php

Jones, S. *Rock Formation: Music, Technology and Mass Consumption*, London, Sage, 1992

Jordanger, V., Popov, A., Aas Rustad, S., and Vitvitsky, A. *The North Caucuses Dialogue Project: Report on the IPC Two-Years Project 2004–2006.* Trondheim, Building Peaces, http://buildingpeaces.org/filer/TheIPCtwoyearproject2004–2006.pdf

Juslin, P. N., and Sloboda, J. A. (eds.). *Music and Emotion: Theory and Research*, Oxford, Oxford University Press, 2001

Kahn, D. *Noise, Water, Meat: A History of Sound in Art*, Cambridge, MA, MIT Press, 1999

Kański, J. 'Über die Aufführungsstile der Werke Chopins: Einige allgemeine Probleme der Aufführung auf Grund von Schallplattenaufnahmen', in Z. Lissa (ed.), *The Book of the First International Musicological Congress devoted to the Works of Chopin: Warszawa 16th–22nd February 1960*, Warsaw, PWN Polish Scientific Publishers, 1963, pp. 444–54

Katz, M. *Capturing Sound: How Technology Has Changed Music*, Berkeley, University of California Press, 2004

'The phonograph effect'. PhD thesis, University of Michigan (1999)

Kazdin, A. *Glenn Gould at Work: Creative Lying*, New York, E. P. Dutton, 1989

Kealy, E. 'From craft to art: The case of sound mixers and popular music', *Work and Occupations*, 6/1 (1979), 3–29

'The real rock revolution: Sound mixers, social inequality, and the aesthetics of popular music production'. PhD thesis, Northwestern University (1974)

Keil, C. 'Motion and feeling through music', *Journal of Aesthetics and Art Criticism*, 24 (1966), 337–49

'Participatory discrepancies and the power of music', *Cultural Anthropology*, 2 (1987), 275–83.

'The theory of participatory discrepancies: A progress report', *Ethnomusicology*, 39/1 (1995), 1–19

Keith, C. and Feld, S. *Music Grooves: Essays and Dialogues*, Chicago, University of Chicago Press, 1994

Kelly, A. *His Master's Voice: The German Catalogue: A Complete Numerical Catalogue of German Gramophone Recordings Made from 1898 to 1929 in Germany, Austria, and Elsewhere by the Gramophone Company Ltd = Die Stimme seines Herrn*, Westport, CT, Greenwood, 1994

Kennedy, R. *Jelly Roll, Bix, and Hoagy: Gennett Studios and the Birth of Recorded Jazz*, Bloomington, Indiana University Press, 1994

Kernfeld, B. (ed.). *The New Grove Dictionary of Jazz*, London, Macmillan, 1988

Kershaw, A. 'Bob Dylan: How I found the man who shouted "Judas"', *Independent* (23 September 2005), www.independent.co.uk/arts-entertainment/music/features/bob-dylan-how-i-found-the-man-who-shouted-judas-507883.html

Kershaw, B. *The Politics of Performance: Radical Theatre as Cultural Intervention*, London, Routledge, 1992

Kertz-Welzel, A. 'The "magic" of music: Archaic dreams in romantic aesthetics and an education in aesthetics', *Philosophy of Music Education Review*, 1 (2005), 77–94

Kivy, P. *The Possessor and the Possessed: Handel, Mozart, Beethoven and the Idea of Musical Genius*, New Haven, Yale University Press, 2001

Korner, A. (roundup of new releases of 'Negro gospel music'), *The Gramophone* (June 1960), 46

Kusek, D., and Leonhard, G. *The Future of Music: Manifesto for the Digital Music Revolution*, Boston, MA, Berklee Press, 2005

Lacasse, S. 'The phonographic voice: Paralinguistic features and phonographic staging', in A. Bayley (ed.), *Recorded Music: Performance, Culture, and Technology*, Cambridge, Cambridge University Press (forthcoming)

Laing, D. *One Chord Wonders: Power and Meaning in Punk Rock*, Milton Keynes, Open University Press, 1985

Lake, S., and Griffiths, P. (eds.). *Horizons Touched: The Music of ECM*, London, Granta, 2007

Landau, J. *It's Too Late To Stop Now*, San Francisco, Straight Arrow, 1972

Lanza, J. *Elevator Music: A Surreal History of Muzak, Easy-Listening and Other Moodsong*, Ann Arbor, University of Michigan Press, 2004

Lash, S. M., and Urry, J. *Economies of Signs and Space*, London, Sage Publications, 1994

Lastra, J. *Sound Technology and the American Cinema: Perception, Representation, Modernity*, New York, Columbia University Press, 2000

Latour, B. *Reassembling the Social: An Introduction to Actor-Network Theory*, Oxford, Oxford University Press, 2005

Lebrecht, N. *The Life and Death of Classical Music*, New York, Anchor, 2007

Leech-Wilkinson, D. *The Changing Sound of Music: Approaches to Studying Recorded Musical Performances* www.charm.kcl.ac.uk/studies/chapters/intro.html

The Modern Invention of Medieval Music, Cambridge, Cambridge University Press, 2002

'Musicology and performance', in Z. Blazekovic (ed.), *Music's Intellectual History: Founders, Followers and Fads*, New York, RILM (forthcoming).

'Portamento and musical meaning', *Journal of Musicological Research*, 25 (2006), 233–61

'Sound and meaning in recordings of Schubert's "Die junge Nonne"', *Musicae Scientiae*, 11/2 (2007), 209–33

Lena, J. C. 'Meaning and membership: Samples in rap music, 1979 to 1995', *Poetics*, 32/3–4 (2004), 297–310

Leppert, R. *The Sight of Sound: Music Representation and the History of the Body*, Berkeley, University of California Press, 1995

Lesiuk, T. 'The effect of music listening on work performance', *Psychology of Music*, 2 (2005), 173–91

Lewisohn, M. *The Beatles Recording Sessions: The Official Abbey Road Studio Session Notes 1962–1970*, New York, Harmony Books, 1988

Lindberg, U., Guomundsson, G., Michelsen, M., and Weisethaunet, H. *Rock Criticism from the Beginning: Amusers, Bruisers and Cool-Headed Cruisers*, New York, Peter Lang, 2005

Lochner, L. P. *Fritz Kreisler*, New York, Macmillan, 1950

Lockard, C. A. *Dance of Life: Popular Music and Politics in Southeast Asia*, Honolulu, University of Hawaii Press, 1998

MacDonald, R. A. R., Hargreaves, D. J., and Miell, D. (eds.). *Musical Identities*, Oxford, Oxford University Press, 2002

MacKenzie, D., and Wachjman, J. *The Social Shaping of Technology*, second edition, Buckingham, Open University Press, 1999

Maisonneuve, S. 'Between history and commodity: The production of a musical patrimony through the record in the 1920–1930s', *Poetics*, 2 (2001), 89–108

Manovich, L. *The Language of New Media*, Cambridge, MA, MIT Press, 2001

Manuel, P. *Cassette Culture: Popular Music and Technology in North India*, Chicago, University of Chicago Press, 1993

Marcus, G. *Mystery Train*, New York, Dutton, 1975

Maré, G. *Ethnicity and Politics in South Africa*, London, Zed Books, 1993

Marmorstein, G. *The Label: The Story of Columbia Records*, New York, Thunder's Mouth Press, 2007

Marsh, D. *Glory Days: Bruce Springsteen in the 1980s*, New York, Pantheon, 1987
 The Heart of Rock and Soul: The 1001 Greatest Singles Ever Made, New York, NAL, 1989

Martin, C. ' "We feed off each other": Embodiment, phenomenology and listener receptivity of Nirvana's *In Utero*'. MA dissertation, Bowling Green State University (2006)

Martland, P. 'A business history of the Gramophone Company Ltd (1887–1918)'. PhD thesis, University of Cambridge (1992)

Massey, H. *Behind the Glass: Top Record Producers Tell How They Craft the Hits*, San Francisco, Backbeat Books, 2000

Mathieson, K. *Giant Steps: Bebop and the Creators of Modern Jazz*, Edinburgh, Canongate, 1999

McLuhan, M. *Understanding Media: The Extensions of Man*, London, Routledge, 2001 (1964)

Meintjes, L. 'Paul Simon's *Graceland*, South Africa, and the mediation of musical meaning', *Ethnomusicology*, 34/1 (1990), 37–74
 'Reaching overseas: South African sound engineers, technology and tradition', in P. D. Greene and T. G. Porcello (eds.), *Wired for Sound*, Middletown, CT, Wesleyan University Press, 2005, pp. 23–46

Sound of Africa! Making Music Zulu in a South African Studio, Durham, NC, Duke University Press, 2003

Melchior-Bonnet, S. *The Mirror: A History*, New York, Routledge, 2002

Messing, S. *Schubert in the European Imagination*, volumes I and II, Rochester, NY, University of Rochester Press, 2006–7

Middleton, R. *Studying Popular Music*, Philadelphia, Open University Press, 1990

Miller, D. *Materiality*, Durham, NC, Duke University Press, 2005

Miller, R., and Boar, R. *The Incredible Music Machine*, London, Quartet/Visual Arts, 1982

Milsom, D. *Theory and Practice in Late Nineteenth-Century Violin Performance*, Aldershot, Ashgate, 2003

Molenda, M. 'Production values: Listen to the music', *Electronic Musician* (April 1996), 69

Moorefield, V. *The Producer as Composer: Shaping the Sounds of Popular Music*, Cambridge, MA, MIT Press, 2005

Morris, C. 'We're an American band', *Pulse* (April 1996), 45

Morton, D. *Sound Recording: The Life Story of a Technology*, Westport, CT, Greenwood Press, 2005

Mowitt, J. 'The sound of music in the era of its electronic reproducibility', in R. Leppert and S. McClary (eds.), *Music and Society*, Cambridge, Cambridge University Press, 1987, pp. 172–97

Mugan, C. 'With the rise of downloads are albums now dead?', *Independent* (29 June 2007), www.independent.co.uk/arts-entertainment/music/features/with-the-rise-of-downloads-are-albums-now-dead-455056.html

Musgrave, M., and Sherman, B. D. *Performing Brahms: Early Evidence of Performance Style*, Cambridge, Cambridge University Press, 2003

Myers, K. *Index to Record Reviews*, Volume IV, Boston, MA, G. K. Hall and Co., 1978

Nettl, B. *The Study of Ethnomusicology: Twenty-nine Issues and Concepts*, Urbana, University of Illinois Press, 1983

Nombuso Dlamini, S. 'The construction, meaning and negotiation of ethnic identities in KwaZulu-Natal', in A. Zegeye (ed.), *Social Identities in New South Africa: After Apartheid*, Cape Town, Kwela Books, 2001, pp. 195–222

North, A. C., David, J., and McKendrick, J. 'The influence of in-store music on wine selections', *Journal of Applied Psychology*, 2 (1999), 271–6

O'Connell, C. *The Other Side of the Record*, New York, Alfred A. Knopf, 1947

O'Hara, K., and Brown, B. (eds.). *Consuming Music Together: Social and Collaborative Aspects of Music Consumption Technologies*, New York, Springer, 2006

Ong, W. *Orality and Literacy*, London, Methuen, 1982

Osborne, R. 'An historical anatomy of the vinyl record', PhD thesis, London Consortium/Birkbeck College (2008)

Owsinski, B. 'You don't know jack', *EQ* (May 1996), 55

Paddison, M. *Adorno's Aesthetics of Music*, Cambridge, Cambridge University Press, 1993

Page, T. (ed.). *The Glenn Gould Reader*, New York, Vintage, 1990

Pandit, S. A. *From Making to Music: The History of Thorn EMI*, London, Hodder and Stoughton, 1996

Parakilas, J. (ed.). *Piano Roles: Three Hundred Years of Life with the Piano*, New Haven, Yale University Press, 2002

Parsonage, C. *The Evolution of Jazz in Britain, 1880–1935*, Aldershot, Ashgate, 2005

Patmore, D., and Clarke, E. 'Making and hearing virtual worlds: John Culshaw and the art of record production', *Musicae Scientiae*, 11/2 (2007), 269–93

Pederson, S. 'Beethoven and masculinity', in S. Burnham and M. P. Steinberg (eds.), *Beethoven and His World*, Oxford, Princeton University Press, 2000, pp. 313–31

Peirce, C. S. *Collected Writings*, C. Hartshorne, P. Weiss and A. Burks (eds.), eight volumes, Cambridge, MA, Harvard University Press, 1931–58

Perlman, M. 'Golden ears and meter readers: The contest for epistemic authority in audiophilia', *Social Studies of Science*, 5 (2004), 783–807

Pettan, S. (ed.). *Music, Politics, and War: Views From Croatia*, Zagreb, Institute of Ethnology and Folklore Research, 1998

Phelan, P. *Unmarked: The Politics of Performance*, New York, Routledge, 1993

Philip, R. *Early Recordings and Musical Style: Changing Tastes in Instrumental Performance, 1900–1950*, Cambridge, Cambridge University Press, 1992

  Performing Music in the Age of Recording, New Haven, Yale University Press, 2004

  'The romantic and the old-fashioned', in E. Kjellberg, E. Lundkvist and J. Roström (eds.), *The Interpretation of Romantic and Late-Romantic Music: Papers Read at the Organ Symposium in Stockholm, 3–12 September 1998*, Uppsala, Uppsala Universitet, 2002, 11–31

Pinnock, T. '20 years of The English Concert', *Early Music News*, 174 (May 1993), 1

Plant Armstrong, R. *The Affecting Presence: An Essay in Humanistic Anthropology*, Urbana, University of Illinois Press, 1971

Porcello, T. G. 'Music mediated as live in Austin: Sound, technology, and recording practice', in P. D. Greene and T. G. Porcello (eds.), *Wired for Sound: Engineering and Technologies in Sonic Cultures*, Middletown, CT, Wesleyan University Press, 2005, pp. 103–17

  'Sonic artistry: Music, discourse, and technology in the sound recording studio'. PhD thesis, University of Texas at Austin (1996)

  'Speaking of sound: Language and the professionalization of sound-recording engineers', *Social Studies of Science*, 34/5 (2004), 733–58

Prendergast, M. *The Ambient Century: From Mahler to Trance – the Evolution of Sound in the Electronic Age*, London, Bloomsbury, 2000

Pulling, M. J. L. (ed.). 'The magnetophon sound recording and reproducing system'. British Intelligence Objectives Subcommittee, B.I.O.S. Final Report No. 951 (1946)

Randolph, D. 'Records in review', *High Fidelity*, 3/1 (March/April 1954), 49

Rayner, F. J. W., Vaseghi, S. V., and Stickells, L. 'Digital signal processing methods for the removal of scratches and surface noise from gramophone recordings', in *Archiving the Audio-Visual Heritage – A Joint Technical Symposium*, Berlin, Stiftung Deutsche Kinemathek, 1988, pp. 109–11

Read, O., and Welch, W. L. *From Tin Foil to Stereo: The Evolution of the Phonograph*, Indianapolis, Howard W. Sams, 1959

Reger, S. N. 'The string instrument vibrato', in C. E. Seashore (ed.), *The Vibrato*, Studies in the Psychology of Music 1, Iowa City, University of Iowa, 1932, pp. 305–43

Repp, B. 'Diversity and commonality in music performance: An analysis of timing microstructure in Schumann 's "Träumerei"', *Journal of the Acoustical Society of America*, 92/5 (1992), 2546–68

Reyes Schramm, A. 'Music and tradition: From native to adopted land through the refugee experience', *Yearbook for Traditional Music*, 21 (1989), 25–35

Richerson, P. J., and Boyd, R. *Not by Genes Alone: How Culture Transformed Human Evolution*, Chicago, University of Chicago Press, 2005

Ritosalmi-Kisner, K., and Rooney, D. D. 'Minneapolis Symphony Orchestra/ Minnesota Orchestra: A discography of recordings, 1924–2003', *ARSC Journal*, 34/2 (2003), 160–93

Robertson, C. A. 'Jazz and all that', *Audio* (October 1957), 49

Rolling Stone Record Review. New York, Pocket Books, 1971

Rose, T. *Black Noise: Rap Music and Black Culture in Contemporary America*, Hanover, NH, Wesleyan University Press, 1994

Rosenberg, W. Review of Lukas Foss and the Zimbler Sinfonietta, *Bartók: Divertimento for Strings, HiFi-Stereophonie*, 7/9 (1968), 670

Rothenbuhler, E. and Peters, J. D. 'Defining phonography: An experiment in theory', *Musical Quarterly*, 81/2 (1997), 242–64

'Reminiscing – the stereophonic record', *Journal of the Acoustical Society of America*, 77/4 (1985), 1332

Rust, B. *The American Dance Band Discography*, New Rochelle, Arlington House, 1975

Jazz Records, 1897–1942, fourth edition, New Rochelle, Arlington House, 1978

Sackville-West, E., and Shawe-Taylor, D. *The Record Guide*, London, Collins, 1951

The Record Year: A Guide to the Year's Gramophone Records Including a Complete Guide to Long-Playing Records, London, Collins, 1952

Samson, J. 'Chopin, Fryderyk Franciszek', section 11: Reception, *Grove Music Online*, L. Macy (ed.), www.grovemusic.com

Sanders, A. (ed.). *Walter Legge: Words and Music*, London, Duckworth, 1998

Schaeffer, P. *Traité des objets musicaux*, Paris, Editions du Seuil, 1966

Schmidt Horning, S. 'Chasing sound: The culture and technology of recording studios in America, 1877–1977'. PhD thesis, Case Western Reserve University (2002)

Schutz, A. 'Making music together', in *Collected Papers*, volume II, The Hague, Nijhoff, 1971, pp. 159–78

Schwarzkopf, E. *On and Off the Record: A Memoir of Walter Legge*, London, Faber and Faber, 1982

Scott, H. H. 'The design of dynamic noise suppressors', *Proceedings of the National Electronics Conference*, volume III, Chicago (3–5 November 1947), p. 25

Shank, M. and Schirch, L. 'Strategic arts-based peacebuilding', *Peace and Change: A Journal of Peace Research*, 33/2 (2008), 217–42

Shennan, S. *Genes, Memes and Human History*, London, Thames and Hudson, 2002

Shipton, A. *A New History of Jazz*, New York, Continuum, 2007

Sidran, B. *Talking Jazz: An Oral History*, New York, Da Capo, 1995

Simons, D. *Studio Stories*, San Francisco, Backbeat, 2004

Sleeper, M. B. 'By way of introduction', *High Fidelity*, 1/1 (Summer 1951), 6

Sloboda, J., A. Lamont and A. Greasley, 'Choosing to hear music', in S. Hallam, I. Cross and M. Thaut (eds.), *Oxford Handbook of Music Psychology*, Oxford, Oxford University Press, 2009, pp. 431–40

Small, C. *Musicking: The Meanings of Performing and Listening*, Hanover, NH, Wesleyan University Press, 1998

Smith, G. *Lost in Music*, London, Picador, 2000

Sperber, D. *Explaining Culture: A Naturalist Approach*, Oxford, Blackwell, 1996

Steiner, G. *Real Presences*, London, Faber and Faber, 1989

Sterne, J. *The Audible Past: Cultural Origins of Sound Recording*, Durham, NC, Duke University Press, 2003

Stockfelt, O. 'Adequate modes of listening', in D. Schwarz, A. Kassabian and L. Siegel (eds.), *Keeping Score: Music, Disciplinarity, Culture*, Charlottesville, University of Virginia Press, 1997, pp. 129–46

Suleri, S. *The Rhetoric of English India*, second edition, Chicago, Chicago University Press, 1992

Sundberg, J., Friberg, A., and Frydén, L. 'Rules for automated performance of ensemble music', *Contemporary Music Review*, 3/1 (1989), 89–109

Sutherland, S. Review of the Sugarcubes's *Life's Too Good*, *Melody Maker* (23 April 1988), 38

Swidler, A. 'What anchors cultural practices', in K. D. Knorr-Cetina, T. R. Schatzki and E. Savigny (eds.), *The Practice Turn in Contemporary Theory*, London, Routledge, 2001, pp. 74–92

Symes, C. *Setting the Record Straight: A Material History of Classical Recording*, Middletown, CT, Wesleyan University Press, 2004

Szwed, J. *So What: The Life of Miles Davis*, London, William Heinemann, 2002

Tamm, E. *Brian Eno: His Music and the Vertical Color of Sound*, London, Faber and Faber, 1990

Taruskin, R. 'The pastness of the present and the presence of the past', in N. Kenyon (ed.), *Authenticity and Early Music*, Oxford, Oxford University Press, 1988, pp. 137–207

Text and Act: Essays on Musical Performance, New York, Oxford University Press, 1995

Taylor, T. *Global Pop: Global Music, Global Markets*, London, Routledge, 1997

Strange Sounds: Music, Technology and Culture, London, Routledge, 2001

Théberge, P. *Any Sound You Can Imagine: Making Music/Consuming Technology*, Hanover, NH, University Press of New England, 1997

'The "sound" of music: Technological rationalisation and the production of popular music', *New Formations*, 8 (1989), 99–111

Thompson, E. 'Machines, music, and the quest for fidelity: Marketing the Edison phonograph in America, 1877–1925', *Musical Quarterly*, 79 (1995), 131–71

Thompson, J. *Ideology and Modern Culture*, Cambridge, Polity, 1990

Todd, N. 'A model of expressive timing in tonal music', *Music Perception*, 3 (1985), 33–58

Toop, D. *The Rap Attack: African Jive to New York Hip-Hop*, London, Pluto, 1984

Toynbee, J. *Making Popular Music*, London, Arnold, 2000

Trythall, S. 'Live music in hospitals: A new "alternative" therapy', *Journal of the Royal Society for the Promotion of Health*, 3 (2006), 113–14

Urmson, J. O. 'The ethics of musical performance', in W. Thomas (ed.), *Composition–Performance–Reception: Studies in the Creative Process in Music*, Aldershot, Ashgate, 1998, pp. 74–92

Van Tassel, E. 'Recordings', *Early Music*, 12 (1984), 125–9

Verna, P. 'Marching to his own drum sound, Hugh Padgham beats a path to the top of the industry', *Billboard* (27 July 1996), 54

Wallis, R., and Malm, K. *Big Sounds from Small Peoples: The Music Industry in Small Countries*, London, Constable, 1984

Ward, E. 'Rock Critics RIP!', *American Way* (Autumn 1988), 72–6
'Where have all the rock critics gone?', *Austin Chronicle* (August 1988), 14

Waters, S. 'The musical process in the age of digital intervention', online paper, Music Department, University of East Anglia: Advanced Research in Aesthetics in the Digital Arts, 2000, www.ariada.uea.ac.uk/ariadatexts/ariada1/content/Musical_Process.pdf

Watkinson, J. *The Art of Digital Audio*, third edition, Oxford, Focal Press, 2001
RDAT, Oxford, Focal Press, 1991

Watts, A. *Cecil E. Watts: Pioneer of Direct Disc Recording*, London, Agnes Watts, 1972

Weber, W. 'Did people listen in the 18th century?', *Early Music*, 4 (1997), 678–91
'From miscellany to homogeneity in concert programming', *Poetics*, 2 (2001), 125–34

Welch, C. Review of Genesis's ... *And Then There Were Three*, *Melody Maker* (1 April 1978), 20

Wellburn, R. G. 'The early record review: Jazz criticism's first-born child', *Annual Review of Jazz Studies 3*, New Brunswick, Transaction Books, 1985

Widmer, G. 'In search of the Horowitz factor: Interim report on a musical discovery project', *Proceedings of the 5th International Conference on Discovery Science*, London, Springer Verlag (2002), pp. 13–21

Wiener, A. *The Beatles, the Ultimate Recording Guide*, New York, Facts on File, 1992

Williams, C. 'Does it really matter? Young people and popular music', *Popular Music*, 2 (2001), 223–42

Williams, F. F. 'Records and music in Germany', *The Gramophone* (December 1923), 126–7

Williams, R. *Long Distance Call*, London, Aurum Press, 2000

Wilmsen, E., Dubow, S., and Sharp, J. (eds.). 'Ethnicity and identity in Southern Africa', *Journal of Southern African Studies*, special issue, 20/3 (1994), 347–53

Wilson, J. S. 'Creative jazz', *New York Times*, 5 April 1953, X9

Wilson, P. 'Home recording', *The Gramophone* (March 1931), 513–14

Wimbush, R. (roundup of miscellaneous and dance music releases), *The Gramophone* (June 1940), 16

Wishart, T. *On Sonic Art*, revised edition, London, Harwood Academic Publishers, 1996

Witkin, R. W. *Adorno on Popular Culture*, London, Routledge, 2002

Zak, A. *The Poetics of Rock: Cutting Tracks, Making Records*, Berkeley, University of California Press, 2001

Zaslaw, N. 'Toward the revival of the classical orchestra', *Proceedings of the Royal Musical Association*, 103/1 (1976), 158–87

Discography

Ansermet, Ernest and the Decca String Orchestra. *Ernest Ansermet Conducts Handel.* Koch Historic 3-7708-2H1 (1996)

Baillie, Isobel, Leslie Heward and the Hallé Orchestra. *Handel:* Messiah *('I know that my redeemer liveth').* Columbia DX 1036 (1941)

Basie, Count. *April in Paris.* Verve MG-V 8012 (1955)

Belafonte, Harry. '*Banana Boat [Song] (Day-O)'.* His Master's Voice 45 POP 308 (*c.* 1957)

Bellezza, Vincenzo and the Rome Opera Chorus and Orchestra. *Verdi:* La traviata. Columbia DX 1324/38 (1949)

Boston Symphony Orchestra. *The First Recordings of the Boston Symphony Orchestra.* BSO Classics 171002 (1995)

Boult, Sir Adrian and the Scottish National Orchestra. *Elgar: Symphony No. 2 in E-flat Major.* Waverley SLLP 1022 (1963)

Busch, Fritz and the Glyndebourne Festival Chorus and Orchestra. *Mozart:* Don Giovanni. HMV DB 2961/83 (1936)

Busch Quartet. *Beethoven: Quartet in A Minor, Op. 132.* HMV DB 3375/9 (1937) *Beethoven: Quartet in C-sharp Minor, Op. 131.* HMV DB 2810/4 (1937)

Busser, Henri and the Paris Opéra Chorus and Orchestra. *Gounod:* Faust. HMV C 2122/41 (1932)

Carmichael, Hoagy and the Happy Harmonisits. *Hoagy Carmichael: The First of the Singer Songwriters. Key Cuts 1924–1946.* JSP Records JSP918 (2004) *Those Fabulous Gennetts Vol. 2.* Timeless CBC 1–080 (2002) *Washboard Blues.* Gennett 3066A (1925)

Caruso, Enrico. *Puccini:* Tosca *('Recondita armonia' and 'E lucevan le stelle').* HMV DA 112, Victor Matrices 8347 & 8346 (1909)

Coates, Albert and the London Symphony Orchestra. *Borodin: Symphony No. 2 in B Minor, third movement – Andante.* IMG 5 75486 2 (1929)

Debussy, Claude. *Claude Debussy: The Composer as Pianist.* Pierian Recording Society, Pierian 0001 (2000)

Emerson String Quartet. *Mendelssohn: The Complete String Quartets.* Deutsche Grammophon B0006TN9G2 (2005)

Fall, the, Joy Division, John Cooper Clark and Steel Pulse. *Short Circuit – Live at the Electric Circus.* Virgin VCL 5003 (1978)

Finzi, Christopher, Wilfred Brown and the English Chamber Orchestra. *Finzi:* Dies Natalis. World Record Club/Recorded Music Circle CM 50 (1963)

Formby, George. *George Formby: England's Famed Clown Prince of Song.* JSP Records, JSPCD 1901 (2004)

Foss, Lukas and the Zimbler Sinfonietta. *Bartók: Divertimento for Strings*. Turnabout Vox TV 34 154 S (*c.* 1967)

Fricsay, Ferenc and the Berlin Philharmonic Orchestra. *Tchaikovsky: Symphony No. 6 in B Minor*. Deutsche Grammophon Gesellschaft DGM 18104 (1954)

Galli-Curci, Amelita, *et al. Donizetti: Lucia di Lammermoor ('Chi mi frena') and Verdi: Rigoletto ('Bella figlia dell'amore')*. HMV DQ 102 (1927)

Gavin Bryars Ensemble. *Gavin Bryars: After the Requiem*. ECM Records ECM1424 (1991)

Gilels, Emil. *Haydn: Piano Sonata in C Minor, Hob. XVI:20*. Le Chant du Monde LDA 8310-1 (1960)

Gilels, Emil, Leonid Kogan and Mstislav Rostropovich. *Beethoven: Piano Trio in B-flat Major, Op. 97*. Monitor MC 2010 (1956)

Goodman, Roy and The Hanover Band. *Beethoven: Symphony No. 6, 'Pastoral'*. Nimbus NI5099 (1988)

Gui, Vittorio and the Glyndebourne Festival Chorus and Orchestra. *Mozart:* Le nozze di Figaro. HMV ALPS 1312 & ALP 1313/5 (1955)

Gulda, Friedrich, Hans Swarowsky and the Orchester der Wiener Staatsoper. *Mozart, Piano Concertos No. 21, K. 467 and No. 27, K. 595*. Concert Hall M 2319 (*c.* 1963)

Harnoncourt, Nikolaus, Hans Gillesberger and the Concentus Musicus Wien, Wiener Sängerknaben, Chorus Viennensis. *J. S. Bach: Mass in B Minor BWV232*. Telefunken Das Alte Werk SKH 20 (1968)

Heaton, Roger. *New Music for Multi-tracked Clarinets*. Clarinet Classics CC0009 (1994)

    Tom Johnson: Rational Melodies, Bedtime Stories. Ants AG12 (2006)

Hendrix, Jimi. *Jimi Hendrix: Live at Woodstock*. MCD 11987/111 987-2 (1999)

Hilliard Ensemble, the. *Gesualdo: Tenebrae*. ECM New Series 1422/23 843 867-2 2CDs (1991)

Hogwood, Christopher and the Academy of Ancient Music. *Mozart: Symphonies*. L'Oiseau Lyre 452 496-2 (1997)

Isigqi sesiManjemanje. *Lomculo Unzima*. LP RPM Records, AFRLP 029 (1992)

Karajan, Herbert von and Berliner Philharmoniker, with various soloists. *Beethoven: 9 Symphonien*. Deutsche Grammophon DGG 4290362 (1963)

Karajan, Herbert von and the Philharmonia Orchestra and Chorus. *Mozart:* Così fan tutte. Columbia 33CX 1262-4 (1954)

Katims, Milton and the Budapest Quartet. *Mozart: Quintet in C Major, K. 515*. Columbia ML 4034 (1945)

Klemperer, Otto and the Philharmonia Orchestra. *Beethoven: Symphony No. 5 in C Minor*. Columbia 33C 1051 (1955)

Lawrence, Carol and others. *Bernstein:* West Side Story – *Original Broadway Cast Recording*. Columbia OM 5230 (mono, 1957), OS 2001 (stereo, 1958)

Lawson, Colin, Roy Goodman and The Hanover Band. *Mozart: Concerto for Basset Clarinet K. 622*. Nimbus 6228 (1990)

    Weber/Spohr: Clarinet Concertos. Classic FM 75805 57019 2 (2001)

Levin, Robert, Christopher Hogwood and the Academy of Ancient Music. *Mozart: Piano Concertos K. 482 and K. 488*. L'Oiseau Lyre 452 052-2 (1996)

Menuhin, Yehudi, Christopher Lee and the English Symphony Orchestra. *Prokofiev: Peter and the Wolf*. Nimbus 5192 (1991)

Menuhin, Yehudi with Rudolf Barshai and the Bath Festival Orchestra. *Mozart: Sinfonia concertante in E-flat Major, K. 364*. HMV ASD 567 (1963)

Moiseiwitsch, Benno, Leslie Heward and the Hallé Orchestra. *Grieg: Piano Concerto in A Minor*. HMV C 3264/7 (1941)

Moreschi, Alessandro. *Alessandro Moreschi, the Last Castrato: Complete Vatican Recordings*. Pavilion Pearl Opal CD 9823 (1987)

Muck, Karl and the Boston Symphony Orchestra. *Tchaikovsky: Symphony No. 4*. BSO Classics 171002 (1995)

Parrott, Andrew, Taverner Players Orchestra, Taverner Choir and Taverner Consort Choir. *Una Stravaganza dei Medici – Florentine Intermedi*. EMI Reflexe 47998 (1986)

Phillips, Peter and The Tallis Scholars. *Obrecht: Missa Maria zart*. Gimell CDGIM032 (1996)

Prohaska, Felix and the Vienna Chamber Choir and State Opera Orchestra. *Bach: Cantatas BWV78 and BWV106*. Vanguard/Bach Guild BG 537 (1954)

Rachmaninov, Sergei, Leopold Stokowski and the Philadelphia Orchestra. *Rachmaninov: Piano Concerto No. 2 in C Minor*. Biddulph LHW 036 (1997)

Reinecke, Carl. *Mozart: Piano Concerto No. 26, K. 537, 2nd mvt*, Welte 237 (1905)

Richter, Sviatoslav. *Schumann: Humoreske in B-flat Major, Op. 20*. Monitor MC 2022 (1956)

Sabajno, Carlo and the Chorus and Orchestra of La Scala. *Verdi:* Rigoletto. HMV C 1483/97 (1927/8)

Sabata, Victor de and the Chorus and Orchestra of La Scala. *Puccini:* Tosca. Columbia 33CX 1094/5 (1953)

Schiøtz, Aksel and Gerald Moore. *Schumann:* Dichterliebe. HMV DB6270/2 (1946)
  Schubert: Die schöne Müllerin. HMV DB6252/9 (1945)

Serkin, Rudolf, Adolf Busch and Hermann Busch. *Schubert: Piano Trio in E-flat Major, D929*. HMV DB 2676/80 (1935)
  Schubert: Piano Trio No. 2, Op. 100. Electrola E 80 792 (1963/4)

Sex Pistols. *Never Mind the Bollocks*. Virgin Records V2086 (1977)

Smetana Quartet. *Beethoven: Quartets in C Minor, Op. 18 No. 4 and C Major, Op. 59 No. 3*. Westminster WST 14119 (1959)
  Janáček: Quartet Nos. 1 and 2. Electrola SME 91442 (1965)
  Shostakovich: Quartet No. 3. Supraphon SV 8223 (1961)

Solti, Georg and the Vienna State Opera. *Wagner:* Der Ring des Nibelungen *(Ring Cycle)*. Decca 414 100-2 (1958–65)

Stokowski, Leopold and the Philadelphia Orchestra. *Stravinsky:* Petrushka. HMV DB 3511-4 (1937)

Tansini, Ugo and the EIAR Chorus and Orchestra. *Donizetti:* Lucia di Lammermoor. Parlophone R 20454/66 (1939)

Toscanini, Arturo and the New York Philharmonic-Symphony Orchestra. *Beethoven: Symphony No. 7 in A Major*. HMV DB 2986/90 (1936)

Turner, Bruno with Pro Cantione Antiqua and the Hamburger Bläserkreis für alte Musik. *Ockeghem: Missa pro defunctis*. Archiv Produktion 2533 145 (1973)

Umzansi Zulu Dancers. *Zindala Zombili*. Izimpande IZI003 (2007)

Various artists. *A–Z of Conductors*. Naxos 8558087-90 (2007)

Various artists. *A–Z of Pianists*. Naxos 8558107-10 (2007)

Various artists. *A Factory Sampler*. Factory Records FAC 2 (1978)

Various artists. *Great Pianists of the 20th Century*. Philips 462 845-2 (1999)

Various artists. *A Manchester Collection*. Object Records OBJ 003 (1979)

Various artists. *The Record of Singing*: Vol. 1, 12 LPs, EMI RLS 724 (1977, reissued with a supplementary record in 1982); Vol. 2, 13 LPs, RLS 743 (1979); Vol. 3, 13 LPs, EMI EX 2901693 (1984); Vol. 4, 8 LPs, EMI EX 7697411 (1989)

Various artists. *Street to Street – A Liverpool Album*. Open Eye OE LP 501 (August 1979)

Various artists. *Unzipping the Abstract*. Manchester Musicians' Collective MMC 1 (1980)

Various artists. *The Violin on Record*. Pearl BVA I and II (1990)

Willcocks, Sir David, the Jacobean Consort of Viols and the Choir of King's College, Cambridge. *Gibbons: 'Glorious and powerful God'*. Argo ZRG 5151 (1958).

Index

Cambridge Companions to Music

Topics

Composers